Managerial and Supervisory Principles

FOR PHYSICAL THERAPISTS

Managerial and Supervisory Principles

FOR PHYSICAL THERAPISTS

LARRY J. NOSSE, MA, PT, ATC
Associate Professor
Department of Physical Therapy
Marquette University
Milwaukee, Wisconsin
President, LJN Therapy, SC
Wauwatosa, Wisconsin

DEBORAH G. FRIBERG, MBA, PT
Vice President, Operations
Executive Director, WakeMed Rehab
WakeMed
Raleigh, North Carolina

PETER R. KOVACEK, MSA, PT
President and Chief Executive Officer
Kovacek Management Services, Inc.
Principal, The Focus Group, Inc.
Harper Woods, Michigan
Clinical Faculty
Wayne State University
Detroit, Michigan
Oakland University
Rochester, Michigan

With a contribution from
DONALD OLSEN, MMSc, EdD, PT, OCS
Principal
Homestead Orthopedic Physical Therapy
Cedarburg, Wisconsin
Wisconsin Orthopedic Rehabilitation Consultants
Milwaukee, Wisconsin
Adjunct Clinical Faculty
Department of Physical Therapy
Marquette University
Milwaukee, Wisconsin

Williams & Wilkins
A WAVERLY COMPANY

BALTIMORE • PHILADELPHIA • LONDON • PARIS • BANGKOK
BUENOS AIRES • HONG KONG • MUNICH • SYDNEY • TOKYO • WROCLAW

Editor: Eric Johnson
Managing Editor: Linda Napora
Marketing Manager: Tara Williams
Project Editor: Robert D. Magee

351 West Camden Street
Baltimore, Maryland 21201-2436 USA

Rose Tree Corporate Center
1400 North Providence Road
Building II, Suite 5025
Media, Pennsylvania 19063-2043 USA

Printed in the United States of America

First Edition, 1999

Library of Congress Cataloging-in-Publication Data

Nosse, Larry J.
    Managerial and supervisory principles for physical therapists /
Larry J. Nosse, Deborah G. Friberg. Peter R. Kovacek : with a
contribution from Donald Olsen.
        p.   cm.
    Includes bibliographical references and index.
    ISBN 0-683-30254-X
    1. Physical therapy—Practice.   2. Physical therapists—
    Supervision of.   3. Physical therapy—Management.   I. Friberg,
    Deborah G.   II. Kovacek, Peter R.   III. Olsen, Donald.   IV. Title.
    RM713.N674   1998
    615.8′2′068—dc21   98-29592
                                                             CIP

To purchase additional copies of this book, call our customer service department at **(800) 638-
0672** or fax orders to **(800) 447-8438.** For other book services, including chapter reprints and
large quantity sales, ask for the Special Sales department.

Canadian customers should call **(800) 665-1148,** or fax **(800) 665-0103.** For all other calls orig-
inating outside of the United States, please call **(410) 528-4223** or fax us at **(410) 528-8550.**

Visit Williams & Wilkins on the Internet: **http://www.wwilkins.com** or contact our customer
service department at **custserv@wwilkins.com.** Williams & Wilkins customer service representatives are available from 8:30 am to 6:00 pm, EST, Monday through Friday, for telephone
access.

99 00 01 02
1 2 3 4 5 6 7 8 9 10

◫ Preface

Managerial and Supervisory Principles for Physical Therapists has been written for physical therapists and student physical therapists with little or no formal preparation in business. Its purpose is to provide the knowledge required for dealing successfully with the day-to-day demands physical therapists face or will face as they pursue their careers. The principles are equally applicable to physical therapy practitioners working in large and small health care organizations. Key management concepts are related to physical therapy practice at both the organizational and clinical departmental level.

This text makes liberal use of examples that demonstrate the application of management principles to the practice of physical therapy. The authors are physical therapists, and the examples used in this text are derived from the authors' collective experience in the field. However, these basic principles apply to the management of any health care business.

Today's health care environment requires all physical therapists to make the kinds of decisions that only managers made just a few years ago, as managerial skills have become a basic part of the practice of physical therapy. Because physical therapy brings both cost and revenue to a health care organization, it is part of the business of health care. Understanding service-related business concepts is important to the cohesive functioning of a physical therapy department.

In reading the first chapter, readers will quickly begin to appreciate that the practice of physical therapy is only one part of a much larger health care delivery system. This larger health care delivery system is charged with delivery of quality health care services to large numbers of people. An understanding of health care business principles, particularly those associated with managed health care, will enhance the physical therapists' ability to deliver appropriate services in an efficient and effective fashion. Ultimately, to be successful, physical therapists need to de-velop management and business-related skills, in addition to clinical therapeutic skills. Physical therapy is a part of the business of health care. Business and technical knowledge and skills are complementary in an environment of continuously increasing pressures to do more, better, in less time and with fewer resources. This is the situation physical therapists face now and in the foreseeable future.

This text will help physical therapists meet today's challenges and future challenges inherent in the U.S. health care delivery system. The book has been organized as follows: Chapter 1 deals with the present health care system. Chapters 2 through 13 present the core business and management principles. Chapter 14 applies the presented business principles in the context of private physical therapy practice. Chapter 15 presents a view of the future of the health care system and physical therapy.

Several features will facilitate learning:

Key Words at the beginning of each chapter help the reader become familiar with new terms.
Discussion of values and motivation provides a framework for balancing the rights of patients and the need to operate financially viable organizations. See Chapter 2.
Card sort exercise in Chapter 2 aids the reader in identifying personal motivations served by individual/personal values.
Discussion of the future of the health care system and physical therapy, including recommendations for physical therapists to enhance their employability. See Chapter 15.
Appendix A contains a continuous case study, a role play, based on a single story line. The case study characters are introduced in the first role play scenario and reappear at various times as significant changes take place in their professional lives. The role play exercises can be used in a variety of ways. They can be used to facilitate group discussion or to provoke individual thought. The role play offers the reader an opportunity to engage in the cognitive processing and integration of core material from each chapter.

We wish to both acknowledge and thank the exceptional, dedicated, anonymous reviewers who helped us sharpen our focus and our writing.

We welcome your comments about this book. Comments can be sent to us care of the publisher. Your input is a valued part of our continuous commitment to quality. Our goal is to put the managerial skills for successful physical therapy practice in your hands.

L.J.N.
D.G.F.
P.R.K.

Contents

3   MARKETING   43

4   ORGANIZING AND ENGAGING PEOPLE IN THE WORK SETTING   60

5   DEALING WITH DIFFERENCES   77

6 ORGANIZATIONAL STRUCTURE AND CONTROL FOR BUSINESS SUCCESS   88

7 MONEY MATTERS: HEALTH CARE FINANCIAL MANAGEMENT   113

8   MONEY MATTERS: MAXIMIZING FINANCIAL PERFORMANCE 148

9   FACILITY PLANNING 185

10 INFORMATION MANAGEMENT 205

11 OUTCOMES: WHAT TO COLLECT AND WHAT DOES THE INFORMATION MEAN 221

12 PLAYING IT SAFE: MANAGING RISK 247

13 GETTING ADVICE: CONSULTANTS 267

14 ENTREPRENEURSHIP: OWNERSHIP AND PRIVATE PRACTICE PHYSICAL THERAPY 278

Donald Olsen, MMSc, EdD, PT, OCS

15   FUTURES 299

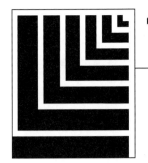

1

THE HEALTH CARE DELIVERY SYSTEM

PREVIEW

The American Health Care delivery system has been in continuous transition as the American people search for better ways to finance the cost of health care. Their goal is access for all, so that they may enjoy the benefits of health care services without the potential risk of financial devastation. Since the creation of the Medicare and Medicaid programs in 1965, the rate of change within the health care delivery system has continued to escalate. The period from 1965 through 1980 was one of tremendous growth and development. Unlimited funding, available through the third party payment system and coupled with growing consumer demand, fueled the expansion of the health care system into the world class system it is today. Efforts to regain control of the cost of health care began in the 1980s. Changes in payment methodology once again brought about significant change in the health care delivery system. Health care financing system reform efforts aimed at improved access and cost control have continued into the 1990s. As American health care providers work to respond, the impact of change experienced by those providing and receiving health care continues.

KEY WORDS

Ambulatory Care: refers to services that require less than a 24-hour period for delivery and recovery, after which the patient is ready for discharge home.

Beneficiary: an individual who is enrolled and is eligible to receive health care insurance coverage under the Medicare and/or Medicaid programs.

Best Practices: approaches to care delivery identified when the practices of clinical care providers are reviewed and analyzed to identify those that produce the best clinical and financial outcomes. Best practices are used to guide the practices of other clinicians.

Coverage Guidelines: written descriptions of the types of service and terms under which health care services qualify for payment under a health insurance plan.

Deductible Payments: the portion of the health care costs that must be paid by the subscriber before their health plan assumes any financial responsibility for covered health care services.

Disease Management: a term used to describe utilization management efforts that are targeted at controlling the cost of care for patients who have a chronic disease or disability.

Geriatrician: a physician who specializes in the provision of health care to the elderly.

Health Care Provider: an individual or organization that provides products and/or services used to maintain or improve health.

Integrated Delivery Network (IDN): an affiliated group of health care providers who together are able to meet the comprehensive health care needs of patients within a specific geographical region.

Health Maintenance Organization (HMO): a health insurance plan that assumes responsibility for all of the subscribers' health care cost for a fixed, all inclusive price. The HMO is responsible for the quality and cost of care provided to en-rollees. To control both of these elements, the HMO restricts enrollee choice of health care providers to those who have participation agreements with the plan. The group of participating providers is sometimes referred to as a panel.

Physiatrist: a physician who specializes in physical medicine and rehabilitation.

Reference Laboratory: provides highly specialized analytic services and accepts referral work from other laboratory providers.

Participating Provider: a provider of health care products and/or services who has applied, met criteria for participation and has a signed agreement with a government or private health care insurance plan for the provision of specific health care services to its enrollees (beneficiaries).

Plan Member (Enrollee): an individual who is enrolled in a health care plan and is entitled to receive health care coverage under an individual or group insurance plan for a specific period of time.

Provider Participation Agreements: contracts between health care providers and government or private health care insurance plans for the provision of specific health care services to its enrollees (beneficiaries).

Subscriber: is the individual who holds or joins a group that holds, or subscribes to, an insurance policy for health care coverage. A subscriber may enroll others under the policy or into the group that holds the policy. An employee who enrolls for insurance as an employment benefit is the subscriber. All of the employer's employees and those they enroll will be part of the employer's group.

Third Party Payer: refers to employers, health insurance plans or any other entity that pays health care providers for services provided to another party, the patient. The consumer (the first party) unable to pay for services of the provider (the second party) relies on the health care plan (the third party) for payment (1).

INTRODUCTION

To appreciate the demands faced by today's health care professionals, the reader must first understand the environment in which those professionals must function. That environment is best described as change, both rapid and continuous within the health care system. The greatest single impetus for this change has been the continued escalation of health care costs (2). From 1980 to 1985, national expenditures for physician and hospital services increased from 148.4 to 250 billion dollars. These same expenditures were expected to increase by another 53% over the next 5 years (3). At the same time, a national shift to low paying service sector jobs was leaving an increasing number of people without health care insurance. Health care providers were then forced to shift the growing cost of providing health care services to the uninsured and underinsured to corporate and government payers who could pay. As a result, businesses were faced with significant increases in the cost of providing health care benefits to workers. Meanwhile, the rate of growth in health care spending threatened the government's ability to meet other financial demands and control the growing federal deficit.

In the early 1980s, both the government and private industry took action to control their health care expenditures. Medicare adopted a fixed rate payment system for inpatient hospitalization. Private businesses turn to managed care. These and subsequent efforts of third party payers to control the cost of health care have fostered the current environment of rapid and continuous change.

Change brings threat, challenge and opportunity. The health care delivery system has responded by changing its structure, facilities, work force composition and the process of health care delivery. At times, the magnitude of change has left health care providers in a state of turmoil. Demands for change have also offered the opportunity to assess the relative value of various elements of the care delivery process.

To be successful in such an environment, today's health care professionals must be armed with both the skills of practice managers and clinicians. To contribute to the change process, clinicians must demonstrate the value their services bring to the health care delivery process. Leadership in today's health care environment requires a willingness and ability to create opportunities for improvement through change and the desire to help others to do the same. Our hope here is to guide those who choose to lead and, for those who follow, help them to understand and support their leaders, so that both may find success.

HEALTH CARE DELIVERY SYSTEM

The health care delivery system encompasses a multitude of diverse organizations. Collectively, these organizations provide the products and services consumed to maintain and/or improve the health of individuals. Some organizations are involved directly in the delivery of health care. Hospitals, home care agencies, public health departments, physicians, nurses and, of course, physical therapists are all involved directly in the delivery of health care services. Other organizations provide products and services that support the process of health care delivery. A pharmaceutical company, medical equipment manufacturer, a medical researcher and medical waste disposal company are all examples of indirect health care providers. All of these organizations are a part of the health care delivery system.

The health care delivery system has evolved significantly over the last 25 years. Delivery has moved beyond the physician's office and hospital. Today, patients have access to a variety of services delivered in diverse settings. Care providers may be categorized by either type of setting or type of care provided. In addition to setting and type, there is often a need to define the health care delivery system in terms of the patient care process or the continuum of care.

Providers by Type of Care

There are several descriptors used to define type of care. The major categories are preventive care, primary care, and specialty care. A health care provider may deliver one or all types of care. A physical therapist, for example, may teach workers about back injury prevention, provide the primary evaluation to monitor previously injured or high risk workers and provide specialty care for workers following acute back injury.

Preventive Care

Preventive health care includes such things as wellness programs, health screenings, health education and immunizations. Preventive health care as a part of the health care delivery system has gained importance as the cost of corrective care has increased.

Primary Care

Primary care, the front-line of the health care delivery system, is most often the initial point of patient contact with the health care delivery system. Primary health care providers have direct access to the patient. Traditionally a general practice physician, the role of primary care provider has been extended to include other health care providers. Medical specialists, such as geriatricians, pulmonologists and physiatrists, have expanded beyond their roles as consultants to provide primary care to special patient populations. Nonphysician providers, including such professionals as the advanced practice nurse, social worker, and physical therapist, are also developing expanded roles as primary care providers.

Specialty Care

Specialty care provides services, equipment and facilities not offered at the primary care level. Specialized medical management, diagnostic laboratory, imaging, surgical and rehabilitation services, sports medicine, day care, hospice, respite, and substance abuse are all examples of specialty care services.

Type of Setting

When grouped by setting, services are categorized as ambulatory (or outpatient), inpatient and home care. Ambulatory care settings are designed to meet the needs of patients who are able to arrive for and depart from the care setting on the day of service. Inpatient care settings offer 24-hour skilled medical care. Home care refers to all health care provided in the patient's residence. Residence should be defined broadly, as a private home, residential care setting, supervised living and homeless shelter may all qualify as a patient's residence.

Ambulatory Care

Ambulatory care settings offer a variety of preventive, primary and specialty services. Over the past several years, many services that had been delivered exclusively to inpatients are now available to patients in ambulatory settings. The shift toward ambulatory care has resulted in increased convenience for both care providers and patients. In some cases, the shift has increased the efficiency and decreased cost of care delivery. The cost efficiency of ambulatory care over inpatient care has not proved to be universal. Public health departments, wellness and health education centers, imaging and surgical centers, rehabilitation clinics, physician offices, specialty care clinics and day care centers are all examples of ambulatory care settings.

Inpatient Care

Inpatient care is provided in acute care, post acute and skilled nursing facility settings. Acute care providers offer two levels of specialized service provision: secondary and tertiary care. Medical specialty services, diagnostic laboratories, general and routine surgical services, women's health services, pediatric services and inpatient rehabilitation are all examples of secondary care. The tertiary acute care provider offers an even greater degree of sophistication in the provision of specialized health care services. A tertiary medical provider functions as a regional referral center for other primary and secondary providers. Services that may be available through a tertiary provider include a reference laboratory, advanced radiological imaging, a cardiovascular and/or transplant surgical service, trauma center, heliport and air rescue service, specialized intensive care, burn care and mobile transport service with advanced life support capabilities.

Postacute inpatient care meets the needs of patients who continue to require a skilled level of inpatient care but who do not require the intensity and/or variety of services available in the secondary or tertiary acute setting. Surgical recovery centers, longer term rehabilitation centers, long-term care hospitals, skilled nursing facilities and inpatient hospice care are examples of postacute inpatient care.

Home Care

Home care is the fastest growing segment of the health care delivery system. Home care refers to the provision of medical equipment and/or health care services to patients in a home setting. Figures 1.1 to 1.3 present the types and settings for patient care.

Continuum Of Care

The diversity of service types and settings is indicative of two initiatives: to improve the effectiveness of health care services by providing patients with better access to the variety of specialized care needed throughout the care and recovery process; and to improve the cost efficiency of care delivery by matching the resources used with care

required. Both initiatives support the growth of ambulatory and home based care options. In theory, this diverse array of services can be organized around the patient to provide a continuum of care driven by changes in a patient's care requirements. As the health care delivery system has moved beyond the physician office and hospital, management priorities have changed. Figure 1.4 demonstrates the magnitude of this change.

Ideally, services along the continuum of care are coordinated among the providers so that the patient's transitions between continuum service settings are smooth and progressive. The

The Health Care Delivery System		
Ambulatory Care		
Prevention	Primary Care	Specialty Care
Public Health	Physician Care Internal Medicine Pediatrics Geriatrics Family Practice	Physician Care
Health Education	Non-physician Care Nurse Practitioner, Physical Therapist, etc.	Ambulatory Surgery / Radiological Imaging Centers
Wellness & Fitness	Patient Education	Adult Day Care Centers
Health Research	Urgent Care	Sports Medicine Clinics
Industrial Health	Routine Outpatient Diagnostics	Outpatient Rehabilitation Facilities

FIGURE 1.1. The health care delivery system: ambulatory care.

The Health Care Delivery System		
Inpatient Care		
Acute Care	Post-Acute Care	Nursing Home/ Transitional Living
Community Hospital Tertiary Medical Center	Surgical / Medical Recovery Centers	Skilled Care Nursing Rehabilitation
Women's Health	Rehabilitation Ventilator Dependent Care	Intermediate Care
Rehabilitation / Substance Abuse	Brain Injury Care Centers	Alzheimer's Care
Orthopedics Neurosciences	Birthing Centers	Residential Living
ENT Cardiology Urology etc	Hospice Care Respite Care	Community Re-entry Services

FIGURE 1.2. The health care delivery system: inpatient care.

continuum of care model is at the core of the health care industry's move toward the development of integrated delivery networks (IDN). An IDN is a horizontally and vertically integrated health care delivery system. Horizontal integration means the network includes two or more like providers such as hospitals. Horizontal integration may be necessary to cover large geographical regions or accommodate existing patient preferences. Vertical integration means that the network includes a variety of services that make up a comprehensive health care delivery system as defined in Figures 1.1 to 1.3. As a result, IDNs offer a full continuum of care and serve a specific geographical region. Figure 1.5 depicts a model IDN in relation to patients and third party payers.

HEALTH CARE SOCIAL PHILOSOPHY AND PUBLIC POLICY

Access to health care has been and continues to be of great importance to the American public.

The Health Care Delivery System		
Home Care		
High Tech Care	Skilled Nursing & Rehab Care	Supportive Care
Durable Medical Equipment	Patient / Family Education	Housekeeping
Infusion Therapy	Wound Care	Personal Care
Parental Therapy	Disease Management (Diabetic Care, Pulmonary Care, etc.)	
Chemo Therapy	Hospice Care	

FIGURE 1.3. The health care delivery system: home care.

Over the years, prevailing public opinion and social philosophy about the accessibility of health care has continued to evolve. Throughout this period, the core issues have remained unchanged: financial accessibility and cost of health care. The structure of the health care delivery system has and will continue to be shaped by changing social philosophy regarding health care.

As early as the 1920s there was concern about the ability of the individual to pay the costs of hospitalization. The first hospital prepayment plan was founded in 1929, at the start of the great depression, by Dr. Justin Ford Kimball of Baylor University. The plan was established to help the University Hospital, as it was in serious financial trouble because patients were not paying their bills. The prepayment plan was successful.

The idea quickly caught on around the country. This was the beginning of the health care third party payer system of today. The consumer (the first party), unable to pay for services of the provider (the second party), relies on the health care plan (the third party) for payment (1). As the number of prepayment plans grew, standards of performance were established through efforts of the American Hospital Association, among others. Several plans organized under what is now known as the Blue Cross-Blue Shield (BCBS) Association (The Blues). The Blues plans continued to grow. Today, the BCBS plans are the largest group of associated health care insurers in the United States (1).

Up until World War II, the individual was usually responsible for the BCBS premium payment.

Traditional Priorities		New Priorities
Acute Inpatient Care	→	Continuum Of Care
Treating Illness And Injury	→	Maintaining Health And Wellness
Care Of Each Patient	→	Care Of A Patient Population
A High Volume Of Patient Care	→	A Large Number Of Covered Lives Under Contract
Filling Inpatient Beds	→	Providing The Right Care In The Right Setting
Managing An Organization	→	Managing A System of Care
Coordinating Services	→	Managing Care

FIGURE 1.4. Changing priorities for the delivery of health care. (Adapted from a presentation by Douglas E. Henson, Mayo Clinic at the National Association for Home Care, 14th Annual Meeting and Home Carexpo, October 8, 1995.)

During WW II, to counter the freeze on wages, employers began offering health plan premium payment as an alternative to increased wages. Following World War II, the practice of employer-sponsored health insurance continued and spread. Health insurance became a fringe benefit under most union contracts. With the cost of health care now disassociated from the user, there was decreased control of health care service utilization. Because the purpose of the prepayment plans was to improve payment to hospitals, the basis for payment of health care services was service utilization. Fueled by increased utilization and a reliable payment system that rewarded providers for service delivery, the health care delivery system grew.

Period 1965 through 1980

A review of public health care policy shows clearly the relationship between social philosophy and changes in the health care delivery system during this period of growth. The prevailing social philosophy regarding access to health care was one of entitlement. Popular opinion supported the position that all persons were entitled to equal access to the highest quality of health care services available. Popular opinion was reflected in public policy adopted during that period (4). The two most important pieces of health care legislation of that time period were Title XVIII and Title XIX of the Social Security Act. Both pieces of legislation were intended to improve the accessibility to health care for the elderly, disabled and poor. This legislation, establishing Medicare and Medicaid, represented many years of discussion to balance the special interests of hospitals, doctors, unions, business and insurers.

Medicare

Title XVIII of the Social Security Act was signed into law in 1965. It is considered to be the

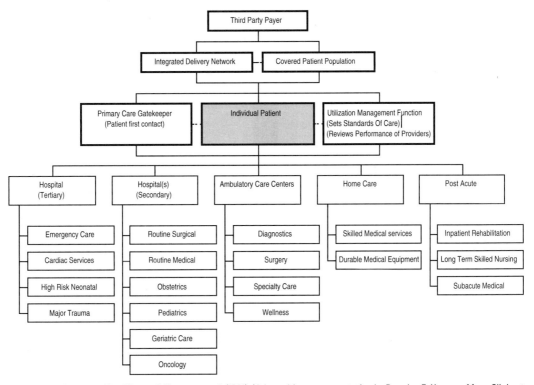

FIGURE 1.5. Integrated healthcare delivery network (IDN). (Adapted from a presentation by Douglas E. Henson, Mayo Clinic at the National Association for Home Care, 14th Annual Meeting and Home Carexpo, October 8, 1995.)

Most significant piece of health care legislation ever passed by the U.S. Congress (5). Medicare was targeted to provide for the health care needs of the elderly. Later, the Medicare program was expanded to provide coverage to others, including persons with a permanent disability. The Social Security Administration (SSA) Amendments of 1972 enacted special eligibility provisions. These provisions affected the Medicare participation of persons with qualifying disabilities or chronic renal disease (1). Provider payment under Medicare was to follow the pattern established by the Blues. Payment was to be based on a reasonable cost basis.

Medicaid

Medicaid, established by Title XIX of the Social Security Act, is a state administered program intended to provide access to health care services to the poor, elderly and the disabled persons. Medicaid can be supplemental to Medicare for individuals eligible under both programs. The Medicaid program is optional at the state level. For states choosing to participate, expenses of the program are shared between the state and federal government. Provider reimbursement was to be based on a reasonable cost basis. Participating states are required to meet program established minimum coverage requirements, but may expand coverage beyond the minimum. As a result of this flexibility, Medicaid benefits vary among states (1, 4–5).

The Blues

As the largest provider of prepaid health care plans, the creation of Medicare had a great impact on the Blues. Yet, the federal government needed the claims handling capabilities of the Blues and other large insurers. The support of the insurers was garnered through the financial arrangements structured to obtain their services to manage the program. These insurers became Medicare's fiscal intermediaries (1). Medicare fiscal intermediaries function as the administrative agent for the Health Care Financing Administration (HCFA), which is responsible for the administration of the Medicare program.

Cost: The Impetus For Change

Under the reasonable cost payment methodology of Medicare, Medicaid, and other insurers, health care providers were financially rewarded for providing more services at a greater cost. Naturally, health care utilization grew. The health care delivery system grew. Consumers, free from financial responsibility for health care service utilization, were encouraged to utilize all of the services that an expanded health care delivery system had to offer. It is no wonder that the cost of health care services continued to rise. By the mid 1970s, the cost burden of health care began to get the increasing attention of employers as well as state and federal government (1). The cost burden of health care had shifted from the patient and philanthropic funding sources to the government and the employers. Table 1.1 demonstrates the shift in funding sources from 1965 to 1980. Employers, now paying 30 percent of the growing cost of health care, were struggling with the rising cost of health care benefits. The cost of the Medicare and Medicaid programs had increased government's share of the cost of the health care burden to 29% (6).

Under cost-based reimbursement, the payer is totally responsible, at financial risk, for the cost of health care provided to consumers covered under their health plan. As the cost and utilization of health care services rise, payer costs increase. This increase is passed along to employers or, in the case of the government, to the taxpayer. Yet, the payer has no control over service utilization or the cost of health care services. On the other hand, neither the consumers nor the providers of health care services have any incentive to stem the growth of health care costs.

Period 1980 to 1990

The 1980s saw a new era of evolution for the health care industry. The entitlement philosophy of the 1960s was challenged by the public response to the rising cost burden of health care. In the early 1980s, employers and the government took action to contain the utilization and cost of health care. Supported by public opinion, third party payer efforts to control the cost of health care resulted in major changes in the health care delivery system. Payers adopted the following five strategies to control costs.

1. Insurance plans shifted from the traditional full choice insurance model to more restrictive managed care models.
2. Plan design and payment methods were modified to limit and shift financial risk from the plan to patients and providers.
3. Utilization management programs were developed to control the use and cost of services.
4. Payers began using performance outcome measurement to evaluate and select providers.
5. Provider participation was limited by restrictions on service coverage and payment.

The Move To Managed Care

Payers had to gain control over the utilization and the cost of health care services. They needed to manage access, the cost and quality of health care services. The result was a shift from the traditional insurance plans to managed care insurance plans. Because managed care plans vary greatly, there is no single definition of managed care (7). The American Managed Care And Review Association (AMCRA) defines managed care as a comprehensive approach to health care delivery that encompasses planning and coordination of care, patient and provider education, monitoring of care quality, and cost control (8).

Under managed care, the consumer of services, the patient, gives up the exclusive right to

TABLE 1.1
Percent Of Expenditure For Health Services And Supplies By Payer Type

PAYER TYPE	PERCENT EXPENDITURE BY YEAR	
	1965	1980
Federal Government	10.9%	17.0%
State and Local Government	11.5%	11.9%
Business	17.4%	30.0%
Household and Philanthropy	60.2%	41.1%

(Derived from the work of Levit KR, Freeland MS, Waldo DR. Health spending and ability to pay: Business, individuals and government. Health Care Financing Rev 1989;10(3):1–11).

choose health care providers and services. The health care service provider loses its exclusive role as decision maker regarding the health care delivery process. Managed care plan administrators now find themselves in the middle of the health care delivery process with the power to evaluate the health care delivery process, to choose the right location, the level, and type of care needed to achieve desired health outcomes at the least possible cost (7). The transition from traditional to managed care insurance plans has been dramatic. AMCRA now reports that the percentage of the American population covered under some from of managed care plan exceeds 41% of the population (8).

The three major types of managed care organizations (MCO) are the Health Maintenance Organization (HMO), Preferred Provider Organization (PPO) and the Point-Of-Service Organization (POS). An HMO offers comprehensive health care service coverage of hospital and physician services for a prepaid, fixed fee. An HMO may either employ or contract with health care service providers. Generally, plan members must receive needed services from plan providers. Commonly, access to plan providers is controlled by a primary care physician (PCP) who acts as a gatekeeper. When the physicians are employed by the managed care plan, it is called a staff model HMO. When physician groups are contracted by the managed care plan, it is called a group model HMO. When individual physicians contract with the HMO to provide services, it is referred to as an Independent Physicians Association (IPA).

A preferred provider organization (PPO) is a network of health care providers who have contracted with a managed health insurance plan to provide services to plan members. Members of the PPO accept discounted rates and agree to comply with preauthorization and utilization review requirements of the managed care plan. In return, PPO members hope to receive an increased volume of business. Plan enrollees are either required or receive financial incentives to use the PPO members long-term (9). Access to specialists may be controlled by a PCP who acts as a gatekeeper.

POS plans offer a network of providers who have contracted with a managed health insur-

ance plan to provide services to plan members. Plan members who wish to use health care providers outside of the network or to access specialists directly may do so if they are willing to pay an additional fee. For example, the co-payment for a physician office visit may be $10 for network providers and $20 for out-of-network providers.

Limiting And Shifting Financial Risk

Early payer efforts were directed at limiting and shifting the financial risk for health care utilization and cost from themselves to the consumer and the provider of health care (10). The goal of risk limits and cost shifting was simple. If the consumer and provider were at financial risk for the utilization of health care services, they would have an incentive to join payers in the effort to control utilization and cost. Payers approached risk shifting in several ways.

CHANGING PAYMENT METHODS

Payment methodology was changed in ways that placed providers and consumers into positions of financial risk for the cost of health care services. An early and important effort to limit or cap payer financial risk came from the federal government in the form of the Tax Equity and Fiscal Responsibilities Act of 1982 (TEFRA). TEFRA (Public Law 97–248) was an effort to control the growing cost of the Medicare program. Under TEFRA, Medicare cost-based reimbursement method for inpatient acute hospitalization was changed to a prospective per case payment methodology. This system became known as the prospective payment system (PPS). PPS uses the patient's primary diagnosis to categorize them into a diagnostic-related group (DRG). Each DRG represents a mutually exclusive grouping that is used to assign a case payment rate. The case payment rate is preset. The provider is paid at the fixed rate regardless of the cost incurred caring for a patient. If the cost incurred in caring for a patient is greater than the fixed DRG payment, the provider loses money. If the care of a patient costs less than the DRG payment, the provider makes money. The PPS system was designed to provide a financial incentive for hospitals to control resource utilization and cost. In doing so, the system served to limit the financial risk of the Medicare program.

PPS is an example of case rate reimbursement. Other payment methods adopted to limit risk and control costs were daily (per diem), and capitation payments. Under per diem payment methodology, the provider is paid a fixed rate per day of care. Under capitated payment methodology, a provider contracts with a health plan to provide all of a specific type of care to a specific group of people in return for an agreed upon payment. The provider assumes full financial responsibility and risk for provision of the agreed upon service to the specified group. Therefore, the provider has a financial incentive to control the amount of service provided. Payment methodology is discussed in more detail in Chapters 7 and 8.

THE CONSUMER PAYS MORE OF THE BILL FOR HEALTH CARE

Payers increased the consumer's financial risk and share of the cost burden through the use of higher deductible and co-payments. Deductible payments are set amounts an enrollee has to pay before their health insurance assumes financial responsibility for covered health care services. A deductible is commonly a flat dollar amount, i.e., $2,000 per coverage year. The consumer is financially responsible and must pay all or part of their health care bills until the deductible is met. In this example, the consumer is at risk to pay up to $2,000 per year for the health care services they receive. Co-payments are made by the patient to the provider to cover that portion of health care charge that the patient must pay on an ongoing basis. Co-payments may be limited by use of annual deductible requirements. Under some health insurance plans, there are no annual limits on co-payments. Co-payments may be a set dollar amount, i.e., $10 per office visit, or a percentage of the total service charge, i.e., 20% of the patient's bill. Co-payments often vary by type of service received.

Utilization Management

Utilization management refers to practices and processes employed to influence the use of health care services by a patient or patient population. Utilization management efforts may be used by payers as well as health care providers to control service utilization and cost. Efforts have been aimed at controlling both the amount and type of services provided.

Care management is a term used to describe the clinical management of health care rsources. It is a form of utiliza-tion management. Care management systems use a variety of approaches to manage the care of individual patients and/or larger patient populations. The following are examples of care management approaches.

1. Use of a primary care gatekeeper.
2. Use of case management to coordinate and control the care provided to individual patients.
3. Second opinion requirements.
4. Preauthorization requirements for coverage of care.
5. Concurrent utilization review for appropriateness of care.
6. Retrospective review for appropriateness of care.
7. Use of standardized, diagnosis specific plans of care.
8. Application of best practice guidelines.
9. Service coverage restrictions and limitations.
10. Wellness and prevention activities.

To ensure that utilization management efforts are maximally effective, payers and providers target patients and patient populations that have the potential to generate high health care costs. In that way, utilization management has the potential to yield the greatest cost reductions. There are two types of patient populations that have the potential to generate high health care costs.

The first category includes a small number of patients who utilize a high volume of health care services. For example, patients recovering from catastrophic injury or experiencing end stage renal failure are likely to use a disproportionate amount of health care services. To minimize the overall utilization of care, case management may be used to insure that the patient receives only appropriate services at the right time, and in the right setting. The second type of patient population that is targeted for utilization management has high volume. When a large number of individuals within a patient population require the same type of care, such as patients undergoing total joint replacement or having acute back injuries, there may be the potential for over utilization of the services. The use of gatekeepers, second opinion reviews, service use criteria, prevention, and preauthorization requirements are likely to minimize the number of patients using services. Use of best practice guidelines, standardized plans of care (often called care paths, critical paths or care maps) and retrospective review can be used to decrease the cost of providing care to patients who do require services.

Utilization management efforts have evolved, becoming more effective over time. Initially, the focus of utilization management was largely on controlling the amount of health care services used. That focus has expanded. Experience has shown that reduction of health care costs over the long-term requires attention to not only how much care is delivered but, how, when, and where care is delivered. This concept may be best explained through an illustration. In the 1970s, a person with an uncomplicated, acute back injury was routinely treated with a period of bed rest, followed by several weeks of physical therapy. The typical physical therapy plan of care included a few weeks of heat and massage. Later, exercises and patient education were initiated.

Twenty to thirty visits was the normal course of care. Initial utilization management efforts to control the cost of this care would have been to limit the number of physical therapy visits. Limiting visits without changing the what and when of care might result in a short term reduction in cost. Unfortunately, it is just as likely to result in an increased number of repeat injuries and total cost over time. In contrast, altering the plan of care to include earlier intervention, more aggressive exercise, patient education and a strong follow-up plan has a better probability of producing a short term reduction in the total number of physical therapy visits without an increase in long-term utilization.

Disease management is the term used to describe utilization management efforts that are targeted at controlling the cost of care for patients with chronic disease or disability. The goal of disease management is the reduction of health care service utilization and cost. The strategy is the coordinated utilization of health care services to stabilize the patient's condition and minimize expensive complications and exacerbations in the disease process. Disease management addresses service utilization over the life of patient rather than during a single episode of care. It is a good example of how health care utilization management has changed over time.

It should be noted that the utilization management practices of payers have sometimes been challenged by both payers and consumers. Some payers have responded by adopting the guidelines developed by the National Committee on Quality Assurance (NCQA). The NCQA is a managed care accreditation organization. The NCQA accredits managed care organizations on all aspects of the health plan's operations related to the delivery of health care. The NCQA review process covers utilization management, credentialing, member services, preventive health care, and medical records maintenance. NCQA accreditation may be a factor in an employer's decision to offer a specific managed care plan to its employees (11).

Provider Accountability For Performance Outcomes

The focus on utilization management has also changed the way health care services are evaluated. Where health care providers had always focused on the discrete tasks of health care delivery, payers began to focus on the process and outcomes of the health care delivery process. Access to increasingly sophisticated information systems has facilitated this change. Today, providers are being held accountable for their performance outcomes. Multi provider performance assessment systems are being used to compare the performance of one provider against the performance of similar providers. This information is being used by providers to guide their continuous improvement of clinical care processes and service outcomes, as well as to market services to managed care plans. Performance outcome information is being used by managed care plans as the basis for contracting with select providers.

Restrictive Guidelines For Provider Participation

Another method employed by payers to gain control over the health care costs is an increased use of restrictive guidelines governing provider participation under their insurance plans. Such restrictions have been incorporated into provider participation agreements and legislation that restrict certain health care provider business practices. Two areas that have received special attention from the federal government are referral for profit relationships and service over utilization. The Ethics in Patient Referrals Act of 1989 (also know as the Stark Law) and the Medicare and Medicaid Patient Protection Act (also referred to as the anti-kickback law) are two areas of law which restrict the business practices of health care providers in an effort to control over utilization and the cost of health care services. The anti-kickback law provides for fines and imprisonment for any entity that would knowingly and willfully offer, pay, solicit or receive remuneration to induce business reimbursed under Medicare or state health care programs. The intent is to stop the payment of any kind of financial inducement in return for the referral of patients whose services are paid for out of public funds (12). Financial enticement to obtain referrals increases the cost of care as well as the potential for over utilization of a service.

Similarly, the Stark Laws target referrals for certain services made by physicians to any Medicare or Medicaid providers with which the physician (or immediate family member) has a financial relationship. Services included under the Stark Law include physical therapy, occupational therapy, durable medical equipment services and supplies, prosthetics, orthotics and prosthetic devices and supplies and home health services (12). There are a number of exceptions to these general statements.

The federal government is taking the control of health care fraud and abuse very seriously. Each health care practitioner is responsible for knowing fully their responsibilities under these laws. Readers are encouraged to research these topics more fully.

Health Reform In The 1990s

The 1990s saw the beginning of renewed public debate about the financing of health and access to health care for all citizens. The impetus for renewed public concern was twofold. First, there was a growing public concern about the 38.9 million uninsured Americans (13). The uninsured are a group composed largely of workers and their dependents employed in low wage service and agriculture industries as well as the employees of small firms (14). Second, there was a growing public realization that job instability and the continuing elimination of well-paid jobs had resulted in decreased financial security for the middle class American. An unexpected employment change accompanied by an interruption or loss of health care insurance coverage could result in serious economic hardship (7). For both of these reasons, the 1990s brought renewed pressure to reform the financing of health care.

The Clinton Administration, responding to public demand, set in motion a series of efforts aimed at health care reform. Those efforts failed to produce an overall reform of health care financing. However, the anticipation of change resulted in significant changes in the health care delivery system. Health care providers have been pushed by the Clinton Administration's view that the future lies with managed care (7). They have responded by developing structures that are suited to the management of health care services provided to large patient populations. Essentially, the restructuring efforts of providers that have occurred in anticipation of reform have resulted in change without health care financing reform.

Health care provider driven changes have also included efforts to bypass the administrative controls and cost associated with operating health care insurance plans. Providers are looking at opportunities to regain control of their environments through establishing provider operated managed care organizations. Employers and providers are also looking at opportunities to bypass third party payers entirely through direct contracting. Medicare and, in some states, Medicaid, is moving toward the use of Medicare managed care plans as an alternative to the traditional Medicare/Medicaid insurance program. Medicare is also experimenting with best practice centers to provide high volume, high cost services. The Medicare Centers of Excellence demonstration projects are currently focused on the high volume patient populations undergoing coronary artery bypass grafting and total joint replacement procedure and are limited in number. The reader will note the focus on two high volume, high cost patient populations. The Centers of Excellence demonstration projects use a capitated payment method. Providers are selected based on historical ability and patient outcomes.

THE SEAL OF APPROVAL: EXTERNAL OVERSIGHT

Governmental Regulation And Review

Health care providers have historically been subject to external oversight. Oversight has come in the form of government regulatory compliance reviews and voluntary accreditation reviews. Regulatory compliance reviews are performed by federal, state and local governmental agencies or their representatives. Regulatory reviews can occur as a condition of participation in government-funded health care programs such as Medicare and Medicaid. They can also occur as a condition of continued operation as a state or local government approved health care provider. Reviews performed as a condition of continued operation may involve annual reviews for continued licensure, facility safety inspections or compliance with state licensure requirements for medical professionals such as nursing.

The purpose of health care regulation is to protect the interests of the public. Independent professionals and organizations involved in the delivery of health care services are held accountable to the public through the enactment and enforcement of regulations that set community standards for health care service delivery. Government regulations affect most of the operating practices of heath care providers, including organizational structure, business and financial management practices, service documentation, service evaluation, personnel practice and facility design. Full cooperation with the regulatory review process is mandatory. Failure to participate and/or cooperate could result in cancellation of a provider's participation agreement for government-funded health programs or loss of licensure to operate. Health care regulation is administered by several different departments of the federal, state and local government. At the federal level, the most notable is HCFA. HCFA is responsible for the operation of the Medicare program. The Office of the Inspector General (OIG) is responsible for situations involving Medicare fraud and abuse. At the state and local level, one or more departments of the government are responsible for health care oversight. For example, a State's physical therapy licensure board is responsible for oversight of physical therapy practice.

Accreditation And Quality Review

In addition to regulatory review, many health care service providers voluntarily participate in external review processes. Often these review processes result in some from of accreditation. Accreditation signifies that the organization has met the performance standards established by the accrediting organization. The Joint Commission on Accreditation of Healthcare Organizations (JCAHO) is probably the best known health care accreditation organization. JCAHO offers accreditation for hospitals, skilled nursing facilities, ambulatory care, home care agencies, hospice, and home care equipment providers. In the field of rehabilitation, CARF, the rehabilitation accreditation commission, is the largest accreditation organization. Accreditation is used as an indicator of quality. As such, a specific accreditation may be required by a payer as a condition of plan participation or for participation in the delivery of specific services. For example, a hospital may be required to have JCAHO accreditation. In addition, the hospital's inpatient or other rehabilitation programs may be required to have CARF accreditation. In most cases, accreditation remains a voluntary review process. However, the number of payers that require provider certification is growing. Some states are requiring provider accreditation as a condition of operation.

Professional Associations

Professional associations are also a source of external review for health care service providers. Professional associations set standards for professional practice. Professional associations may offer an accreditation or certification to its members.

As long as professional association membership is voluntary, so is participation in professional association practice oversight activities.

THE HEALTH CARE INDUSTRY RESPONDS

The health care delivery system has been shaped by the social philosophy and public policy related to health care financing. The types and settings for health care have grown and developed in response to the financial incentives created by the third party payer system. A review of the continuum of health care services presented in Figures 1.1 to 1.3 quickly demonstrates the expansion of the health care delivery system from the physician and hospital-based delivery system of the 1960s.

Period 1965 Through 1980

During the period of 1965 through 1980, the energies of the health care delivery system were focused on growth and development. Both the supply of and demand for health care grew. This period resulted in many changes, including:

- An increase in the capacity, capabilities, number and types of health care providers.
- An increase in the number of persons accessing the health care delivery system.
- An increase in the amount of care provided to each individual accessing the health care delivery system.
- The development of new and improved health care delivery processes and technology.

The structure of the health care delivery system, characterized by small independent physician group practices operated as independent businesses, remained largely the same during this period. Larger, multi specialty clinics were developing but were not the norm. Hospitals provided secondary and tertiary care. Ambulatory and specialty care was provided at the physician's office or in a hospital setting.

Period 1981 To 1990

During the 1980s and 1990s, cost containment pressure forced both hospitals and physi-

cians to examine the care delivery process. Early cost reduction efforts focused on the reduction of inpatient hospital utilization. There were several notable changes that resulted from these early efforts (4).

- Decrease in the average length of stay of inpatient hospitalizations. Neu indicated that the average length of stay for Medicare patients dropped 20.4 percent within the first years after the implementation of PPS (15).
- Decrease in the use of routine diagnostic testing during inpatient hospitalizations.
- Shift toward use of outpatient diagnostic testing and treatment.
- Use of postacute services such as home care and skilled nursing care increased (15).

The impact on both hospitals and physicians resulting from these changes was significant (4). Following are four notable results.

1. A decrease in inpatient hospital bed utilization resulted in excess hospital bed capacity. Hospitals that previously operated with beds 90% full might now operate with 50% of their inpatient beds full.
2. Hospitals and physicians began to experience decreased profits. This occurred because while both the volume of business and the amount of payment were declining, the cost of operating a health care business continued to rise. Some hospitals faced financial losses for the first time.
3. Decreased profits meant financial limits on new investment in technology and facilities.
4. Providers began to openly compete for a larger share of the health care market. To remain financially sound, hospitals needed to fill excess capacity. More patients were needed to keep beds full as length of stay decreased.

Hospitals responded to these challenges in a variety of ways. Common responses included:

- Cost reductions. Initial attempts at cost reduction included staff reductions and structural reorganization.
- Diversification. New payment methods created incentives to develop alternative care options which could be used to reduce hospital length of stay and produce additional revenue. Common areas for diversification included inpatient rehabilitation (which was exempt from PPS), home care, ambulatory care, and long-term care. From 1985 to 1996, there was a substantial increase in the number of inpatient rehabilitation facilities, long-term care hospitals, skilled nursing facilities, compre-

hensive outpatient rehabilitation facilities and outpatient physical therapy providers certified to provide services under the Medicare Program. Table 1.2 shows the number of facilities certified under the Medicare program in 1985 and in 1996. These numbers do not include providers who choose not to participate in the Medicare program. There was a 20% increase in the number of hospitals providing home care between 1985 and 1989 (16).

- Organizational restructuring. Where previously hospitals had been at the center of the health care delivery system, there was an emerging view that hospitals were the anchors for much larger diversified health care systems. Hospitals began to restructure through horizontal and vertical integration with other providers. Horizontal integration was accomplished through consolidation with like providers in the marketplace. For example, the affiliation of several hospitals to form a regional network is horizontal integration. This allowed one larger health care delivery system to cover larger geographical regions, provide a more comprehensive package of services and thus capture a greater portion of the market share. Vertical integration was used to link together a full continuum of services under one umbrella. A health care system that offers primary care, hospital care, ambulatory care, home care, rehabilitation and long-term skilled nursing care would be vertically integrated. Systems that are vertically integrated can provide patients with the convenience of one-stop shopping. Patients are able to receive all of their care from one source. Service integration supports care management efforts.

- New attention to traditional marketing strategies. Traditionally, hospitals and physicians relied on word of mouth, the prestige of their practice and cutting edge technology to attract physicians and their patients. There was more than enough business to go around. When they found themselves in a position of needing to compete for market share, they turned to more traditional consumer marketing.

- A change in the health care delivery system that developed in the same time frame was the proliferation of entrepreneurial alternative providers. Physicians and others looking for alternative sources of revenue began to provide services traditionally provided only in the hospital setting such as diagnostic radiological imaging. Another example of such a care alternative is the non-hospital based urgent care center. During this period, the profession of physical therapy experienced success in several states as it pushed for legal recognition as a direct access provider. Table 1.2 clearly demonstrates the growth in the number of outpatient physical therapy practices.

The 1990s

The continued growth of managed care and efforts toward the reform of health care financing have kept health care providers focused on change. Restructuring of the health care delivery system has continued. Health care providers have continued to come together through affiliations, mergers and acquisitions to form ever larger provider networks.

Managed care contracting practices now favor a limited number of providers who can cover large geographical regions. To accommodate, health care delivery networks are expanding to cover regional and national patient populations. Another phenomenon has been the growth of national, publicly traded, for-profit health care corporations. These corporations operate nation wide networks of hospitals, skilled nursing facilities, ambulatory care centers, physician and outpatient rehabilitation services practices.

Smaller, independent providers are finding it increasingly difficult to capture and hold a share of the patient market. To survive, many independent providers have joined together to form specialty service networks. Their goal is to get and/or keep a piece of the managed care market. Independent physicians are experiencing the same pressures and are rapidly moving to join large multi-specialty practices. These large physician groups may join larger health care systems or compete for managed care business on their own. More physicians are seeking secure employment

TABLE 1.2

Estimates of The Number of New Medicare Certified Rehabilitation Providers, Skilled Nursing Facilities and Longterm Care Hospitals in 1985 and 1996

TYPE OF PROVIDER	1985	1996
Rehabilitation Hospital, PPS Exempt	68	195
Rehabilitation Units, PPS Exempt	386	841
Long-term Care Hospitals, PPS Exempt	86	181
Skilled Nursing Facilities (SNF)	6,725	13,591
Comprehensive Outpatient Rehabilitation Facilities (CORF)	86	386
Outpatient Physical Therapy Providers	827	2,327

Source: Health Care Financing Administration; Bureau of Data Management and Services, Baltimore, MD.

relationships with larger health care organizations. Employers and providers are both looking at opportunities to by-pass third party payers entirely through direct contracting. Efforts to manage the delivery of care continues. There is an increased emphasis on disease management and the control of cost in the long-term rather than solely focusing on episodic care consumption.

Care standardization efforts are continuing. The refinement and use of alternative levels of care remains a primary strategy of providers operating under risk arrangements. Medicare and, in some states, Medicaid, is moving toward the use of managed care plans as an alternative to the traditional Medicare/Medicaid pre-payment program. Medicare beneficiaries would choose to receive all their care through a managed care provider. Medicare would pay the monthly premium. Many believe that the incentive to enroll will be the provision of insurance plan paid medications. Medicare beneficiaries must pay for their medications directly under Medicare's general coverage guidelines.

Medicare is also experimenting with best practice centers of excellence to provide high volume, high cost services. The Centers of Excellence demonstration projects are limited in number and only involve beneficiaries who undergo coronary artery by-pass grafts and total joint replacement surgery at this time.

The Centers of Excellence demonstration projects take the concept of DRG case payments one step further. The Centers of Excellence receive one bundled payment for all related physician and hospital services provided to the patient from pre-operative care through discharge. Medicare efforts to move away from cost based reimbursement have continued. HCFA has announced its intent to began to change Medicare payment for home care, inpatient rehabilitation and skilled nursing care from a cost based to fixed payment system by the year 2000. The Balanced Budget Act of 1997 has confirmed this initiative and set target dates for every setting except long-term care hospitals. Several states have announced their plans to convert Medicaid to a managed care model. Providers have already begun to respond to these anticipated payment changes.

THE HEALTH CARE PROFESSIONAL MUST ALSO RESPOND

New Skills For A New Time

All of these changes have had a significant impact on the people who deliver health care. Health care providers have been and will continue to be challenged to produce the same or better patient outcomes with fewer resources. Direct care professionals are being required to gain an entirely new set of care management skills in addition to clinical practice skills. Health care managers are required to have a level of leadership ability once expected only from organization leaders. These demands have left more than one health care professional in turmoil. But the demands have also provided the opportunity for clinical managers to step forward and become actively involved in designing the health care delivery system of the future. Decision making is being pushed down from management to the front lines of care delivery. Managers have become mentors, facilitators and educators for staff who are more involved in making organization decisions.

Accountability For Patient Outcomes

Health care professionals are facing increased demands for performance accountability. The outcomes of the health care services are being compared among clinicians. The best practices of health care providers are being modeled. The less effective are being asked to improve. The topic of performance outcomes will be covered in depth in Chapter 11.

Hard Times For The Independent Practitioner

Independent practitioners are facing increased difficulty making an adequate income. While the reimbursement rate for service delivery is steadily declining, the cost of operating a private practice continues to increase. Only those practices that are actively growing and/or are large enough to spread out administrative expenses will remain successful. This scenario makes independent practice an easy target for acquisition by larger organizations. Chapter 14 will focus on business planning skills which are essential for the independent practitioner's success.

Generalists, Specialists And The Use Of Professional Extenders

Health care professionals have also been challenged by industry changes related to the use of generalists, specialists and professional extenders. The current payment trend is toward limiting the financial benefits of specialization in favor of better compensation for generalist practitioners. This balancing is most evident for physicians, but is also reflected in the lack of increased compensation for advanced degrees and clinical specialists in other professions, including physical therapy. There is a growing trend in the medical and allied health professions to use more professional extenders. Physical Therapist Assistants and Therapy Aides are examples of professional extenders. The use of professional extenders brings down the cost of care delivery by increasing the productivity of the better paid professional. This trend is affecting physical therapy as well as other professions.

Impact On The Practice Of Physical Therapy

In our view, the profession of physical therapy has, overall, benefited from the change process. We believe this to be true for several reasons.

1. The demand for physical therapy services has continued to grow since the creation of the Medicare and Medicaid programs in 1965. The demand for physical therapy services grew as the number of elderly and disabled people gained better access to health care through enrollment in the Medicare and Medicaid programs. Physical therapy service demand also grew along with the expansion of the health care services made possible by the growth of the private third party payer system and employer sponsored health care benefits. Under Medicare PPS reimbursement, the importance of physical therapy in ensuring timely and safe discharge was recognized. The demand for physical therapy grew in contrast to other professions that experienced down sizing. Finally, the growth in alternative care settings including inpa-

tient rehabilitation, home care and long-term skilled care created new, expanded markets for physical therapy services.
2. The profession of physical therapy has enjoyed a good reimbursement history making it a service that is attractive to organizational providers and independent practitioners alike.
3. The average rate of compensation for physical therapists became disproportionately higher than that of similar professions due to an ever present shortage of physical therapists in the face of growing demand.
4. The challenges of managed care have provided the opportunity for physical therapists to demonstrate the value of their services toward the goal of reducing the long-term costs of many chronic, disabling conditions.

In sum, the profession of physical therapy has become stronger and better recognized because the health care delivery system has been challenged. Although the overall impact of change has been positive, there are very real challenges ahead. The same factors that have benefited physical therapy professionals have made physical therapy an attractive target for managed care reductions in the future. As the use of physical therapy grows, the efforts of managed care to control that growth will escalate. Because physical therapy is well reimbursed, physical therapy services are an attractive investment for individuals and corporations. As a result the small, private practitioner will face significant challenges in the future.

Finally, as the supply of physical therapists increases and the growth in demand for physical therapy services stabilizes, the shortage of physical therapists will diminish. According to a recent study commissioned by the American Physical Therapy Association, this will result in a softening of the demand for physical therapists and a decline in compensation (17). This topic will be covered in more detail in Chapter 15, Futures.

SUMMARY

Health care professionals have faced significant and continuous changes in the health care delivery system over the past 3 decades. A constant through all of this change has been the commitment among health care professionals to meet the challenges and, in doing so, meet the needs of their patients.

To be successful in the future, health care professionals must stack the deck. They must prepare themselves with skills that have never been required of health care professionals in the past. This book has been written with the belief that, armed with appropriate skills, physical therapists will meet and exceed today's expanded expectations.

The concepts presented in this, and other chapters, may be explored more fully through the use of a continuous case study, a role play, presented in Appendix A. The role play has been designed to demonstrate how management concepts may impact the clinical setting on a daily basis. The intent of the role play is to provoke thought and build a connection between theory and practice of physical therapy in today's health care environment.

REFERENCES

1. Berman HJ, Kukla SF, Weeks LE. The Financial Management of Hospitals. 8th ed. Ann Arbor, MI:Health Administration Press, 1994:96–99,143.
2. Tokarski C. 1980s prove uncertainty of instant cures. Mod Health Care 1990;8(Jan):51–58.
3. American Hospital Association: Council On Long Range Planning And Development. The Environment of Medicine. Chicago: American Medical Association, 1989; Publication no. OP-223/9:15–23.
4. Nosse LJ, Friberg DG. Management Principles for Physical Therapists. Baltimore:Williams & Wilkins, 1992:4.
5. Rhienecker P. Catholic health care enters a new world. Health Prog 1990;June:31–36.
6. Levit KR, Freeland MS, Waldo DR. Health spending and ability to pay: Business, individuals and government. Health Care Financing Rev 1989;10(3):1–11.
7. Hughes, EFX. New Leadership in Health Care Management: The Physician Executive, II. Tampa, FL:The American College of Physician Executives, 1994: Chapter 1.
8. Managed Care Overview. Washington, DC: The American Managed Care And Review Association Foundation, 1994–1995.
9. Report of Managed Care Focus Meeting. Section For Metropolitan Hospitals, American Hospital Association. 1989;Oct:16.
10. Kiesler CA, Morton TL. Psychology and public policy in the health care revolution. Am Psychol 1988;43 (12):993–1003.
11. Boyd J, Kelley L. Health Law 2000: Regulation, litigation, or strangulation? Health Affairs 1996; Fall 15 (3):31–34.
12. Murer CG. Medicare fraud and abuse. REHAB management 1997;June/July:103–104.
13. Pear R. Increase found in those without health coverage. The New York Times; December 15, 1993:A1.
14. Blendon RJ, Donelan K, Lukas CV, et al. Caring for the uninsured and the underinsured: The uninsured and the debate over the repeal of the Massachusetts Universal Health Care Law. Journal of the American Medical Association 1992; Feb 287 (8):1113–1117.
15. Neu CR, Harrison SC. Posthospital Care Before and After the Medicare Prospective Payment System. Santa Monica: Rand, vi.
16. American Hospital Association. Vision, Values, Viability: Environmental Assessment-1989/1990. Chicago; American Hospital, 1988:60–72.
17. American Physical Therapy Association. APTA workforce study looks at supply and demand of PTs. PT Bulletin 1997;May 12(20):1.

2

VALUES AND MOTIVATIONS

PREVIEW

The placement of this chapter early in the book reflects five of the authors' beliefs about the impact of values on human behavior. These beliefs are:

1. Values propel important human behaviors.
2. At its core, health care is a human-to-human endeavor.
3. Health care personnel should prize values that reflect motivations to meet the needs of those in their care.
4. Behavior of health care personnel should reflect an appreciation of values focused on the welfare of others.
5. The above four beliefs should apply to all members of health care organizations.

Such strong belief statements certainly require explanations. To add substance to the discussion of values (what is important), we add the concepts of morality (duties and obligations) and ethics (morality based rules and ideals). The organization of the this chapter flows from a theoretical description of the influence of values on personal behavior to practical applications of the theoretical concepts in health care organizations. The concepts of values, morality and ethics will be integrated as they apply to an individual health care professional and to health care organization managers. Laws are excluded from the discussions because the focus is on choosing to do what is morally right based on ethical principles rather than out of concern of a legal penalty.

Practical examples are provided to engage the reader to think about identifying values, assessing situations for moral and ethical content, and resolving such issues in health care organizational contexts. A role-playing situation is included in Appendix A.2 to facilitate integration and engender thought about moral issues and ethical principles in physical therapy work environments.

KEY WORDS

Code of Ethics: guidelines formulated by members of a group with common interests that express the group's ideals and moral code or obligations to the public to self-regulate while advancing the interests of the group.

Culture: people who come together to achieve a common purpose.

Ethical Principles: guidelines or rules based on moral philosophies used to compare alternative options.

Ethics: branch of philosophy focusing on morality (see morality below). Ethics relate to what ought to be done in the ideal sense.

Mission Statement: written document identifying why an organization exists. This statement tells the reader what the business does (products, services), who the customers or patients are, the geographical location(s) where the business operates, its specialty, and it expresses the collective aspirations (goals) of the organization. This statement also may contain values related to interpersonal relations.

Moral Issues: conflicts stemming from human interactions that involve matters of fairness, harm, just claims and rights.

Morality: in its most general form morality involves assumptions about what is good and right, and duties or obligations present in a situation. Moral obligations are behavior related. These behavioral obligations are universal and apply without exception to everyone alike.

Motivation: a psychological construct term that refers to biological, interpersonal and societal goals people strive to fulfill. Values (see below) support motivations.

Motivational Types of Values: empirically derived groups of values that serve different motivations. A value typology that groups values according to their common motivational goal.

Self-View: a constructed word meaning all aspects of one's psychological self. Groups also have self-views. Self-view is a global cognitive concept that is sustained by engaging in behaviors that are congruent with self-view.

Stakeholder: any individual or group with something to gain or loose as a result of a decision.

Strategic Plan: the result of an organizational planning process which is intended to fulfill the organization's values, mission, and move the organization toward the realization of its vision (see below).

Values: words expressing enduring goals that carry sufficient psychological reward to serve as guiding principles in the life of a person, group or culture. Values stimulate emotions, serve as cognitive standards for judging and justifying actions, and lead to actions that fulfill desired personal, social, and societal motivational goals.

Value Priority: relative importance given by an individual or group to the motivational goal served by a particular value.

Values Statement: a document adapted by the highest managerial level of an organization that focuses on moral issues. A values statement, also known as a philosophical statement, proclaims the organization's beliefs about morality, i.e., what behaviors are right and what behaviors are wrong.

Vision Statement: a simple, brief, written inspirational document intended to advance a futuristic view of an organization to its members and other stakeholders.

INTRODUCTION

We visualize an ideal health care organization as one in which personal and group decisions are made based on balanced considerations. These considerations include knowing what the organization values, having a desire to treat others fairly and recognizing that it takes resources for the organization to realize its goals. Our approach in this chapter is to emphasize what should be rather than what is. We take this approach without losing sight of the necessity of a business to have a margin of profit to carry out its purposes.

In managing the provision of health care services, there are many kinds of decisions that must be made. People who stand to gain or lose something when decisions are made have something at stake. They are called stakeholders. The principal stakeholders in health care are patients. Employees, vendors and visitors are also stakeholders. Even competitors may be considered stakeholders. In the current and near future health care environment, today's competitors are likely to be tomorrow's associates (see physical therapy practice, Chapter 15). Under this scenario, it is reasonable to treat competitors to some extent as stakeholders.

The ideal being suggested above is that health care decisions be made after a balanced consideration of what is good for all stakeholders. In addition to accurate factual information, balanced consideration of options requires:

- Knowledge of the values that are being advanced by the actualization of a particular solution.
- Personal and collective willingness to act morally, i.e., meet obligations to others.
- Guidance from an organization's leadership.
- Guidance from external stakeholders, e.g., professional associations like the American Physical Therapy Association (APTA).

The maxim that evolves from the idealistic vision outlined above is: meet stakeholders' needs, prosper by positive means and compete honestly (1). From an organizational perspective, this statement means, prospering by working hard, paying great attention to details, providing superior service (see Chapters 3, 14), striving for win-win solutions (see Chapter 4), and being persistent (see Chapter 14). This maxim opposes the idea of profiting by win-lose solutions in which calculated means, even though they might be legal, are used to cause potential or actual harm to stakeholders (1).

Why this concern for others? How far does this concern reach? What does this concern have to do with clinical practice? Can health care organizations advance themselves if they treat others, including competitors, fairly? To help answer these kinds of questions, in the following sections, we discuss important antecedents to human behaviors. The most important of these antecedents are personal values and organizational values. The following discussion therefore dimensionalizes values and related psychological concepts to develop a framework for dealing with the practical matter of balancing obligations to stakeholders and self-interests in the work place.

PERSONAL GUIDANCE: UNDERSTANDING PERSONAL VALUES

The term value has two general meanings. One is economic and tangible, and the other is psychological and intangible. Economic value is usually directly measurable by objective means such as financial worth. The psychological perspective of value is cognitive and emotion related. Psychological value can only be inferred from other behaviors. One way values are discovered is by asking people what is consistently important to them or what principles guide their choices in all of their life roles. Psychological values are defined in this chapter by words people attach to goals that provide psychological reward. Value words reflect enduring beliefs that serve as guiding principles for making choices among available options for fulfilling personal, social, and societal goals, i.e., motivations (2).

In this book, the term value is used in the economic and psychological sense. Usually, the context is clarified in the discussion. In this chapter, the emphasis is on the psychological perspective of values and the relationship between values and personal, organizational and professional behaviors. It is important to explore the psychological concept of values because it is generally believed that values influence human behavior, particularly when choices must be made between emotion stimulating options (3).

VALUES THEORY

Values have often been categorized situationally, for example, family values, work values, and cultural values. Values have also been traditionally dichotomized into moral and non-moral categories. Moral values carry obligation such as duty and justice. Non-moral values reflect social conventions such as being respectful to important people or personal preferences like the make of car one chooses to buy. Studying values in these restricted contexts has resulted in attention being given to individual or a few value terms and a segmented understanding of values. Such approaches have failed to produce a generalizable theory of values that reasonably explains how all values interrelate to influence behaviors (3).

Over the past dozen years, a unique approach to the study of values has emerged. Rather than emphasize a hierarchy among individual values as had been done, this approach began with the hypothesis that there was a logical organizational structure among groups of values. It was assumed that groups of values were related and this relationship would be statistically demonstrable. This hypothesis was tested in international studies involving more than 20,000 participants from different cultures and backgrounds. The results supported the generalizablity of the organizational theory of values (4). This theory of values offers a new perspective on how values interrelate and their connection to motivations and overt behaviors. A second benefit of this theory stems from the diversity of the groups who were studied. The theory has application in cross-cultural situations. An understanding of the general structure of values systems can help health care managers gain insight into work place issues such as motivation and ethics across cultures.

Generalizable Values Theory

The Theory of the Universal Content of Values defines values as words reflecting individualistic or collective goals which are evaluated on a scale ranging from unimportant to supremely important (5). Two central ideas of this theory are:

1. Values are organized according to common goals called motivations.
2. Motivations and their component values are organized in a continuum of interrelationships that is logical.

The basic logic is within a values continuum, some values support motivations that are more or less achievable together. These complementary values are also opposed in varying degrees to the fulfillment of motivations served by some other values (2). Research has supported this continuum of complementary and oppositional value-motivation relationships. Analyses of the data have provided statistical confirmation of a continuum involving 10 groups of values. Each group of values was named for the common motivational goal they advanced.

Continuum of Motivational Types of Values

Figure 2.1 is a circle graph representing the idealized continuum of relationships among 10 categories of value priorities. Two types of analyses are used to develop such a graph. One analysis is based on intercorrelations between value importance ratings. The other analysis is a set of rules used by the investigators to determine where to place the partition lines on a graph's surface (5).

The numbers in Figure 2.1 represent intercorrelations among importance ratings of selected values plotted on X and Y axes. Table 2.1 names and defines the numbered values in Figure 2.1. Table 2.2 defines the motivational terms noted in the figure. Plotting the intercorrelations as de-

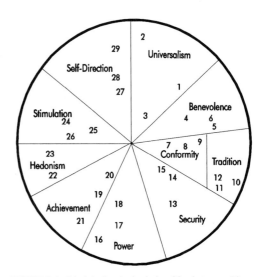

FIGURE 2.1. Model of typical relationships between 10 motivational types of values. Modified from Schwartz S. Are there universal aspects in the structure and contents of human values? Journal of Social Issues 1994;50:24.

TABLE 2.1

Definitions of Selected Value Terms and Their Typical Motivational Goal Classification

EXAMPLE VALUES	DEFINITIONS	MOTIVE GOAL
1. A world of beauty	beauty of nature and the arts	universalism
2. Broad-minded	tolerant of different ideas, beliefs	
3. Protect the environment	preserving nature	
4. Helpful	working for the welfare of others	benevolence
5. Honest	genuine, sincere	
6. Forgiving	willing to pardon others	
7. Politeness	courtesy, good manners	conformity
8. Honoring parents, elders	showing respect	
9. Self-discipline	self-restraint, resist temptation	
10. Devout	holding religious faith and belief	tradition
11. Accepting life as it is	submitting to life's circumstances	
12. Respect for tradition	preserving time-honored customs	
13. National security	protection of my nation from others	security
14. Social order	stability of society	
15. Family security	safety for loved ones	
16. Social power	control over others, dominance	power
17. Authority	the right to lead or command	
18. Wealth	money, material possessions	
19. Successful	achieving goals	achievement
20. Capable	competent, effective, efficient	
21. Ambitious	aspiring, hard-working	
22. Pleasure	gratification of desires	hedonism
23. Enjoying life	enjoying, food, leisure, sex, etc.	
24. Daring	seeking risk, adventure	stimulation
25. A varied life	challenge, novelty and change	
26. An exciting life	stimulating experiences	
27. Creativity	imagination, uniqueness	self-direction
28. Curious	interested in everything, exploring	
29. Freedom	freedom of action and thought	

 TABLE 2.2

Names and Definitions of the 10 Motivational Goals that Values Serve

MOTIVE TERMS	DEFINITIONS
UNIVERSALISM	Appreciation, tolerance, understanding and protection for the welfare of all people and nature
BENEVOLENCE	Enhancement and preservation of the welfare of people with whom one is in frequent contact
CONFORMITY	Restraint of actions and impulses likely to upset or harm others and violate social expectations or norms
TRADITION	Acceptance, commitment and respect for the customs and ideas that traditional culture or religion provide
SECURITY	Harmony, stability and safety of self, relationships and society
POWER	Prestige and social status, control over resources and people
ACHIEVEMENT	Personal success earned by demonstrating competence according to social standards
HEDONISM	Sensuous gratification and pleasure for oneself
STIMULATION	Challenge, excitement and novelty in life
SELF-DIRECTION	Independent thought and action

Adopted from Schwartz S. Are there universal aspects in the structure and contents of human values? Journal of Social Issues 1994;50:22.

scribed above gives each value a unique two-dimensional location in space. The circle configuration allows the continuum of interrelationships among groups of values to be clearly presented. Values whose intercorrelations with all other values under consideration are most alike serve the same motivation. They are represented on the graph as numbers near each other. Values numbered 10–12 (Fig. 2.1) are examples of values with similar intercorrelations with all other values. These three values also demonstrate the concept of oppositional relationships between values. While values 10–12 (Fig. 2.1) are similarly well correlated with the same values, they are similarly poorly or negatively correlated with other values, e.g., numbers 24–26. This finding is interpreted to mean that these trios of values serve goals or motivations that are oppositional. It is not likely that both motivations could be fulfilled together.

The second feature of the graph is the partition lines which divide the circle into distinct regions (Fig. 2.1). The 10 slices include the values representing 10 distinct motivational goals found in many cultures. Table 2.1 presents the definitions of the numbered values contained within each slice in Figure 2.1. The complete list of values that have been studied can be found in reference five. Table 2.2 presents the definitions of the 10 motivational types of values listed in Figure 2.1. Together these definitions complete the essential information needed to appreciate the organizational framework of values within a motivational continuum.

There are five practical points relevant to managing people that can be drawn from the discussion so far:

1. The importance of values is that they serve to facilitate engaging in behaviors that satisfy motivations. The crucial content aspect that distinguishes among values is the type of motivational goal they express (3).
2. Motivations are identified vicariously though statistical relationships among values.
3. No single value leads to engaging or not engaging in a particular behavior. A person's value system, i.e., all the values a person recognizes, are likely involved in the weighing of options expected to satisfy a particular desire, need or goal.
4. People from the same culture hold similar values

as individuals, however, they differentially rate the importance each value has as a guiding principle in their lives.
5. People in one culture may prize the same values as people in another culture. However, these values may serve different motivational goals in each culture.

The preceding five points are based on the assumption that when asked, people know what is important to them and that they can rate their value priorities upon request. This assumption can be challenged by personal experience. We all have stopped at times to ask ourselves such questions as, What do I want? What is important here? Why do I want that to happen? Understanding what we value is not always clear. Making choices between desirable options is difficult without giving thoughtful consideration of why one option should be chosen over another. An understanding of personal values is needed to make difficult choices.

EXPLORING PERSONAL VALUES

One way to gain insight into personal values is through a card sorting exercise. An example exercise is described in Table 2.3. The reader is reminded that this example involves only a sample of the value terms that have been studied. For the complete list of values used in the international studies, see reference five.

A variation of the preceding card sort exercise is to use different value terms. There are several other sources of defined value terms that can be consulted (6,7). To carry out the card sort exercise, follow instructions 1 through 6 in Table 2.3. Remember to use the new value terms at step 3. The chosen values, if different from those in Table 2.1, have not likely been categorized by motivational type. To determine the common factors supported by prioritized values requires introspection on the part of the person carrying out this exercise. Self-questioning can help uncover patterns from prioritized values. Look at each of the value terms rated most important.

- Ask, "What would I gain if this value were realized?"
- Write down the answers.
- Repeat the question a second time.
- If the answer changes, reflect this on the answer list.

TABLE 2.3
Instructions for Values Card Sort Exercise

SUPPLIES NEEDED:
Scissors, a copy of Table 2.1, 8 index cards and a marker
INSTRUCTIONS:
1. Use the 8 index cards to make a 1-8 rating scale Number each card. Annotate cards 1, 4, 5, and 8 as follows:
   • Card 1 represents the few values that are not important as guiding principles in your life.
   • Cards 4 and 5 represent values that are important in your life.
   • Card 8 represents the few values that are supremely important as guiding principles in your life.
2. Place the cards in numerical order so card 8 (most important) is located closest to you and card 1 (not important) located furthest from you.
3. Cut each of the example values and their definitions from Table 2.1.
4. Consider all of the sample value terms
   • Pick out the few values you rate 8 (supremely important).
   • Pick out the few values you rate 1 (not important).
   • Place these values face up on the appropriate rating card.
5. Sort the remaining values according to their relative importance as guiding principles in your life. Try to distinguish as much a possible between values by using all the rating options.
6. Review all of the values and re-rate them as necessary.
7. Note which values you gave the highest ratings. Consult Table 2.1 to see which motivational types of values you identified as most important as guiding principles in your life.
8. Assess the results. Do you agree or disagree? Is there a pattern? What surprised you? What was confirmed?

• Review the list and ask, "Are there any answers that seem similar?"
• Ask, "Can these answers be combined?"
• If necessary, repeat the questioning process until a few central goals summarize the aims of the prioritized values.

The final goals extracted by the card sort can be considered the ends served by the prioritized values. It should be realized that the card sort exercises, while theory based, are not valid measurement instruments. The purpose of their inclusion here is to facilitate deeper thinking and discussion about personal and later, professional and organizational values and motivations.

HARD QUESTIONS: WHAT IS RIGHT?

The preceding theory of values is basically a way of framing a psychological concept. The theory recognizes that values have an evaluative function. Values felt to be very important facilitate engaging in behaviors that serve certain motivational goals. The theory however makes no judgement as to which values or motivational types of values are more or less preferable. Questions which ask what is good and bad, right and wrong (8) and whether or not one has an obligation to do this or that are in the realm of moral philosophy. A more common name for moral philosophy is ethics (9).

CHANGING THE FOCUS FROM VALUATION TO OBLIGATION

There is a difference between expressing what you would like to do because it is personally desirable (valuation) and expressing what you ought to do because of duty or obligation (morality). This statement recognizes a change in focus from thinking about self-interest to thinking about obligations to others. There are general situations which involve moral issues (10):

• When the welfare of an individual or a group is in question.
• When justice is a concern.
• When human rights are in question.

Moral obligations are universal. They compel everyone, without exception, to do what is good or right (11). Moral obligations are distinguishable from personal preferences like the clothing style and social conventions like addressing a physician as doctor.

External pressure to prize certain values or motivations increases when those values or motivations are widely shared in a culture. Most members of a culture share values that deal with moral obligations. However, whether or not these obligations are met, is ultimately dependent on a person's motivation to act morally, i.e., their will to act morally (11). Some moral obligations are clear to most people. For example, doing something to save someone's life is a universal moral obligation. Other moral obligations are subtler. These situations have more nuances making recognition sometimes difficult (1).

DEALING WITH MORAL ISSUES

When moral issues are identified, they are often emotionally difficult to resolve (1). This is assumed to be the case because moral issues involve making choices between two or more conflicting motivations that are important aspects of a person's self-image. Second, the results of moral issue deliberations are seldom resolvable in ways that honor the interests of all stakeholders equally. These types of resolutions, sometimes called win-win solutions, are difficult but not impossible to formulate. A process for dealing with moral issues is described next using a manager as the example moral agent.

A Process to Deal with Moral Issues

The first step in dealing with a moral issue is recognizing that there are moral obligations inherent in a situation. Managers may find this difficult. Typically managers have developed problem identification and decision-making skills in traditional areas of business. Traditional management skills include budgeting, controlling, coordinating, directing, integrating, organizing, planning and staffing. The general decision-making paradigm used to solve traditional management-related issues involves three steps:

1. Identify the problem.
2. Identify alternative solutions.
3. Choose the best alternative from among the options.

Having decision-making preparation places a manager in an advantageous position to solve a variety of types of problems. However, problems with underlying moral causes can be very subtle. Moral issues often involve assumptions about duties outside of traditional areas of managerial preparation. Failure to recognize nuances associated with moral issues may hinder a manager or others from accomplishing step one of the general problem solving process, i.e., identification. For example, problems such as patient complaints, employee grievances, higher than expected productivity, incident reports, and resignations may involve problems in areas managers are used to encountering. It is also possible that these problems are related to moral issues or they may involve a mixture of issues. Managers are trained to and rewarded for looking at problems in the context of business operations such as those noted above. As a result, traditional management issues are often the sole focus of the problem solving process (1). Moral matters may not be considered as related causes of operational problems. The matter of moral problem identification is further complicated when those involved are unprepared or unwilling to deal with such problems (1).

There are several practical suggestions presented in Table 2.4 to assist managers and others to begin to recognize and identify moral issues.

Making Moral Decisions

Once a moral problem is identified, progress toward a solution can be made. However, solving moral problems requires more steps than were noted in the initial general problem-solving model. Five main steps have been identified in a moral reasoning process (1):

1. Analyze the situation based on ethical principles.
2. Weigh options according to how well they meet the most situationally relevant ethical principle(s).
3. Justify the identified ethical principle(s) on the basis of most likely outcomes.
4. Choose the course of action that is best for stakeholders.
5. Evaluate the outcome of the process.

This process is dependent on familiarity with four primary ethical principles applicable to the behavior of health care personnel: Autonomy, beneficence, justice and nonmaleficence. These principles are defined and summarized in Table 2.5.

It is helpful to know what kinds of ethical problems are typical before beginning to look for

TABLE 2.4
Selected Methods for Discovering Moral Issues

METHODS	COMMENTS
Ask: Is there a legal problem here?	Laws are minimal societal standards. Something illegal is also a violation of someone's rights. Moral obligations require honoring the rights of others.
Review professional literature on business and professional ethics.	There are contemporary discussions and case studies with expert comment to help managers and clinicians deal with contemporary moral issues.
Review professional codes of ethics and accompanying interpretive practice documents.	These documents express the obligations of members of a professional association. As the practice of the profession evolves, new issues are encountered. The professional documents are often revised to meet changes in professional practice.
Consult knowledgeable people.	Some health care organizations have an ethics committee. Advice can be sought from such a group.
Educate yourself.	Take a continuing education or academic course in ethics or moral development. Volunteer to serve on professional committees that deal with ethical behavior.
Brainstorm with peers.	Discuss issues with those you trust. A fresh point of view may be gained. A friend may have had prior experience with a similar issue that may be helpful in dealing with the current issue. Discussing an issue may re-frame it so its nature becomes clearer.
Apply the golden rule.	If there is concern about the moral aspects of a situation take a third party stance. Ask, what would a person who respects others do in the particular situation. Compare your mental solution to what occurred or may occur.
Use your intuition.	If a problem exists, and there is no legal concern, and no business principle seems to apply, consider the possibility that the problem may be related to a moral issue.

TABLE 2.5
Four General Ethical Principles Applicable to Health Care Environments

	ETHICAL PRINCIPLES	COMMENTS[a]
Autonomy	(Respect for self-determination)	For this principle to be honored, the stakeholder must be told the truth, promises kept and information that is shared, and legal, must be treated as confidential.
Beneficence	(Balance harms and benefits)	To honor this principle a person in power has a duty to act positively on behalf of the stakeholder. This entails balancing potential and actual risks on behalf of a stakeholder unable to do this alone.
Justice	(Fairness)	This principle requires those in power to share resources and allocate benefits according to need, merit and valid claims.
Nonmaleficence	(Do no harm)	This principle requires those in power to avoid causing harm to stakeholders. This includes using methods that minimize harm to stakeholders when harm is unavoidable.

[a]Adopted from Darr K. Ethics in health services management. 3rd ed. Baltimore, MD: Health Professions Press, 1997:24–26.

them. In health care, these problems are commonly found in the following areas (1, 12):

1. Conflicts between duties, e.g., do no harm, be truthful.
2. Conflicts between rights, e.g., patient's autonomy versus beneficence.
3. Conflicts between responsibilities, e.g., to patient and to employer.
4. Conflicts between character traits , e.g., compassion versus honesty.

Looking for moral content in these above areas can be helpful in dissecting moral issues.

They provide a framework for analyzing situational conflicts for moral implications.

A Quantification Method

Once the ethical problem has been identified and analyzed, a quantified moral reasoning process can be carried out. Table 2.5 defines four ethical principles that can be used to guide the process. This process results in a numerical score that can be used to compare alternative solutions in terms of their relative fulfillment of ethical principles. The instructions for this method are as follows:

1. Identify the problem (duties, rights, responsibilities, traits).
2. Identify all reasonable solutions (at least two).
3. Identify the ethical principles related to each solution (autonomy, beneficence, justice, nonmaleficence).
4. Rate the identified ethical principles from least important (rated 1) to most important (rated 4).
5. Make a form like Table 2.6 to do calculations.
6. Follow the instructions in Table 2.6 and calculate the relative contribution of each solution to meeting the prioritized ethical principles.
7. Sum the relative contribution of each option.
8. Choose the option that most promotes the ethical principles identified in the situation.

There are issues that require this time consuming process because they seriously jeopardize the well being of stakeholders. When there are multiple options and numerous stakeholders, then the quantified process has much to offer as a guide to ethical decision making.

A Quick Screen

There are ethics-related issues that are not complicated by having many stakeholders or several options to consider. There are also times when a decision has to be made in public and immediately. An expedient approach may be warranted for such situations. This approach involves carrying out an ethical issue screen. Screening involves a yes or no response to the following three questions (13):

1. Is the act legal? (If yes, proceed to question two).
2. Is there, or will there be, a big winner and a big loser?
3. Am I comfortable with what has occurred or is likely to occur?

The analysis of the responses to these questions is straightforward. Ethical requirements are usually more demanding than laws; therefore, an illegal act is also unethical. A response of no to the first screening question terminates the screening process but demands followup action. If an illegal act has been carried out, then it must be reported to organizational and legal authorities. If the illegal act is being contemplated, then a no response to the legal question clearly warns against carrying out the action. Acts determined to be legal should be screened further using the remaining questions.

The second question is concerned with fairness or justice. It assumes that when someone gains markedly more from a transaction than others involved in the transaction, it is a win-lose situation.

TABLE 2.6

Form for Calculating the Relative Contribution of Three Behavioral Options Toward Fulfilling Important Ethical Principles

OPTIONS	PRINCIPLE RATED 1 ($\downarrow$ IMPORTANT)	PRINCIPLE RATED 2	PRINCIPLE RATED 3	PRINCIPLE RATED 4 ($\uparrow$ IMPORTANT)	TOTALS
X	+	+	+	=	
Y	+	+	+	=	
Z	+	+	+	=	

[a]The highest ratings reflect relatively greater importance. Rate each ethical principle from least important to most important for the situation. Rate each option on each ethical principle in accord with its perceived promotion of each principle. Rate the option contributing the least to the promotion of each principle 1. Rate the option contributing the most 3. Multiply the principle ratings by the option ratings and sum horizontally to obtain the total for each option. The option with the greatest total promotes the important ethical principles to a relatively greater extent than the other options.

Win-lose situations should be looked at more closely. Such situations can occur through deceitful actions as well as through shrewdness. Win-lose situations can also occur by design. A person guided by ethical principles would find it emotionally difficult to carry out actions that lead to gains acquired unfairly or result in serious harm to others. This assumption leads to the next question.

The third question asks a person how they are likely to feel if or after the act occurs. This question assumes several things. First, it assumes a person has a moral foundation that allows them to know right from wrong. Second, it assumes that a person desires to do what is right. This is an assumption that the person has a moral conscience. Finally, it also assumes that the person has moral will, i.e., they are motivated to make ethical choices. A person who sees oneself as an ethical person will likely experience psychological discomfort if they break an ethical rule.

The preceding screening questions provide food for thought. They offer a quick, simple way to assess single or related actions. Applying these questions to everyday situations can facilitate thinking about the moral side of past, present and anticipated actions. Asking these questions regularly increases sensitivity to moral issues and it may shorten the time needed to identify basic moral issues.

A Role Playing Method

The final method to be discussed focuses on the ethical principle of justice. The golden rule, do unto others as you would have them do unto you, guides a decision-maker through a process designed to identify just solutions. This method is very different from the two prior methods. A decision-maker is asked to take on two roles. One role requires taking the perspective of a stakeholder. The second role requires taking the perspective of an impartial observer.

Throughout the role play, the decision-maker is supposed to be thoughtful, thorough and honest in their analysis of the options under consideration. The general instructions for the role player are (14):

1. Imagine that you are in each person's position.
2. State all the morally supportable claims that could be made by each person in this situation.

3. Now change roles. Be an impartial observer. Imagine you do not know which person you are.
4. As the impartial observer, weigh the merits of the claims made by each person in the situation.
5. Identify which claims you, the unbiased observer, would uphold.
6. Finally, apply the golden rule. Would you accept the decisions you made if you were the stakeholder(s)?

The main assumption of this method is that morality is best determined by subjecting a situation to examination based on values that prioritize justice-related goals. The ideal outcome of this type of assessment is a balanced or just solution. A just solution is possible if the decision-maker is willing and able to see the situation through the eyes all the stakeholders. This ability occurs in stages and can be facilitated by opportunities to take multiple role perspectives (15) as well as through a mentoring relationship with experienced moral decision makers (11).

SUMMARIZING PERSONAL GUIDANCE: A MODEL

The relationships between values, motivations, morality and ethical principles have been only loosely integrated in the preceding discussions. These concepts have not been blended in a reasonable way to explain their interactive influences on human behaviors. To conceptually relate the value-motivation-moral-ethical information discussed thus far, a rational model is offered. Figure 2.2 is a model to help conceptu-

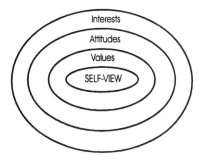

PERSONAL GUIDANCE

Interests

Attitudes

Values

SELF-VIEW

FIGURE 2.2. A conceptual model of the interrelationships of important factors guiding personal behaviors.

alize relationships among values, motivations and other behavioral antecedents. To functionally unite these terms, the model incorporates a construct named self-view. This psychological construct can be envisioned as representing what one believes about one's self. Included within self-view is a person's motivations and their moral will, i.e., their desire to make moral choices. Self-view, like other global psychological constructs, e.g., ego, self-esteem (16), self-concept (17), and personality (18), evolve from cultural influences, life experiences, and individual or group interpretations of these influences and experiences (19). An important purpose of self-view is to clarify the function of values. This values function is to sustain self-view by maintaining harmony among self-view and other behavioral influences like attitudes and interests (16). This is the gatekeeper or evaluative function that has been ascribed to values. By controlling antecedent influences on behavior, values can be helpful in sustaining harmony between self-view and actions. To recognize this important filtering function, the term values is located in the ring adjacent to self-view in Figure 2.2, and attitudes and interests are located in the outer rings. The more centrally located values reflect the belief that values temper attitudes and interests as well as their influence on self-view (16).

Personal self-view may be inferred from several measures. These include measures of values, attitudes and interests. Self-view can also be inferred from observed behaviors, such as the activities that are given priority (values-motivations), what is said regarding general categories of people, objects or ideas (attitudes) (16), and work preferences (interests) (20).

When harmony exists among self-view, values, attitudes and interests, psycholgical comfort would be expected to occur. For maximal comfort, other guidance systems must also be in harmony. In the case of health care professionals, two additional important circles of influence exist. These are the guiding influences of professional associations and managers in the work place. These sources of behavioral guidance will be discussed in turn.

PROFESSIONAL GUIDANCE: MORE ON ETHICS

Behavioral guidance for health care personnel also comes from professional associations such as the APTA. This association, and others like it, are offically recognized organizations representing members of specific professions. In general, professional associations advocate for their membership to the public, in governmental arenas, and to third party payers (see Chapters 7 and 8). Professional organizations often help provide guides to enhance the ethical behavior of members. These professional behavioral guides are stated in a written document called a code of ethics and interpreted in supplemental documents. Codes of ethics serve three general purposes (21):

1.   Define member obligations to the public.
2.   Self-regulation.
3.   Self-manifestation.

A code of ethics identifies the values of members of the association with respect to meeting the preceding purposes. A code stipulates the moral rules and ideals members of the association are to follow or aspire to in such areas as patient care, professional interactions, economic matters and marketing. A well developed code of ethics clearly states (22,23):

*   Moral rules of the profession, e.g., specific duties related to avoid causing harm.
*   Moral ideals of the profession, e.g., encouragement to carry out positive actions toward others to prevent or relieve discomfort.
*   Defines violations (interpretations) of moral rules in the profession.
*   Responsibility of members to police themselves and impose sanctions on offenders.

In subscribing to standards of professional behavior, an association member is contracting with society to limit his or her own self-interest in moral situations (24, 25). Only members of the organization are obligated to this contract. Licensed practitioners in the same field who are not members have not entered into this contract. These individuals are therefore not directly bound to follow the standards of behavior. However, professional codes of ethics can indirectly affect licensed professionals who are not members of their professional associations in at least two ways. The first way is through licensure laws. The second way relates to consumer preference. Licensure laws often adopt elements of a profession's code of ethics as the standard for defining morally acceptable behavior. The practical implication of this is that a licensed professional is likely to be held to the standard of their representative professional organization (personal communication, 3/27/97, Kathy Lewis). Purchasers of services want to know that they are receiving high quality care delivered in an ethical manor. Verification of credentials of perspective employees or service providers is receiving much attention today (see Chapters 1 and 12). Service purchasers may require providers to follow the code of ethics of their professional association as one means of assuring quality care.

Code of Ethics

A professional organization's code of ethics clearly identifies the moral rules its members must follow. These rules are specific to a particular profession. Only informed members of a profession can substantively determine what the moral rules are in their field. These moral rules are often stated as "do not's". The APTA Guide to Professional Conduct (Appendix B) states, for example, that physical therapists shall not engage in conduct that constitutes harassment or abuse of, or discrimination against, colleagues, associates, or others (26). The basic precepts of morality also advocate striving for actions that promote the welfare of others. These are ideals that association members are encouraged to realize. These ideals are often stated as nice to do's. An example of such an ideal would be: physical therapists shall support quality education in academic and clinical settings (26).

Moral rules can be interpreted as the minimal standards of behavior that all members of a profession are required to follow. Moral rules are duties. As duties, they must be followed impartially. Those who break moral rules should be punished. Typically, this punishment is by public an-

nouncement naming those who have been expelled from the association. Moral ideals, on the other hand, are behavioral aspirations that members are encouraged to achieve. Moral ideals differ from moral rules in that they encompass areas that are not always under the control of the member wishing to act in a positive manner toward others. At best, members of professional organizations can but strive to attain moral ideals. The attainment of moral ideals is encouraged but there is no punishment for failing to attain them (23).

The above distinction between moral rules (universal do not's) and moral ideals (nice to do's) is important because of the sanctions that are invoked for breaking moral rules. Unfortunately, professional codes of ethics do not always clearly distinguish between moral ideals and moral rules. Furthermore, moral ideals are sometimes transformed into specific duties, i.e., moral rules. For example, relieving pain is a moral ideal for many health care personnel. By adding the specific situations and circumstances under which pain is to be relieved gives relieving pain the status of a moral rule.

Typically, only common moral issues are addressed in a code. As a result, it becomes important to identify the underlying bases for the selection of the issues addressed in a code. These bases include the stated values of the profession and ethical principles. Once a profession's core values are identified, they provide generalizable guidance in interpreting situations that are not addressed or inadequately addressed by the code or its interpretive documents. For example, the values in Table 2.6 were extracted from the current APTA Code (Appendix C) (27) Code of Ethics and Guide (26). Clearly, these values can be interpreted as supporting motivations that benefit patients and other stakeholders. A more thorough look at the code and guide is needed to distinguish moral rules from moral ideals.

1997 APTA CODE OF ETHICS AND GUIDE FOR PROFESSIONAL CONDUCT

The current APTA code is the fifth version since 1935. The format of the code includes a preamble and eight statements of principle. To assist members in interpreting the code there is a guide containing 54 primary interpretive statements. There is no formal listing of core values for physical therapists as there are for some similar health care groups (28, 29). Therefore, the values in the code and guide have to be extracted from the written information (Table 2.7).

Analysis of APTA Code and Guide

The content of the APTA code preamble, eight statements of principle and interpretive guide will be reviewed. The focus of the review is to identify the underlying values and ethical principles important to the APTA as an organization and its membership.

The APTA code preamble makes clear that ethical principles are the underpinnings of the code and that all active and presumably student physical therapist members of the association shall be bound to uphold the principles. The strength of this obligation upon members is reinforced by the use of the legalistic term shall (3). Each of the code statements of principle and their associated conduct guide statements is assessed below. The key value terms found in these documents are identified along with the relevant ethical principle(s) (Table 2.5).

Statement 1. Physical therapists respect the rights and dignity of all individuals.

Assessment: The related interpretive statements in the guide show that respect for dignity and freedom of everyone in the work place was the intent of the statement. Also, expressions of the value confidentiality or keeping secrets are noted. These values come from the ethical principle of autonomy.

Statement 2. Physical therapists comply with the laws and regulations governing the practice of physical therapy.

Assessment: Laws and regulations are intended to protect the public from harm. The predominant values extracted from the interpretive guide are doing what is good for others and avoid harming others. The ethical principles here are beneficence and nonmaleficence. Another viewpoint is that laws that prohibit unqualified (unlicensed) individuals from practicing physical therapy protect the autonomy of the profession.

Statement 3. Physical therapists accept responsibility for the exercise of sound judgement.

Assessment: The importance of this statement is evident in the 15 interpretive statements that divide responsibility into four categories. The underlying values in the statement and the related guide interpretive statements include doing what is good for the patient in the clinical sense, doing what is good for the patient and others in the fiscal sense, and fairness. All four ethical principles are implicated here. Which principle predominates is situation dependent.

Statement 4. Physical therapists maintain and promote high standards for PT practice, education, and research.

TABLE 2.7

Value Terms Extrapolated from the 1997 APTA Code of Ethics and Guide for Professional Conduct and their Assumed Motivational Goals

VALUE TERM AND DEFINITION	LIKELY MOTIVATION(S) SERVED[a]
AUTONOMY (Self-determination)	Self-direction
BENEFICENCE (Do good)	Benevolence
CONFIDENTIALITY (Keep legal secrets)	Benevolence
EQUALITY (Treat like cases alike)	Universalism
FIDELITY (Loyalty)	Benevolence
DIGNITY (Support other's esteem)	Benevolence, Conformity
JUSTICE (Fairness, just payment)	Universalism
NONMALEFICENCE (Do no harm)	Universalism, Conformity
SELF-DETERMINATION (Use judgement)	Self-direction
PURSUE EXCELLENCE (High standards)	Achievement
SOCIAL JUSTICE (Pro bono service)	Universalism
VERACITY (Truth, give accurate information)	Benevolence

[a]See Table 2.2 for definitions of motivational types of values.

Assessment: The interpretive statements reflect doing what is good for all those with whom the member interacts in the clinic, classroom or research setting. The ethical principles are autonomy, beneficence and nonmaleficence.

Statement 5. Physical therapists seek remuneration for their services that is deserved and reasonable.

Assessment: The values are fairness and doing good for all stakeholders, i.e., patients as well as third party payers. Benevolence, justice and nonmaleficence are ethical principles supporting statement five. Interpretive statements specifically address situations in which private practitioners and employed therapists must be just and fair to those they serve. A secondary interpretation of the guide statements could be that physical therapists themselves are due reasonable payment for their services and they should advocate for their own due reward.

Statement 6. Physical therapists provide accurate information to the consumer about the profession and about the services they provide.

Assessment: Doing good and being truthful or fidelity are the values supporting statement six. The underlying ethical principle is autonomy. Competent consumers must have the appropriate information to make their own decisions.

Statement 7. Physical therapists accept the responsibility to protect the public and the profession from unethical, incompetent, or illegal acts.

Assessment: The value doing good is represented in this statement. Autonomy, nonmaleficence and beneficence are the ethical principle bases for this statement. The clinical and fiscal nature of doing good is summarized in the interpretive statements.

Statement 8. Physical therapists participate in efforts to address the health needs of the public.

Assessment: The value from which this statement emerges is social justice. The ethical principle of justice, distributive justice to be more specific, is clearly the basis for this statement. Pro-bono services are specifically mentioned in the guide.

Summary of the APTA Code and Guide

The APTA code and guide use primarily mandate language (3). This mandate is demonstrated by the use of the word shall in the preface and guide over 30 times. The most frequently identified underlying value was doing good for others. This value was presumed to underlie 19 interpretive statements relating to patient care matters and 10 interpretive statements associated with fiscal matters. The ethical principle supporting doing good for others is beneficence. In the context of the code and guide, this principle encourages caring for all stakeholders.

In relation to the topic of management, it is interesting to note the frequency of guide statements with a monetary connection. Controlling financial self-interest is very evident in the APTA code and guide. At least 19 of 54 (35%) of the APTA guide statements are related to business or billing matters. The APTA code and guide clearly give recognition to that fact that physical therapy is one aspect of the business of delivering health care services.

PROFESSIONAL GUIDANCE: A MODEL

The preceding discussion on professional ethics completes the foundation for guiding professional behaviors. Figure 2.3 summarizes the functional interrelationships between the components of the professional guidance system. The discussion of this figure parallels the discussion of Figure 2.2. The personal guidance and professional guidance discussions are closely related because it is by personal choice that a person joins an association and formally accepts additional moral obligations.

Self-view in Figure 2.3 includes the association's view of itself, its motivations, moral rules and ideals. The association's values serve to sustain its self-view and influence the contents of its code of ethics and its interpretive guidelines.

The particular behaviors that have been emphasized have concerned interpersonal relationships related to providing physical therapy services. To complete the behavioral guidance discussion, the influence of the work environment

FIGURE 2.3. A conceptual model of the relationships between important factors guiding professional behaviors.

must also be considered. This consideration expands the discussion to the guiding influences provided by managers, boards of directors and owners of health care businesses. The next section focuses on values and moral guidance in an organizational setting.

Organizational Guidance

Broadly defined, a culture is a group of people who come together to achieve a common purpose. Organizations are essentially groups of people brought together to achieve common purposes. People bring to the work place their personal values and system of ethics, also known simply as ethic (1). Organizations have values, an ethic, norms, shared meanings, and traditions (30). The personal values and ethic of each individual employee combine with the organization's ethic, norms and traditions to give each organization a unique culture that distinguishes it from similar organizations (30). An organizational culture is not usually formalized through policies and procedures. Organizational culture is most often acquired in an informal way. It is an interpersonal environment that takes shape over time. New members learn the culture by interacting with those who have already been acculturated (see culture, Chapter 6). At the cultural level, the personal values and personal ethic of managers have powerful influences on members of the organization (1). Formally, management carries the responsibility for the ethical behavior of all members of the organization. Management is also responsible for the organization's success. Meeting these dual responsibilities can be challenging.

CONFLICTING VALUES EQUALS CONFLICTING MOTIVATIONS

Health care businesses, like other businesses, operate according to general business principles. These principles form a framework that allows products and services to be marketed (Chapter 3), delivered in an organized manner (Chapter 6), and bills collected and payments made (Chapters 7 and 8). Businesses must make more money than they spend or they will be unable to continue operations. The need to bring in money from the sale of services, e.g., physical therapy, or products, e.g., crutches, creates the potential for conflict between values serving opposing motivational goals. For example, conflicts can arise between motivations related to fostering human relationships (see universalism and benevolence, Tab. 2.1) and motivations related to making money (see power and achievement, Tab. 2.1). Balancing these potentially conflicting motivations requires consideration of the welfare of everyone likely to be affected by decisions, i.e., stakeholders. In Figure 2.4 the term stakeholders represents everyone whose interest decision-makers are morally obligated to consider. From an organizational point of view, the stakeholder picture is complicated because there are multiple stakeholders. In addition, the organization must sustain itself financially to do its work. These dual obligations are depicted at the top of Figure 2.4. How the organization balances these obligations depends on their guiding precepts. These organizational precepts are stated in three documents called a values statement, a mission statement and a vision statement. In Figure 2.4, these statements are located within the fulcrum part of the figure to represent their role in balancing responsibilities to many stakeholders. How these documents interrelate to guide behaviors throughout an organization will be discussed in depth.

CONCEPTUAL MODEL: ORGANIZATIONAL, PERSONAL AND PROFESSIONAL GUIDING INFLUENCES

The values and ethic most clearly reflected in organizational cultures are those management chooses to have reflected (1). Management at all levels of an organization has the responsibility for the ethical behavior of all members of the organization. Management is also responsible for the organization's success. These dual responsibilities can be difficult to deal with. An organization's managers have the moral obligation to set appropriate examples through their actions (1). It is important that they set moral examples by making decisions that reflect evenhandedness by holding all to the same obligations regardless of rank, tenure, gender, race or religion.

The moral issue that managers focus on is ultimately a reflection of their personal values and motivations. Managers have authority given to them by the organization and the power to use authority to meet organizational objectives (see Chapter 6). To support taking a moral stance and

FIGURE 2.4. The organizational documents which give behavioral directions for dealing with various responsibilities in a balanced fashion.

to act according to ethical principles, the manager relies on three main sources of guidance. Two of the sources have already been discussed, personal values and ethic, (Fig. 2.2) and professional association behavioral documents (Fig. 2.3). The third component is the organization's fundamental documents. Figure 2.5 is a model depicting all three behavioral guides. The figure represents the circles of influence on the behaviors of health care professionals. Imagine the top circle in Figure 2.5 as representing an individual health care manager or clinician. Envision the left circle as the professional association(s) an individual belongs to. Think of the right circle as representing an organization's collective power group, i.e., mid to executive level managers, owners, and board members. Next, look at the terms located within the same rings in each circle. These terms are intended to reflect similar degrees of influence on behaviors. Beginning with the central common model element, self-view, each part of Figure 2.5 will be integrated. The major discussion will focus on the organizational circle because the personal and professional portions of the figure have already been discussed in depth.

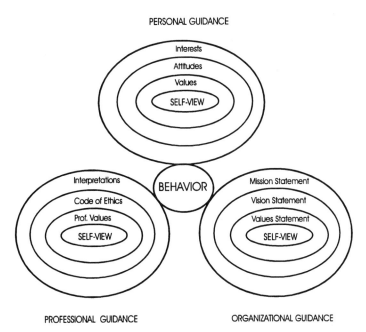

FIGURE 2.5. A conceptual model of the major sources of influence which guide the personal, professional and work-related behaviors of health care personnel.

Organizational Self-View

In the organizational portion of Figure 2.5, the central self-view construct represents a collective concept of what the organization thinks of itself. It is a collective concept because it reflects the combined thinking of many contributors. Organizational self-view includes the organization's view of itself and its personal, social, and societal motivations and its moral will. Organizational motivations are most clearly expressed in an organization's fundamental documents. Basically, these documents contain the proclaimed values, future vision and purpose of the organization (1). Self-view can also be inferred from the results of the outcomes of organizational activities, the rewards and punishments the organization administers to its members and how the organization deals with competitors.

Fundamental Documents

Fundamental documents are called fundamental because they give direction to all members of an organization as they carry out their current duties and plan for the future (31). See Chapters 6, 9 and 14 for additional discussions on fundamental documents. In an ideal world, organizations would develop three fundamental documents i.e., values, vision, and mission statements to provide guidance and direction to all members of the organization (1) (Figs. 2.4, 2.5). Guidance is needed as members of the organization make and carry out plans to meet the objectives of the organization. A vision is needed to encourage longterm efforts in a particular direction. The larger the organization, the more important guidance and direction become (see Chapter 6). Ideally, the first fundamental document to be developed would be a values statement (1). The importance of the values statement is reflected in Figure 2.5 by its placement in the ring closest to organizational self-view.

Values Statement

An ideal values statement would express the moral consciousness of the organization through the identification of its core values and principle beliefs. A values statement is an organization's proclamation regarding what behaviors are right, what behaviors are wrong or what behaviors are acceptable and what behaviors are not (1). Other names for values statements are philosophical statements (1) and philosophy (Chapter 14). The rationale for developing a values statement first is to provide a moral-ethical context for the development of the other fundamental documents (1).

A values statement is formulated by an organization's board of directors, chief executive officer or owner(s). It may or may not reflect the input of other stakeholders within and external to the organization. It proclaims what the organization prizes in terms of human relationships. In a sense, the values statement is the organization's written conscience. It makes clear to everyone in the organization the importance of being concerned for the well being of all those with whom members of the organization interact. This concern, if taken as a principle, requires consistency in its application. Concern for others extends to patients, staff, peers, venders, and competitors (1). The utility of a values statement is that it sets boundaries and offers guidance to all members of the organization as they make decisions and carry out their duties. It can reduce behaviors that can harm the organization (see Chapter 12). If the organizational values and motivations are understood and shared by members of the organization, there will likely be sufficient cohesion, cooperation and understanding to realize the desired goals.

Vision Statement

The second document flowing from the values statement is a vision statement (1). The placement of the vision statement in Figures 2.4 and 2.5 reflects subservience to the values statement. Although a vision statement is future oriented (also see Chapter 15), the values and principles that serve as the foundation for the organization will influence that future. A vision statement expresses aspirational and inspirational messages about what the organization would like to become (32). This statement is usually created by the leader(s) of an organization. There may or may not be contributions from others within and external to the organization. The vision is shared in writing and verbally with the organization's members and other stakeholders. The purposes of a vision statement are to inspire stakeholders to look forward to what can be achieved and to enlist their support and efforts to make the envisioned possibilities realities (32). See Chapter 15 for additional information on the process of developing a dynamic vision statement.

Mission Statement

The third fundamental document is called a mission statement. A mission statement is the operationalization of a vision statement (1). This means the mission statement translates the vision into tangible terms for a given time period. A mission statement describes the organization's purpose. This is what the organization produces, sells, who the customers are and to some degree, how people are treated by members of the organization. Specifically, a mission statement (1,33):

- States the collective goals of the organization
- Offers general guidance with respect to interpersonal relationships
- Explains what its services are
- Explains what its products are
- Serves as a communication tool which explains what the organization's business is to people within and external to the organization.

A mission statement, like the other fundamental statements, is a product of the efforts of executive level managers, boards of directors and owners to define and guide the organization. Like a vision statement, a mission statement must complement and comply with the precepts stated in the values statement. If there is no separate organizational values statement, a mission statement may include specific values that are held in esteem (31) in the organization. In larger organizations, there are individual departmental mission statements that complement the overall organizational mission statement. Departmental mission statements are developed by department managers and staff and focus on the specific endeavors of the department. This departmental document is also known as a scope of service statement. In terms of what the department produces and sells, this state-

ment describes the department's activities, how they are operationalized, who the customers are, and how these activities contribute to the overall mission of the organization. It should be clear that a departmental mission statement is in harmony with, and complementary to, the organization's fundamental documents. Table 2.8 presents an example of the interrelationships between the fundamental documents and a strategic plan. A single part of the philosophical statement is used to show these relationships. See Chapters 6 and 14 for more on strategic plans.

Reality

Not all health care organizations have developed all three fundamental documents. Organizations are more likely to have mission statements than values statements. Large organizations that have many employees, have been in operation for some time and have found the guiding worth of having all three documents are likely to have developed them. A small, new organization such as a sole proprietorship private practice (see Chapters 6 and 14) may only have some general rules of operation that are transmitted to others informally. Another reality is that mission statements often contain values along with a description of what the business does (1). A potential problem with combining values and mission is the same problem any dual-purpose tool has, it may not serve all needs equally well (31).

It is common for an organization's managers to put more effort into describing the organization and what it does (mission) than how its members ought to treat stakeholders (values and ethics). Values and ethics may also be considered as after the fact add-ons to the mission. This approach hardly offers behavioral direction to members of the organization. The more logical order in the process of formulating the fundamental documents is to focus on the ethical grounding of the organization first (1). A middle ground for dealing with the issue of ethical guidance is to extract the values from the mission statement and list them as the organization's values. Regardless of where an organization chooses to state its values and moral position, the purpose is the same: to provide behavioral guidance for everyone in the organization.

TABLE 2.8

Example of the Interrelated Contributions of Fundamental Documents on a Strategic Plan

EXCERPT FROM THE VALUES STATEMENT

In all our endeavors we prize most highly the involvement of stakeholders in formulating and enacting plans that affect them.

EXCERPT FROM THE VISION STATEMENT

Within the next 5 years the members of XYZ Outpatient Services will accomplish what others wish for. That is, as a group, we will have high regional name recognition, exceptional patient and physician satisfaction ratings and a 25% share of the region's outpatient market.

EXCERPT FROM THE MISSION STATEMENT

Our purpose is to deliver excellent health care services in a unique, individualized and participative manner at a reasonable cost. The provision of services under these conditions requires and encourages creative involvement of physicians, staff, patients and their agents in all aspects of the care planning and delivery process. Among the products and services that we can provide to help achieve our overall goal are educational in nature.

EXCERPT FROM THE STRATEGIC PLAN

The north end of the first floor will be remodeled this month. A media department and classroom will be located in the space. A media person will be employed within one month. Within three months, under his/her direction, each department will have developed educational materials in multiple formats including audio and videotapes, picture books, automated slide shows, recorded phone messages and component parts of our internet home page. The products produced initially will deal with the commonest health care problems seen by each department and their related current treatment alternatives. A panel of current and former patients and their family members or caregivers and physicians will be employed as actors and reviewers of the materials. Within six months each department manager will designate two individuals as their educational coordinators who will act as instructors and managers of the instructional materials. These coordinators will form an education committee to deal with coordination, evaluation and long term educational planning. Within one year, example materials will be used as part of the treatment program of most patients. Selected materials will be submitted for consideration for presentation at appropriate professional meetings held in this region. To facilitate the implementation of this plan each department will receive a 0.5% increase in their budget to cover costs directly related to this endeavor.

Values and mission statements underscore what the organization deems important in human relationships and what the business does. However, these statements are too general to identify who should do what, where, when, and how in the every day operation of the business. More specific plans are needed (also see Chapter 6).

Strategic Plans

The most tangible expressions of an organization's fundamental documents are strategic plans. These plans are called strategic plans because they identify the strategies to be used to meet the overall organizational mission. Every component of a large organization formulates strategic plans for accomplishing its part of the total organizational mission. For example, there are specific strategic plans for making, marketing and selling products or services that support the organization's overall strategic plan (see Chapter 3).

Managers who are closely related to the delivery of services and production of goods formulate strategic plans. Because staff will be implementing strategic plans, it is important that they also be involved in their development at the department level. This involvement may add useful insights that would be otherwise missed. Involvement in planning of those who will ultimately be responsible for enacting the plan is likely to increase compliance with the plan (see Chapter 4).

Strategic plans are more objective than fundamental documents because they call for observable, measurable, and assessable actions. As will be discussed in Chapter 11, the outcomes of strategic plans are an important means of assessing progress and identifying problems within and outside the organization. Strategic plans also have an important connection to the discussion of values and moral issues. These plans are the documents most closely related to the actual delivery of services. If an additional circle representing strategic plans were to be added to the organizational guidance portion of Figure 2.5, it would encircle all of the other elements of the organizational guidance system. This circle would

reflect strategic plans as flowing from the fundamental documents and being guided by them.
The actions the plans call for would therefore be
balanced. The strategic actions would meet the
organization's obligations to all stakeholders.

SUMMARY

This chapter presented a theory and a conceptual
model relevant to guiding personal, professional
and organizational behaviors. The main constructs in the discussions were personal values,
motivations served by values, moral obligations,
ethical principles, and moral will. The end product of the theory and conceptual model include
practical means of exploring values, identifying
motivations, heightening sensitivity to moral issues, considerations in moral issue decision
making and making choices that balance obligations and self-interests. The foundation for behavioral guidance set in this chapter will be useful for analyzing the information presented in
subsequent chapters.

   To further thought about values, motivations,
ethics, and moral issues related to management
and physical therapy, the reader should review
the Chapter 2 role play in Appendix A.

REFERENCES

1. Darr KJ. Ethics in Health Services Management. 3rd
    ed. Baltimore MD:Health Professions Press, 1997:
    32–33,39, 41, 45–46, 48, 53.
2. Schwartz SH, Bilsky W. Toward a universal psycho-
    logical structure of human values. Journal of Personal-
    ity and Social Psychology, 1987;53:550–562.
3. Schwartz S. Value priorities and behavior: Applying a
    theory of integrated value systems. In Seligman C, Ol-
    son JM, Zanna MP, eds. The Psychology of Values:
    The Ontario Symposium, Volume 8. Mahwah, NJ:
    Lawrence Earlbaum, 1995:1–24.
4. Schwartz SH, Sagiv L. Identifying culture-specifics in
    the content and structure of values. Journal of Cross-
    Cultural Psychology, 1995;26:92–116.
5. Schwartz SH. Universals in the content and structure of
    values: Theoretical advances and empirical tests in 20
    countries. In Zanna M, ed. Advances in Experimental
    Social Psychology Volume 25. Orlando, FL: Academic
    Press, 1992:1–65.
6. Braithwaite VA, Scott WA. Values. In Robinson JP,
    Shaver PR, Wrightsman LS, eds. Measures of person-
    ality and social psychological attitudes. Vol. 1 in Mea-
    sures of Social Psychological Attitudes Series. NY,
    NY: Academic Press, 1991:661–753.

7. Marques JF, Miranda MJ. Developing the work impor-
    tance study. In Super DE, Verko B, eds. Life Roles,
    Values and Careers. International Findings of the Work
    Importance Study. San Francisco, CA: Jossey-Bass,
    1995:62–74.
8. Kurtines WM, Gewirtz JL. Moral development: An in-
    troduction and overview. In Kurtines WE, Gewirtz JL,
    eds. Moral Development an Introduction. Boston,
    Mass: Allyn & Bacon, 1995:1–15.
9. Murphey MG, Berg I, eds. Values and value theory in
    twentieth-century America. Philadelphia, PA: Temple
    University Press, 1988:3–11.
10. Laupa M, Turiel E. Social domain theory. In Kurtines
    WM, Gewirtz GL, eds. Moral Development an Intro-
    duction. Boston, Mass: Allyn & Bacon, 1995;455–473.
11. Berkowitz MW. The Education of the Complete Moral
    Person. Aberdeen, Scotland: Gordon Cook Founda-
    tion, 1995.
12. Purtilo RB. Ethical considerations in physical therapy.
    In Scully RM, Barnes MR, eds. Physical Therapy,
    Philadelphia, PA: JB Lippincott, 1989:36–40.
13. Blanchard K, Peale NV. The Power of Ethical Man-
    agement. NY, NY: Fawcett Crest, 1988:7–20.
14. Reimer J, Paolitto, DP, Hersh, RH. Promoting Moral
    Growth from Piaget to Kohlberg. 2nd ed. NY, NY:
    Longman, 1983:83–116.
15. Kohlberg L. Moral stages and moralization: The
    cognitive-developmental approach. In Lickona T, ed.
    Moral Development and Behavior: Theory, Research,
    and Social Issues, NY, NY: Holt, Rinehart and Win-
    ston, 1976:31–53.
16. Rokeach M. The Nature of Human Values. NY, NY:
    Free Press, 1973:4–25.
17. Campbell JD, Trapness PD, Heine SJ, Katz IM,
    Lavallee LF, Lehman DR. Self-concept clarity: Mea-
    surement, personality correlates, and cultural bound-
    aries. Journal of Personality and Social Psychology
    1996;70:141–156.
18. Mayton DM III, Ball-Rokeach SJ, Loges, WE. Human
    values and social issues: An introduction. Journal of
    Social Issues 1994;50:1–8.
19. Dennison D. Corporate Culture and Organizational Ef-
    fectiveness. NY, NY: Wiley, 1990:2.
20. Harmon LW, Hansen JC, Borgen FH, Hammer AL.
    Strong Interest Inventory Applications and Technical
    Guide. Stanford, CA: Stanford University Press 1994:
    2–7.
21. Mooney MM. The code for nurses: A survey of its con-
    tent, constitutive structure, and usefulness to the nurs-
    ing profession. [Dissertation]. Washington, DC: The
    Catholic University of America, 1980:5–6.
22. Hall JK. Nursing Ethics and Law. Philadelphia, PA:
    W.B. Saunders, 1996:29,52.
23. Gert B. Morality, moral theory, and applied and pro-
    fessional ethics. Professional Ethics,1992;1:5–24.
24. Griener GG. Moral integrity of professions. Profes-
    sional Ethics 1993;2:15–38.
25. Pritchard MS. Good works. Professional Ethics 1992;
    155–177.

26. American Physical Therapy Association. Guide for professional conduct. Physical Therapy 1997;77: 1629–1631.

27. American Physical Therapy Association. Code of ethics. Physical Therapy 1997;77:1628.

28. American Association of Colleges of Nursing. Essentials of college and university education for professional nursing. Final report. Washington, DC: Author, 1986.

29. American Occupational Therapy Association. Core values and attitudes of occupational therapy practice. American Journal of Occupational Therapy 1993;47: 1085–1086.

30. Harquail CV, Cox T, Jr. Organizational culture and acculturation. In Cox T, ed. Cultural Diversity in Organizations: Theory, Research and Practice. San Francisco, CA: Berrett-Koehler, 1993:161.

31. Nosse LJ, Friberg DG. Management Principles for Physical Therapists. Baltimore, MD: Williams & Wilkins, 1992:28, 142, 220–225.

32. Hoyle JR. Leadership and Futuring: Making Visions Happen. Thousand Oaks, CA: Corwin Press, 1995:20.

33. Cross W. Prentice Hall Encyclopedic Dictionary of Business Terms. Engelwood Cliffs, NJ: Prentice Hall, 1995:253.

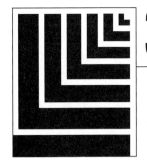

3

MARKETING

PREVIEW

Few areas of management have as much impact on the eventual success or failure of a business as does marketing, the process of matching programs and services to the customers who are likely to want or need them. This chapter will build upon the previous discussion of healthcare environment and personal and professional values to help the reader develop and promote high quality programs and services that are likely to succeed. The emphasis throughout this chapter will be on satisfying customer needs and wants as opposed to simply finding customers who need the services that are already available.

This chapter will review the key components of marketing that will help the reader develop an appreciation of the important role that marketing plays in the daily decisions of the clinical manager and proactive practitioner.

KEY WORDS

Customers (clients): individuals or groups who directly or indirectly may need or want to use a product or service.

Forecasting: the process of using scientific systems and data to predict changes in a market.

Market Mix: the combination of those factors that determine a market strategy: product or service, price, place and promotion.

Market Orientation: a philosophy seen in companies that hold that the main task of the organization is to determine the needs and wants of target markets and to satisfy them through design, communication, pricing and delivery of appropriate and competitively viable products and services (1).

Market Share: the percentage of the entire market that is served by a single organization.

Market Segmentation: the process of dividing a market into submarkets according to target market characteristics.

Marketing: the process of planning and executing the conception, pricing, promotion, and distribution of ideas, goods, and services to create exchanges that satisfy individual and organizational objectives (2).

Marketing Campaign: the process by which a marketing strategy is executed.

Niche Marketing: the targeting of a specific group (subset) of consumers with a product or service.

Opportunity Cost: the potential that is lost because of the path you take.

Product Line: a group of similar products that are often functionally presented together or thought of as a collective.

Service Line: groups of similar services or treatments that are often functionally presented together or thought of as a collective.

Target Market: a selected group who share specific characteristics that may affect their interest in a specific product or service.

INTRODUCTION

People who choose similar careers often share common personal characteristics and career goals. People choose to become physical therapists for quite varied reasons. In our experience, physical therapists commonly share two career goals: the desire to help others and the desire to succeed. In this chapter, we attempt to demonstrate that professional success is the reward for meeting customer needs for products and services. Businesses often refer to their customers as their market. Marketing is the area of business practice that encompasses the activities a business undertakes to develop, expand and keep customers.

Marketing is more than selling. It is the process that includes planning, design and development of products and services. It also includes the pricing, promotion and distribution of products and services to the customer. The marketing process begins with identification of customers and their needs (2). This means providing an appropriate type and quality of care at a time, place and cost that meets clients' wants and needs. Additionally, in choosing their services, potential clients must also be aware of the practice's existence, what services are available and the potential benefits of the services available.

Marketing allows a business to accomplish all of this in an efficient and effective manner. Marketing is defined as the process of planning and executing the conception, pricing, promotion, and distribution of ideas, goods, and services to create exchanges that satisfy individual and organizational customers.

MARKET ORIENTATION

A company with a market orientation is "an organization that holds that the main task of the organization is to determine the needs and wants of target markets and to satisfy them through design, communication, pricing and delivery of appropriate and competitively viable products and services" (1).

In contrast to a market orientation, several other possible orientations may describe an organization. They include:

A product orientation holds that the major task of an organization is to pursue efficiency in production and distribution. A product orientation holds that the major task of an organization is to put out products that it thinks would be good for the public.

A sales orientation holds that the main task of the organization is to stimulate the interest in potential consumers in the organization's existing products and services.

When effective, a strong market orientation will result in physical therapy programs that are responsive to the needs of the populations they are intended to serve. There will be strong relationships between the physical therapy practice and its customers that serve the interests of all parties involved.

Programs and services will serve and attract specific segments or subsets of customers. Physical therapy programs will be developed to meet the identified needs of potential customers rather than to meet the need of a physical therapy practice for prestige or to follow the latest technological fad.

The marketing concept will permeate the entire practice in all its affairs. The marketing oriented practice will address all aspects of its services in evaluating old programs or designing new ones (3).

Market Orientation: The Road to Success?

A market orientation will help the organization achieve success most efficiently in a changing environment. Customers have choices in the health care marketplace. The preferred choices will be based on the individual values of the customer. Many times these values are closely related to various, sometimes unrelated factors, such as convenience, image, and cost. To be successful in any business, it is necessary to know the customers, yourself, and the competition. It is necessary to recognize that all of these factors are in a continuous state of change. The market-oriented business has embraced this concept and incorporated it into everything it does. The successful practice will also be sensitive to the wishes of consumers and produce or provide what the customers want, need, or can be persuaded to believe that they need.

It is easy to assume that wants and needs related to physical therapy do not change, but they do. Keeping up with consumer demand allows a practice to show that their service has special value, which will earn either a premium price and hence higher profits or allow the practice to secure a larger market share of the overall physical therapy market. Market share is defined as the percentage of a total market that is served by a single organization. Figure 3.1 illustrates a changing market share in a market with a cadre of three competitors.

In traditional product marketing, added value can be derived from being fashionable. For example, the right look, location or affiliation might make a product fashionable. This is not enough for service marketing, especially health care services. Current marketing trends suggest that physical therapy services are best offered to spe-

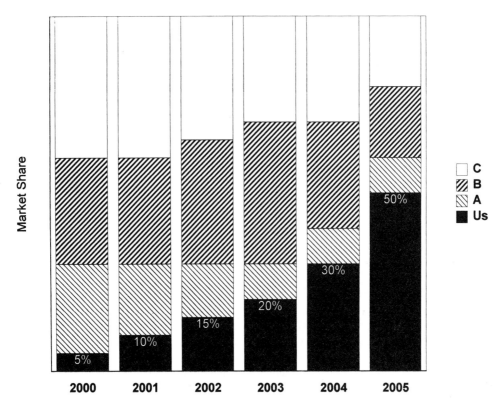

FIGURE 3.1. Market share years 2000-2005

cific groups with very specific messages based on the perceived needs and wants of that target market. Groups of similar services or treatments are often functionally lumped together into a service line or product line. Chapter 4, Organizing and Engaging People, describes the various ways to structure organizations, including product and service lines.

Market-Oriented Planning and Information

Internal Information

The driving force behind any marketing strategy should be business objectives. Business objectives will be based on the organization's mission and values statements (See Chapter 2). Table 3.1 reflects some sample business objectives for a typical physical therapy practice.

 TABLE 3.1
Business Objective

Sample Business Objectives for Our Practice
• Provide quality clinical care
• Provide cost effective and competitively priced clinical care
• Innovate through clinical research
• Provide charity care to those within our service area who cannot afford our services

External Information

Marketing is a basic business function. Successful marketing begins with focused listening. As illustrated in Figure 3.2, there are many audiences to which practice members must listen. Clients, competitors, payers, boss and referrers are but a few. The practice members must also listen intensely to the health care and physical therapy environment for potential changes in areas such as health care related legislation that may affect the practice's financial well being.

Product and service design begins with programs that will meet the needs and wants of current and/or potential customers. Without an intense focused listening process, the practice will be forced to make assumptions about the markets served. These assumptions, if inaccurate,

can lead to wasteful and expensive mistakes and misdirections in strategy. In addition to the obvious financial costs of misguided programs, there are also opportunity costs that come from not being able to develop and provide alternate programs. The potential that is lost due to choices made and the path taken is defined as an opportunity cost.

Successful physical therapy practices have translated this focused listening into a market-oriented approach. They try to produce a product or service that meets the needs of their customers. Having developed products and services that meet these needs, they then try to provide the product or service at a profit.

Successful practices are also adaptive. There would be little point to producing products or services that are not able to keep up with consumers' wishes. Physical therapy practices primarily provide services (therapy and consultation), but products, such as exercise equipment, adaptive equipment for the home, and patient education materials, may be a significant component of what is offered to clients and others served.

What Is A Market?

The idea of a market, a place where buyers and sellers meet, is an ancient one. Originally, there may have been a two-way exchange of goods or services (barter). This is now likely to be an exchange of money or credit for products or services. The idea, however, remains the same. The seller wants to sell for a high price. The buyer wishes to buy for the lowest price. In physical therapy and all of health care, we often refer to the seller as a provider and the buyer as the client or payer.

Special Customer Considerations In Health Care Marketing

The traditional market forces of supply and demand that typically control interactions between buyer and seller may not apply to health care. The provider (seller) is at a relative advantage because the provider often plays the role of diagnostician or need-identifier for the client (buyer). This places the consumers of

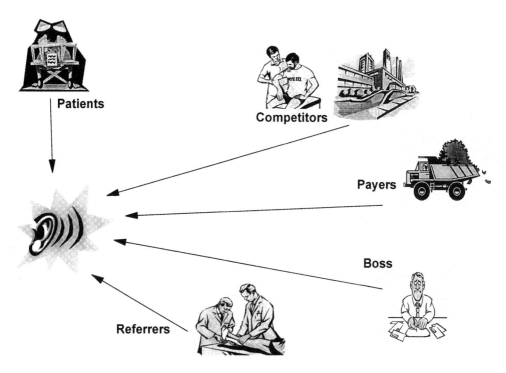

FIGURE 3.2. Focused listening

health care services at a relative disadvantage. For this reason, the ethical health care provider must act in the client's best interest first. Additionally, the payer for health care services is often not the patient themselves. Payment often comes from a third party such as an insurer, employer, government agency or some other third party.

Customers

Previously, we referred to the need to develop a process to assure focused listening to the needs of the customer (Fig. 3.2). There are many potential definitions of customer. There are many additional customers that can be identified.

All of these customers may, in some way, influence the health care transaction. The influence of all these customers creates many, sometimes conflicting, market forces. These market forces need to be balanced for the health care transaction to be mutually beneficial to all involved parties. A very important factor in this transaction is the financial balance. In today's health care en-

vironment, those who purchase health care often are able to exert the greatest influence on this balance. In most cases, the person receiving the care is not the individual who is directly paying for the majority of the bill. The actual payer is a third party, i.e., a person or organization that is not involved in the provision or receipt of the care.

This, so called, third party payer system in health care has a tremendous effect on the balance of power and on the eventual provision of health care. Figure 3.3 illustrates the relationships in the third party payer system.

In health care, market forces rely on a number of parties behaving rationally, including:

1. The provider considering costs, competition, possible profit and technology.
2. The consumer considering the price of the product, tastes, availability of similar products, the price of other products and utility (to self).
3. The payer considering all of the above in terms of the payer's business interests.
4. The regulators, local, state and national, attempting to serve the needs of and protect the interests of the public.

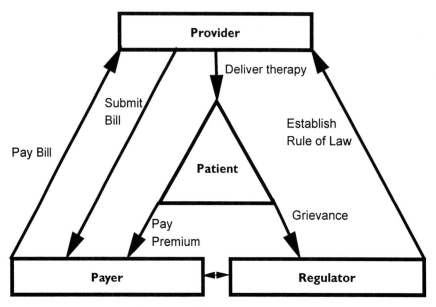

FIGURE 3.3. Third party payer system

The eventual payment rate for the service will depend upon achieving an equilibrium among all these factors and the relationships of the four parties involved in the third party payer system. Failure to achieve equilibrium may result in the consumer, payer or regulating agency being dissatisfied.

Foremost among the factors that will affect this equilibrium are the relationships and expectations among the four parties involved. Understanding those relationships and expectations is key to understanding the marketplace of health care.

Expectations and Relationships in the Third Party Payer System

PATIENT-PAYER

- Client pays premium to insurer to become a member of a pool of insured people.
- Insurer establishes a mechanism to pay provider(s) to care for client's health care needs.
- Mechanisms are developed to allow for resolution of conflicts that arise between the parties.

PATIENT-PROVIDER

- Client chooses a health care provider (choice may be limited by many factors, including which pool of insured people they join).
- Provider delivers health care services to client.
- Client authorizes insurer to pay fees to provider for services rendered.

- Mechanisms are developed to allow for resolution of conflicts that arise between the parties.

PAYER-PROVIDER

- Provider agrees to deliver health care services to members of payers' insured pool.
- Payer and provider negotiate a rate and mechanism of reimbursement for the delivery of services.
- Provider notifies payer of services delivered or proposed to be delivered to members of the insurance pool.
- Payer reimburses provider (directly or through client) as negotiated.
- Mechanisms are developed to allow for resolution of conflicts that arise between the parties.

REGULATOR-PROVIDER AND PAYER

- Regulator establishes laws, guidelines and requirements concerning appropriate mechanisms for delivery of health care services.
- Regulator acts to serve the needs and protect the interests of the public (clients).
- Provider delivers health care services within the established guidelines.
- Payer administers the health insurance program within the established guidelines.
- Mechanisms are developed to allow for resolution of conflicts that arise between the parties.

PATIENT-REGULATOR

- Client chooses to live within the regulator's geographic jurisdiction.

- Regulator oversees delivery of health care and insurance services to the client including acting as ombudsman for clients.
- Client notifies regulator of any significant deviation or digression from the established procedure or outcome.
- Mechanisms are developed to allow for resolution of conflicts that arise among the parties.

Market Segmentation

Market segmentation is the process of splitting the known market for a product or service into separate parts. Consumers within these segments may be categorized in a variety of ways; by age, social class, life style, setting, geography, avocation or purchasing habits.

In physical therapy, we may segment consumers by client, referral source, other provider, payer or employer. We may also subdivide clients into more discrete segments, by how, for example, they may use physical therapy services. There are different clients, for example, who may use aquatic therapy, sports injury care, incontinence therapy, wound care, spine care, occupational services, pediatric therapy, intensive care unit therapy, or pain management.

Table 3.2 lists some of the potential ways to segment the physical therapy market. Practices with a market orientation of a product will attempt to make their product particularly attractive to one or more of these market segments listed in Table 3.3. Market research will help identify the features that most appeal to any one segment. Table 3.4 shows several examples of market segmentation and the differentiating factor that defines the specific segments. Examples of services that may be offered to each segment are included.

Niche Markets

Niche marketing is the targeting of a specific group (subset) of consumers with a product or service. In recent years, a number of specialty practices have developed in physical therapy. These are often related to the provision of a specific type of therapy. Examples of niche markets in physical therapy include aquatics, wound care, balance and vestibular training, incontinence therapy, myofascial release, cardiopulmonary, wellness and sports injury care. Niches have been developed in a wide variety of business areas, both service and product.

Basics of Marketing—The Marketing Mix

The marketing mix is the combination of factors which are used to market any product or service. Figure 3.4 illustrates the basic marketing mix. The five key factors in the mix are:

1. Characteristics of the product itself.
2. Type of promotion used to sell it.
3. Price charged for it.
4. Place(s) chosen to sell it.
5. Manner in which the product or service is packaged, i.e. its features.

The term marketing mix refers to the tool kit that organizations use to match consumer needs with products and services. It is a combination of all the critical factors that must be included in determining a marketing strategy. For obvious reasons, these five key factors are often known as the five Ps of marketing.

1. Product/services.
2. Packaging (features).

TABLE 3.2
Potential Physical Therapy Customers

CLINICAL CUSTOMERS	REIMBURSEMENT CUSTOMERS	INTERNAL CUSTOMERS	OTHER CUSTOMERS
Clients	Case managers	Board of trustees	Employers
Referrers	Insurance companies	Administration	Community groups
Referrer's office staff	Managed care companies	Suppliers	Supporters
Former clients		Employees	Regulators
			Colleagues

3. Pricing/positioning.
4. Place (refer to facility planning chapter).
5. Promotion/communication.

Figure 3.5 illustrates the marketing mix for services. In the service sector, an additional three Ps can be identified which are:

6. Physical evidence of quality or effectiveness provided by the environment offered by the service business.
7. Personnel providing the service and the way they are selected and trained.
8. Processes offered by the service and the extent to which they instill a sense of confidence in the client, referrer or payer.

TABLE 3.3
Potential Factors for Market Segmentation in Physical Therapy

Age	Geographic Location
Gender	Employment Status
Type of Therapy Needed	Nature of Disability
Socio-economic Factors	Shared Vision or Belief
Vocation	Avocation
Child-bearing Status	Previous Experience with PT
Affiliation with Community Group	Transportation Method
Risk of Future Health Problems	Behavioral Factors
Relationship with Referrers	Projected Benefit of PT to Client

Most service organizations spend a considerable amount of time and money assuring that the above three Ps meet the needs of their customers. The essence of marketing is the composite of the processes that go into assuring that these eight factors match the needs and wants of the customers in our chosen markets.

Products and Services

Within physical therapy, product and service lines are often developed to most effectively promote and provide services. Rather than consider a single product or service that the organization currently offers or is considering offering, it is often helpful to combine a group of related products and/or services that are offered to a target market segment together as a product or service line. A service line is composed of the various product and service components that are directed by the practice to a specific targeted marketplace.

Most products and service lines have a limited life, with distinct stages within that life. This is called the product life cycle. A product life cycle is generally represented as a curve as shown in Figure 3.6 that is divided into four areas: introduction, growth, maturity and decline.

Demand, volume and profitability will rise and fall throughout the life cycle, and each stage will require different marketing strategies.

Most products and service lines will have a life cycle that follows the stages of introduction, growth, maturity and decline. The periods of

TABLE 3.4
Examples of Market Segmentation

MARKET SEGMENT	DIFFERENTIATING FACTOR	EXAMPLE SERVICE
Parents of children with developmental disabilities	Significant familial stress due to the increased demands of caring for an ill or handicapped child.	Pediatric therapy provided in a day rehab model with significant parental respite components.
Adult children whose elderly parents currently live independently but who are beginning to have difficulty with independent mobility or self care	Middle-aged children of elderly parents are often in the period of having highest discretionary income. Concerns of needing to consider assistance for a parent now or in the future is very stressful.	Fall prevention programs for independent senior citizens, especially those with a tendency toward balance or orthopedic problems.
Clients under age 45 who have suffered a CVA	Most clients with CVAs are older. There may be a sense of isolation among younger clients post CVA.	Young adult CVA survivor support group.

greatest profit will be the growth and maturity stages, while both introduction and decline will have relatively low profitability.

During the Introductory Period, sales are slow and profits are small, as the service line establishes itself. During the Growth Period, there is rapidly increasing market acceptance and escalating sales. Maturity marks a slow-down in growth, although volume and profit may remain at high levels for a long time. Decline is marked by falling sales and profit erosion.

The mix of marketing components is developed in an evolutionary manner according to the sequence illustrated in Figure 3.7. The various stages of the product life cycle will require different marketing mix strategies. Unless the provider has good reason to allow a service line to decline, the end of the maturity period will be marked by extension activities, as the practice attempts to prolong the life cycle of the service line. These extension activities might include such strategies as widening the scope of service, redesigning a component of the service line, or attempting to enter new market segments. The aim will be to extend the life of the service line without incurring any additional significant costs.

Within a practice, there may be multiple service lines at various stages of development and progression along the product life cycle. Because each stage of the product life cycle brings with it different opportunities, challenges and re-

FIGURE 3.4. Basic marketing mix

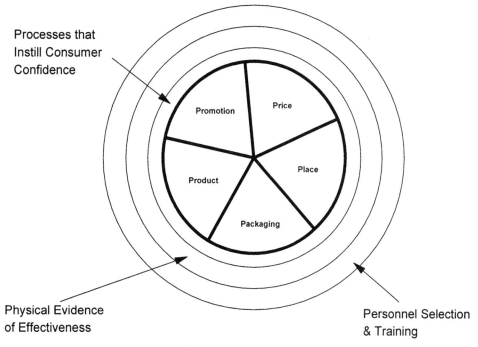

FIGURE 3.5. Service market mix

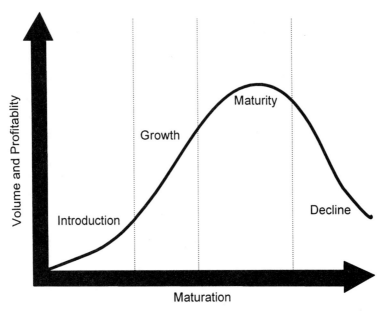

FIGURE 3.6. Product life cycle

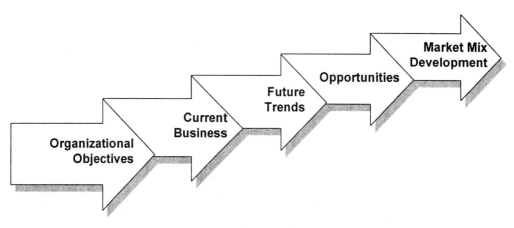

FIGURE 3.7. Marketing mix strategy

wards, it is necessary to develop a well balanced portfolio of services from each of the four stages of the product life cycle. The product mix matrix in Table 3.5 illustrates the various types of products that can be identified according to their rel-ative market growth and market share and prof-itability.

Practices should adopt a strategy whereby their product portfolio includes items across all the stages of the product life cycle and across all mar-

 TABLE 3.5
The Product Mix Matrix

		RELATIVE MARKET SHARE & PROFITABILITY	
		HIGH	LOW
MARKET	High	Stars	Problem Children
GROWTH	Low	Cash Cow	Dogs

TABLE 3.6

Comparison of Competitors by Cost and Volume

COMPETITOR	COST	VOLUME
Our Practice	Medium	Low
A	Low	Low
B	Medium	High
C	High	Medium

ket segments and profit levels. This enables some products at the early and expensive part of the life cycle to be financed by those at the profitable and cash-generating middle and end of the cycle.

Understanding your practice's position within the existing market is also needed. Many pairs of factors can be used to compare yourself to your competition. Table 3.6 shows a comparison of a practice to competitors A, B, and C based on client volume and cost to the payer.

There are many other factors that you could use to compare your practice to your competition. Each is identified in the components of the marketing mix. No factor, by itself, gives a complete picture.

Pricing

Organizations must decide on an overall pricing strategy that reflects the values and objectives of the organization. This pricing strategy is part of the marketing mix of the overall organization and will be linked to the scope of services, the clinical locations, and the promotional aspects of marketing the practice. The pricing strategy sets a framework within which some slight adjustments or tweaking can occur as conditions change. These adjustments are referred to as pricing tactics. Pricing tactics are minor adjustments that should not cause a major deviation from the overall pricing strategy. An example of a pricing strategy, is to ensure that you're less expensive than your competitors. Such a strategy could be realized by offering special methods of pricing such as capitation or case rates, rather than typical per treatment or per visit pricing (these concepts are fully explained in Chapters 7 and 8). Similarly, a practice that has a premium pricing strategy will have higher and less flexible pricing strategies. Premium pricing is usually only successful, however, should there

exist a demonstrable, quality differential between your practice and others.

BUNDLING

Another tactic used by some businesses is to price items in combination with their complements or other products. In consumer products, for example, razors could be priced very cheaply, but razor blades could have a high price. This tactic ensures a suitable profit from the combination of razors and blades, though one item (razors) does not make the business very much money. In this case, the cheaper item has been used to encourage the consumer into the market so that they will be more likely to purchase the more profitable blades. When done in health care, this is often referred to as bundling. It is also seen in physical therapy when a practice negotiates case rates or per visit pricing.

Additional information on fee structures and pricing is covered in Chapter 8, Money Matters.

The actual price of the services will be decided by a variety of factors. The provider will determine how much it costs to produce a service and which other costs have been incurred in reaching the marketplace. The client, insurance company or managed care organization will determine how much the service is desired or needed, whether or not an alternative is available, and the competitive price. In much of health care, the actual price paid by the consumer is intensely negotiated and based on many factors that may or may not be directly involved in the delivery of services.

Price must also be considered in light of the perceived quality and the potential successful outcome of the services. Quality, if adequately defined, is an excellent way to differentiate physical therapy services within a market place. High quality care is more valuable to consumers and stakeholders and, therefore, should demand a higher price.

Table 3.7 may help the reader understand appropriate pricing methodologies. Table 3.8 illustrates the interaction of price and quality in developing a pricing strategy.

Forecasting

Forecasting is the process of projecting what is most likely to occur during a future period. A

TABLE 3.7
Physical Therapy Pricing Methodologies

MODEL	HOW IT WORKS	ADVANTAGES DISADVANTAGES
Treatment pricing	Payment based on type and quantity of procedures provided.	Tends toward high cost to clients. Very easy to track and document.
Visit pricing	Payment based on number of client contacts.	Eliminates costs of high intensity visits. Shifts some risk to provider.
Case pricing (case rates)	Payment based on type and number of cases cared for.	Shifts more risk to provider. Eliminates costs of high intensity clients.
Population pricing (capitation)	Payment based on type and number of potential cases.	Shifts most risk to provider. Eliminates costs of high volume of clients in the population.

TABLE 3.8
Quality and Price Strategy

| QUALITY | PRICE | | |
	HIGH	MEDIUM	LOW
High	Premium Strategy	High Value	Super Value
Medium	Over Charge	Medium Value	Good Value
Low	Rip Off	False Economy	Economic Strategy

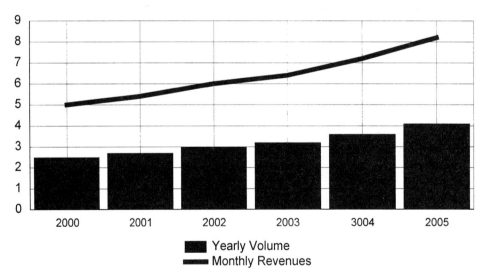

Yearly Volume
Monthly Revenues

Projections as of 1/1/2000

FIGURE 3.8. Forecasting

significant amount of uncertainty is always involved in forecasting.

The market oriented organization must not simply define a marketing mix for the current business period. The marketing mix components must also be clearly defined for future periods (Fig. 3.8). This involves anticipating what will change or remain the same over time. To do this effectively, systems and processes must be developed to forecast future events and possibilities.

All health care providers need to plan for the future and make decisions that have consequences at a later date. As physical therapy practices operate in an uncertain environment, it is in their own interest to try to predict some of the future events. Predicting what will happen to volume of services provided, payroll expenses, the size of the market, the types and level of payment, and so on, will help the practice plan for the future. Sometimes it is possible, by looking at past information, to see trends developing. Knowledge of trends can help the organization remove some uncertainty. One way of looking at trends is to use time series analysis, which tries to negate seasonal fluctuations.

Figure 3.9 illustrates a yearly analysis that smoothes out these fluctuations. This is particularly important if the business has a seasonal trend to sales, such as a pediatric physical therapy practice that might see significant shifts in demand at various times in the school year, or involvement in pre-participation physicals for sports therapy in high schools, colleges and universities. This sort of analysis is dependent on having access to good, reliable data and points out the need to develop strong data collection processes and systems (see Chapters 10 and 11).

Sources of Forecasting Information

Physical therapy practices have internal and external sources for forecasting information. The internal sources will cover financial accounts, commissioned reports and predicted trends from records kept within the normal course of business operations. The use of standardized practice analysis tools will assist in developing a strong database of internal clinic data. Table 3.9 details a practice Report Card developed by The Focus Group, Inc. to be used to systematically collect clinical and operational data for a typical hospital-based practice.

Information of value for forecasting includes volume, responsiveness to referrals and demographics of community and patients.

Trend data can be used to forecast such things as future volumes, customer mix, utilization,

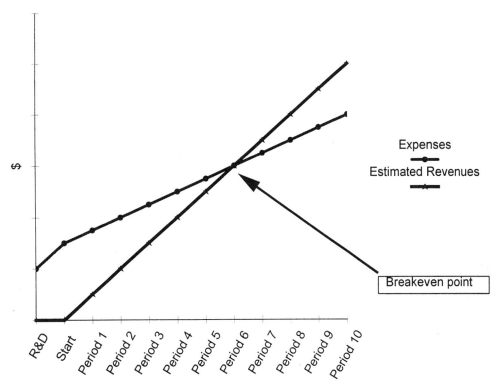

FIGURE 3.9. Sample cost benefit analysis

TABLE 3.9
Hospital-Based Physical Rehab Report Card

DISCIPLINE = PHYSICAL THERAPY			MONTH 1	MONTH 2	MONTH 3	YTD	AVERAGE
Volume	Treatments		6,010	5,800	6,800	18,610	6203
	Budget Treatments		6,000	6,000	6,000	18,000	6000
		Variance	100.17%	96.67%	113.33%	103.39%	
	Visits		1,939.00	1750	2200	5,889	1963
	Budget Visits		2000	2000	2000	6,000	2000
		Variance	96.95%	87.50%	110.00%	98.15%	
	New Patients		105	118	145	368	123
Staffing	Clinical FTE-Therapist		14.2	13.8	11.7		13.23
	Clinical FTE-PTA		3	4.1	4.1		3.73
	Clinical FTE-Aide		2	2.2	3.5		2.57
	Non Clinical FTE-Office		3.4	3.6	2.4		3.13
	Total Clinical FTE		19.2	20.1	19.3		19.5
	% Therapist		74%	69%	61%		68%
	% Assistant/Other		16%	9%	16%		14%
	% Aide/Tech		14%	16%	30%		20%
Finance	Total Expense		$ 83,100	$ 84,300	$ 75,900	$243,300	$81,100.00
	Clinical Payroll		$ 46,000	$ 47,000	$ 41,000	$ 134,000	$ 44,666.67
	Office Payroll		$ 23,250	$ 23,250	$ 22,250	$ 68,750	$ 22,916.67
	Payroll Expense-Total		$ 69,250	$ 70,250	$ 63,250	$ 202,750	$ 67,583
	Receivables		$ 875,000	$ 925,000	$ 1,010,000		$ 936,667
	Accounts Receivable days		97	106	99		100.80
Productivity	Treatments/FTE/Month		423.24	420.29	581.20		474.91
	Visits/FTE/Month		136.55	126.81	188.03		150.47
	Treatments/FTE/Day		19.87	19.73	27.29		22.30
	Visits/FTE/Day		6.41	5.95	8.83		7.06
Patient Mix	Diagnosis Mix:Ortho		65%	67%	71%		68%
	Diagnosis Mix:Neuro		25%	22%	20%		22%
	Diagnosis Mix:Peds		10%	11%	9%		10%
Payer Mix	Payer Mix: Fee for Service		21%	19%	17%		19%
	Payer Mix: Cost Reimbursed		47%	48%	46%		47%
	Payer Mix: Managed Care		32%	33%	37%		34%
Referrer Mix	Referrers		31	36	41		36.00
	1st Time Referrers		3	6	8		5.67
Treatment Mix	% Non Modality		81%	76%	74%		77%
	% Superficial Heat		13%	15%	19%		16%
Calculations	Visits Per Case-Ortho		14.00	12.00	13.00		13.00
	Budget V/Case		12.00	12.00	12.00		12.00
		Variance	117%	100%	108%		108%
	Visits Per Case-Neuro		21.00	18.00	16.00		18.33
	Budget V/Case		16.00	16.00	16.00		16.00
		Variance	131%	113%	100%		115%
	Cost Per Case-Ortho		$ 791.43	$ 714.41	$ 523.45		$ 676.43
	Budget Cost/Case		510	510	510		
		Variance	155%	140%	103%		
	Budget Cost/Case		510	510	510		510%
		Variance	0%	0%	0%		
	FTE Per Case		0.135	0.117	0.081		0.11
	Budget FTE/Case		0.09	0.09	0.09		0.09
		Variance	150%	130%	90%		
Outcomes	Satisfaction Rating		97%	94%	91%		94%
	Critical Outcome data A						0%
	Critical Outcome data B						0%
	Critical Outcome data C						0%
	Critical Outcome data D						0%

outcomes, cost per visit or cost per case. This type of data is very helpful in planning activities.

External data focuses on those market factors that are not within the direct control of the practice managers. These include competitor and environmental analysis.

One of the most frequently used analysis tools that includes both internal and external data is the Strength, Weakness, Opportunity, Threat analysis. This is also known as the SWOT analysis (4). Table 3.10 provides a sample SWOT analysis tool. In this analysis, each of the four factors are thoroughly detailed using internal and external data sources. The SWOT analysis allows the organization to identify:

- Strengths: basic internal building blocks upon which to develop further programs and services.
- Weaknesses: internal areas for improvement.
- Opportunities: external situations that could be used to the practice members' advantage.
- Threats: external situations that could negatively impact the future development of the practice.

Sources of data outside the organization include government information, trade associations and private companies that specialize in providing information.

External information may be expensive to acquire; however, it can be worth the expense to remove some of the uncertainty of the future. Despite having the best information, no business can predict everything that will happen, as there are always surprises.

The main purpose of marketing tools and analyses is to clarify the future for the organization so that it is possible to develop an effective marketing strategy. It is hoped that such information will provide real solutions to current and future client and customer problems.

Using Marketing Dollars Wisely

Once the practice group has identified target markets and matched them with products and the messages to communicate, the next step for marketing is to promote the product or service to targeted customers. Promotional communication can become very expensive and complicated.

The Promotional Mix

Communicating your message to your potential market involves the development of a promotional mix. A promotional mix is the blending of personal and nonpersonal selling by marketers in an attempt to accomplish promotional objectives (1). The promotional mix is also known as the communication media mix.

Communication Methods And Media

Public relations is often a major part of the marketing strategy for a company. It may have several objectives, including the creation of a positive corporate image for a company, image enhancement or referral development. Public relations activities might involve the company in community activities, or in sponsoring sporting events, all to bring the company's name into the public eye in a positive way. Public relations departments in large companies have several different groups to whom they address their communications.

A corporate identity is important for a company which provides a variety of services, but which wants the market to recognize that all the differing products belong to one company. Corporate identity should be directly derived from the values that the company holds. However, corporate identities only work positively for a company while the company has a good general image for

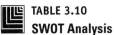

TABLE 3.10
SWOT Analysis

| PRODUCT | INTERNAL FACTORS | | EXTERNAL FACTORS | |
	STRENGTH	WEAKNESS	OPPORTUNITY	THREAT

quality, an image for being ethically sound, or no public image at all. Once a company has lost its reputation for one product, then a well known but negative corporate identity can be a liability, as consumers may reject all products belonging to that corporation. It can be very difficult to disentangle a specific product from others which are tied together with a strong corporate identity. For example, strong open heart surgery, oncology and transplant programs may transfer a credibility to other programs offered by your organization, including physical therapy. Programs that may not be as strong as the higher profile programs may be perceived to be better than they actually are because they are offered by a quality organization.

There are four components that comprise the promotional mix: advertising, personal selling, sales promotion and public relations.

Advertising is paid, non-personal communication channeled through various media by business firms who are in some way identified in the advertising message and who hope to inform or influence a target market. In physical therapy and health care, advertising is often done through print media, such as newspapers and magazines or through broadcast media, such as radio and television. Some health care organizations are also beginning to use the Internet for advertising purposes.

Personal selling is the interpersonal influence process involving a seller's promotional presentation conducted on a person-to-person basis with a potential customer. In health care and physical therapy, personal selling is often seen when a practice hires personnel or uses staff members to directly contact insurers, referrers and other potential customers to inform them of the availabilities and capabilities of the practice.

Sales promotion is marketing activities that stimulate consumer purchasing and seller effectiveness. Sales promotion includes trade shows and expositions, demonstrations, and various nonrecurrent selling efforts. In health care, the most common sales promotions are health fairs, community outreach programs and other special promotional activities such as sponsorship of a sporting event or charity benefit.

Public relations is a more global term that encompasses a practice's communications and relationships with its various customers, including the professional media. Publicity is the process of stimulating demand for services by placing commercially significant news or obtaining favorable media representation not paid for by an identified sponsor.

All marketing activities have costs associated with them, even if only opportunity costs. Table 3.11 details the comparative value of the various promotional components. To effectively determine the value of marketing and the potential for financial success of a product or service, an organization will want to determine the risk of proceeding with a marketing plan. These known expenses should then be compared to the projected revenue from the program. The point at which these two lines intersect will determine when the project will be at the break even point (Fig. 3.9).

THE MARKETING CAMPAIGN

Once all components of the marketing mix have been decided, it will be necessary to plan a marketing campaign. This should be undertaken in a manner similar to any significant project in business. Project management tools should be used in the planning and implementation of the plan.

POTENTIAL MARKET WITHOUT CAMPAIGN INTERVENTION

Marketing does not create markets, but rather uses information to understand and communicate to markets that are already in existence. To fully evaluate the impact of the marketing campaign we need to consider what would happen if no formal marketing program was enacted. Because there will be no incremental costs associated with a campaign that does not exist, there is no need to perform a cost benefit or break even analysis. However, to evaluate the real impact of the campaign, we only need to consider the incremental revenue that is likely to be realized because of the marketing campaign.

CAMPAIGN BUDGET

Part of the decision to implement a marketing plan is to consider the costs involved in implementation of the marketing campaign and the development of any new or revised service lines. Care must be taken in the development of the

TABLE 3.11
Comparative Value of Various Promotional Components

PROMOTION	TYPE	RELATIVE COST	ADVANTAGES	DISADVANTAGES
Advertising	Non-personal	Depending on media, can be very expensive or relatively inexpensive.	Communicates to largest audience with relatively little individual effort. Allows control over the message.	Many in audience may not be potential customers. Difficult to measure results.
Personal selling	Personal	Most expensive per individual contact.	Helps develop relationship. Allows flexible presentation to meet target needs and preferences.	Expensive. Highly trained and qualified personnel can be difficult to attract and manage.
Sales promotion	Non-personal	Ranges from quite inexpensive to very expensive, depending on format and scope.	Event-marketing can gain immediate attention of potential customers. Can build relationship with customers.	Easily imitated. Can be difficult to find creative approach that will attract customer attention.
Public relations	Non-personal	Relatively inexpensive, Publicity is free.	Credible to customers because it is not paid advertising.	Can present organization in positive or negative light. Difficult to control, time and measure results.

plan to include a realistic estimate of the costs. The development of a budget for marketing is not significantly different than any other budget. Refer to Chapter 7 for additional information on budgeting.

EVALUATION OF THE MARKETING CAMPAIGN

The final step in managing any project is to evaluate its impact. This information should assess both successes and failures. Were the specific goals met? Did the project meet budget for costs and timeliness? What can be learned from this project that can be used to improve performance for the next time? These and related questions and answers should be formalized into a written evaluation process.

SUMMARY

Marketing is a forward thinking, intentional process. It is necessary to emphasize the marketing process throughout the organization. This will be a critical factor in developing a market-oriented organization. There are no short cuts to effective listening, good program design and effective clinical implementation.

A strong marketing program is managed as a project. Good project management skills are needed. Because a marketing program is based in effective listening and should include the ongoing collection and analysis of internal and external data, it is necessary to develop systems to manage the information requirements of a marketing project. Chapter 10, Information Management, will help you develop such systems.

Attention to the marketing decisions in an organization will allow the missions to be accomplished through successful matching of targeted audiences and the products and services offered by the organization. Role Play 3 in Appendix A provides the reader with a scenario with a marketing focus. This role play allows practice in application of the principles presented in this chapter.

REFERENCES

1. Boone LE, Kurtz DL. Contemporary Marketing. New York, NY: CBS College Publishing, 1986.
2. Kottler P. Marketing for Nonprofit Organizations. Englewood Cliffs, NJ: Prentice-Hall, Inc., 1982.
3. MacStravic RE, Marketing Healthcare. Germantown, MD: Aspen Systems Corporation, 1977.
4. Peters JA. Strategic Planning Process for Hospitals. Chicago, IL: American Hospital Association, 1985:67.

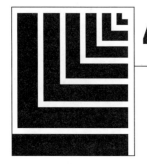

4

ORGANIZING AND ENGAGING PEOPLE IN THE WORK SETTING

PREVIEW

The American health care industry is under continuous pressure to change the way health care is delivered. Our customers, those who pay for health care, including government, business, tax payers and patients, are the source of this pressure. What our customers want is quality health care at a price they can afford. Their needs have changed and, in their view, the health care industry was unwilling or unable to respond. So to control health care related costs, our customers have adopted their own cost containment strategies. These strategies have been effective in significantly decreasing the reimbursement for health care services (1). The topic of health care reimbursement will be reviewed more fully in later chapters. For our purposes here, an important outcome of cost containment pressure is a need to find new and better ways to maximize productivity. In health care this means we have to find improved ways of organizing and engaging people in the work of the organization.

KEY WORDS

Chief Executive: the highest ranking member in the management structure. Usually the owner or person accountable to the owner or board of directors of a business.

Cross-functional: organizational work, processes, groups that involve representatives from diverse departments, disciplines and/or job categories.

Entrepreneur: someone who is willing to take risks or try new things in pursuit of business gains.

Human Resources: members of an organization as a potential input to produce an output. It recognizes people as an asset to the organization. Human resources may also be the name of the organizational segment that manages employee related functions such as recruitment and benefits.

Input: represents the resources used to produce an outcome.

Leader: a term used in reference to any individual who has the ability to lead others regardless of organizational position and/or authority.

Management: the formally recognized leadership of an organization.

Management Style: the behaviors a manager exhibits as a leader within the organization (e.g., dictatorial, collaborative, controlling, influenced by others, etc.).

Manager: any individual who has been assigned organizational authority to direct other members of the organization.

Output: what is produced when resources are used.

Productivity: the relationship between the value of resources used (INPUT) to the value of what is produced (OUTPUT).

Scope: the breadth of the organization or part of an organization. Scope may range from a small element of the organization up to and including the entire organization.

Senior Management: often called executive management, refers to those individuals near the top of the management structure. Senior managers often report directly to the chief executive or another member of senior management.

Vision: an organization's view of what it can and should strive to become in the future.

INTRODUCTION

The why and how of managing people has been, and continues to be, a focus of concern for organizations. Managers have been presented with theory after theory in an ongoing effort to discover the secret to maximizing the potential contribution of employees toward the success of the organization. Management theories and practices have evolved as assumptions about human behavior and the potential contribution of employees have changed over time.

Over the past 50 years, assumptions about human behavior have shifted dramatically. At the start of this period, management based its practice on the assumption that employee contribution was a reflection of how well management could standardize and control their work. Current theory indicates that employees' contribution reflects management's ability to provide required education, tools, autonomy and support so the employee might determine the best way to get the job done. These assumptions and their implications for organizational leaders are obviously on the opposite ends of the spectrum. This chapter will explore both theory and management practice related to organizing and engaging people in an effort to maximize their contribution to organizational performance. Chapter 5, Dealing With Differences, will add another important perspective to group management.

ACHIEVING THE ORGANIZATIONAL VISION THROUGH PEOPLE

An organization is, by definition, "a group of people united in a relationship and having some interest, activity, or purpose in common" (2). People are the fundamental element of every organization and determine the purpose of an organization. Their values shape an organization, creating the vision of what their organization can and should strive to accomplish. People are responsible for organizational action or inaction.

Without people, an organization would not exist. Without the commitment and resultant effort of people, an organization could never perform at its full potential or reach its vision. The key to organizational success lies with its members. For this reason, the leadership of successful organizations commit both attention and resources to organizing and fully engaging its members in the purpose, values, vision and activities of the organization.

Few would disagree that the greatest challenge of today's leaders is engaging and directing the commitment and energy of people. Leaders who are recognized as exemplary are those who recognized "that great leadership is not merely a series of mechanical tasks but a set of human interactions" (3).

THE CONCEPT OF PRODUCTIVITY

To fully appreciate a discussion of leadership in the context of maximizing the contribution of employees is to understand that the contribution sought is employee productivity. Productivity is determined by relating the cost of resources used (INPUT EXPENSE) to the value of the outcome produced (OUTPUT PRICE). If an organization spends more to produce a product or service (INPUT EXPENSE) than the customer is willing to pay (OUTPUT PRICE), it will lose money. If it continues to lose money, it will cease to exist.

The concept of productivity can be applied to any and all of an organization's resources, including human resources. Health care is a human resource intensive industry, meaning that a high percentage of health care cost comes from employing people. This is certainly true for the practice of physical therapy. Salaries, benefits, recruitment, training, retention, employee health, and workers' compensation are all examples of employee related expenses. With the output price of health care declining, health care providers must control the cost of human resources to be successful. The cost of human resources can be reduced if employee productivity is increased (4).

LEADERSHIP

Organizational leadership can take many forms. The goal of leadership is to stimulate organizational action in a desired direction. This occurs when an organization gives some members the power to direct and/or influence the actions of other members. Leaders can be followed voluntarily out of loyalty, respect, and trust or, out of fear of undesirable consequences.

Three common characteristics explain why individuals might be recognized as leaders.

1. They have the commanding authority, by virtue of ownership or appointment, to set and direct an organization along a course of action.
2. An individual member is recognized as having knowledge, experience and/or abilities which exceed those of others.
3. Someone acts to guide the way for others by taking a risk or going first.

Regardless of the reason, leaders are characterized by their ability to move others to action. The power and influence of a leader may extend to the entire organization or be limited to one other member. Some leaders are better at influencing desired actions than others. Some leaders rely solely on organizational authority. Successful organizations recognize the value of its leaders and routinely invest in their development.

Formal and Informal Leaders

Organizations generally have many leaders. Leaders may be formally recognized by the organization through title, assigned responsibility and/or inclusion in direction-setting activities. Organizations establish formal leadership structures (management structures) to coordinate the efforts of employees, maximize overall productivity and carry out strategies (4).

The titles of president, vice president, director, manager, supervisor, and coordinator are all used to identify formal management positions. The responsibility of persons with these titles varies among organizations. Any of these titles may be applied to physical therapy management.

Organizational performance may also be influenced by informal leaders. Informal leaders demonstrate the ability to influence the actions of other organization members, but are not recognized formally within the organization's leadership structure. The formal leadership structure may not recognize or may be reluctant to place a value on the influence of informal leaders. The decision to ignore recognized informal leaders should be made with great caution. It is very important for all members of an organization to stay committed to a common organizational purpose and vision. An informal leader who is able to influence others to act in a way that limits or directly opposes management's direction can waste resources, decrease productivity and negatively impact organizational success.

Informal leaders should be recognized as a potential resource or risk. Often, through recognition and inclusion, the influence of an informal leader can be used to increase organizational performance. If not, they should be encouraged to consider changing roles or possibly, leaving the organization.

Through the remainder of this chapter you will note that the words leader and manager are used interchangeably. Although both terms are used frequently, when the term manager is used it is intended to designate that category of leaders who hold formal organizational authority and responsibility to lead people.

Leadership: Art, Science Or Both?

Are great leaders born or do their abilities come from education and experience? Often this question is raised because employees are so seldom completely satisfied with the performance of their organization's leaders. Although technically proficient and experienced, they just do not meet employees' expectations. So what do employees expect from their leaders?

Teal (5) summarizes these expectations well. At the top of the list are the more traditional skills: finance, resource allocation, product development, marketing, service delivery, technology and technical proficiency. Employees also expect leaders to be masters of strategic planning, persuasion, negotiation, speaking, writing and listening. They expect them to make decisions, take responsibility for outcomes, and make lots of money to share. Leaders are expected to do it all while continuously demonstrating the qualities of leadership: vision, passion, sensitivity, commitment, insight, intelligence, ethical behavior, charisma, courage, tenacity and, at times, humility. Practicing organizational leadership in a

manner that "meets employee expectations requires people to display on an everyday basis the combined skills of St. Peter, Peter the Great and the Great Houdini." (5) It's no wonder that so few organizational leaders consistently meet employee expectations. No doubt some leaders are recognized as great because they do meet this superhuman challenge. But there are others who are considered great leaders despite the fact that they fail to meet many employee expectations. It is this last group that Teal might say have mastered the art of the human side of management.

ORGANIZATIONAL LEADERSHIP: ROLES, RESPONSIBILITIES AND COMPETENCIES

Leadership Roles

Mintzberg, in writing on the nature of managerial work, identified three roles assumed by organizational leaders: interpersonal, informational and decisional (6). Mintzberg's work provides a convenient framework for review of the multiple roles leaders must play in today's organizations.

The Interpersonal Role

Under the interpersonal role, Mintzberg included the roles of figurehead, leader, and liaison (6). The figurehead role is both external and internal to the organization. Leaders must carry out their responsibilities in a manner that continuously models the values, mission and philosophy of the organization. They are a role model for others. The role of leader encompasses creating a shared vision, setting standards, motivating employees, and facilitating desired organizational changes. As liaisons, leaders must advocate for, and promote, the organization. They must build and maintain beneficial relationships inside and outside the organization.

The Informational Role

Mintzberg's informational role includes the leadership functions of researcher/learner, disseminator/spokesman, and listener. As a researcher/learner, organizational leaders must continually obtain and manage information about the external environment, the organization, it's customers, and employees. Information must be analyzed to evaluate external opportunities and threats as well as organizational strengths and weaknesses. Information must be disseminated and others educated to benefit the organization. Finally, leaders must listen to ideas of others (6).

The Decisional Role

The decisional role incorporates the roles of an entrepreneur, disturbance handler, resource allocator and negotiator. This role considers the responsibilities for innovation and encouraging openness for the exploration of new ideas. The skills of facilitator, team leader, and team builder are necessary to encourage cooperation and collaboration within and between organization divisions. Two key competencies fall under resource allocation, planning and administration. It is under these functions that the activities related to organizational operations are found, including productivity management (6).

Leadership Roles And Organizational Position

Each role applies to all organizational leaders. A specific focus is determined by position within the management structure. Zuckerman (3) and Mintzberg (7) indicate that the primary responsibility for managing information, adapting to environmental demands, providing vision and strategic direction rests with the chief executive and senior members of the management structure. Research supports the idea that the focus and time spent in performing each of the three roles varies by position within the management structure. One such study examined the perceptions of hospital-based executives (multiple business and/or care units), administrative (business units) and clinical leaders (patient care units) to assess differences in responsibility for and time spent in Mintzberg's three roles (6,8). The findings of this study indicate that executive leaders assume primary responsibility for ensuring appropriate external relations, planning and decision making for the organization. Though administrative and clinical leaders assume primary responsibility for the internal interpersonal

roles, the study found, many spent a similar amount of time in planning and decisional roles.

Table 4.1 provides an overview of leadership roles with related competencies and skills. Using Mintzberg's framework (6), it is intended to provide a more detailed summary of leadership roles. It also provides a point of reference for leaders to evaluate their preparation to fulfill these roles.

THEORIES ABOUT MANAGING PEOPLE: PAST TO PRESENT

Assumptions about human attitudes, aptitudes and behaviors are the foundation upon which people management theories and related management practices are built. As research and experience contribute to our knowledge of human behavior, approaches to achieving maximum employee contribution change. Miles (9) provides a conceptual model for understanding the evolution of management theory. He recognizes three basic models of management theory and suggests that most, if not all, management theories fall in line with one of these models. His three models of management theory include the traditional, human relations and human resource models. These models are reflective of knowledge and experience gained over the last 50 years. Because our own experience suggests that practices reflective of all three models are seen in today's organizations, an overview of the underlying assumptions, characteristics, and representative theories of all three models are viewed as relevant to the leaders of today.

The Traditional Model

Miles (9) applies the theories of Darwin to describe assumptions underlying the traditional model of managing people. People of superior ability should lead and direct others of lesser ability. Max Weber (10) promoted the concept of work standardization and job specialization at all levels of the organization. The assumption was that peak performance was achieved when each employee was required to perform a minimum number of standardized tasks on a repeated basis. Organizational performance results from

TABLE 4.1

The Roles Of An Organizational Leader

ROLES INTERPERSONAL	COMPETENCIES/SKILLS
FIGUREHEAD (ROLE MODEL)	> DEPORTMENT
Leader (visionary)	> Creating a shared vision
	> Change facilitation
	Stress management
	> Motivation
	> Set standards
Liaison	> Advocacy
	> Relationship management
	> Organization promotion
INFORMATIONAL	
Researcher/Learner	> Information collection
	Industry trends
	Market trends
	Organizational
	assessment
	Self knowledge
	> In touch with customers and
	employees
	> Analysis/problem
	identification
	> Computer skills
Disseminator/	> Communication
Spokesman	Writing skills
	Presentation skills
	> Educator
Listener	> Openness to influence
DECISIONAL	
Entrepreneur	> Risk taking
	> Innovation
	> Flexibility
Disturbance Handler	> Problem resolution
	> Team building
Resource Allocation	> Planning
	> Administration
	Financial management
	Productivity management
	Quality management
	Workload management
	Time management
	Customer service
	management
	Facility management
	> Organizational ability
	> Making decisions
	> Human resource
	management
	Personnel selection
	Personnel development
	Employee relations
	delegation
Negotiator	> Conflict management

management's ability to provide a decent physical environment, to design efficient tasks and to provide close supervision.

An example of the traditional model can be found in the writing of Fredrick Taylor (11). Based on his scientific observations and analysis of work activities in an industrial setting, he postulated that even skilled workers required the guidance of supervisors to achieve optimal performance of standardized tasks. Employee recognition equaled adequate pay. Workers were thought to be incapable of independently designing or carrying out their work. Under the traditional model, the management style would be authoritarian and directive. Employees would be discouraged from giving input and making decisions on any level. Work would consist of standardized tasks performed under the watchful eye of the manager.

The Human Relations Model

Miles' (9) human relations model is reflective of management theories that identify the importance of dealing with needs of individual workers. This model promotes the demonstration of concern and consideration for employees' feelings and personal needs. Employees are kept informed and have the opportunity to give input on routine matters. Management is encouraged to use additional non-monetary rewards such as recognition. Management's intent is to make employees feel good. This model falls short of substantial inclusion of the employee in the decision-making process.

The Human Resource Model

The human resource model also recognizes the importance of meeting workers' needs for recognition, inclusion, attention and contribution. But, the model goes even further. It recognizes that workers want the opportunity to develop and use all of their skills. Miles' human resource model contends that employee satisfaction comes not from external reward, but from a sense of accomplishment (9). Under this model, organizations receive greatest benefit when they encourage full participation of all employees. An organization's leadership is challenged to provide an environment that supports and facilitates maximum involvement to produce maximum contribution and productivity.

Herzberg's Two Factor Theory is an example of a human resource model (12,13). Herzberg theorizes that there are two categories of job attitude factors that influence performance. He labels these categories satisfiers and dissatisfiers. Organizational and job factors that lead to employee dissatisfaction are hygiene factors. Hygiene factors need to be present to avoid employee dissatisfaction, but their presence does not lead to employee satisfaction. Alternately, when present, job satisfiers act as employee motivators. Herzberg postulates that the higher the level of employee satisfaction, the greater their level of cooperation and productivity. Table 4.2 provides a listing of those job factors that Herzberg defined as dissatisfiers and satisfiers.

A CONTINUUM OF MANAGEMENT STYLES: PUSH, PULL OR LEAD

Miles'(9) three models represent a continuum of management styles in which the manager's role moves from one of total control, the dictator, to one of total collaboration with employees at all levels of the organization, the democrat. This continuum of management styles is represented in Figure 4.1. As indicated in the figure, as the management style moves toward the democratic

TABLE 4.2

The Two Factor Theory of Job Satisfaction

FACTORS LEADING TO JOB DISSATISFACTION AND SATISFACTION

DISSATISFIERS	SATISFIERS
• Administration	• Achievement
• Benefits	• Advancement
• Interpersonal Relations	• Growth Potential
• Job Security	• Interpersonal Relations
• Organizational Policy	• Power
• Salary	• Recognition
• Supervision	• Responsibility
• Interpersonal Relations	• Salary
	• Status

or human resource end of the continuum, the influence of employees over their work increases.

As noted at the outset of this discussion, it has been the authors' observation, having had the opportunity to work with and observe many organizational leaders over the past years, that the full continuum of management styles is evident in today's organizations. This most certainly includes health care organizations. In fact, the same manager might be observed using different styles at different times. Management theories that promote and defend the use of varying management styles are said to fall under the contingency model (9).

The Contingency Model

It takes little interaction with today's managers to realize that the search for the one 'best' approach that will work for all managers in all situations to motivate all workers to maximum productivity is ongoing. This has lead to the development of theories that propose that the right management approach is contingent on situational factors.

The work of Tannenbaum and Schmidt (14) suggests that management style may be viewed in terms of the situational forces that influence it. These forces come from the situation, the employee(s) and from the manager. Table 4.3 lists some of the situational forces that may influence management style.

Situational forces may work in concert, thereby moving the manager's style toward the same end of the management style continuum. Or, the forces may be conflicting, which makes it difficult to choose between approaches. Pressures that result from multiple situational forces can be complex, challenging the abilities of even the most skilled organizational leaders. Figure 4.2 depicts Hersey and Blanchard's Life Cycle Theory (15). The Life Cycle Theory suggests that management style should be primarily determined by employee maturity. Assessment of employee maturity is based on achievement motivation, task-relevant education, ability to do the work required, and willingness to take responsibility. The diagram suggests that at the point at which average group maturity is low,

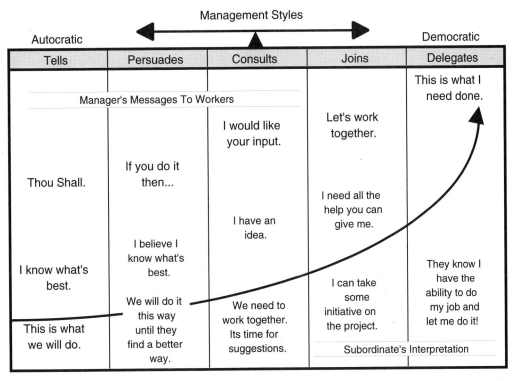

FIGURE 4.1. The Continuum Of Management Styles. Modified from Nosse LJ, Friberg DG. Management Principles for Physical Therapists. Baltimore, MD: Williams and Wilkins, 1992:48.

TABLE 4.3
Factors Influencing Management Style

	SITUATIONAL FACTORS	
MANAGER	**EMPLOYEE/WORK GROUP**	**SITUATION**
Values	Values	Organizational:
Competencies	Competencies	Ownership
Skills	Education	Purpose, Vision
Experience	Skills	and Values
Leadership	Experience	Strategies
Tendencies	Level of Satisfaction	Culture
Situational Comfort	Level of Interest in Job	History
Sense of Security	Acceptance of	Environment
History of	Responsibility	Practices
Performance	Availability	Resources Available
Perceived Risk	Expectations of the	Job Characteristics:
Confidence in	Manager	Scope
Employees		Urgency
		Importance

management should adopt a highly directive style. As the group maturity increases, a highly supportive management style should be incorporated with the highly directive approach. In this way, management continues to ensure the performance of the work group while beginning the transition to a more democratic style. As the group maturity continues to increase, manage-

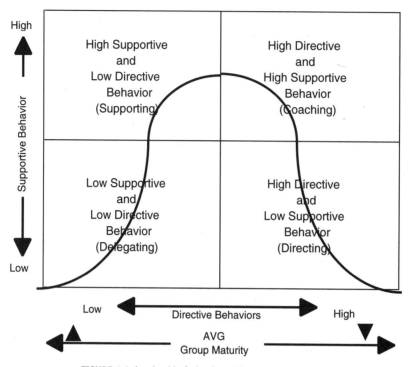

FIGURE 4.2. Leadership Styles Based On Group Maturity.

ment's directive behaviors should decline. This transition continues until, at full maturity, management style is highly supportive with a low directive component. This cycle may repeat itself as group composition and membership, the task or the organization change over time.

The implication of the Life Cycle Theory (15) is that employee and/or work group factors may impact management style more than manager or situational factors. As we continue this discussion, the reasons for this should become more evident. Contingency models do not provide all the answers on how best to manage people toward maximum performance. They do suggest that managers can and should modify their approach to leadership based on the situation. Even if current theory does not leave struggling managers with the one 'best' way, it does provide some guidelines for action.

Managers seek information about managing people for one reason: to assist them in their never ending effort to maximize employee productivity. If you accept the concept that situational factors should and often do determine the best management approach, then managing the variables of the situation seems to be an obvious place for managers to focus their effort. That is not to say that all variables can or should be controlled. The intent is to identify key variables that can be controlled so that, in complex situations, the manager is most likely to adopt the best approach. The fewer the variables, the more likely that will happen. So what can a manager do to control situational factors?

A review of Table 4.3 indicates that there are situational factors and pressures that can be minimized through management action. Organizations spend a lot of time talking about motivating employees toward higher productivity. The manager who is successful at controlling situational variables, particularly the employee/work-group factors, may still utilize the continuum of management styles, but they will have already taken a giant leap toward motivating employees to high performance. The opportunities for action will be .expanded upon more fully later in this chapter during the discussion of practice implications for health care managers.

ACHIEVING MAXIMUM PRODUCTIVITY THROUGH WORK TEAMS

Why Work Teams?

At the same time the health care industry has been struggling to meet new customer expectations, there has been an increasing awareness and interest in the success of Japanese organizations toward motivation of employees to continuously achieve high levels of productivity. Ouchi (16) observed Japanese organizations and reported that the success of those Japanese organizations was due to their collaborative management style. These organizations placed great value on their employees, as employees were consulted on issues that affected them and their work.

Employee participation was achieved through the use of a group process. Work teams would meet regularly to review operations, identify opportunities for improvement and make changes necessary to improve quality and productivity. These teams were referred to as quality circles. The concept of quality and productivity improvement throughout the organization and empowerment of employee work groups caught on quickly. Following the lead of other American organizations, the health care industry began to turn its attention away from the individual employee to the work team as a unit so that major productivity improvements could be derived.

Team Formation

A work group consists of individuals who are organized together to perform a set of assigned tasks. Within work groups, individuals may be performing the same task or components of a larger task. For example, Group A may transport patients to and from a care setting while Group B transports, prepares patients to receive care, performs the care, prepares and transports the patient back to the starting location. Group A members perform the same task. Group B members perform a process made up of several tasks.

Work groups may be together on a permanent basis or assemble to tackle a specific, time limited task. They can be cross-functional, including representatives from many departments or represent one department such as the physical therapy department. Work groups have many names. Intact team, department, committee, council, task force, project team, process improvement team, hot teams, steering committee and management group are just a few of the names organizations use to describe work groups (17). Organizing people into a work group is the starting point but it takes more than structure to turn a group of employees into a functioning work team.

Transformation: Work Group To Work Team

For a work group to become a highly productive work team it takes commitment and a lot of hard work. There are steps that management can take to increase the chances of a successful transformation from an individual to a team focus.

1. Group members must have and understand what is expected from them by the organization.
2. They should be aware of the barriers they face.
3. The team must adopt work rules to achieve its task.
4. The team must be structured and positioned within the organization to achieve expected performance.
5. Members must have the needed skills, knowledge and experience to perform the tasks required.

Performance Expectations

The first thing a team needs is specific performance expectations that are defined in terms of quantifiable outcomes. Performance expectations may originate with management or with the team. Expectations should be consistent with the basic purpose and vision of the organization. Performance expectations may have a broad scope that affects the entire organization or a narrow scope that affects a small part of the organization. Whatever the source or scope, performance expectations must be clear and concise. There should be no room for differing interpretations of the expected outcomes.

Performance Constraints

The team should be aware of any known constraints that they must accommodate to meet their performance expectations. Constraints should be identified and defined. Common constraints faced by work teams in health care organizations include:

- Limited resources such as money, equipment, space, or information.
- The availability of qualified employees.
- Time restrictions.
- External restrictions that are outside the organization's sphere of control. External restrictions affecting health care organizations come in many forms such as licensure laws, wage and salary guidelines, service certification requirements, customer needs and building codes.

Work Rules

The next step is for the team to agree upon a common set of work rules. Work rules are tools that team members can use to anticipate the actions of other members. They provide structure for group interactions and group tasks. Clinical care protocols, policies, procedures such as scheduling procedures and defined decision-making processes such as standard assessment tools are all forms of work rules.

Rules do not need to limit team creativity, flexibility or responsiveness to change. In fact, rules about how the team will respond to new ideas could increase members' comfort with sharing ideas. Work rules may limit the individuality of team members. However, team performance should be enhanced even in times of change and uncertainty. This happens because members can count on the support, stability and predictability of the group. Finally, work rules do not need to be and should not be etched in stone. To the contrary, rules should be flexible, changing as the needs of the team, organization and its customers change. In fact, changing the work rules of the health care delivery process is exactly what some of our customers are expecting providers to do.

Team Structure

Significant attention should be paid to the structure of the team. Team structure would include such things as member roles, membership characteristics (also see Chapter 5), and group size. The team structure should reflect performance expectations and constraints. The objective is to assemble the right people to get the job done.

MEMBER ROLES

Work teams mirror larger organizations in that its members are assigned to perform specific roles. Team roles include a leader, members, and often, support staff and a facilitator. An individual team member may perform one or more role. Assignment and definition of team roles will help members understand their contributions to the group process.

The team leader is responsible for getting the work done. The team leader should also be an active member in the group process. In the group decision-making process, team leaders have no more authority than any other member regardless of management authority. Leaders can be appointed by the organization or selected by the group. Generally, the team leaders' areas of responsibility will be significantly affected by the work of the group.

The facilitator is responsible for managing group dynamics, the process and reinforcing group work rules. The facilitator often is required to break down barriers that limit the group process and progress. Frequently encountered barriers include status of members, conflicting goals, member characteristics, information, lack of group process skills and failure to follow established work rules. The team leader or a member may function as the facilitator. Or, the facilitator may be a neutral outside party who is not considered a team member.

MEMBER SELECTION

Members contribute their energy, ideas, talents and skills toward meeting the team performance expectations. Considerations for member selection should start with the team's performance expectations. The work to be done, people affected, organizational priority, time available and the individual's ability to contribute to a successful outcome are some of the considerations related to the performance expectations. Constraints may also play into the choice of members. Members who have the potential to limit or remove constraints would be highly valued. The constraint may be limited availability of desirable members. Team member balance, fit and diversity (see Chapter 5) should also be considered. Table 4.4 provides a list of factors that may influence the choice of members.

TABLE 4.4
Work Team Member Selection

FACTORS FOR CONSIDERATION		
PERFORMANCE EXPECTATIONS	KNOWN AND POTENTIAL CONSTRAINTS	GROUP BALANCE, FIT AND DIVERSITY
Defined Work To Be Done	Define Constraints To Be Accommodated	Group Dynamics and Process
• Scope of impact	• Organizational values, vision and culture	• Group process skills
• Priority	• Divergence from norms	• Leadership skills
• Time available	• Resources	• Worker representation
• Potential contribution	• Member availability	• Diversity of group member work, styles, skills
• People Affected	• Information access	• Education
• Functions Affected	• Potential for internal resistance	• Skills
• Roles within the group	• External factors	• Experience
		• Organizational position
		• Knowledge of the organization

GROUP SIZE

There is no magic formula for determining the best group size. The most productive teams are those no larger than they need to be to get the job done. Each member should represent added value. Group size should not be used to limit participation in any individual or work group whose work is influenced by the decisions of the work team.

Information

The value of information has long been recognized. Information is an organizational asset. As noted in Chapter 3, Marketing, those organizations that have and know how to use information about customers, the environment, and itself, will have a competitive advantage in the marketplace.

In 1954, Drucker wrote that employees who lack information "necessary to control, measure, and guide his own performance" also "lack both the incentive and means to improve their performance" (18). Access to the right information at the right time affects the performance of a work team the same way it does an individual. It serves to define performance expectations and constraints in objective terms. It can be used to educate and align team members. Information is needed for the team to assess their performance. It is the foundation for setting direction and decision making. Information gives a team the power to maximize their performance.

Information is a source of power (19). It positions an organization to be more influential in its environment and marketplace. It offers the potential to limit the success of competitors. Information is also a source of internal organizational power. Unfortunately, this can create the potential for individuals who control the flow of information to have more organizational influence and personal success. A powerful incentive may exist to keep information from others (19). Information can be withheld by restricting access, delaying access or failing to educate others so they have the skill to understand and to use information to improve performance. The practice of withholding information to control and limit the activities of others is a common criticism directed at today's organizations. It is a practice that limits the productivity of an organization.

Stages Of Team Development

When all of the right elements are in place, when group members understand what they are to do, the barriers they face, resources available, how the group will be structured and whom they will work with, then the group will be well positioned to become a high performance work team. Weber (20) provides us with the "Forming-Storming-Norming-Performing" model (Table 4.5) that describes how groups pass through stages as they develop into highly productive work teams. LaPenta and Jacobs (21) expand on the model by providing insight into leadership issues, team/task issues, interpersonal issues and group behavioral patterns

TABLE 4.5
Team Development: Stages, Issues And Behavior Patterns

ISSUES/BEHAVIORS	STAGES			
	FORMING	STORMING	NORMING	PERFORMING
Leadership Issues	* Dependence	* Independence * Cliques	* Interdependence	* Interdependence
Group Tasks	* Membership * Roles * Similarities * Differences	* Decision-making Process * Power * Influence	* Building relationships	* Productivity
Interpersonal	* Inclusion	* Control	* Affection	* Affection
Group Behaviors	* Seek similarities * Anger * Frustration * Polite * Vague * Confused	* Set work rules * Create order * Attack leader * Negative about task demands	* Cohesion * Negotiation	* Growth * Understanding * Team work

that correspond to each developmental stage. Table 4.5, modeled on the work of LaPenta and Jacobs, provides an overview of developmental stages and related issues.

A Performing Work Team: Would You Know It If You Saw It?

Performing work teams share certain characteristics that differentiate them from work groups. When a work team is at a high performance level, members demonstrate an obvious commitment to their shared purpose. Open communication and a collaborative working style between members will be the norm. When members disagree, the group will employ a comfortable, established approach to conflict resolution. The team will use an established decision-making process. Once decisions are made, the team will demonstrate a common level of support and dedication to action. Morale will be high. Often, group dynamics will be characterized by a sense of excitement. Most important, the team will exhibit a high level of productivity.

Work Teams And Productivity

Enhanced productivity can be attributed to the work team structure that gives individuals the opportunity to develop a broader focus of their roles, responsibilities and contribution to the organization. Because performing work teams have an established process for information sharing and broad organizational networks, team members will have more and better information upon which to base decisions. Inclusion in the decision making process enhances member buy-in to team commitments and change initiatives. As a result, members are likely to work harder to engage others in the team's efforts. Team pressure and support help team members to maintain their level of commitment and follow through over time. All of these factors contribute to productivity. Such characteristics of a high performing team would not be duplicated were the focus on individual performance.

Self-Directed Work Teams

Self-directed work teams are different from other work teams. They lack a formal team leader. In the absence of a team leader, team members share responsibility for most or all aspects of the team process. Also referred to as work cells, self-directed work teams are organized around a specific work process (17). More prominent in manufacturing, the use of self-directed work teams is growing within the health care industry (17). Use of self-directed work teams is often viewed as an opportunity to reduce the number of employees without reducing productive capabilities. Self-directed teams operate with a high degree of autonomy. Increased member collaboration and subsequent reduction in conflicting influences that may occur within self-directed work teams has the potential to provide many organizational benefits.

- Simplified operations
- Increased responsiveness to customer needs
- Decreased needs and cost related to management and support services
- Improved quality
- Increased employee satisfaction
- Increased productivity

The authors' own experience with self-directed work teams is that they have been marginally successful. Group maturity, the prior establishment of cooperative working relationships and the group interaction skills of the team members were observed to have a significant impact on the long-term success of self-directed teams.

PRACTICE IMPLICATIONS FOR HEALTH CARE MANAGEMENT

Management's goal is to assure the success of the organization. Management cannot accomplish that goal without the support and effort of each employee. But how does a manager promote a high level of organizational support from employees? Organizational leaders are challenged to use all available resources to facilitate employee commitment and motivation. The following discussion is an attempt to provide some direction toward the practical application of the concepts shared in this chapter.

Know Yourself And Prepare For The Future

A personal assessment of management competencies and skills is a good place to start. Self-awareness can position a manager to build on strengths and remediate areas of weakness. Experts predict that change within the health care industry will continue at an increasing rate well into the future. As organizational structures and demands change, so do the skills required of its leaders. It is essential for health care leaders to

know what is needed, embrace the challenge and evolve their own behaviors and practices to meet new demands. In the past, it was enough for managers to direct, teach tasks, plan, problem solve and control operations.

Knowledge of the task is still a common reason new physical therapy managers are selected. But knowledge of the task is not enough. Today, physical therapy managers must focus on creating a vision, developing employees' self-management skills, and team building. The roles of coach, enabler, team member, and team leader will be today's keys to future success (17).

Self-assessment may sound like an easy task, but, in fact, objective self-assessment is not routinely part of the preparation of organizational leaders. Often new managers receive little or no preparation at all. An objective self-assessment can help both the manager and the organization. A self-assessment should include feedback from superiors, peers and subordinates. It should use objective, standardized testing. If properly done, a self-assessment can provide a manager with insight into their values, personality characteristics, leadership competencies, leadership tendencies, and management abilities. Self-assessment can provide insight into how a manager's performance is perceived by others and how they function in a group or team setting. Self-awareness should increase confidence and make it easier to share decision-making authority with other employees and peers. The resources needed to complete a self-assessment may be available through an employer, professional organizations, management development courses or management consultants.

Have The Right People And Prepare Them Well

Managers must know the capabilities of employees, peers and superiors. Employees cannot be productive if they don't know how to do the job. Managers are responsible for having people available who are capable of maximum performance (22). Managers can meet this responsibility only if they have an effective employee recruitment, selection, training, orientation and performance evaluation process. There are several benefits that come from an effective staff recruitment and development program.

1. Having the right number of qualified employees is the only effective way to meet the organization's performance goals.
2.. Employees who work under the conditions created by long-term staffing shortages have the potential to become less satisfied, less productive and ultimately leave the organization.
3. A shared knowledge of employee qualifications, experience and past performance will raise the level of situational comfort for both manager and employee(s).
4. Employees will have the skills to meet performance expectations.
5. Managers will make better situational assessments and decisions.

Each of these benefits has the potential to improve both the manager's and the organization's performance.

Keep Good Employees

Of equal importance is management's responsibility for employee retention. Organizations must invest substantial resources in training and developing people so they are prepared to do the work required. As an organization's investment in developing employees goes up, so does the value of the employee as an asset of the organization. It is a real loss when a valued employee leaves the organization. Management is responsible for providing a work environment that motivates employees to remain with the organization. Herzberg's work provides some practical guidance (12,13). A supportive environment starts with the basics (22).

1. Employee compensation, including wages and benefits, should be competitive for the market area and type of position.
2. Strategic and financial management practices should be sound, resulting in reasonable job security.
3. Management style should reflect the situation and the needs of the employees.
4. Positive relations among employees, and between management and employees should be fostered.
5. Management should provide clear goals, objectives and performance expectations.

6. Employees should be provided with the right tools, equipment and facilities.
7. Employees should be free from unnecessary organizational barriers.
8. Employees should be provided with opportunities for achievement and advancement.
9. Management should be generous with its recognition and rewards.

Herzberg's list of satisfiers can guide management as they, with their employees, work to create the right environment (13). Without a supportive environment, employees will be unlikely to perform at maximum levels.

Know Your Business

Knowledge of the work is an essential management competency. What resources are required? What resources are available? What are the job characteristics? Is the scope small, such as registering a patient, or large, like the selection and set up of a new registration system? What barriers exist within the organization that may limit choice of approach? If skilled employees are not available, the manager may need to select a more autocratic or directing style because the potential for developing a successful team is limited. What external influences may need to be considered? Professional licensure laws, accreditation requirements and/or customer requirements may restrict the options available. As this knowledge is required, a manager might prepare and support others in their efforts to improve task efficiency and outcome.

When a manager lacks the required knowledge or skill, it is their responsibility to get the assistance that they need. Use of internal and external consultants is discussed in Chapter 13.

ORGANIZATIONAL PERFORMANCE IMPROVEMENT

A discussion about organizing and engaging people would not be complete without inclusion of the concept of organizational performance improvement. Individual and group performance improvement efforts can have an impact on the performance of organizations. As the previous discussion moved from individual to group based performance, there was a clear message that individuals working as part of a team have the potential to out perform a similar group of individuals working alone. So, if this compounding effect works when we move from individual or work group to work team, then does it also work when performance improvement initiatives are focused on the organization as a whole? Proponents of organizational performance improvement say the answer is a resounding yes.

Organizational performance improvement has also arisen out of the efforts to understand the success of Japanese companies. It is true that the Japanese used work teams to engage and improve the performance of its employees. But, what may be more important, is the use of work teams as a way to focus the efforts of the entire organization on two complementary strategic directions. First, to continuously improve the quality of the product. Second, to continuously improve service to the customer. Both are strategies needed by market-driven organizations. How quality improvement and service improvement efforts lead to increased productivity merits additional attention.

Quality Improvement/Service Improvement

Organization wide efforts to improve quality, often referred to as Total Quality Management (TQM) or Continuous Quality Improvement (CQI or QI), have been shown to improve organizational performance by improving the way products and/or services are produced and supported.

Within an organization, opportunities to improve product and service quality as well as production efficiency can be identified in many ways. Most commonly, opportunities are identified through the collection and analysis of data from internal and external sources. Internally, improvement initiatives may be identified from problem logs, work process delays, expense overruns, system failures, work group complaints, complaints from others affected (internal customers), error rates, rework costs, wasted supplies, canceled appointments, inventory levels, duplication of work, etc. Chapter 11 provides a comprehensive review of information that can be used to measure and improve an organization's performance outcomes.

Externally, opportunities for improvement may be identified through contact with customers, obtaining industry benchmarks or observation of other organizations. The inclusion of external information sources, particularly customers, will focus improvement efforts on service. As discussed in Chapter 3, market orientation starts with identification of customers needs. The customer's definition of quality and service should drive quality improvement initiatives.

Improvement initiatives and resulting benefits can be large or small. If initiatives are successful, "efficiency and productivity rise, and customer as well as employee satisfaction (or delight) soars" (17). To be successful, quality improvement efforts in an organization should follow some practical guidelines.

1. Quality improvement efforts should use a work team approach.
2. Team formation and support should be an organizational priority.
3. Team process should be defined and followed.
4. Data should be collected and analyzed to determine and validate the cause of the problem and/or the opportunity to improve performance.
5. Input should be sought from those who are affected by the improvement effort.
6. Improvement strategies should be based on fact not intuition.
7. Improvement initiatives should be well planned, implemented and monitored to see if they produce expected quality improvements.

Models for organizational quality improvement programs can be found throughout management literature.

Organized quality improvement programs have been recognized as an important management tool. In health care, QI has replaced many of the traditional quality control and quality assurance activities. The Joint Commission on Accreditation of Health Care Organizations (JCAHO) requires demonstration of an operating, organization-wide plan for performance improvement. As a result, knowledge of quality improvement is essential for health care managers working in hospital, long-term care, rehabilitation center, and home care settings throughout the country.

SUMMARY

The roles of an organizational leader are complex and multi-faceted. Role model, visionary, researcher, evaluator, communicator, educator, planner, problem solver, administrator, motivator, and arbitrator are just a few characteristics of this role.

One of the critical factors impacting organizational success is productivity. The key to productivity in labor intensive health care organizations is worker commitment and effort. Organization leaders are accountable for organizational productivity. They fulfill this responsibility by adopting a management style and organizational structure that facilitate employee engagement and productivity. There is a continuum of management styles a leader might adopt. From autocratic to democratic, a leader may use a singular approach or modify their style and actions based on the situation. Organizational structure should support workers' efforts and, where feasible, encourage members of work groups to develop into high performing work teams. In this way, the potential productivity of individual workers can be realized.

The concepts presented here, and elsewhere throughout the book, may be explored more fully through the use of a continuous case study, a role play, presented in Appendix A. The role play has been designed to demonstrate how management concepts may impact the clinical setting on a daily basis. The intent of the role play is to provoke thought and build a connection between theory and practice of physical therapy in today's health care environment.

REFERENCES

1. Kiesler CA, Morton TL. Psychology and public policy in the "health care revolution". Am Psychol 1988; 43(12):993–1003.
2. Macmillian Contemporary Dictionary. New York: Macmillian Publishing,1973:710.
3. Zuckerman HS. Redefining the role of the CEO: Challenges and conflicts. Hospitals and Health Services Administration. 1989; Spring 34:1: 26–38.
4. Porter ME. Operational effectiveness is not strategy. Harvard Business Review 1966; November–December: 61–77.
5. Teal T. The human side of management. Havard Business Review 1996;November-December:35–44.
6. Mintzberg H. The Nature of Managerial Work. New York: Harper and Row, 1976.
7. Mintzberg H. The Structuring of Organizations. Englewood Cliffs, NJ: Prentice Hall, 1979.
8. Brandt EN, Broyles RW, Falcone DJ. Roles of hospital administrators in South Carolina. Hospital & Health Services Administration 1996,Fall 41:3:373–383.
9. Miles RE. Theories of Management: Implications for Organizational Behavior and Development. New York: McGraw-Hill, 1975.
10. Gerth HH, Mills CW. From Max Weber: Essays in Sociology. New York: Oxford Press, 1958:196–244.
11. Taylor F. The Principles of Scientific Management. New York: Norton, 1967.
12. Herzberg F, Mausner B, Snyderman B. The Motivation to Work. 2nd ed. New York:Wiley, 1959.
13. Herzberg F. Work and the Nature of Man. Cleveland: World, 1966.
14. Tannenbaum R, Schmidt WH. How to choose a leadership pattern. Harv Bus Rev 1973;May–June:162–180.
15. Hersey P, Blanchard KH. Management of Organizational Behavior. Englewood Cliffs, NJ:Prentice Hall, 1972.
16. Ouchi W. Theory Z: How American Business Can Meet the Japanese Challenge. Reading, PA: Addison-Wesley, 1981.
17. Clemmer J. Firing on All Cylinders. Burr Ridge, IL: Irwin, 1992.
18. Drucker,P. The Practice of Management. New York, NY: Harper & Row, 1954.
19. Case J. Open-Book Management. New York, NY: HarperCollins, 1994.
20. Weber RC. The group: A cycle from birth to death. In Porter L, Mohr B (Eds.). Reading Book for Human Relations Training. Alexandria, VA: NTL Institute, 1982.
21. LaPenta C, Jacobs GM. Application of group process Model to performance appraisal development in a CQI environment. Health Care Manage Rev 1996;21(4): 45–60.
22. Schemerhorn JR. Improving health care productivity through high-performance managerial development. Health Care Manage Rev 1987;12:49–55.

5

DEALING WITH DIFFERENCES

PREVIEW

This chapter will assist the reader in understanding and appreciating two very important concepts: diversity and conflict management. Diversity in the workplace includes cultural, age, gender, socioeconomic, racial, and sexual orientation diversity, among others. The main focus in addressing these issues will be to realize the value of diversity as a source of organizational innovation and contribution.

The second concept that is addressed is the management of conflict that may arise within the organization. A significant role in any manager's work life is to anticipate conflict, develop plans to minimize, direct or avoid conflict, and to manage conflict. In this chapter, we will present a conceptual framework for dealing with conflict within an organization. Conflict can be beneficial when appropriately managed or directed.

The reader will learn why diversity of all types within the workplace does not detract from the work of the organization, but it actually enhances the overall value of the workforce. Diversity creates an environment of increased innovation, creativity, and eventually, success. This chapter deals with an important issue: how to prosper as an organization due to diversity of viewpoints, interests, aspirations, expectations, skills, perspectives and a multitude of other attributes that allow people to have different insights and different frames of reference.

KEY WORDS

Civil Rights Act (1964): Title VII established the Equal Employment Opportunity Commission (EEOC) to define and enforce acceptable employment policies and practices as they affect minorities and women.
Cultural Diversity: the representation, in one so-cial system, of people with distinctly different group affiliations of cultural significance.
Culture Group: an affiliation of people who collectively share certain norms, values, or traditions that differ from those of other groups.
Culture Identity Groups: groups of individuals

that are different from the majority group in which the differentiating factors are based on shared norms, values, and common socio-cultural heritage (i.e., subjective culture).

Majority Group: numerically the largest group represented in the social system, typically the group in power.

Managing Diversity: planning and implementing organizational systems and practices to manage people so that the potential advantages of diversity are maximized while the potential disadvantages are minimized.

Minority Group: group with fewer members than the majority group, lower status or less power in the social system compared to the majority group.

Phenotype Identity Groups: groups of individuals that are different from the majority group in which the differentiating factors are physically and visually observable. For example, gender-specific groups, racial-ethnic groups, and persons with differing abilities.

Prejudice: an attitudinal bias and tendency to prejudge something or someone on the basis of some differentiating characteristics. Although prejudice may be manifested as either a positive or negative predisposition, it is most often defined as a negative predisposition.

INTRODUCTION

Among definitions of diversity are the quality of being diverse, variety, multiformity, and difference. In general, none of these terms typically evoke emotional reactions. However, if something or someone being different results in some type of change, then emotions may be aroused. The logical question is, "What is the trigger for concern?" Is it merely that someone or something being different is emotionally unsettling? Is it that differences or a difference bring(s) about change and change is what is the concern?

Using a computer analogy, all humans have the same hardwiring/chips, i.e., innate reflexes, which are used to initiate a developmental sequence, which in turn allows for exploration, enrichment and unique learning experiences. These unique learning experiences are akin to software, i.e., unique programs. We all begin with the same hard wiring that leads to unique experiences which give us somewhat different software.

Having a wide variety of software is helpful to computer users in meeting daily needs as well as solving special problems. In this same sense, having diversity, i.e., people with different skills, interests, experiences, values, and other attributes is critical to solving current and future problems. It is a way of combating group think, i.e., everyone agreeing on an issue because they are products of the same experiences. In a country whose demographics are changing rapidly, in a market that is unpredictable and hostile (see

Chapters 7 and 8), in a business that is essentially borderless, to have employees of one mind, to have uniformity instead of multiformity, is undesirable. It is detrimental to growth.

Diversity among managers at all levels, among staff, among customers, among products and among services is good for business. Difficulties that arise from diversity of values, frames of reference and other sources of uniqueness are manageable if they are recognized.

VALUES

Chapter 2 presented the idea that values serve motivations and that similar values can serve different motivations for different people. If one believes, as many do, that human wants, i.e., the spectrum of human motivations, are similar world wide (1), then one might more easily focus on commonalties among people than differences.

Values, the principles that guide peoples' lives, are seen by each of us as worth advocating, because they lead to something desirable. Values, when challenged, carry an emotional charge. They cause thinking, weighing of alternatives, and they stimulate behaviors that are expected to lead to fulfillment of particular motives or desires. To appreciate and use the many positive contributions that a diverse workforce can bring to an organization, one has to become aware that different people advocate for different values.

Values clarification is one way of becoming sensitive to diversity of values (see Chapter 2 for other methods). In general, the clarification process involves recognizing that everyone has different values and even when values are the same, different people may impart differing degrees of importance to the same values (2). By recognizing one's own values and the ordered importance of each and discussing prized values with others, one can gain an appreciation that the values others will defend, even though they may be different, are just as important to them as ours are to ourselves.

The difficulty with this approach to understanding value diversity is that it makes values relative. In a relativistic sense, no value is more important than another. Everyone's values are equal. If I value winning and I cheat, no one has the right to criticize because I prize winning.

The buck has to stop somewhere. All values do not lead to equally worthy ends. This is where making a distinction between moral and nonmoral values becomes useful. Moral values are those which deal with justice, rights, claims and, in general, advocate for the golden rule. What places a value in this category is a person's intentions. For example, consider autonomy, dignity, and other human respect related values. One who is moral honors these values as beneficial to others with whom they interact. One who prizes these values because they perhaps result in wealth due to the contributions of others is doing so from a different perspective. So, while the discussion of values is often entered into when talking about racial, gender, ethnic and other types of diversity, values are not the issue; motivation is. As discussed in Chapter 2, the key question is, what does honoring value x provide a person? A moral manager fosters an environment that is just, caring, and benevolent. In return, a moral employee does what is just for all concerned, is caring to all with whom they interact, and is benevolent when others are not able to make their own decisions.

Recognizing the tremendous variation in values that are held by various cultures throughout the world, a key question that must be asked about these differences in values is, "When is different just different, and when is different wrong?" (3).

In addressing this question, the concept of cultural relativism must be considered. This concept holds that no culture's ethics are better than any other's. Therefore, there are no international rights and wrongs. Cultural relativism suggests that "when in Rome, do as the Romans."

An additional concept to consider is ethical imperialism. In direct contrast to cultural relativism, this concept suggests that the appropriate action is the same regardless of the culture in which the action is performed. Although this concept can be very attractive, it does not take into account many of the differences in what is considered acceptable or unacceptable behavior in various cultures throughout the world.

Ethical imperialism is based on absolutism, which holds that there is a single list of truths that can be expressed with one set of concepts and that this requires exactly the same behaviors throughout the world. In this model, there is a lack of respect for different cultures and cultural traditions. An additional concern with absolutism is that there is no global standard of ethical behavior (3).

DIVERSITY

A cultural diversity program, sometimes known as a multiculturalism initiative, is a process designed to promote awareness, understanding, and appreciation of one another among people of various cultures. Ethnicity, race, gender, class, religion, sexual orientation, physical ability, and age make people unique individuals with different contributions to make to an organization. A goal of diversity programs within organizations should be to promote increasing awareness of different cultures that are part of the organization as a whole in building an environment in which everyone within the organization, regardless of race, religion, gender, sexual orientation, economic background, or physical ability has the opportunity to develop and realize his or her potential to contribute to the organization.

Much has been written related to cultural diversity over the past few years. There are several reasons for this phenomenon. In the 1990s, approximately 45% of all net additions to the labor force will be nonwhite individuals and almost two-thirds will be female (4). It is estimated that by the year 2000, a majority of public school-age children in the United States will be nonwhite (4). In addition to these demographic trends, organizations are beginning to emphasize the importance of cross-cultural teams as a basis for competitive advantage. An additional factor that demonstrates the relevance of diversity is the increasing emphasis within organizations on global marketing and multinational business operations. The recent passage of the Americans With Disabilities Act has also driven the movement toward diversity within organizations for persons with differing abilities.

Although all of the above factors related to the various types of diversity are very important, for the purposes of this chapter, the critical concept will be the acceptance of those whom we might consider "other". Whether that "other" is an individual from another culture, a person whose age differs significantly from ours, someone of the opposite gender, a member of a different socioeconomic group, an individual from a different race, or someone whose sexual orientation differs from ours, is irrelevant. What is important is that the differences that people bring to our relationship with them do not detract from the worth of that relationship, but rather the differences enhance the worth of that relationship. This is also true of that individual's relationship with an organization as a whole.

The goal of a diversity management program should be to maximize the benefits that people with differing backgrounds, or who identify with different sociocultural groups, bring to the organization. Diversity management should include overt actions to develop a climate within the organization that recognizes value differences rather than represses them. An alternate way of viewing this goal is to look at diversity management as systems and practices to manage people so that the potential advantages of diversity are maximized within the organization while the potential disadvantages are minimized (4).

As was mentioned in the discussion of values and diversity, many managers believe that there is a moral imperative to successfully managing diversity. For example, in the United States the dominant sociocultural group has, historically, been white males. This represents a certain prejudice against people of color and females. In a 1990 study by the American College of Health

Care Executives and the University of Iowa, men and women who entered the same field at the same time and who achieved similar education levels were compared. It was identified that women did not achieve parity with men in salary, position level, or job satisfaction (5). In a 1996 followup to the 1990 study (5), the following findings were reported:

- The salary gap continued. Women continued to earn less.
- Men advanced further within organizations.
- While a gender gap continues to exist in health care management, it may be narrowing in some areas.
- Men and women are perceived to have different management skills.
- Men and women experience similar job satisfaction rates.
- Women have more home and family obligations.
- Healthcare has many of the same gender gap problems that are found in other service fields.

Several authors have claimed that a more diverse workforce will increase organizational effectiveness. Diversity in the workforce, according to these authors, will improve morale, bring greater access to new segments of the marketplace, and enhance worker productivity (4,6). These authors feel that diversity is basically good for business. However, at times, attempts to increase diversity in the workplace have backfired, bringing increased tension between employees and interference with organizational success (6). Many managers assume that diversity will naturally lead to increased representation of groups that are traditionally under-represented within the workplace. However, if the only benefit of diversity programs was to increase representation in the workforce of traditional minority groups, the connection to increased organizational performance would not be clearly established.

How and Why Do Organizations Choose Diversity as a Goal?

One of three choices is typically made by organizations as they move toward the management of diversity.

Quality and Fairness Paradigm

The first option is to seek quality and fairness in the workforce. In this option, members of minority groups are encouraged and expected to blend in with the majority group. In these situations, there is the assumption that the primary value that these minority groups bring to the workplace is an understanding and knowledge of their own people. Obviously, this assumption is limited and can be, in the long run, inconsistent with true diversity management. This perspective is often referred to as the discrimination and fairness paradigm. In this paradigm, leaders within the organization attempt to right previous wrongs that have been propagated upon the minority groups. A major focus of the organization's diversity efforts will be compliance with equal employment opportunity requirements.

In 1964, Title VII of the Civil Rights Act established the Equal Employment Opportunity Commission (EEOC) to define and enforce acceptable employment policies and practices as they affect minorities and women. This was an important step forward for people of color and women. It allowed people who felt they were discriminated against to bring complaints to their employers based on EEOC guidelines.

Additional efforts, in the quality and fairness paradigm, are often focused toward instituting mentoring and career development programs for specific members of previously under-represented groups. In this paradigm, according to some authors (6), the staff becomes more diversified but the work itself does not. This is because the discrimination and fairness paradigm insists that everyone is the same. With its emphasis on equal treatment, it puts pressure on employees to make sure that significant differences between them do not count. Such "workplace paradigms" channel organizational thinking in powerful ways. By limiting the ability of employees to acknowledge openly their work-related but culturally based differences, the paradigm actually undermines the organization's capacity to learn about "and improve its own strategies, processes, and practices" (6).

Access and Legitimacy Paradigm

The second, and more effective, option is to recognize that diversity is more than increasing representation of a minority group. The real value, in this option, is to understand that the value of diversity comes from the varying perspectives and approaches to work that members of different minority groups bring to the workplace (6). This perspective is referred to as the access and legitimacy paradigm.

A major focus of the access and legitimacy paradigm is the recognition of an increasingly multicultural world. Companies utilizing this paradigm identify a NEED for a diverse workforce demographic. A diverse workforce will understand and serve culturally diverse markets better. In this model, diversity is not a question of fairness, it is a requirement for improved business performance, relationships and practices.

Learning and Effectiveness Paradigm

The third option incorporates aspects of the first two, but goes beyond them by analyzing the benefits of diversity from the perspective of diverse approaches to work itself. This perspective is often referred to as the learning and effectiveness paradigm (6).

A major advantage of the learning and effectiveness paradigm is the recognition that members throughout the workforce frequently make decisions and choices based on their cultural background. Companies that use this paradigm develop systems that enable the organization to incorporate employee perspectives into the primary work of the organization. This means that these companies adopt a diverse perspective of their primary tasks, market definition, strategies, products, mission, long-term vision, business practices, and organizational culture. We believe that this third paradigm, the learning and effectiveness paradigm, is most appropriate for long-term success of health care organizations.

There are eight conditions that are necessary for making the shift to a learning and effectiveness paradigm for any organization (6). Table 5.1 lists these conditions.

In the area of health care and, specifically, physical therapy, it is necessary to recognize the value of diversity training both from a management and patient care perspective. Examples of cultural sensitivity in patient care include the ability to detect changes in the integument of patients who are persons of color and the many cultural mores that exist throughout the world con-

TABLE 5.1
Organizational Conditions Needed For a Learning and Effectiveness Diversity Paradigm

1. The organization must understand that a diverse workforce will result in multiple perspectives and approaches to work. The organization must value this variety of opinion and insight.
2. The organization must recognize that different perspectives will present organizational learning opportunities and challenges.
3. High standards of performance must be expected from everyone within the organization.
4. Personal development must be stimulated by the organizational culture.
5. The organization must value openness, debate, and constructive conflict.
6. All workers must feel valued.
7. There must be a well defined and well understood organizational mission statement.
8. The organization must support decentralized decision-making in a nonbureaucratic structure.

Adopted from Thomas RR. Beyond the race and gender: Unleashing the power of your total work force by managing diversity. American Management Association 1991:16–33.

cerning touching and other intimate contact between clinicians and patients (7).

There are several key components to a diversity program. Among these components, typically, are the following five elements (8).

1. Fostering awareness and acceptance of individual differences.
2. Fostering greater understanding of the nature and dynamics of individual differences.
3. Helping members of the workforce understand their own feelings and attitudes about people who are different.
4. Exploring how differences among members of the workforce might be developed into opportunities and assets for the organization.
5. Enhancing relations between members all through the workforce who are different from each other.

For the organization that effectively manages diversity, there are many benefits (9). These benefits occur at the personal, interpersonal, and organizational levels. They include the following:

1. Attracting and retaining the best available human resource talent.
2. Increasing overall flexibility of the organization.
3. Gaining and keeping a greater market share by including a larger potential market of customers.
4. Reducing costs.
5. Improving the quality of management.
6. Creating and innovating more powerfully.
7. Solving problems more effectively.
8. Increasing productivity.
9. Contributing to social responsibility.

Elements of Culture

Many authors have documented the myriad differences among the cultures of the world. The purpose here is not to reiterate all those differences. However, it will be helpful to understand how cultures differ. One author (9) suggests that there are nine major areas that need to be examined to understand any one cultural group (Table 5.2). These areas of cultural distinctiveness should be considered when attempting to understand the values, mores, and behaviors of any given cultural group.

Each of the nine defining areas listed in Table 5.2 should be used to better understand cultural distinctiveness and how these differences can best benefit the organization. Using these areas of cultural distinctiveness to stereotype or to encourage individual members of any group to be considered as merely a member of the collective should be discouraged.

One of the concerns that comes from recognizing that there is distinctiveness in various segments of the workforce is that these differences may not be valued. They may become a source of conflict. In the next section, the role of the manager in conflict resolution and change management is addressed.

Conflict

In any situation in which there are differences of opinion, and especially in situations in which people are passionate about their feeling and be-

TABLE 5.2
Areas of Cultural Distinctiveness

1. Locus of control
2. Individualism versus collectivism
3. Achievement versus affiliation
4. Equality versus hierarchy
5. Risk-taking versus security seeking
6. Single task time use versus multiple task time use
7. Personal distance and space
8. Direct versus indirect communication
9. Industrial versus agricultural versus post industrial economic system

Adopted from Carr-Ruffino N. Managing Diversity: People Skills for a Multicultural Workplace. San Francisco, CA: Thompson Executive Press, 1996:41.

liefs, there is likely to be conflict. The workplace is often a site of conflict.

Conflicts arise for many reasons. Differences between members of the workforce can be caused by many different factors, among which are cultural differences. To learn to manage conflict, it is necessary to define it. Conflict can be described as a battle, the opposition of mutually exclusive impulses, desires or tendencies, a controversy or a disagreement. Not all conflict is a negative experience. Conflict is an outgrowth of the diversity that characterizes our thoughts, attitudes, believes, perceptions and social systems and structures. A key factor in managing conflict is to realize that every individual has influence and power in determining whether the conflict becomes negative. When conflict does not become negative, it presents an opportunity for growth and development. Attitudes and beliefs about conflict have a significant impact on one's ability to develop conflict management and conflict resolution skills. Attitude shifts, helpful to the resolution of conflicts, shift from viewing conflict negatively to viewing it positively. Several example shifts of this type are listed below (10).

1. A disruption of order to an outgrowth of diversity that holds possibilities for growth and for improving relationships.
2. A battle between incompatible self-interest to one of a relationship.
3. An isolated event that may define a relationship to a single occurrence within a long-term relationship that can help to clarify that long-term relationship.

4. A struggle between right and wrong to a confrontation between differences in specific aspects of a total relationship.

Conflict resolution involves entering into a relationship in which highly developed negotiation skills are needed. This relationship could involve spouses, a parent and a child, a student and a teacher, a therapist and a therapist assistant, a clinician and an external case manager, or a manager and an employee. Negotiation relationships involve at least two negotiation associates, not opponents. Each negotiation associate has very specific responsibilities (11). These include:

- The responsibility to develop ideas to resolve the issues over which the conflict arose.
- The responsibility to develop a better relationship.
- The responsibility to be a good partner.

There is also the responsibility to develop better negotiation skills, which can be improved with practice. The basic building blocks for developing negotiations skills are those that develop effective listening, relationship-building, innovative joint problem-solving skills (11). Problem-solving skills are no different in negotiation situations than are they in clinical problem-solving situations. The basis for problem solving in both clinical and negotiation situations has been defined by the American Physical Therapy Association (APTA) (12,13). The APTA model of problem solving presented in Figure 5.1 should be used whenever possible in negotiation and other conflict resolution situations.

Role and Importance of Language

Conflict resolution and other negotiation sessions are based in part upon the use of language. This language is, at best, an imprecise method for communication. Language usage can vary in different cultural groups. To be effective in conflict resolution situations, each of the parties involved should be as skilled as possible in understanding not only the words communicated, but also the message intended. This will typically involve both verbal and nonverbal communication. Especially in the area of nonverbal communication, cultural differences can arise and lead to increased levels of conflict or misunderstanding.

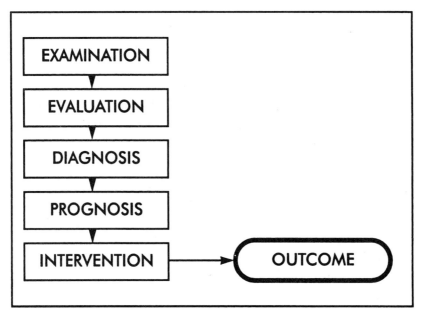

FIGURE 5.1. Elements of problem solving. From American Physical Therapy Association. Chapter one: Management of physical therapy patients. Physical Therapy 1995;75:711–719. Reproduced by permission.

Sources of Conflict

One of the keys to effective conflict resolution is to understand the sources of conflict. Foremost among the sources are varying personal and professional needs, varying perceptions, self-interest, power, differences in values, principles, feelings and emotions, and internal conflicts (10). There are several known ineffective methods of conflict resolution. Five ineffective methods of conflict resolution are discussed below.

1. The first ineffective conflict resolution method is the conquest approach, in which the conflict becomes a battle to win, a struggle to gain an advantage in the relationship or to dominate. Unfortunately, the conquest approach creates a winner and a loser in the relationship. This prevents the relationship from being sustainable (8).
2. The next ineffective conflict resolution method is the avoidance approach. One using this approach believes conflicts will go away if everyone pretends that the conflicts do not exist. The avoidance approach merely postpones the conflict and usually allows it to become exacerbated. This approach is not an effective long-term strategy (10).
3. The third method is the bargaining approach, in which the parties view conflict resolution as a game in which there are demands, interests and

other currencies that are traded. Success is defined by how much each party concedes. This approach also creates a winner and a loser in a relationship. It is common for both parties to perceive themselves as having lost something in the conflict. This prevents the relationship from being sustainable (10).
4. The fourth ineffective conflict resolution method is the band aid approach. In this approach, the parties are so uncomfortable with conflict that they accept whatever quick-fix solution they can find. This approach is rarely effective, as it creates the illusion that the problems that brought about the conflict have been addressed, but they have not. This approach produces a lack of confidence in conflict resolution for both parties. Although there may be short-term rewards in this approach, the long-term usefulness of the strategy is limited (10).
5. The last ineffective conflict resolution method is the role player approach. In this method, the parties assume predefined roles such as boss and employee or parent and child. Although there are situations in which decisions and discussions must be made in the context of such roles, this approach allows the parties to unnecessarily hide behind their roles. This makes it necessary to deal with stereotypes rather than relationships or issues. The role player approach can perpetuate ineffective relationships and short circuit effective conflict resolution (10).

The Conflict Partnership Process

The Conflict Partnership Process offers an effective conflict resolution method (10). Table 5.3 lists the background beliefs of this method. Table 5.4 lists the steps of the Conflict Partnership Process for effective conflict resolution. The result of successful conflict resolution is improved relationships in which differences and conflicts are dealt with in ways that nurture mutual development (10). These are team decision-making models as well.

Alternative Methods for Conflict Resolution

Although a single method for conflict resolution has been presented, there are many other

TABLE 5.3
Beliefs of the Conflict Partnership Process for Effective Conflict Resolution

1. We, not me versus you
2. Conflicts are dealt with in the context of an overall relationship
3. Effective conflict resolution should improve the overall relationship
4. Effective conflict resolution results in mutual benefit, i.e., a win-win situation
5. Relationship building and conflict resolution are connected

Adopted from Weeks D. The Eight Essential Steps to Conflict Resolution: Preserving Relationships At Work, At Home, and the Community. NY, NY: Putnam Books, 1992:63–67.

TABLE 5.4
Steps of the Conflict Partnership Process For Effective Conflict Resolution

1. Create an effective atmosphere
2. Clarify perceptions
3. Focus on individual and shared needs
4. Build shared positive power
5. Look to the future, then learn from the past
6. Generate options for resolution of the conflict
7. Develop possible actions and intermediate steps to action
8. Make mutual benefit agreements

Adopted from Weeks D. The Eight Essential Steps to Conflict Resolution: Preserving Relationships At Work, At Home, and the Community. NY, NY: Putnam Books, 1992:70.

alternatives that are available. The basis for all of these alternatives should be the desire to create win-win situations for all involved parties. Consensus or team-building activities allow the involved parties to focus on those areas in which they agree. Our experience suggests that the typical conflict situation involves parties who have more commonalities than differences. By focusing on the common areas that the parties share, it is often possible to develop improved relationships and hopefully improved relations.

Majority rule is an alternative method to consensus building that recognizes that the parties will continue to have differences but allows the majority of the group to make decisions for the group as a whole. This is the most common mechanism for decision making in a democratic society. It is necessary for all members of the society to agree to a democratic process before implementation of a majority rule conflict resolution process. The interests and concerns of minority groups are often not adequately addressed in a majority rule decision process. Additionally, there are often concerns about majority rule processes becoming overly political and cumbersome.

Decisions can also be decided in a democratic process requiring unanimity or homogenous consent. In this situation, all of the group members must agree with the decision. By definition, there is no minority group in unanimous consent circumstances. This situation is relatively rare. Although it can be suggested that unanimity is a noble goal, it is unlikely that it would be possible to successfully make many decisions if unanimity was a requirement.

An alternative method of conflict resolution involves mediation. In mediatative situations, an outside mediator facilitates interaction between the parties who then strive toward a mutually acceptable solution. It is necessary to understand that the mediator does not represent either party. It is critical for the mediator to be perceived by all parties as supportive of resolution of the conflict but impartial to all parties. In some circumstances, binding mediation, a situation where the mediator not only facilitates the resolution of the conflict but also adjudicates the final decision regarding the resolution, is involved. In binding mediation, both parties agree to abide by the decision of the mediator who acts as judge. It is also possible for mediation to be facilitated by a panel of mediators. Mediation should be used only when the parties involved cannot resolve their conflict by themselves.

Special skills and training are necessary to function effectively as a mediator. There may be times in which a manager may be called upon to mediate conflict between employees. These situations should always be approached with great caution. It is often advisable for outside, disinterested parties to function as mediator rather than internal, potentially biased parties, such as managers.

Managing Change

Change within an organization can be a very difficult process. Change involves alteration of personal, team, and organizational values, attitudes, beliefs, and behaviors. Each change process involves individuals and groups who must not only adopt new ways of doing things, but must also relinquish old, familiar ways of acting and thinking (14). Often, change involves not only behaviors of individuals but also the total culture of the organization (15). This can be difficult, especially if the organization does not want to change its culture.

To effectively manage change, one must first understand it. Although the process of change is generally quite unpredictable, the responses of individuals to change are often quite predictable. Figure 5.2 illustrates the process individuals go through as they move toward acceptance or change. The first stage is denial, followed by resistance, a sense of a new awareness and finally commitment. Each individual and each group of individuals will move sequentially through each of these four stages. Effective change management focuses on processes to assist individuals and groups of individuals in moving through each of these stages more comfortably and more quickly.

One of the most effective strategies for managing change is to convert changes imposed upon the work team into change that is perceived as initiated by individuals within the work team or by the work team itself (14). This allows the members of the work team to avoid feeling as if they are the victims of change. It allows members of the work team to feel greater ownership and responsibility for the organizational changes.

One of the most difficult areas for managers, in helping staff adapt to change, is overcoming resistance to change. To effectively overcome resistance to change, it is necessary to understand the causes of resistance, which include personal self-interest, misunderstanding the facts of the change, differing assessment of the impact of the change, lack of trust caused by previous ineffective leadership or change programs, and overall low tolerance or poor skills for managing change in the work team (14).

SUMMARY

In this chapter we have presented a review of diversity issues relevant to the health care workplace. The main focus has been to develop an appreciation for the potential contribution that a diverse workforce can bring to an organization. It is the authors' hope that the reader will fully appreciate the positive opportunities that are available to learn from one another when there is a diverse workforce.

In addition to the opportunities that workforce diversity brings, there is the potential threat of conflict. This chapter has addressed conflict resolution, and presented a model for effective resolution of conflict in the workplace. A model for effective change management that can be implemented in many workplace settings was also presented. Role-play five, in Appendix A, pre-

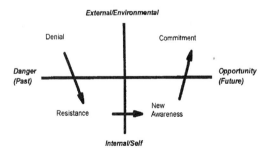

FIGURE 5.2. Acceptance of change. From Managing Change. Kovacek Management Services, Inc., 1994. Reproduced by permission.

sents a scenario involving differences. Readers are encouraged to use this role-play to strengthen their skills in dealing with workplace situations involving conflict based on differences in the style used to manage people.

REFERENCES

1. Schwartz SH. Are there universal aspects in the structure and contents of human values? Journal of Social Issues 1994;50(4):19–45.
2. Raths LE, Harmin M, Simon SB. Values and Teaching, 2nd ed. Columbus, OH: Charles E. Merrill, 1977:26–29, 33–35, 47.
3. Donaldson TS. Values in tension: Ethics away from home. Harvard Business Review 1996(Sept/Oct):48–62.
4. Cox T, Jr. Diversity in Organizations: Theory, Research & Practice. San Francisco, CA: Berrett-Koehler, 1995:3, 17, 24, 27–39.
5. Weil PW, et al. Exporting of the gender gap and health care management. Healthcare Executive 1996(Nov/December):18–21.
6. Roosevelt TR. Beyond the Race and Gender. Unleashing the power of your total work force by managing diversity. American Management Association 1991:16–33.
7. Arriaga RL. Cross cultural considerations. Rehab Management 1994;9(5):99–101.
8. Thomas DA, Ely RJ. Making differences matter: a new paradigm for managing diversity. Harvard Business Review 1996(Sept/Oct): 79–90.
9. Carr-Ruffino N. Managing diversity: People Skills for a Multicultural Workplace. San Francisco, CA: Thompson Executive Press, 1996:21.
10. Weeks D. The Eight Essential Steps to Conflict Resolution: Preserving Relationships at Work, at Home, and the Community. NY, NY: Putnam Books, 1992.
11. Grey PM, Kovacek PR. The skill of artful negotiation. PT Magazine 1997;5(2):26–30.
12. American Physical Therapy Association. Chapter One: Management of physical therapy patients. Physical Therapy 1995;75:711–719.
13. American Physical Therapy Association. Chapter 1: Who are physical therapists, and what do they do? Physical Therapy 1997;77:1177–1187.
14. Kovacek PR. Managing Employees in Changing Times. Harper Woods, MI: Kovacek Management Services, Inc., 1995.
15. Pritchett P, Pound R. High Velocity Culture Change: A Handbook for Managers. Dallas, TX: Pritchett and Associates, 1993.

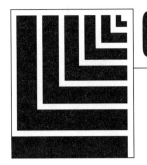 **6**

ORGANIZATIONAL STRUCTURE AND CONTROL FOR BUSINESS SUCCESS

PREVIEW

In earlier chapters, we read about the relationship of an organization's purpose, values and vision to its strategic direction. It is management's responsibility to move an organization along a strategic direction by setting and achieving goals and objectives. Management is accountable for the organization's success. Except in the smallest organizations, managers meet these responsibilities and achieve success largely through the efforts of others.

Management success is dependent on the ability to lead others toward maximum performance. Managers must put into practice the values of the organization, creating an organizational culture that will support and guide each employee in the performance of their work. The structure of the organization, and methods chosen to control and direct employee activity, reflects management assumptions about employee behavior and performance. These are two of the many situational factors that a manager must take into account when making decisions about how to structure and control the work of the organization.

Chapter 6 provides the reader with an appreciation for the impact of organizational structure and work design on the success of a business. Common structural configurations, as well as methods to control and coordinate work, will be reviewed. Internal and external factors that may influence management decisions about the organization and control of work are identified. The reader will develop a practical understanding of why and how organizational structure and work design improve or limit an employee's performance.

KEY WORDS

Board of Directors: also referred to as a Board of Trustees, is the governing body of an organization.

Dividend payments: made when a company distributes net revenue to its owners based on the number of shares of stock owned on or before a specified date.

Expenses: costs incurred by a business.

Gross revenue: the sum of all the income earned by a business.

Incorporation: the process by which a business venture receives recognition as a legal entity.

Investment: the money paid for the purchase of financial instruments such as stock for personal gain.

Net revenue: equal to gross revenue less total expense for a specific time period.

Organizational restructuring: occurs when the management of an organization changes the relationships between employees in one or more segments of the organization or the relationships between segments of the organization.

Organizational culture: the set of behavioral norms that guide the actions of an organization's employees.

Organizational structure: how the segments and employees of an organization relate to each other in the performance of their work.

Performance benchmarks: local, regional, national or international industry standards against which the performance of a similar organization can be compared. For example, a therapy practice can determine if it offers competitive outcomes if it compares its performance to the outcomes achieved by other providers for similar services.

Profit: positive net revenue. Other terms used to describe a positive net revenue include excess of revenue and positive contribution.

Venture capitalist: an investor who provides business financing in return for an ownership interest in the company. The goal of a venture capitalist is to make a profit on money invested.

Work design: the process of determining the work processes and specific job duties of the employees of an organization.

INTRODUCTION

Whenever two or more individuals work together to accomplish a single task, there is a need to coordinate their efforts. Coordination creates a common understanding of the work to be done and how individuals will work together to achieve a common goal. Coordination is needed to develop a shared understanding of the goal, define performance expectations, establish a work plan, assign responsibility and coordinate assignments between individuals. As the numbers of employees increase, the need for coordination will increase (1).

By definition, an organization is an administrative or functional structure. Organizing is the act of applying systematic planning and a unifying effort toward the arrangement of independent elements into an interdependent whole (2).

Chapter 6 focuses on the topics of organizational structure and work design. As Chapter

6 progresses, the reader will appreciate that decisions about organizational structure and work design are dynamic. The same factors that influence management to adopt any specific organizational structure will subsequently be influenced and possibly changed by the adopted structure. Organizational and work design are a management responsibility. To manage these dynamic processes, managers must be familiar with the many factors that might or should influence their decisions about organizational structure and work design. At the same time, the manager must understand how the organizational structure and work methods impact the organization's ability to perform under varying circumstances.

Knowledge of organizational structure and work design is of particular importance to health care managers. The rapid rate of change in the external environment of health care organizations can be readily observed. Management efforts to accommodate external change have left many health care organizations in a state of continuous organizational restructuring. Increased market and competitive pressures in health care have lead to increased organizational complexity. Each time the organizational structure and/or work methods change, the division and methods for the coordination of work may also change. While management and employees learn new jobs and develop new relationships, work coordination and productivity can decrease. At the same time, growing organizational complexity increases the need for effective work coordination. Under these circumstances, organizational performances become more dependent on a management ability to understand, support and assist the change process (3).

Finally, business success depends on management's ability to maintain a work force that is prepared to work effectively under a continuously changing set of performance expectations. Therefore, a review of human resource management practices and skills related to work design, setting performance standards, performance appraisal and performance management have been included in this chapter.

CHARACTERISTICS OF BUSINESS STRUCTURES

There are many ways to approach a discussion of organizational structure. Structural references commonly used to describe health care organizations include legal structure, tax status, and operating structure. These references define the organization in different ways. Legal structure defines some elements of ownership, the relationship of owners, type of business, and/or the purpose of the organization. Tax status helps define the organization's purpose and relationship with its owners as well as other individuals and organizations. The operating structure provides insight into the organization's response to all of the internal and external factors that influence its success.

Legal Structure

There are various legal structures under which an organization can be formed. The best legal structure for a business is determined by its business objectives. Incorporation is the process by which a business venture receives recognition as a separate legal entity. Legal recognition is desirable should the business owners wish to separate the organization's legal and financial affairs from their personal, legal and financial affairs.

This section will provide an overview of sole proprietorship, partnership, the limited liability corporation, and the corporation. These structures are common to health care businesses. Our intent here is to provide a general understanding about the variety of options available. This information should not be applied to any specific situation.

Business incorporation is governed by state law. As a result, the rules and regulations governing business incorporation can vary between states. Anyone desiring more information about business incorporation in a particular state should seek advice from an attorney or other knowledgeable source.

Sole Proprietorship

A business, run by an individual or family, which does not adopt a formal business structure, is, by default, a sole proprietorship. This designation would apply to any unincorporated business, including professional private practices of lawyers, accountants and therapists. Under a sole proprietorship, the business and the person are legally one and the same. The owner may be required to register the sole proprietorship with a government office. A sole proprietorship, easy and inexpensive to form because you can do it yourself, provides the owner full control and all the profit. For tax purposes, business profit is treated as the owner's personal income.

Disadvantages of a sole proprietorship include unlimited liability. The owner is directly liable for all the debts and expenses of the business, meaning the owner's personal assets, such as their savings and house, are at risk. The only available protection is through insurance. At this time, a sole proprietorship can not provide tax-free benefits such as health or life insurance to the owner. A sole proprietorship may also have more difficulty raising capital than other types of business organizations (4).

Partnership

A partnership is a simple way to structure a business with one or more other persons. There are no legal requirements to forming a partnership. When two or more persons come together for the purpose of doing business, they are considered partners from both a legal and tax perspective. Local government may require a partnership to be registered. Like the sole proprietorship, a partnership is easy and inexpensive to form because you can do it yourself. The partners have shared control. Profit is divided between the partners. For tax purposes, business profit is treated as personal income. Partners pay taxes on the profit at their own tax rates, even if they differ. Disadvantages of a partnership include unlimited liability. The partners are directly liable for all the debts and expenses of the business. Again, each partner's personal assets are at risk. Partners are jointly and severally liable. That means that all partners are liable for the full extent of any liability, even if it resulted from the actions of their partner(s). Shared liability would apply to all aspects of business operations. In the case of a physical therapy practice, any potential liability, such as a malpractice claim, would be the responsibility of each and every partner regardless of the partner or employee at fault. The only available protection is through insurance. As was the case with a sole proprietorship, a partnership may have some difficulty raising capital. At this time, a partnership cannot provide tax-free benefits such as health or life insurance to the partners.

There is one type of partnership that offers the protection of limited liability for some owners. Called a limited partnership (4), it allows some partners to limit their liability to the amount of their investment in the partnership. Partners with limited liability are called limited partners. At least one partner, called a general partner, must be at full risk with unlimited personal liability. The limited partners are 'silent' and may not be involved in the day-to-day operation of the partnership. The general partner(s) has complete control.

Even though there are no legal requirements, it is advisable to have a partnership agreement. This agreement can delineate the purpose, structure and membership of the partnership. It can address partnership funding, management structure, profit and loss distribution, partnership termination, and other operating arrangements. It should delineate what each partner will do and how they will be compensated. Partners can have differences. To protect the business and the partners, a partnership agreement should be executed by a lawyer (4).

The Corporation

When it is desirable to legally separate a business from its owners, the business can be incorporated. There are three types of corporations to consider: C corporation, S corporation and the limited liability corporation.

C CORPORATION

A C corporation is a legal entity, distinct from its owners, and must be formed under state law. This option is more expensive, in part, due to incorporation fees. An attorney is not required, but is usually advisable. The advantages of a corporation include limited personal liability. The corporate structure offers ease of ownership transfer and will continue to exist without the initial owners. Corporations have the easiest time raising capital. As a legal entity, corporations are subject to income tax on profits. If the after-tax profits are distributed to the owners, the distributed funds are subject to a second tax paid at the owner's income tax rate. This double tax can be costly. Other disadvantages of a C Corporation include more regulation and more legal restrictions (4).

S CORPORATION

The S Corporation offers both limited personal liability and pass through tax treatment for federal income tax purposes. The S Corporation is the only alternative for a one-person company looking for limited liability without the liability of corporate taxes. Other advantages include continuity of existence without the original owner and ease in raising capital. Disadvantages are similar to the C Corporation, including high regulation and legal restrictions. The S Corporation also has ownership restrictions. Shareholders are limited to 35 individuals who are U.S. citizens or resident aliens (4).

LIMITED LIABILITY CORPORATION (LLC)

The newest type of corporation, the LLC is only an option in some states. The LLC is owned by its members. It combines some advantages of a partnership and a corporation. The LLC is more like a partnership in that it allows the benefit of pass through income. Profit is divided among the partners and treated as personal income for tax purposes. There is no corporate or double tax. One disadvantage is the newness of this option and lack of legal testing. It is more costly to set up than a partnership.

Tax Status

A business can be either for-profit or not-for-profit. Tax status is determined by two factors: the purpose of a business and how the business uses its profits. The need to make a profit is fundamental to all businesses. Money is required for a business to sustain itself and achieve its purpose. To grow and prosper, a business must earn more than it spends. It must make a profit. When money is earned through the sale of services and products, interest on investments, or contributions from external sources, it is called gross revenue. When money is spent it is an expense. Gross revenue minus expenses is called net revenue. When net revenue is positive, the business has made a profit. Profit increases the value of the business. A negative net revenue or loss would decrease the value of the business.

The nature of the business and how profit is used will determine tax status. Does money provide the means to achieve a purpose? Is making money the purpose itself? For example, Clinic A makes money by providing services to patients with the financial means to pay for care. The money is used to pay the expense of providing care to those who cannot pay and to provide an up-to-date outpatient facility for all residents of the community. Clinic B makes money by providing services to patients with the financial means to pay for care. The money is used to provide an income for the owner-operator. Both of these businesses provide high quality care, what differs is the purpose of the business and the use of profits. In this example, the Clinic A will likely qualify for tax exempt status. while the Clinic B would not.

The For-Profit Business

The for-profit business provides goods and services for the purpose of making money for its owners. Both private and publicly traded businesses can be for-profit. For-profit businesses pay taxes on profits. Profits remaining after taxes can be used to improve the financial position of individual owners. The for-profit business may choose to distribute the remaining profit directly to its owners through a dividend payment. Alternately, it can retain the money to increase the value of the owner's holdings. Under some legal structures, an owner may claim profit as personal earned income. This is done so the profit can be taxed at the owner's personal income level. Otherwise, the profit would be taxed first at the corporate level and then again as earned income. Many health care businesses are for-profit. Therapy and other private practices are often for-profit. There are national, publicly traded, for-profit health care corporations that operate hospitals, longterm care facilities, home health agencies, and therapy contract services.

The Not-For-Profit Business

A not-for-profit business is designated as tax exempt. It is exempt from all forms of federal, state and local taxes, including income tax, property tax and sales tax. A business must apply to the Internal Revenue Service for a tax exemption. Exemptions are granted to businesses whose primary purpose is some form of community service.

Not-for-profit businesses may not provide financial benefit to any private individual or for-profit business. The payment of reasonable compensation to an owner-employee, other employees or corporate owners does not fall under this restriction. Not-for-profit businesses are required to retain and reinvest excess revenue into the business to support its mission. The following are examples of businesses that are frequently designated as tax exempt:

- Health care organizations
- Religious communities
- Churches
- Professional associations
- Government operated businesses
- Charitable organizations
- Community service organizations

Over the past few years, increasing attention has been paid to the public cost of tax exempt organizations. The public cost is a combination of lost tax revenues and the expense of government services, such as fire and police protection, used by tax exempt organizations at public expense. Many not-for-profit businesses, including health care providers, are being challenged to demonstrate that the community benefit equals or exceeds public cost. As communities face an increasing financial burden for the provision of health and social services to the poor, the demand for accountability is likely to increase. Health care organizations risk loss of their tax exempt status if they fail to provide a reasonable level of community service or financial relations with for-profit businesses.

Operating Structure

Mintzberg (5) describes the organization of human activity as the act of balancing two opposing requirements, the first, the division of work between employees; and, the second, the coordination of the work of two or more employees to achieve a common goal. An organization's operating structure provides the framework for both work division and work coordination. There are numerous ways to divide the work of the organization. Three methods are available to coordinate work between individuals (5). They are:

1. Work Standardization
2. Supervision
3. Mutual Accommodation

All three methods of work coordination are used by health care organizations to coordinate the efforts of employees. Management's decisions about operating structure are influenced by factors both internal and external to the organization. Table 6.1 provides listing of both internal and external factors. There is dispute over the relative importance and the interrelationship of any of these factors in determining a specific organization's structure.(3,5–8). Knowledge of work coordination methods and an understanding of the potential impact of these factors will help managers determine the operating structure that best fits their situation.

Work Coordination

There are three basic methods that businesses can use to coordinate the work of employees. They are work standardization, supervision, and mutual accommodation.

 TABLE 6.1
Factors Influencing Operating Structure

INTERNAL	EXTERNAL
Ownership	Industry trends
Mission	Performance benchmarks
Purpose	Environmental stability
Values and philosophy	Environmental complexity
Production technology	Market stability
Strategic direction	Market competition
Competitive strategies	Environmental predictability
Age	Legal climate
Size	Legislative climate
History	

STANDARDIZATION

Work standardization can be approached from three points (5).

1. Work processes and tasks
2. Work output
3. Worker skills

Standardization reduces the need for direct supervision and mutual accommodation because it reduces the variation between the performance of employees. Performance consistency also reduces the need for direct or frequent communication between workers. Work processes and tasks can be standardized through the use of such things as policies, procedures, work (treatment) protocols, or standardized work (treatment) plans. For example, a physical therapist's work may be standardized through the use of written guidelines for the delivery of a treatment procedure such as ultrasound. The use of a standardized treatment program guiding the course of care for a patient following joint replacement is another example.

The use of output (outcome) standardization is on the rise in health care. If the treatment protocol for care of the patient with a joint replacement used mobility status and range of motion to guide care and determine discharge, then it would be an example of outcome standardization. Outcome standardization will be discussed in detail in Chapters 10 and 11.

Skill standardization through education, training and licensure are fundamental elements for work coordination for health care organizations. Standardization reduces the need for supervision or mutual accommodation (5). The requirement that employees meet job qualifications such as physical therapy licensure, experience and/or postgraduate education are all examples of skill standardization methods. Application of on-the-job competency testing is another example of skill standardization.

SUPERVISION

Supervision refers to the control and direction of the work of one or more employees by another employee. Supervision can be used to coordinate the work of the organization. When this occurs, the supervisor must have direct knowledge of the work of a group of employees. The supervisor would then direct the employees to perform their work in a manner and time frame which complements the work of others in the work group. The supervisor is responsible for the coordination of the work of the group.

MUTUAL ACCOMMODATION

Mutual accommodation is the simplest method of work coordination. Mutual accommodation results from the ongoing interaction between individuals. This interaction results in continuous adjustment between individuals toward the achievement of their shared goals. This method of work coordination is common in simple organizations. It may also be the most effective method of work coordination for the most complex situations. Management should consider the alternative methods of work coordination whenever organizational structure might be changed or performance fails to meet expectations. Organizational structure must be supported by the way work is divided and the method for coordination of those divided efforts. Table 6.2 provides an overview of the work coordination methods used in therapy practice. If it does not implement work coordination, the business will not perform to its maximum capabilities. Strategic goals may not be met.

Internal Factors Influencing Operating Structure

OWNERSHIP, PURPOSE, VALUES AND VISION

The three basic types of ownership are private, public and governmental. All three types of ownership arrangements are used in the health care industry.

Private Ownership

Private ownership implies that the business is owned solely by an individual, a group of individuals or another privately owned business. The owners have the right to establish the purpose of the organization. The owner's purpose could be anything from provision of a financial return, personal employment, meeting a community need to supporting a special philanthropic interest. An owner may be involved directly in the

TABLE 6.2
Production Technology And Work Coordination In Therapy Practice

PRODUCTION TECHNOLOGY	WORK STANDARDS	SUPERVISION	MUTUAL ADJUSTMENT
Unit Production			
Professional Education	X		
Advanced Certification	X		
Assessment Practices	X		
Treatment Algorithms	X		
Clinical Resource Staff		X	X
Advanced Training	X		
Patient Care Conferences		X	X
Treatment Teams			X
Flexible Schedules			X
Mass Production			
Licensure Requirements	X	X	
Policies and Procedures	X		
Treatment Protocols	X		
Standardized Care Plans	X		
Job Descriptions	X		
Performance Standards	X	X	
Staff Schedules	X	X	
Practice Guidelines	X		

management of the business or rely totally on employed managers. Health care practitioners, such as therapists, own health care businesses. Privately owned businesses often have more autonomy in making business decisions. Owners are more likely to share a common vision of the organization's purpose. Private religious organizations often own health care businesses. Chapter 14 will provide additional information about the management of a private practice business.

Unless you are one of the founding members, an ownership interest in a private organization can only be obtained by sale or transfer of an ownership interest by the existing owner(s). Often, the conditions for sale or transfer are restricted by the business' articles of incorporation. Articles of incorporation are the set of legal documents that define the structure of a business (4).

Public Ownership

Public ownership implies that the stock representing an ownership interest is traded to members of the public through a stock exchange. A publicly traded business is owned by a group of diverse individuals who have elected to invest in the business through the purchase of stock.

They are the stockholders. Management of publicly owned businesses are accountable to the stockholders to provide a return on their investment. A return on investment can be provided through an increase in the value of the investment or through provision of investment income such as a dividend. In addition to the laws that govern all health care providers, publicly traded businesses are governed by the rules and regulations established by the National Securities Exchange Commission.

Government Ownership

Businesses can also be owned by local, state or federal governments. Under government ownership, a health care organization is owned directly by the government body and indirectly by the citizens who reside within that government's jurisdiction. The governing body of the jurisdiction, either directly, through government employees or contract arrangements, are responsible for operating the business in a way that meets the needs of the community. For example, a county government may own a hospital, a home care agency and long-term care facility or other health care business.

Government-owned health care businesses are often required to follow a special set of rules and regulations governing the operations of all government businesses within a local or state jurisdiction. This may affect how the business manages its human resources, purchases resources or invests in facilities and capital equipment. Government ownership may provide advantages and/or disadvantages to the health care business. There is a current trend toward privatization of government-owned health care businesses such as hospitals. The benefits of privatization, either to the organization or the community, require a case specific assessment.

Ownership Sets the Foundation

In our society, individuals are held accountable for their actions. As long as an individual complies with society's laws, they are free to make decisions about how to conduct their personal affairs. It is a personal choice to adhere to any other external set of standards. In the same way, a health care business is held accountable to act in accordance with the laws governing its actions. As long as a business functions within the requirements of the law, it is accountable only to its owners. Therefore, the purpose of any health care business is established by its owners.

Management's overall accountability is to meet the needs of the owners. As a result, organizational structure and work design find their foundation in the purpose, values, vision, as well as the defined needs of its owners. The impact of these characteristics are illustrated by comparing two therapy organizations. The first company is a large, multi-site, multi-disciplinary therapy corporation. Its clinics are all located in high density urban or suburban settings and are owned by six business partners. Partners A, B and C are therapists. Partner D is an attorney. Partner E is a business leader. Partner F is a private venture capitalist. Partner F owns 45% of shares of the business. The remaining 55% ownership shares are split evenly among the other five partners. The owners make decisions by voting their share of the business. One share equals one vote. A majority vote wins. When the owners have differing opinions on what should be done, Partner F will determine the outcome with 45% of the voting shares unless all of the other partners vote together against him. Partner F's purpose is to maximize his return on investment by increasing the value of the business.

The second business is owned by a single, private practitioner, located in a small, rural community. A sole proprietorship, owned and operated by one therapist, it provides therapy services under contract to the local hospital and nursing home. The owner has total control over the purpose and strategic directions of the business. The owner's purpose is to treat patients and earn an income. Both of these businesses are privately owned and provide therapy services. But it is unlikely that each would define the purpose, vision and strategic directions of their businesses in the same way.

PRODUCTION TECHNOLOGY

Businesses can be differentiated by the type of work and the technology they use to produce their product. There are three types of production technology systems that can define a business: unit, mass, and process production systems (9).

Unit Production

Unit production describes a production system that is based on customer-specific requirements. This would include the production of prototypes or a customer-specific product. Health care is provided on a patient-specific basis. Guided by the outcomes of the patient assessment process, each patient is provided with services to meet their specific care needs. The work order for each patient is a physician order or a patient plan of care. As such, direct health care service provision is a unit production business.

Mass Production

Mass production describes a business that produces a large volume of similar product. Producers of health care products such as walkers or wheelchairs are a good example of a mass production health care business. The description of mass production can also apply to some health services functions. Laboratory tests, radiology exams, even certain elements of therapy service, are mass produced. The distribution of these mass-produced products and services is a function of the unit production process.

Process Production

Process production describes the production technology of large quantities of liquid, gas or other continuous flow products such as electricity. Process production is common to utility companies, telephone and communications companies. Process production technology is not typical to health care delivery.

PRODUCTION TECHNOLOGY AND WORK COORDINATION

Production technology will influence the type and division of the work to be performed. How work is divided will determine the need for work coordination. We see the delivery of health care as a hybrid, a blending of unit and mass technology. At the customer level, there is a plan of care that has been designed to meet patient specific requirements. To produce the care required, many highly standardized components of care are combined with a smaller number of more customized components. Table 6.2 provides examples of standardization and customized work coordination methods associated with unit and mass production that are common to therapy practice.

CULTURE

Culture is the term used to describe the patterns of social interaction that define the norm within the organization (10). An organization's culture reflects the values, direction and purpose of the owners and top executives. Employees are socialized to the organization's culture through formal orientation and ongoing interactions with other employees. Culture is learned and then shared with others. Goffe and Garth (10) describe two types of human relations: sociability and solidarity. Sociability is a measure of the true friendliness between employees. Solidarity is a measure of the organization's ability to pursue shared objectives quickly and effectively. Goffe and Garth indicate that an organizational culture with high sociability and high solidarity, a communal organization, is a "appropriate culture for organizations that interface with their environment through multiple connections involving customers, the government, competition and research institutes" (11). This description closely fits that of many health care organizations.

SIZE AND AGE

Mintzberg (5) summarized several hypotheses regarding the relationship between the size and age of an organization. His observations indicated that as organizations age, size also increases. Increased size often leads to greater division of labor, a larger, more complex management structure, differentiation of organizational subunits, and a more dominant organizational culture.

By personal observation, we question whether there has been a reversal in the practice of continuously increasing the size of the management structure as the organization grows. In health care, management downsizing and a movement toward flatter management structures have become a common method of cost reduction (10,11). The movement toward less supervision has resulted in a greater reliance on standardization and mutual accommodation for work coordination. Standardization has been increased through such things as standardized care plans. The use of mutual accommodation is supported by the use of human resource focused management methods, work teams and continuous quality improvement methods.

External Factors Influencing Operating Structure

External factors, by definition, are things that originate or act from outside the organization (2). There are numerous external factors that impact health care organizations.

*   Customers
*   Competitors
*   Political climate
*   Governmental regulation
*   Economic climate
*   Technological innovation
*   Demographic shifts

The extent of the impact can be understood by assessing the condition of the health care environment for stability, complexity, market diversity and hostility (3).

STABILITY

The stability of the environment is related to the rate and predictability of environmental change. The greater the rate of change and the less predictable, the more unstable. In an unstable environment, businesses have difficulty adopting a strategic direction. Resources and human energy are deviated from productive work into managing change. In an unstable environment, an organization should be structured to respond quickly to varied and unpredictable change. These are often flatter organizations which rely on supervision and mutual accommodation to coordinate the work of employees. Health care organizations exist in an unstable environment (1,3).

COMPLEXITY

A simple environment is one in which external factors such as customers, products, regulations, and competitors, are easily understood. In a complex organization, great technical expertise and in-depth knowledge of all environmental factors are required for success. Generally, this requires the subdivision of complex activities so that they might be more easily understood. Given the diversity of customers and products, the highly technical nature of health care, the required levels and varied types of expertise, the current health care environment must be described as highly complex (1,3).

MARKET DIVERSITY

Markets can be integrated or diverse. An integrated market is one with few products and/or few customers. The greater the number of products and/or customers, the more diverse the organization's market. The more diverse the market, the greater the diversity of the organization's activities. The more diverse the organization's activities, the more effort an organization must invest in work coordination. Market diversity varies between health care organizations. The discussion of health care marketing in Chapter 3 provides in-depth information about the complexity of the health care market place.

HOSTILITY

A hostile environment can arise when an organization faces unpredictable demands from its environment. Such demands might come from its labor force, the government, the community or other external source. There is no doubt the health care environment has and continues to face rapidly changing environmental demands of great proportion (8).

COMMON ORGANIZATIONAL STRUCTURES

There are three basic parts to every organization.

1. Management
2. Operating core
3. Support services

Depending on the size of the organization, owners and employees may function within one or more of the organization's parts. The operating core is the part of the organization that actually does the work (5). As the size of the organization increases, the division of labor will increase. Supervision is the first division of labor in developing organizations. With the addition of supervision, those who do the work are separated from those who supervise the work. Supervision brings the first division of the organization into distinct parts.(5)

As an organization continues to grow, the reliance on support services will increase. Support services can be separated into two groups, the first of which provides technical support. These are technical experts who direct their efforts toward the development of work standards and responding to environmental complexity. A clinical lead or senior therapist might fill this role in a physical therapy practice. The purpose of the technical expert is to enhance the performance of the operating core.

The second group of support functions provides support that is not directly related to the work of the operating core. Marketing, the business office, the mail room and cafeteria are examples of general support functions. As noted earlier, support services represent the third distinct part of an organization's operating structure.

The organizational structure defines the relationships among and between the parts of the organization. The right structure will support the functions of the organization and facilitate performance and will accommodate internal factors and position the organization to respond to external threats and opportunities. In the same way, the wrong structure will impede the performance and the success of the organization. When considering the structure of a specific organization, it is appropriate to ask if form fits function.

The Organizational Chart

The organizational chart is a graphic representation of an organizational structure. Using boxes and lines, an organizational chart presents graphically the relationships between the owners, management, support functions, and operating core departments. Solid lines represent direct reporting relationships. Reporting relationships indicate both communication and top down control. Dotted lines represent communications and/or indirect control (13). An organizational chart can be used to depict a simple or complex organization, and can depict all or part of an organization's structure.

Organizational structures are typically pyramidal representing the hierarchy of the management structure. Depending on the part or parts of the organization depicted, the most senior management position would be placed at the top of the chart. Subordinate positions and departments would follow in order of organizational position from high to low. Traditionally, the organizational chart describes the authority and responsibilities of positions within the organization. Occasionally, an organization will develop a structure that eliminates the typical management hierarchy. An organizational chart may be used to depict such a structure, but it may have little meaning outside of the organization. Additionally, the organizational chart should represent the actual structure, not a desired culture or set of relationships. Figure 6.1 depicts the organizational structure of the sole proprietorship therapy practice described earlier in this chapter.

Operating Structure At Progressive Stages of Organizational Development

As an organization grows and develops, the need to divide and coordinate the work of its employees will grow. As this happens, organiza-

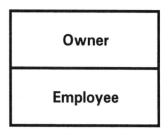

FIGURE 6.1. Sole Proprietorship

tions will pass through classic stages of development. Mintzberg (5) has described five stages of organizational development.

1. Craft stage
2. Entrepreneurial stage
3. Bureaucratic stage
4. Divisional stage
5. Adhocracy (matrix stage)

The Craft Stage

The first stage of organizational development is the craft stage. At this stage, the organization is small, and there is little or no division of labor. The term craft is not intended to describe the work of the organization but rather to describe an organization in which all of the members can effectively perform all of the tasks necessary to achieve the organization's common goal. The work of the craft organization can be coordinated through mutual adjustment, standardization and/or supervision. If there is supervision, it is likely that the role would be defined as a working supervisor where that person commonly performs all the work of the organization along side other organization members. The use of standardization as a method of coordination is largely dependent on the work of the craft organization. Mutual adjustment is more common than supervision at this stage. Figure 6.2 represents the organizational structure of the craft stage of development.

The description of a craft organization fits many small private therapy practices in which the organization consists of one or more therapists who share responsibility for the work of the organization. Work standardization would be a key method of coordination. Standardization would occur as a result of such things as professional education, licensure, standards of practice,

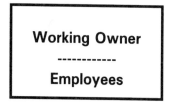

FIGURE 6.2. The Craft Stage

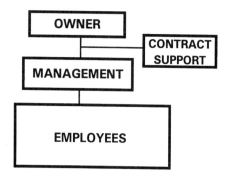

FIGURE 6.3. The Entrepreneurial Stage

policies, procedures and protocols. Mutual accommodation would be sufficient to coordinate the work shared by the therapists.

With luck, the therapists in this example would have the choice to maintain their practice at its current size or take advantage of growth opportunities. If they choose expansion, they will need additional partners and/or employees. Eventually, they will need to expand both the supervisory and support functions of the organization. When that occurs, the organization will move into the entrepreneurial stage of development.

The Entrepreneurial Stage

The second stage of organizational development is represented in Figure 6.3. At the entrepreneurial stage, standardization supported by mutual accommodation can no longer be relied upon to coordinate the work of the organization. Additional supervision and support is required. Further division of labor provides the opportunity to improve performance through increased efficiency. Alternately, it may place the organization at a disadvantage. Additional management layers will lead to greater separation between senior management, employees and the customers. More management can translate into a slower decision-making process. Increased reliance on standardization can decreased flexibility. A longer decision-making cycle, coupled with decreased flexibility, has the potential to make an organization less responsive in a rapidly changing environment.

The Bureaucratic Stage

As the entrepreneurial organization continues to grow, the demand for continued division of labor and a more complex work coordination system increases. At this point, the organization begins to move into the bureaucratic stage. Figures 6.4, A-C illustrate various representations of the

bureaucratic organizational structure, which is characterized by highly specialized employees, a larger, more complex management structure, distinct functional operating segments (departments) structured along lines of specialization, large technical and general support service functions and still more standardization. Bureaucratic organizations, made efficient through high standardization and specialization, can be very successful in a stable environment. However, where the entrepreneurial organization is at risk from decreased flexibility, the bureaucratic organization would require even more effort to respond to environmental changes. Without special mechanisms in place, the lack of ability to respond to change, foster new ideas and stay in touch with customers and employees could significantly interfere with the survival of a bureaucratic organization that found itself in an unstable, hostile and/or competitive market.

Recent and rapid changes in the health care industry have left many large health care organizations in exactly this dilemma. Having found success in a relatively unchanging, but growing market, bureaucratic health care organizations face continuous challenges in adapting to the new health care environment (13).

Only those organizations that can adapt to meet this challenge will be successful. Evidence of this threat can be found in the experiences of health care businesses in areas hardest hit by managed care initiatives. Minneapolis/St. Paul is one of those areas. Between 1981 and 1992, the number of hospitals in the Twin Cities declined from 24 to 19. The number of hospitals not affiliated with a larger health care system declined

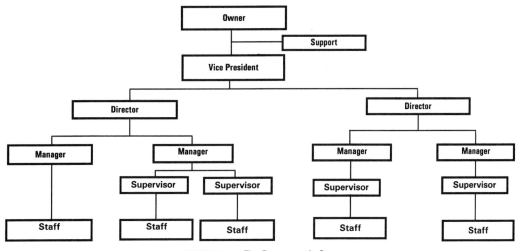

FIGURE 6.4A. The Bureaucratic Stage

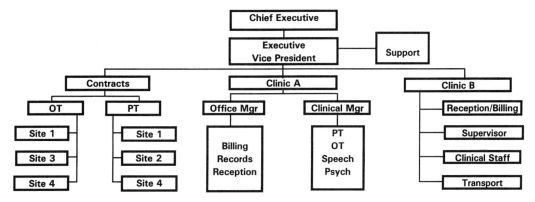

FIGURE 6.4B. A Divisional Model

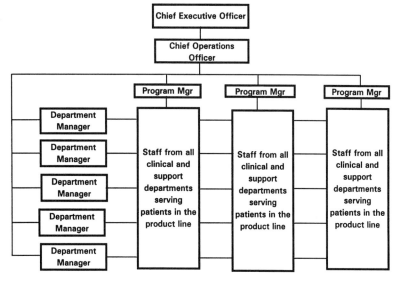

FIGURE 6.4C. A Matrix Model

from 13 to 5. Roughly 62% of the independent hospitals have joined a larger multi-hospital system (14). These figures are representative of a national trend toward health care business failures and consolidations. Increased employee participation in organizational problem solving and the use of work teams are two examples of work design approaches used by bureaucratic organizations to address these weaknesses.

The Divisional Stage (Fig. 6.4B)

An organization that continues to expand through product diversification and/or market expansion may move into the divisional stage of development. This type of business expansion can be achieved through vertical or horizontal integration of the existing business with new or acquired businesses. Or, a company might adopt a divisional structure due to a venture into a completely new line of business. The remaining comments will be focused on the first two options for growth into a divisionalized structure.

HORIZONTAL AND VERTICAL INTEGRATION

Expansion of an organization's current business into new markets is called horizontal integration. A physical therapy practice that acquires or develops additional physical therapy practices to cover a larger geographical region would expand by providing the same service to more customers. The addition of these similar business units is an example of horizontal expansion. Growth in this manner would move the organization into a divisionalized structure.

Business expansion through product diversification, whether by broadening services to the same customer base or by adding a new customer base, is called vertical integration. A hospital that expands through the acquisition of a primary care physician practice, a longterm care facility, and a home care agency is expanding through vertical integration (6). Organizations may have concurrent strategies for growth through both horizontal and vertical integration.

CENTRALIZATION VERSUS DECENTRALIZATION

A key organizational question for the divisionalized organization relates to the centralization of senior management and support functions. If de-

cision making rests largely with management at the corporate (central) office, the organization is centralized. Similarly, if support services are part of the corporate office and have authority over activities of other divisions, they would be described as centralized. To the extent that decision making and support functions are left to the divisions, the organization is decentralized. Full centralization or decentralization should be viewed as a continuum with most organizations resting somewhere between the extremes.

A centralized organization relies on supervision and standardization to coordinate the work between its divisions. Centralized standardization works well for divisionalized organizations whose success is tied to product consistency, such as a nationally known fast food chain. The same concept is equally applicable to a national therapy contract service. If, however, individual divisions must respond to local market demands or provide different products or services, centralization may decrease a division's flexibility and ability to respond to local market conditions. Performance could be impacted negatively.

Additional Structural Models

THE PRODUCT LINE MODEL

Unlike the bureaucratic structure, a product line structure shuns work specific operating units such as a physical therapy department, in preference for product based operating units such as a pain management program. Multiple approaches have been taken to product line structuring. In one case, only a portion of the organization, such as the marketing department, will be organized along product lines. In another case, the entire organization may be aligned with specific products.

A hospital that maintains distinct centralized physical and occupational therapy departments, has managers for both departments with all therapists serving all patient types, would represent a work specific department model. If the same hospital were to reorganize, assign physical and occupational therapy staff to distinct orthopedic, neurologic and geriatric treatment teams and eliminate the department management positions in favor of team supervisors, it would move toward a product line structure. A product line structure is more likely to use mutual adjustment than supervision as a method of work coordination. Standardization would still be used to coordinate work. Instead of department based standards, however, you might see team care plans or other forms of product specific standards of care.

The product line structure focuses the organization's attention outward toward the customer rather than inward toward specialized departments. Products are defined by customer needs. Reasons that an organization might move to a product line model include multiple, different customer markets or a large enough demand for a single product to commit dedicated resources. The use of a product line approach may attract additional customers in need of a specific service or set of services (13,15).

THE MATRIX MODEL (FIG. 6.4C)

The matrix model is another structural model that provides an alternative to the traditional bureaucratic structure. A matrix organization is really a hybrid between the traditional bureaucratic and the product line structure. A matrix organization maintains a specialized department structure, but overlays a product line structure onto the department structure. The product line unit is organizationally equal to the functional departments. The matrix model allows an organization to respond to external factors while maintaining a high degree of internal efficiency (16). The work of a matrix health care organization will be most efficient when coordinated through standardization and mutual accommodation with a lesser reliance on supervision. The matrix model does create a dual system of responsibility and accountability. Staff working in a matrix structure are accountable to meet the expectations of both department and program management. This can become difficult should there be an adversarial relationship between the product manager and the functional manager. Nonproductive conflict can be a difficult problem (16).

ORGANIZATIONAL STRUCTURE AND PRODUCT STRATEGY DECISIONS

The method of work coordination should not be confused with the strategic decision-making process of the organization. At the craft stage of development, the approach to product strategy decisions is dependent on the ownership structure and values. If jointly owned by the employees, a collaborative approach is likely. If solely owned, decision making may be an autocratic process. In a traditional bureaucratic organization, product strategy and alignment of strategy with functional department performance requirements happens at the senior management level. Under the product line model, product strategy development happens at the product unit level. Because there are no functional departments, the product manager is also responsible for direction and coordination of the functional resources that support the strategy. In a matrix organization, the product manager is responsible for product strategy development. The functional department manager participates in the product planning process and is responsible for determining the resource needs required to achieve the performance objectives. In both the product line and matrix models, decision making is pushed down to middle management, resulting in decisions made by people who are closer to the customers and the employees. This enhances the organization's ability to respond to change (16).

PROCESS APPROACH TO ORGANIZATIONAL DESIGN

Reasons To Reorganize

In response to significant environmental pressures, health care organizations have undergone partial or total reorganization to improve the potential for continued success (15,16). Reorganization might be considered when an organization is not meeting quality, productivity and/or financial expectations. A fundamental change in an organization's purpose, vision and/or strategic direction would be another reason for reorganization. Such a change often occurs when an organization is sold, changes its chief executive or merges with another organization. Sometimes organizations change structure simply because reorganizing is a popular thing to do. Reorganization can produce profound organizational change. A true reorganization entails an assessment, and possibly redesign of many organizational functions, such as:

- Employee relationships
- Division of work
- Employee performance expectations
- Work group composition
- Employee skill needs
- Number and type of people employed
- Methods of work coordination
- Work processes
- Work standards (policies, procedures and protocols)

The planning required to implement a successful reorganization is significant. As a result, a poorly planned or implemented reorganization can hurt rather than help the organization (11). For this reason, reorganization should be undertaken only after a comprehensive planning process has been completed.

Reorganization: Part Of The Strategic Planning Process

Reorganization should be undertaken to improve some aspect of organizational performance. However, performance problems that are significant enough to risk the initial disruption of reorganization are unlikely to be corrected by simply rearranging the structural elements of the organization. Reorganization should be one possible outcome of the strategic planning process. It is not a goal to be achieved. Rather, it is but one way to achieve a strategic business objective.

Reaffirm The Vision

Strategic planning should start with the reaffirmation or revision of the purpose and vision of the organization. A successful strategic planning process requires a clear direction for the future. An organization's vision is the target upon which the energies of the organization should be focused (also see Chapter 15).

Complete an Organizational Assessment

The first step in an organizational assessment is an internal and external assessment (8). The internal assessment is used to identify both strengths and weaknesses. The internal assessment should provide a clear understanding of how the organization accomplishes its work.

What type of work is done? How is work divided and coordinated between individuals, departments, divisions? What operates smoothly? Where are the barriers and bottlenecks in work flow? Does the organization meet its performance expectations? The external assessment should be used to determine the current and projected state of the organization's environment. What threats and opportunities face the organization now? What about the future? The reader should refer to Chapter 3 to review the discussion of a SWOT analysis process. All internal and external factors that influence organizational structure should be addressed during the organizational assessment.

Determine Strategic Directions And Set Performance Expectations

Information obtained during the organizational assessment can be used to set strategic directions and performance expectations. Gaps between current performance and performance expectations should define what needs to be done. The work to be done can be expressed as short and longterm goals and objectives. Once management has defined the work to be done, there are two questions that management must ask: Do I have the resources needed to get the job done? Will the organization's infrastructure support the work that needs to be done? If the resources are inadequate, then management will need to obtain additional resources or redefine the strategy. If the infrastructure is inadequate, then reorganization should be considered (17). Again, reorganization means significant change for those affected. All aspects of the infrastructure will experience some degree of change in making a reorganization work.

The relationship between strategic planning and reorganization can be illustrated through use of an example. Our theoretical therapy practice, *Do It All Therapy, Inc.,* is privately owned and has a vision of the future that includes continued growth and expansion. Unfortunately, the company has been losing business for the past six months. An organizational assessment has shown that the volume decline is due to an increase in the number of people enrolled in managed care insurance plans, as local managed care insurance plans have been directing patients to use other therapy providers. Further investigation has shown that *Do It All Therapy, Inc.* will need to provide broader geographical coverage and offer large price discounts to win managed care business from its competitors. To compete for managed care business, *Do It All Therapy, Inc.* will need to open at least two additional clinics. Clinic expansion will require external funding, such as a loan. The added costs related to expansion combined with price discounts will cause a decline in the corporation's profitability. To remain profitable, *Do It All Therapy, Inc.* will need to reduce its expenses. The owner has decided to decrease the number of clerical staff, use more physical therapist assistants and increase the hours of operation. These changes will affect the division of work, number and type of people employed, work group composition, employee relationships, methods of work coordination and work processes. These changes will occur because the corporation's structure will be changed.

The reader should now have an understanding of what structural model(s) will best accommodate and complement the characteristics, strategic direction and environment of an organization. The remaining sections of this chapter discuss development and use of human resource management as it relates to infrastructure.

HUMAN RESOURCE MANAGEMENT IN RELATION TO THE OPERATING STRUCTURE

Work Design Elements

Work design encompasses everything an organization does to structure and regulate the work of its employees. Each employee's work must be defined by the following elements.

1. Work group affiliation
2. Relationships to other employees and/or work groups
3. Specific job duties
4. Work standards such as policies, procedures and protocols
5. Performance expectations
6. Standards by which the employees work will be assessed
7. Education, expertise and skills required
8. Other personal or physical requirements
9. Methods by which the employee's work will be coordinated with the work of others

Each time an organization makes structural changes, all of these elements must be adapted by the new structure. If this is not done, organizational changes are less likely to have the desired impacts.

Work Design Parameters

The work design process has three parameters: job specialization, behavior formalization, and training and professional socialization (5).

Job Specialization

Employee jobs can be specialized in two ways. The first, horizontal specialization, refers to the scope of a job. A position that is highly specialized will include only a few, narrowly defined tasks. The more limited the job, the more specialized it is. A therapist's job that is limited to the treatment of adult patients following joint replacement is an example of high horizontal specialization. Jobs can also be vertically specialized. Vertical specialization relates to the degree of control the employee has over the tasks to be performed. The more vertically specialized the job, the less control the employee has over the work performed. The division of work through horizontal specialization is intended to increase employee, and subsequently, organizational efficiency and performance. The division of work through vertical specialization (supervision) is intended to direct and coordinate the work of employees. Figure 6.5 demonstrates how the concept of job specialization would typically apply to a physical therapy practice. Too often, job specialization is based on the need for control, assumptions about employee capabilities or because employees lack skills necessary to perform the work without division of tasks. Unfortunately, this approach may lead to unnecessary specialization. We refer the reader back to Chapter 4 and the discussion of engaging people for maximum performance. Unnecessary specialization is a barrier to maximum employee contribution by limiting what they are allowed to do. Job design should start with a clear understanding of what the organization requires from its employees. Individual jobs should allow employees maximum latitude and autonomy to get the work done in the most efficient way possible.

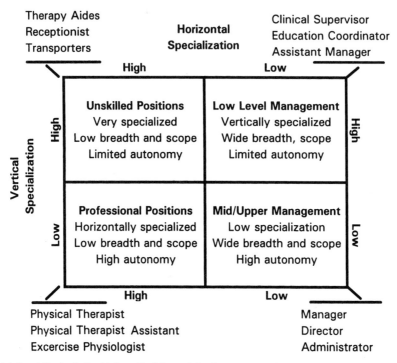

FIGURE 6.5. Job Specialization In Health Care. The job specialization concept as it applies to physical therapy practice. (Modified form: Mintzberg H. The structure of organizations. Englewood Cliffs, NJ: Prentice-Hall, 1979:80).

Both large and small health care businesses have been particularly challenged to reconsider their traditional approach to job specialization. The traditional approach is characterized by a high percentage of specialized employees with limited autonomy. A structure that limits the ability of employees to use all of their skills decreases employees' abilities and willingness to be flexible. This leads to tremendous upheaval when change is needed while decreasing the ability of the business to respond quickly and efficiently to environmental opportunities or threats. In today's environment, health care businesses would be wise to limit specialization whenever possible.

Behavioral Formalization

Behavior formalization is a term used to describe the ways a business can standardize the work of employees (5). The health care industry relies heavily on standardization. Standardization can increase efficiency, but more important to the health care organization, it results in consistency of work performance. When a health care organization makes an error in the delivery of services,

it can have serious and costly consequences (see Chapter 12). The potential for errors is decreased when performance consistency is high. As a result, health care businesses rely heavily on behavior formalization. There are three methods of formalizing behavior: by position, work flow and rules. Job descriptions, standard care plans, treatment referrals, policies, procedures, operating manuals and licensure requirements are all examples of behavior formalization and each should be addressed during the work design process. All are part of the infrastructure that supports the work of the business.

Training and Professional Socialization

Training is the process by which job related skills are taught. The more complex and nonroutine the tasks, the greater the need for training. Training standardizes performance. It can occur inside or outside of the organization. To the extent that training happens outside of the business, the less control the business has over the work methods taught (5).

In health care, training occurs both inside and outside the organization. When basic work methods are learned outside the business, it is incumbent on the business to validate and, where necessary, enhance and standardize work methods used by its employees. In therapy practice, therapists learn basic skills during their professional training. Each time they join a new organization, they can expect to receive an orientation to the way their employer provides therapy services. Written guidelines such as policies and procedures, training, mentoring, job competencies, performance standards and supervision are all commonly used orientation approaches.

The Job Description

The job description represents the outcome of the work design process for an individual employee. As such, it should contain the following information.

1. The organizational relationships of the position. The employee's job title, work group, supervisor, subordinates and relationship to other employees should be defined.
2. A listing of job duties with enough detail of the tasks to be performed and enough latitude to allow for flexibility in responsibilities.
3. A description of the decision making authority (autonomy) of the position. If variable, the degree of autonomy for specific duties should be clear or the mechanism for determining degree of autonomy by task should be clear.
4. Applicable work standards, such as policies and professional standards, should be specified.
5. A description of the minimum qualification such as knowledge, skill, formal education, licensure, physical capabilities, personal resources, and mobility requirements should be specified. All of the minimum requirements should be clearly related to the demands of the job.
6. Responsibility for the work of others.
7. Methods by which work will be coordinated with the work of others.

Performance Standards And Appraisal

The job description defines job duties and related employee capabilities. The performance standards define how the organization expects the duties to be performed and how performance will be measured. Performance standards are the benchmarks against which an employee's performance is to be compared. Performance appraisal is the process of comparing employee performance to the established performance standards for their job. Because employee capabilities vary, so will their ability to perform a specific job. For this reason, performance standards often define a continuum of exceptional to unacceptable performance. Along this continuum, a minimum acceptable level of performance is identified. This approach allows for the identification of performance deficits, opportunities for performance improvement and the recognition of exceptional performance. Both the employer and the employee benefit from the insight that this approach can provide (18). There is no one best performance appraisal system that will work in every situation. But regardless of the system used, it should have the following characteristics:

*   Both employee and employer share a common set of expectations
*   Employees must perceive that the system is an accurate and equitable way to measure performance
*   The system must provide the information required to manage and improve employee performance

Employee appraisal is often used as a basis for compensation adjustment. When that is the case, the need for an objective method of performance appraisal is critical. Figure 6.6 demonstrates how a specific job duty, such as patient evaluation, can be further defined using a range of performance descriptions. The performance descriptions here have been ranked using a five point scale. Level 3 represents the minimum acceptable level of performance. It may be acceptable for employees who are new to a job to perform below the minimum acceptable level of performance for some period of time. When an employee continues to perform below the minimum acceptable level, performance management intervention is required.

Performance Management

Managing employee performance is a key role for the health care manager (19). A performance discrepancy occurs any time an employee is doing something that is different from the expected performance. If an employee is performing better than expected, the discrepancy is positive and the

PERFORMANCE CRITERIA: RATING AND DESCRIPTION

Performance Criteria:
Patient Evaluation And Treatment

Level 5: Exceptional Performance
Independently and appropriately selects and performs
advanced physical therapy evaluation procedures, or
recommends medical evaluation procedures. Routinely
educates other employees on the use of advanced physical
therapy evaluation procedures.

Level 4: Exceeds Expectations
Recognizes the need to perform advanced physical therapy
evaluation procedures. Seeks input from others on the
appropriate implementation of unfamiliar procedures.
Some involvement in staff education on the use of
advanced physical therapy evaluation procedures.

Level 3: Meets Expectations
Completes all basic physical therapy evaluation procedures
independently within the time scheduled. Refers to the
department policy manual for a description of basic
evaluation procedures. Seeks input from others on the
appropriate use and performance of advanced procedures.

Level 2: Partially Meets Expectations
Occasionally requires assistance to select appropriate basic
evaluation procedures. Sometimes requires assistance with
the performance of basic evaluation procedures.
Does not perform advanced evaluation procedures.
Requires indirect and some direct supervision to ensure
quality of patient evaluations.

Level 1: Unsatisfactory Performance
Consistently requires assistance to select and perform
appropriate basic evaluation procedures. Requires
constant direct supervision.

FIGURE 6.6. Performance Discrepancy Analysis Model Modified from: Lachman VD. Increasing productivity through performance evaluation. J Nursing Admin 1984;12(12):11.

employee should be supported and encourage toward continued development. Most often managers are called upon to support an employee so that good performance can become exceptional.

Occasionally, managers must address situations involving negative performance discrepancies. Assuming that the identification of a negative performance discrepancy is based on an objective performance appraisal, the manager must correct the situation. There are two alternatives: correct the discrepancy or replace the employee.

The first step toward resolution is to determine the cause for unacceptable performance. Does it relate to employee ability, support or effort (18)? Resolution of performance discrepancies should be a collaborative process involving the manager and the employee. Figure 6.7 presents a performance discrepancy analysis and remediation process. Using this process, the manager and employee move through a series of remediation steps until the discrepancy is resolved, the employee is transferred to another job within the organization or employment is terminated.

Coaching

When the organizational obstacles and ability have been eliminated as the cause for poor performance, the manager may wish to coach the employee toward improved performance. Coaching is an interactive process used to analyze and improve performance. Coaching should be undertaken with the intent of making the most of a valuable resource, the employee. Coaching takes time and there is no guarantee of a successful outcome (19). To enhance probability for success, the following six steps should be followed:

1. The performance discrepancy must be accurately identified in relation to performance expectations.
2. The manager must help the employee understand why the performance discrepancy is important.
3. The employee must agree that a discrepancy exists.
4. The manager and employee should work collaboratively to develop shared strategies for performance improvement. The employee must commit to an improvement plan.
5. Deadlines for improvement should be agreed upon. The manager must followup on a predetermined schedule.
6. There must be clear and meaningful consequences for lack of improvement.
7. The manager must recognize improvement as it occurs.

Mentoring

When given an employee who is demonstrating exceptional performance, a manager has a unique opportunity to contribute to the future of both the organization and the employee. Through encouragement, support, and the opportunity for development, a manager can contribute to the continued development of the employee. When a manager undertakes this type of supportive interaction, it is referred to as mentoring. As with coaching, mentoring can be a time-consuming process. Both coaching and mentoring can contribute to the success of an organization because both processes result in more productive employees. Exceptional managers may engage in coaching and mentoring activities to some degree with all of their employees (19). Figure 6.7 provides a model for performance discrepancy analysis and remediation.

Employee Retention

Organizations invest time and resources into the orientation, training and development of employees. This investment increases an employee's value to the organization. The loss of an experienced employee can negatively impact organizations in several ways.

* Decreased productivity
* Lost business opportunities
* Lost revenue
* Decreased customer satisfaction
* Decreased employee satisfaction for those remaining

Given the potential impacts, it is in the organization's best interest to retain employees whose performance meets expectations. The impact of employee turnover and importance of employee retention increase when new employees are hard to recruit. The impacts of turnover are compounded when recruitment costs go up and/or positions remain vacant for extended periods. This has been the case with physical therapy for the past several years.

Employee Turnover

Employee turnover, a term used to describe when an employee leaves an organization, is defined as the percentage of employees who have terminated their employment during a specified

QUESTION	RESPONSE
Is there a performance discrepancy? 　　Yes　No ➡ 　　　↓	Continue to appraise performance.
Does the employee know that performance is unsatisfactory? 　　Yes　No ➡ 　　　↓	Provide feedback to the employee.
Does the employee know and understand what is expected? 　　Yes　No ➡ 　　　↓	Provide employee with concise information about performance expectations.
Does the employee have the ability to meet performance expectations? 　　Yes　No ➡ 　　　↓	Provide the employee with training and/or practice.
Does the employee have the organizational support required to meet performance expectations? 　　Yes　No ➡ 　　　↓	Determine what support is needed and provide it.
Do incentives motivate employee to exert effort to meet performance expectations? 　　Yes　No ➡ 　　　↓	Provide incentives which motivate the employee to exert required effort.
Do negative consequences follow nonperformance? Do positive consequences follow performance? 　　Yes　No ➡ 　　　↓	Change consequences.
Could the employee meet the performance expectations if he or she wanted to? 　　Yes　No ➡ 　　　↓	Transfer employee or terminate employment.
Does coaching redirect behavior? 　　Yes　No ➡	Transfer employee or terminate employment.

FIGURE 6.7. Performance discrepancy analysis and remediation. Modified from Nosse LJ, Friberg DG. Management Principles for Physical Therapists. Baltimore, MD: Williams & Wilkins, 1992:87.

period of time. Turnover is often expressed as a percentage. For example, if 2 out of 10 physical therapists working in a department terminate their employment during the year, the department's annual turnover would be 20%. The rate of turnover may be used as a performance outcome measure. The reader is referred to Chapter 11, Outcomes: What To Measure And What Does The Information Mean?

Can Management Control Employee Turnover?

Employees leave organizations for a variety of personal and professional reasons. One study on turnover of physical therapists found that 26% of therapists who had been in the field less than 2 years had between two and five jobs. Seventy-five percent (75%) of physical therapists who had been in the field more than 5 years had between two and five jobs. Our experience suggests that many may leave an organization for reasons unrelated to the work setting. Some turnover can be influenced by management action and some can-

not. Family responsibilities, spouse relocation, return to school, or a change in career are all reasons why employees leave an organization. Managers have little ability to impact turnover that is driven by such personal motivations. Managers should concentrate their efforts on the turnover factors they can influence. Controllable turnover is driven by individual, organizational and environmental factors (21,22). Table 6.3 provides examples of factors that may encourage employee turnover and related management actions which encourage employee retention.

SUMMARY

Management has the responsibility for maximizing the performance of the organization. Business structures have legal, tax and operating structures which define an organization's form and function. Organizational performance is influenced greatly by the organization of its parts into a functioning whole. A planning process should be used by management to determine

TABLE 6.3
Turnover Factors And Management Actions Encouraging Employee Retention

TURNOVER FACTORS	MANAGEMENT ACTIONS ENCOURAGING RETENTION
Poorly defined position responsibilities High stress position	• Clearly define performance expectations • Remove obstacles which interfere with job performance and provide needed resources.
Work that does not utilize employee skills	• Define job prior to employment • Match employee skills with job
Unreasonable performance expectations Limited growth opportunities	• Involve employees in the process of setting performance expectations • Create opportunities for growth and development • Involve employees in the work design process
Lack of recognition for accomplishments	• Recognized good performance • Provide opportunity for peer recognition
Lack of opportunity to express concerns and dissatisfaction Inflexible work conditions Pay inequities Limited autonomy	• Provide formal mechanisms and encourage employees to express work related concerns • Make allowances for flexible work arrangements whenever possible • Use market information to determine wage and benefits programs • Adopt a management style that encourages employee participation and a level of autonomy based on ability.
Open job market	• Develop jobs with competitive compensation and challenging content.
Undesirable work conditions	• Correct work conditions which cause dissatisfaction and correct where possible. • Put in place off setting conditions that decrease the negative impact of undesirable working conditions

Adapted from Nosse LJ, Friberg DG. Management Principles for Physical Therapists. Baltimore, Williams and Wilkins, 1992: 90.

what and how work is to be done. This planning process should look within the organization and outside the organization at the environments that will influence the organization's success. Organizational structure and work design should be dynamic and should change as an organization matures or changes its focus to meet internally and externally driven performance demands. Structure should be linked with and support the organization's product strategy. Work design can be viewed as a fleshing out of the organization's structural skeleton. It is the process of deciding who will do what in relationship to all of the other activities of the organization. The larger and more complex the organization, the more challenging the work design process becomes. The challenge is to balance job specialization with the organization's ability to coordinate the work of many into one unified health care delivery process.

REFERENCES

1. Nosse LJ, Friberg DG. Management Principles for Physical Therapists. Baltimore, Williams and Wilkins, 1992:19–20.
2. Webster's Ninth New Collegiate Dictionary. Springfield. Meriam-Webster, 1986:834.
3. Schneller ES. Accountability for health care: A white paper on leadership and management for the US health care system. Health Care Manage Rev 1997; 22(1),38–48.
4. Weltman B. The Big Idea Book for New Business Owners. New York, NY:Macmillian Spectrum, 1997:52–80.
5. Mintzberg H. The Structuring of Organizations. Englewood Cliffs, NJ: Prentice-Hall, 1979:2.
6. Brown M, McCool BP. Vertical integration: Explo-

7. MacMillan IC, Jones PE. Designing organizations to compete. J Bus Strategy 1984;4:11–26.
8. Liedtka JM. Formulating hospital strategy: Moving beyond a market mentality. Health Care Manage Rev 1992;17(1):21–26.
9. Woodward J. Industrial Organization. "Theory and Practice." Oxford: Oxford, 1965:36–39.
10. Goffee R, Gareth J. What holds the modern company together? Harv Bus Rev 1996; Nov-Dec:134–149.
11. Roach SS. The hollow ring of the productivity revival. Harv Bus Rev 1996; Nov-Dec:81–89.
12. Miles, RE. Theories of Management: Implications for Organizational Behavior and Development. New York: McGraw-Hill, 1975:75.
13. MacStravic RS. Product-line administration in hospitals. Health Care Manage Rev 1986; 11(2):35–43.
14. AHA Guide to the Health Care Field, 1979–1992. American Hospital Association, Chicago, Illinois.
15. Fottler MD, Repasky LJ. Attitudes of hospital executives toward product line management: A pilot survey. Health Care Manage Rev 1988; 13(3):15–22.
16. Timm MM, Wanetik MG. Matrix organization: Design and development for a hospital organization. Hosp Health Serv Admin 1983; Nov/Dec:46–58.
17. Bhide A. The questions every entrepreneur must answer. Harv Bus Rev 1996;Nov-Dec:120–130.
18. Lachman VD. Increasing productivity through performance evaluation. J Nurs Admin 1984;14(12):7–14.
19. Waldroop J, Butler T. The executive as coach. Harv Bus Rev 1996; Nov-Dec:1996:111–117.
20. Harkon DG, Unterreiner AS, Shepard KF. Factors related to job turnover in physical therapy. Phys Ther 1982;62:1465–1470.
21. Smith HL, Discenza R. Developing a framework for retaining health care employees: A challenge to traditional thinking. Health Care Supervisor 1988;7(1):17–28.
22. Abelson MA. Strategic management of turnove: A model for the health service administrator. Health Care Manage Rev 1986;11(2):61–71.

ration of a popular concept. Health Care Manage Rev 1986;11(4):7–19.

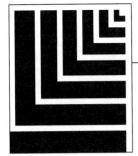

7

MONEY MATTERS: HEALTH CARE FINANCIAL MANAGEMENT

PREVIEW

Truth is, money matters. No health care business can survive long without making money. With survival at stake, it should be easy to understand why financial management is an essential part of every manager's job. Financial management encompasses all of the activities of a business. The goal of financial management is to maximize the wealth of the business and, where appropriate, its owners. There are professional financial managers who have backgrounds in business, finance and accounting. These professionals can support the efforts of the nonfinancial manager in making financially sound decisions.

Chapter 7 provides the reader with an overview of health care finance and financial management systems. Concepts related to the management of revenues and expenses, budgeting and cost control are discussed. The processes used by businesses to keep track of what it spends, earns, owes and is owed will also be covered. Chapter 7 will lay the foundation necessary for the reader to understand the intricacies of health care finance and to use financial information to improve organizational performance. Chapter 8 expands upon topics introduced here, with more practical discussion of ways to maximize financial performance. Chapter 14 focuses on the financial management of a private practice.

KEY WORDS

Accounting: the process of "collecting, summarizing, analyzing, reporting and interpreting, in monetary terms, information about the enterprise" (1).

Case Mix: the mix of patients served by diagnostic category expressed as a percentage of total patients.

Cost: money spent.

Creditor: an individual or company to whom something is owed.

Endowment: wealth that is given to provide a permanent income to an individual or organization.

Enrollee: an individual who has paid a premium for coverage under a health insurance plan.

Entity: for the purpose of financial reporting, a business is considered to be an entity capable of economic action.

Financial report: a statement of financial performance and position.

Industry analysts: individuals whose career is related to the evaluation of the performance trends of a specific industry. They may also perform evaluations of a company's performance in relation to industry standards.

Outlier: events that fall outside of the normal range of variance for similar events.

Philanthropist: an individual who has a natural love of people that is expressed through practical efforts to improve the well-being of others.

Stockholder: an individual or organization that owns stock in a company or corporation.

Wealth: refers to all things having monetary value.

INTRODUCTION

Financial management refers broadly to the actions taken by an organization to obtain and maximize the use of monetary resources. The most obvious aspect of financial management is the gathering and use of financial information. Financial information can be used by a business to improve its performance in three key areas:

First, financial information can be used to assess the relative impact of investment options.

Second, it can be used to improve performance through process management. Accounts management, inventory management, and cash management are processes that, when managed well, can improve financial performance.

Third, good financial information is essential to effective planning (1).

Financial reports, statements of performance and position, are necessary to assess organizational performance (1). Actual performance can be compared to planned performance to guide management decisions. Comparison of past-to-current performance can reveal trends that can be used to predict future performance. The annual financial business plan is called a budget. The budget represents management's best estimate of what will happen in the short-term future. It is the internal benchmark against which day-to-day performance is assessed.

Cost analysis is the process of determining the expense related to the production of a product or service. Cost information can be used to manage expenses and to set prices. This last use is of critical importance for managed care contracting. Historically, access to and the use of financial information has been limited to management. Financial information was often available only on a need-to-know basis. The recent trend toward the use of work teams for problem solving and performance improvement has changed this restricted-use thinking. Many businesses now distribute financial information to employees at all levels of the organization. See Chapter 10 for additional thoughts on this topic. In theory, employees who are knowledgeable about the company's financial position are better able and willing to contribute to performance improvement (2). Employees involved in performance improvement, gain sharing or performance-based compensation programs are more likely to be interested in the success of the organization. They will be prepared to make a greater contribution if they have access to financial performance information.

The information produced by a financial management system is also used by persons outside of the organization. Outside parties use financial information to evaluate the performance and financial viability of a business. An organization's financial information may be used by many outside parties including:

- Government agencies
- Stockholders
- Potential investors
- Creditors
- Philanthropists
- Industry analysts

Any one of these outside users have the potential to impact the success of a health care business (3). The reader will learn about financial management principles as well as financial management practices common to health care businesses. Where possible, common problems or pit falls will be identified. Health care providers encounter some unique financial management issues because there are multiple customers involved in most transactions. This is due to the third party payment system, the involvement of government as a major source of health care reimbursement and the diversity of payment methodology in every health care market. For information regarding the relationship of financial management to the marketing process, the reader is referred to Chapter 3. Topics to be covered in this Chapter will lay the necessary foundation for understanding the in-depth discussion of third party payment presented in Chapter 8.

FINANCIAL MANAGEMENT

Financial management is more than accounting. Accounting is the "process of collecting, summa-rizing, analyzing, reporting and interpreting, in monetary terms, information about the enterprise" (1). In contrast, financial management is the "art of both obtaining the funds that the enterprise needs in the most economic manner and of making optimal use of those funds once obtained" (1). Financial management is the decision-making process, relying on the information provided by a business' accounting process, that allows the entitiy to operate effectively.

Financial Management Services

The services of a financial professional are key to the development of an effective financial management system. Financial management is as much a recognized profession as is physical therapy. Academic preparation for a career in the field of financial management can be through a baccalaureate and/or graduate degree in business administration, accounting or economics. Advanced certification can be achieved through successful completion of a standardized examination prepared by the American Institute of Certified Public Accounts. Designation as a Certified Public Accountant (CPA) can be equated to a Board Certified Specialist designation for a physical therapy professional. The CPA designation offers an assurance of advanced knowledge in the area of accounting and financial management. The CPA designation is often listed as a minimum requirement for financial management positions.

A business can obtain the services of a financial professional by hiring financial management professionals or through the purchase of services from a public accounting service. Employment versus contract decisions should reflect the needs of the organization. It is common for large organizations to obtain financial management services through an employed support service. A smaller business may find it more economical to purchase services on an as-needed basis. Financial management services can be purchased from independent practitioners, local or large national financial services corporations. The reader may refer to Chapter 11 for additional information on the purchase of financial management consulting services.

Financial Reporting

The Financial Accounting Standards Board (FASB) sets the standards for accounting and financial reporting. The FASB defines the objectives of financial reporting in its Statement of Financial Accounting Concepts No.1 (4). FASB defined objectives for financial reporting include:

1. Financial reporting should provide information that is useful to present and potential investors, creditors, and other users in making rational investment, credit and similar decisions.
2. Financial reporting should provide information about the economic resources of an enterprise, the claims to those resources, and the effects of transactions, events, and circumstances that change resources.
3. Financial reporting should provide information about an enterprise's financial performance during a stated period.
4. Financial reporting should provide information about how an enterprise obtains and expends cash, about its borrowing and repaying of borrowed funds, about its capital transactions, and about other factors that may affect its liquidity or solvency.
5. Financial reporting should provide information about how management of an enterprise has discharged its stewardship responsibility for the use of enterprise resources.
6. Financial reporting should provide information that is useful to managers and directors in making decisions in the interest of owners.

Financial Accounting Principles

There are basic principles that guide the way financial accounts are kept. Because these common principles are followed, similar reporting transactions yield similar results. This uniformity in record keeping means that financial accounting records are understandable to all internal and external parties who use them (1). Berman, Kukla and Weeks (1) identify several basic accounting concepts with which managers should be familiar to understand financial data and reports. Their lists of concepts include:

- Entity
- Transactions
- Cost valuation
- Double entry
- Accrual
- Matching

Entity

For the purpose of financial reporting, a business is considered to be an entity capable of economic action. As it is assumed that the entity will be ongoing, financial reporting reflects the assumption of continuity over time.

Transactions

For the financial information of an entity to be accurate all transactions affecting the entity must be recorded. For the purpose of reporting, transactions may be summarized into a manageable level of detail as long as the financial condition and performance of the entity is accurately reflected.

Cost Valuation

The value of transactions must be recorded in a consistent way. Several such options exist, such as the price at sale, the replacement or the purchase price. Accountants have found that "the price paid to purchase an item is the most useful valuation for the purpose of the permanent accounting record" (1).

Double Entry

Each transaction has two aspects: the change in the entity's assets and the change in the source of financing. Both aspects of a transaction should be recorded (1). For example, the purchase of a piece of equipment would be reflected as an increase in the value of equipment owned and a decrease in the cash of the entity and/or increase in accounts or notes payable.

Accrual

The concept of accrual refers to the practice of recording financial transactions within an appropriate period of time. For example, a company following the accrual principle would record the cost of the vacation pay earned by employees as a liability in the period it is earned. This liability is then carried until the employee takes vacation time. When the vacation is used, the liability is reduced. In this way, the expense of the vacation is recorded in the time period it was earned, not when it is paid out. If it were not recorded (accrued) in this manner, the expenses for the period when vacation was earned would be understated, the expenses for the period when vacation time was actually paid to the employee would be overstated and the company's real liabilities would be understated by the total amount of vacation pay owed to employees. For one employee paid $20.00 per hour, a bank of 20 vacation days (160 hours) would represent a liability to a company of $3200. Consistent recording procedures prevent the manipulation of financial performance for an entity during any specific period of time. The rules for transaction recording are:

1) Revenue and expenses should be recorded when services and/or products are sold or costs are incurred
2) Expenses should be recorded during the time period in which the item purchased is used in the production of the entity's goods or services (1).

Matching

To evaluate the actual performance of an entity, income from an activity must be matched with expenses of the same activity so that performance can be assessed. Matching is the only way an organization can determine if a specific product and/or service is contributing to the organization's performance. Comparing the price of a treatment to the cost of delivering the treatment is an example of matching (1).

ACCRUAL METHOD OF ACCOUNTING

The concept of matching is consistent with use of an accrual basis for accounting. The accrual basis requires that revenue be recorded within the period it is earned. Likewise, expenses must be recorded in the period when the resources are consumed for the production of related revenue. For example, payment is received in advance for services to be delivered in three months. Employee salary expense for the delivery of service is incurred during the month of delivery. The revenue should be credited in the same month the services were provided and the expense incurred. Otherwise, a business may think it is performing well in the month cash was received and substantially worse when it pays the related bills (5).

CASH METHOD OF ACCOUNTING

The cash basis is used as an alternative to the accrual method of accounting. Under the cash basis for accounting, revenue is recorded when cash is received and expenses are recorded when bills are paid. This approach fails to match revenue and expenses. It will not support management efforts to determine the costs of individual products and services. It is used on a limited basis in health care, most commonly in small private practices and partnerships (5).

Accounting Conventions

In practice, accounting concepts are modified by accounting conventions. There are both general and industry-specific accounting conventions that guide the design of financial management systems (1). General accounting conventions include the following concepts:

- Relevance: information is relevant if it helps users assess past and future efforts.
- Reliability: information is reliable if it can be verified.
- Neutrality: information is neutral when relevance and reliability determine its use rather than a need to demonstrate any particular result.
- Materiality: the level of detail reflected in financial information should be kept to a level that is useful to the management decision-making process.
- Comparability: to be useful, financial reports should be comparable between organizations and over time.
- Conservatism: when in doubt, financial reporting should error in the direction of underestimating benefits and overestimating the potential costs.
- Costs and benefits: when determining the amount and specificity of information collected, the cost of obtaining and recording information should be weighed against the potential value of the information obtained.

The accounting conventions particular to health care should also be understood. Conventions of importance to health care businesses are allowances for contractual deductions, fund accounting, and funded depreciation. Allowances for contractual deductions are conventions common to health care accounting that address the difference between the price charged for a service and the price paid by third party payers. This approach is taken because the third party payment system for health care services causes prices to be set much higher than the average payment. The amount of payment varies significantly between payers and is seldom under the control of the health care provider. To account for the difference between the amount charged and the amount paid, an account called allowances for contractual deductions is used.

Fund accounting is often found in hospitals and larger health care businesses. Under some conditions, a health care business may need to separate the financial information of one or more sections from that of the total entity. For example, if a health care organization received a philanthropic gift to be used only for the support of a special program or building project, a separate fund would be set up to account for this donor-restricted gift. This separation prevents the co-mingling of restricted with general funds. Types of accounting funds that may be seen in health care are endowment funds, specific purpose fund, plant fund and construction fund. The need for and use of fund accounting should reflect the individual needs of the entity (1). Individual fund accounts are part of a larger financial entity. Therefore, the performance and condition of the fund accounts are included in the financial reports of the total entity.

Funded depreciation is a method that can be used to set aside money for the addition and/or future replacement of buildings and equipment. Funded depreciation occurs when management determines that a certain amount of cash will be set apart from general operating funds to ensure the future availability of building and equipment. This money is usually invested to earn interest to counter the effects of inflation. Although not required, the use of funded depreciation can be a welcome safety net in a rapidly changing environment.

Financial Statements

Information collected through the financial management system is used to support management and others in evaluating and directing the activities of the business. This information is presented in financial statements and reports. Financial statements represent information collected over a specific period of time and/or reported as of a specific date. The specific date is the last date for which information was included. The time frame may vary based on the needs of the organization. Common time frames are yearly, quarterly, monthly and semiweekly. Detailed activity tracking reports may be produced weekly or even daily. Occasionally, the time frame for a report will roll forward. In this case, there is a designated time range such as the most recent 6 months. The time range is consistent from report to report but the months covered change over time. Each time the report is prepared, 1 month would be dropped to add the most recent month's data. This approach can help managers identify subtle performance trends.

Financial reporting does not follow the chronological year. It follows a fiscal year (FY). A FY may follow the calendar year but, can be any 12-month cycle. Once a business has established its FY, it will continue to operate and report performance on that fiscal-year cycle. The FY used by related businesses are often the same, which allows for the comparison and cumulative reporting of financial results among related entities. There are several financial statements that are common to all businesses. These include the balance sheet, income statement and cash flow statement.

Balance Sheet

The balance sheet is a statement of financial condition that provides information about a business' assets, liabilities, and owner's equity as of a specific date. That date is commonly the end of a usual reporting period such as a quarter or year. A balance sheet gives a picture of a business' pluses and minuses at a glance. Figure 7.1 depicts a balance sheet for *Do It All Therapy, Inc.,* as of September 31, 2005. The FY for *Do It All Therapy, Inc.* runs from October 1 to September 31. This balance sheet represents an end of the year status, but includes all activity of the business prior to that date. The format of the balance sheet is represented by the equation:

Total Assets = Total Liabilities and Owner's Equity

ASSETS

"Assets are economic resources which are owned by a business and are expected to benefit future operations" (5). Assets include such things as:

Do It All Therapy, Incorporated Balance Sheet September 30, 2005			
ASSETS		**LIABILITIES AND OWNER'S EQUITY**	
Cash	$45,000	Liabilities:	
Investments	60,000		
Prepaid Expenses	2,000	Accounts Payable	$50,000
Inventories	10,000	Accrued Expenses	5,000
Accounts Receivable	60,000	Notes Payable	225,000
		Total Liabilities	$280,000
Land	40,000		
Buildings	90,000		
Equipment	200,000	Owner's Equity	$227,000
		Total Liabilities and Owner's	
TOTAL	$507,000	Equity	$507,000

FIGURE 7.1. The balance sheet.

- Cash
- Investments
- Prepaid expenses
- Inventories
- Accounts receivable
- Capital assets
- Intangibles

Prepaid expenses include such things as salary advanced or insurance payments made for a future period. Inventories represent the value of supplies or products that will be used or sold during future periods. Accounts receivable represent money that is owed to the business for already delivered products and services. Capital assets include land, buildings and equipment. Sometimes assets are described as intangible, meaning that the asset has no physical substance. Patents, trademarks, copyrights and goodwill are examples of intangible assets (5).

Assets are important in determining the financial health of the organization. For the purposes of reporting, the value of an asset represents its current value to the business. A business views assets as resources available to continue the operation of the business. Potential creditors view a business'

assets as resources available to cover the business debt. For the creditor, more assets mean a better chance of repayment should operation of the business not produce enough income to cover expenses. Creditors value assets both on the value as well as the speed with which the asset can be converted to cash. Cash and assets that can be readily converted to cash are referred to as liquid assets. Assets that require a long conversion period are referred to as fixed assets.

The true value of an asset to a business can change over time and circumstances. A company might find they have assets that are no longer expected to benefit the business in the future. Accounts receivable may go unpaid so long that it is unlikely the debt will ever be recovered. Under these circumstances, the asset should be removed from the books. This reduces total assets and total owner's equity (5).

LIABILITIES

Liabilities are debts of the business. Total liabilities can be thought of as the amount of the business' assets that are owned by its creditors. Liabilities that are repayable within 1 year are considered to be short-term. Liabilities not due or payable in more than 1 year are considered to be long-term liabilities.

Accounts payable are debts payable to individuals who have provided products or services to the business on credit. Outstanding bills for supplies, professional services and cleaning services are examples of debts that would fall under accounts payable. Accrued expenses represent the value of debts that are held for payment in the future (1). The time or need for payment may not be known. As discussed previously, vacation is a good example of an accrued expense. The business owes to its employees the value of their accrued time off. Often, employees are able to bank or use accrued time off at their discretion. Should they terminate their employment, they may or may not be able to claim the value of their banked time. If accrued vacation is paid at prevailing wages instead of the wage at the time of accrual, the value to the employee and size of this accrued debt can grow over time. As long as the employer has the potential to pay for this accrued debt, it is listed as a liability.

Notes payable are loans evidenced by loan agreements indicating the loan amount and interest due at future dates. Amounts owed for lines of credit, start-up capital, and mortgages are examples of debts that would fall under notes payable.

OWNER'S EQUITY

Owner's equity or net worth is the difference between total assets and liabilities. Owner's equity can be a positive or negative value. It represents the portion of the assets that belong to the owner(s). The net worth of the owner(s) can increase in two ways. First, an owner(s) can invest additional resources into the business. Second, net worth can increase as a result of profitable operations.

Income Statement

The income statement is a report on the performance of a business over a specific period of time. It provides a comparison of monies earned (revenues) to monies spent (expenses). The difference between revenues and expenses is the net income or loss from operations during the re-

porting period. A net income indicates that revenues exceeded expenses. The business made a profit. Net worth was increased. A net loss indicates that expenses exceeded revenues. The business lost money. Net worth was reduced. The income statement is represented by the equation:

Revenue − Expenses = Net Income (Net Loss)

Figure 7.2A provides the income statement for *Do It All Therapy, Inc.*, for the fiscal year ending September 30, 2005. Figure 7.2A is an annual income statement. Income statements can be prepared to cover any increment of time but should be prepared at a minimum, once per year. A more frequent time interval should reflect management's need for performance information. The income statement is also called an earnings statement, statement of operations, profit and loss statement, and revenue and expenses statement. The income statement can reflect a past or future time frame. The scope of the income statement, as discussed, is the whole organization. However, the income statement format is also used to reflect the profit (loss) of discrete parts of larger organization. Financial planning, often called budgeting, uses the income statement format to reflect the anticipated performance of each discrete department or function. These discrete departments are usually referred to as cost centers or profit (loss) centers. A true cost center will have an expense budget, but no directly related revenue. A profit (loss) center will have both an expense and revenue budget. Physical therapy departments are profit (loss) centers. Departmental budgets are then combined to form the budget for the whole organization. The income statement is also a key part of any business plan. See Chapters 3, 8, and 14 for additional information on business planning.

REVENUE

Revenue is income. A health care business has several potential sources of revenue.

- Sale of service
- Sale of products
- Gain from investments
- Philanthropic gifts
- Assumption of risk for services

Do It All Therapy, Incorporated Income Statement Year Ending September 30, 2005		
REVENUE:		
Gross Revenue		
Services	$832,818	
Equipment	60,000	
Total Operating Revenue		$892,818
Less:		
Allowance For Deductions		203,563
Gross Revenue Net Deductions		689,255
Non operating revenue		23,000
Total Revenue		$712,255
EXPENSES:		
Salaries	361,421	
Benefits	65,056	
FICA	28,191	
Education	6,300	
Recruitment	5,000	
Professional Services	11,000	
Purchased Services	600	
Supplies	51,095	
Travel	4,000	
Dues	2,000	
Equipment	1,200	
Rent/Lease	20,000	
Utilities	9,000	
Communication	3,375	
Environmental Services	5,300	
Accrued Expenses	40,083	
Insurance	6,100	
Total Expenses		$619,721
Net Income(Loss)		92,534
Taxes		$30,536
Net Income After Taxes		$61,998

FIGURE 7.2A. The income statement.

Do It All Therapy, Incorporated Income Statement Year Ending September 30, 2005		
REVENUE:		
Gross Revenue		
Services	$832,818	
Equipment Sales	40,000	
Equipment Rental	20,000	
Total Operating Revenue		$892,818
Allowance for deductions		
Medicare	88,389	
Medicaid	35,713	
Managed Care	40,177	
Commercial	8,928	
Charity Care	8,928	
Self Pay	21,428	
Total Deductions		203,563
Gross Revenue Net Deductions		$689,255
Non-operating revenue		
Interest Income	3,000	
Education Offerings	20,000	
Total Non-Operating Revenue		23,000
Total Revenue		$712,255
EXPENSES:		
Salaries		
Management	$70,096	
Professional	145,725	
Technical	33,280	
Support	49,920	
Clerical	62,400	
Total Salaries		$361,421
Benefits		65,056
FICA		28,191
Education		6,300
Recruitment		5,000
Professional Services		
Legal	$2,000	
Accounting	3,000	
Marketing	6,000	
Total Professional Service		$11,000
Purchased Services		
Storage	600	
Total Purchase Service		$600
Supplies		
Supplies, General	$4,595	
Supplies, Medical	10,500	
Supplies Sold	36,000	
Total Supplies		$51,095
Travel		$4,000
Dues		$2,000
Equipment		
Small Tools	$500	
Repair	200	
Replace	500	
Total Equipment		$1,200
Rent/Lease		
Equipment	$4,000	
Facilities	16,000	
Total Rent Lease		$20,000
Utilities		
Gas	$4,200	
Electric	4,800	
Total Utilities		$9,000
Communication		
Telephone	$3,000	
Pagers/Cellular Phone	375	
Total Communication		$3,375
Environmental Services		
Maintenance	$500	
Grounds	1,200	
Cleaning Service	2,600	
Linen Service	1,000	
Total Environmental Services		$5,300
Accrued Expenses		
Depreciation	$26,624	
Interest	13,459	
Total Accrued Expense		$40,083
Insurance		
Malpractice	$1,200	
Property/Casualty	1,500	
Auto	800	
Personal Liability	200	
Workers Compensation	2,400	
Total Insurance		$6,100
Total Expenses		$619,720
Net Income(Loss)		$92,535
Taxes		30,536
Net Income After Taxes		$61,999

FIGURE 7.2B. A detailed version of the income statement.

Under the accrual basis of accounting, revenue should be recorded in the period the revenue is made. Under a cash basis, revenue should be recorded when the money is received. Revenue from the sale of services or products is calculated by multiplying the price of the service or product times the number sold. The revenue recorded for items sold at discounted or government established prices should be adjusted by recording a deduction to revenue. Revenue is also classified by its origin. Revenue for the sale of services or product provided by the company is referred to as revenue from operations or, simply, operating revenue. Revenue from all other sources is referred to as non-operating revenue.

Income in return for the assumption of risk is relatively new to health care providers. Income in return for the assumption of risk is a characteristic of a capitated payment arrangement. Under capitation, the health care provider receives a set payment per period of time such as a payment per covered person per month. In return for the payment, the provider agrees to provide all agreed upon services to each covered person for the payment period. The payment amount remains unchanged no matter how much service is delivered. If the provider's expenses exceed the payment, this results in a loss. If no service is delivered, the provider still receives the set payment for the assumption of the risk of providing care. The concept of risk assumption and capitated payment is covered in more detail in Chapter 8. More specific information related to the development of the revenue section of an income statement will be provided later in this chapter.

EXPENSES

An expense is money spent to produce or purchase the services and products sold. Under the accrual basis of accounting, expense should be recorded in the time period the service or item is produced. Under a cash basis, expense would be recorded when the bill is paid. Figure 7.2A clearly shows that there are many more ways to spend money than to make money.

The amount of detail presented in a given version of an income statement depends on the needs of the user. Generally, the more day-to-day accountability a manager has for revenue and expense, the more detail they will require. Figure 7.2B is a more detailed version of the income statement as presented in Figure 7.2A. Managers with direct responsibility for revenue and expenses will typically require the level of detail presented in Figure 7.2B. Information related to the development of the expense section of an income statement and the types and management of expenses will be provided later in this chapter.

Cash Flow Statement

The availability of cash to cover short-term liabilities is of critical importance to a business. The last choice management wants to make is between defaulting on short-term liabilities or liquidation of needed assets. Cash flow management will help a business avoid this situation. A cash flow statement is used to track the sources, use and availability of cash. This financial statement will show how a business' cash position changes over time. Figure 7.3 illustrates the cash flow statement for *Do It All Therapy, Inc.* for the period October 1, 2004 through September 30, 2005. Typically, there are limited sources of cash but many uses. Cash flow statements can be prepared for past, present and future time periods. Cash flow statements that look to the future, called pro forma statements, can help management identify potential problems before they happen.

FINANCIAL ANALYSIS

Information presented in the balance sheet and income statement can be subjected to a variety of analytic techniques to assess a company's performance, financial position and relative financial viability. These techniques include comparative and ratio analysis (1).

Comparartive and Common-Size Financial Statements

More often than not, financial statements are used for comparative analysis. Comparison can be made between elements of the financial state-

Cash Flow Statement
Do It All Therapy, Incorporated
Year Ending September, 2005

Cash Balance, October 1, 2004

Cash in Bank	$39,517	
Petty Cash	500	
Cash Balance		$40,017

Sources of Cash

Cash from Operations	$51,613	
Accounts Receivable	751,910	
Owner Investment	-	
Total Sources of Cash		$803,523

Uses of Cash

Accounts Payable	213,110	
Payroll	495,568	
Owner Withdrawal	25,000	
Capital Purchase	4,862	
Land and Building	60,000	
Total Uses of Cash		798,540
Increase(Decrease) in Cash		$4,983

Cash Balance, September 30, 2005 $45,000

FIGURE 7.3. The cash flow statement.

ment, among time periods or between planned (budgeted) and actual performance. To aid in the comparison of financial statement entries, entries may be expressed in dollar amounts and as a percentage of a total category. For example, salary expense for FY 2005 could be expressed as an amount, $361,421 or a percentage of total expenses 58.3%. When comparative percentages are used to further define elements of a financial statement, then it is referred to as a common-size statement (7). Information on a financial statement can also be expressed for more than one date or period of time. Financial statements that provide information for more than one date or period of time are called comparative. Figure 7.4 illustrates an example of both a common-size and comparative financial statement.

Comparative analysis allows for the identification of trends and financial patterns. It is up to management to determine what information means relative to the performance of the business. In the case of our Figure 7.4 example, the statement shows an improved financial performance over time. Use of the common-size presentation demonstrates the relative expense related to some resources has decline as volume increased. This is an important phenomenon that will be addressed in more detail under the topic of cost-volume-profit analysis.

Financial Ratios

Another technique that can be used to compare financial performance over time, between

Do It All Therapy, Incorporated
Comparative Common-Size Income Statement
Year Ending September 30, 2005 and September 30, 2004

	FY 2005	FY 2004	Common-Size Percentages	
			FY 2005	FY 2004
REVENUE:				
Gross Revenue				
Services	$832,818	$666,254	93%	93.3%
Equipment	60,000	48,000	6.7%	6.7%
Total Operating Revenue	892,818	714,254	100.0%	100.0%
Less:				
Allowance for Deductions	203,563	162,850	22.8%	22.8%
Gross Revenue Net Deductions	689,255	551,404	96.8%	96.8%
Non-operating Revenue	23,000	18,400	3.2%	3.2%
Total Revenue	$712,255	$569,804	100.0%	100.0%
EXPENSES:				
Salaries	361,421	335,124	58.3%	54.8%
Benefits	65,056	60,322	10.5%	9.9%
FICA	28,191	25,805	4.5%	4.2%
Education	6,300	4,500	1.0%	0.7%
Recruitment	5,000	5,000	0.8%	0.8%
Professional Services	11,000	15,000	1.8%	2.5%
Purchased Services	600	480	0.1%	0.1%
Supplies	51,095	40,876	8.2%	6.7%
Travel	4,000	2,500	0.6%	0.4%
Dues	2,000	1,500	0.3%	0.2%
Equipment	1,200	850	0.2%	0.1%
Rent/Lease	20,000	63,300	3.2%	10.3%
Utilities	9,000	9,000	1.5%	1.5%
Communication	3,375	3,375	0.5%	0.6%
Environmental Services	5,300	5,300	0.9%	0.9%
Accrued Expenses	40,083	32,066	6.5%	5.2%
Insurance	6,100	7,100	1.0%	1.2%
Total Expenses	$619,721	$612,098	100.0%	100.0%
Net Income(Loss)	92,534	(42,294)	10.4%	-5.9%
Taxes	$30,536	0	33.0%	0.0%
Net Income After Taxes	$61,998	($42,294)	6.9%	-5.9%

FIGURE 7.4. Comparative and common-size income statement.

elements or between similar business, uses financial ratios. Financial ratio analysis refers to the use of the relationships between two mathematical quantities that have management significance. The idea behind the use of financial ratios is to summarize key financial data in a format that is easy to understand and evaluate (1). Liquidity, capital and activity ratios are types of ratios used to evaluate financial performance.

Liquidity Ratios

Liquidity ratios are used to assess a business' ability to meet its short-term financial obligations (liabilities). Liquidity ratios include:

Current Ratio

$$\text{Current Ratio} = \frac{\text{Current Assets}}{\text{Current Liabilities}}$$

Current ratio is the ratio of current assets to current liabilities. It is a common index of liquidity. The higher the ratio, the better a business is positioned to meet its current obligations (1).

Acid Test Ratio

$$\text{Acid Test Ratio} = \frac{\text{Cash} + \text{Marketable Securities}}{\text{Current Liabilities}}$$

The acid test ratio is the most rigorous test of liquidity. It takes into consideration only cash or those assets that can be immediately liquidated for cash. The higher the ratio, the better the business' potential to meet its current obligations (1).

Days Cash on Hand Ratio

$$\text{Days Cash on Hand} = \frac{\text{Cash} + \text{Short-Term Investment} + \text{Funded Depreciation Reserve}}{\text{Avg. Daily Operating Expense less Depreciation Reserve}}$$

Days Cash on Hand is the ratio of the business' most liquid assets to its average daily operating expenses. This ratio indicates the number of days a business could stay in operation with-

out incoming cash receipts. This ratio is an indicator of performance, but is also impacted by the cash management practices of the business. A higher number of Days Cash on Hand may decrease concern about a business' ability to cover day-to-day expenses. Too high a number may indicate a failure to maximize the potential for income in longer term investments.

Days in Net Accounts Receivable Ratio

$$\text{Days in Net Accounts Receivable} = \frac{\text{Accounts Receivable less Deductions}}{\text{Avg. Daily Operating Revenue}}$$

Days in Net Accounts Receivable is a measure of how long it takes to collect money owed (accounts receivable). A long or lengthening collection cycle can be indicative of future liquidity problems.

Capital Ratios

Capital ratios help assess the financing structure of the organization. Financing structure refers to the mix of debt (liabilities) to equity. Potential creditors will review capital ratios as a way to determine the current level of debt. The greater the proportion of debt to equity, the less likely that creditors will provide additional credit or loans. In addition, the greater the level of debt, the greater the expense of debt service. Debt service refers to debt related interest expense. The higher the debt service costs of a business, the more liquid assets the business must maintain to cover current liabilities. A high-debt service limits a business' resources that could be used for other purposes. Capital ratios include:

Debt Service Ratio

$$\text{Debt Service} = \frac{\text{Net Income} + \text{Depreciation}}{\text{Debt Principal Payment} + \text{Interest}}$$

The Debt Service Ratio is a measure of a business' ability to pay debt related to principal and interest on current debt. The higher this ratio, the better able the business is to cover costs of current debt and to handle additional debt in the future.

Long-Term Debt to Fixed Assets Ratio

$$\text{Long-Term Debt to Fixed Assets} = \frac{\text{Long-Term Debt}}{\text{Net Fixed Assets}}$$

The Long-Term Debt to Fixed Assets Ratio is the proportion of fixed assets that are financed through long-term debt. The higher the ratio, the larger the percentage of fixed assets that have been financed through loans or other forms of financing. Potential lenders use this ratio as an indication of a business' ability to handle additional debt. Potential creditors will become increasingly hesitant to extend a business additional credit as this ratio increases.

Long-Term Debt to Equity

$$\text{Long-Term Debt to Equity} = \frac{\text{Long-Term Debt}}{\text{Equity}}$$

Long-Term Debt to Equity is the ratio of both sources of long-term funding. The higher the ratio, the greater the amount of long-term funding from long-term debt. The higher this ratio, the more difficult it will be to obtain additional long-term financing.

Activity Ratios

Activity ratios help us understand the relationship between a business's revenue and expenses. Using information from both the balance sheet and the income statement, activity ratios measure the use of assets to cover the expenses of the business (1).

Operating Margin

$$\text{Operating Margin} = \frac{\text{Total Revenue} - \text{Total Expenses}}{\text{Total Revenue}}$$

Operating Margin is the ratio of net income to total revenue. Operating margin can be calculated for all or discrete parts of a business. The higher the operating margin, the better. This ratio provides a basis for comparison of the economic performance of one business to industry standards, previous performance and other investment opportunities. Operating margin can also help a

business assess the relative contribution of one operating unit to another.

Return on Assets

$$\text{Return on Assets} = \frac{\text{Income} + \text{Interest Expense}}{\text{Total Assets}}$$

Return on Assets is the relationship of total income to the total investment (assets) of the business. Return on assets can be calculated for all or discrete parts of a business. The higher the return on assets, the better. This ratio provides a basis for comparison of the economic performance of one business to industry standards, previous performance and other investment opportunities. Return on Assets may be used as a criteria for selecting between alternative business strategies.

Performance Indicators

Financial ratios offer a set of standardized assessment tools that allow for the comparison of current financial performance to past performance, current expectations as well as the performance of similar businesses on an individual or industry-wide basis. Skula (8) suggests some additional financial performance indicators that may be of particular value for assessing the performance of a physical therapy practice.

- Volume
  - Referrals
  - Scheduled treatments
  - Completed (billed) treatments
  - Visits
  - Case mix
- Revenues
  - Net revenue per referral
  - Net revenue per visit
  - Net revenue as a percentage of charge
- Costs
  - Labor cost per volume measure
  - Nonlabor cost per volume measure
  - Employee benefits as a percentage of salary
- Efficiency
  - Productive hours paid per billed unit of service (UOS)
  - Non-productive hours paid per UOS
  - Visits per referral
  - Visits per referral by diagnosis, age or other defining factor
  - Billed UOS per visit

Performance indicators can be used to create a report card for business performance. For an example see Chapter 3, Table 3.9. Management should use performance indicators that are meaningful to the organization. Through careful selection, clear performance expectations, sometimes called performance benchmarks, can be established and communicated to members of the organization. Organizational performance indicators should be tracked and trended, and the outcome should be shared with everyone who has a role in meeting performance targets (2).

There is an increasing trend in health care toward the use of industry-performance standards to evaluate the performance of individual health care businesses. Industry-performance standards can help management assess performance in a rapidly changing environment when historical performance has less relevance, set reasonable improvement targets and for competitive positioning. However, the use of external performance standards should be done only with a complete understanding about the source and applicability of the standard. Care should be taken to be sure that selected industry standards are clearly applicable, represent comparable data, and that regional and organizational differences have been identified. Benchmarks should be adjusted accordingly.

Performance assessment, as a part of marketing strategy, was discussed in Chapter 3, Marketing. Several variations of the above noted performance indicators were used in the sample worksheet provided in that chapter, e.g., Table 3.9.

KEEPING THE BOOKS

To be useful, financial information must be accurate. Accuracy is achieved when the recording of financial information consistently follows an understood set of guiding principles. These principles provide direction on how financial information is collected and recorded. In this section, systems necessary to implement those guiding principles will be discussed.

Chart Of Accounts

An account is a category of asset, liability, owner's equity, revenue or expense. A chart of accounts is simply a listing of all of a business' accounts. The chart of accounts is often arranged in financial statement order (6) as is the listing above. The chart of accounts can be viewed as a set of files, with a single file holding only specific types of information that is to be entered into the file at specific times. Each file is identified by a name and numerical code (1). The numerical code is used to classify and to differentiate accounts.

The number and types of accounts will depend on the size, type, and complexity of the business. Management information needs will influence the number and degree of specificity of the chart of accounts. For example, management may wish to have one general account to record revenue from equipment sold. If it is important to know the sales revenue for each type of equipment sold, management may choose to have one account for each type or category of equipment. The total of these equipment revenue accounts would then be combined to determine total revenue from equipment sold. Figure 7.5 provides an example of a chart of accounts at the primary classification level. Each of the major account types from the balance sheet and income statement is assigned a series of numbers that define the characteristics of the account. Within each numerical series, the major accounts are further defined by subgroupings of funds or subgroupings of accounts.

Figure 7.6 provides a more detailed example of numeric coding for the expense category of salaries and benefits. Coding logic that has been used to assign a numeric code to each of the subclasses, such as employee type, is provided. The chart of accounts is specific to a business. Once the logic of the numeric coding is provided, it should be easily understood.

ACCOUNTS RECEIVABLE MANAGEMENT

Accounts receivable management is the financial management of revenue. Good revenue manage-

Do It All Therapy, Incorporated Chart of Accounts Primary Classification September 30, 2005			
Code	**Type**	**Subcode**	**Fund**
100-199	Assets	110 120 130	Operating Fund Capital Equipment Fund Other Funds
200-299	Liabilities	210 220 230	Operating Fund Capital Equipment Fund Other Fund
300-399	Capital Accounts	310 320 330	Operating Fund Capital Equipment Fund Other Fund
400-499	Revenue Accounts	410 420 430	Patient Service Revenue Deductions From Revenue Other Revenue
500-599	Expense Accounts	510 520 530 540 550	Patient Services Support Services Management Services Purchased Services Other Expenses

FIGURE 7.5. Sample chart of accounts.

ment results in the maximization of income from operations. Revenue management involves several activities. These activities include:

- Measuring services and products for sale
- Setting prices for the products and services to be sold
- Setting billing, credit and collections policies and processes
- Invoicing the customer
- Payment receipt management
- Cash management
- Calculation of deductions and allowances
- Payment posting

- Account reconciliation
- Financial reporting

Charge Master (Fee Schedule)

A key element of the accounts receivable management system is the charge master. The charge master is a listing of services and products that the business offers for sale to its customers. Each listing on the charge master, alternately called the fee schedule, is defined by a numeric charge code, description and unit measure of the product or service, and price. As with

Do It All Therapy, Incorporated
Chart of Accounts
September 30, 2005

500-599		**Expense**
		Salaries
531.10		Management
511.10		Therapist
511.12		Technical
521.10		Billing
521.12		Clerical
		Benefits
532.10		Management
512.10		Therapist
512.12		Technical
522.10		Billing
522.12		Clerical
		FICA
533.10		Management
513.10		Therapist
513.12		Technical
523.10		Billing
523.12		Clerical

Summary - Coding Logic

Digit	Meaning	Code	Technical Salaries
1st	Type of Account	5	Expense
2nd	SubGroup/Fund	1	Patient Services
3rd	Account Class	1	Salaries
4th-5th	SubClass/Department	.12	Technical

FIGURE 7.6. Coding logic for a chart of accounts.

the chart of accounts, the charge master will vary based on the size and complexity of the business. It will also vary based on management and customer information needs. The more specific the information needs of management, the more specific the charges. For example, a therapy practice that sells equipment may need a single charge code or several different charges for the items sold. Billing records are often used to track utilization of products and services by patient type. This information is important for managed care contracting.

Operating Revenue

Gross revenue from operations is equal to volume of sales times the price of what is sold. Revenue net deductions is gross revenue less deductions for discounts and other payment allowances. Net revenue is a function of price, sales volume, payer mix and case mix. When financial projections are required, estimates of volume, payer mix and case mix must be made. Payer mix and case mix projections are of great importance to health care providers.

Gross Revenue

Gross Revenue = Units Sold × Selling Price Per Unit

Net Revenue

**Net Revenue =
Gross Revenue − Deductions From Revenue**

Deduction From Revenue

Deductions = Discounts + Payment Allowances

Case Mix and Service Utilization Projections

Case mix refers to the mix of patients by diagnostic grouping. Case mix is used to estimate the volume of services required by patients based on historical service utilization patterns. For example, if *Do It All Therapy, Inc.'s* demand forecast indicates that the clinic will receive approximately 100 referrals for adults complaining of acute back strain, then *Do It All Therapy, Inc.* follows a plan of care that includes, on average, five, 45-minute treatment visits. *Do It All Therapy, Inc.* charges $35 per 15 minutes of treatment. Total charges (gross rev-

enue) for each patient would be $525 ($105 per visit × 5 visits).

To use case mix information, management must have in place a mechanism for tracking the utilization of services by patient diagnosis. Although this may sound simple enough, it requires the development a method of sorting charges by diagnosis. Historically, the patient information and financial data of health care businesses have not been merged. Often, to obtain service utilization by case mix, a manual review of medical records has been required, an approach that is always expensive and often of dubious accuracy. This is a great example of how organization-wide planning could improve the quality of the organization financial information. Chapter 3 provides more detailed information about service-demand forecasting. Chapter 10 provides additional information about information management.

Payer Mix and Deductions From Revenue

Payer mix reflects by percentage of total charges, the source of payment for services and products sold. See Figure 7.7 for an example of payer mix and revenue deduction projections for *Do It All Therapy, Inc.* Assuming the discounts or allowance for each payer type are known, payer mix can be used to project deductions from revenue. In the case of *Do It All Therapy, Inc.,* Figure 7.7 tells us that for patients covered under managed care contracts, the business will collect 85% of what is billed. Continuing with the case of *Do It All Therapy, Inc.* and the 100 adult back strain patients, the method and impact of revenue deductions can be easily demonstrated. If all 100 adult back strain patients had managed care insurance, net revenue per patient would be $446.25 ($525 per patient × .85 of billed charges). If all 100 of the patients with back strain were covered under the Medicaid program, net revenue per patient would be $262.50 ($525 per patient × .50 of billed charges).

Charge and Payment Methodology

Gross revenue equals the volume of products or services sold times the price charged. Unfortunately, in health care, the price charged is rarely the price paid, as the payer for health care is seldom the user of the services. Rather than individual customers, health care providers receive the largest percentage of payment from the government and other large-volume customers. Size and control of the market allows third party payers to negotiate or set payment rates that are standardized across payers and/or below the prices charged by the health care provider. To maximize the amount actually paid, health care organizations need to set charges to accommodate varying payment rates and practices.

WHY CHARGE MORE THAN YOU KNOW YOU ARE GOING TO BE PAID?

A common question for managers new to health care finance is, "Why charge more than you know you are going to be paid?" The reason is a practical one: to maximize revenue under health care's unique third party payer system. Under this system, the major portion of a provider's payment comes from three types of payers:

1. Private health insurance
2. Governmental health payment plans
3. Private payment sources

A minor, but growing percentage of payment, comes from the patient themselves. Commercial (private) health care insurance plans typically use standardized payment schedules that determine the amount that they will pay for a specific health care service. This is called the Usual and Customary Rate (UCR). Often, they will pay the provider charges up to the UCR. The patient is sometimes required to pay the difference. Governmental payers, such as Medicare, use a variety of payment methods ranging from paying some percentage of the provider cost (expenses) to paying a fixed amount per service regardless of the health care provider's cost. Payments from government health insurance programs vary based on type of service, type of provider and patient status. Businesses are required to charge all customers the same price for the same product or service unless there is a real difference in the providers costs of delivery of service to that customer. As a result, the health care provider must set charges to maximize the potential payment from all sources while using one charge level for all patients. All of these factors can be accommodated if the charge rate is set somewhere above the highest payment rate. Contract agreements can then be used to discount services to high volume payers. Volume discounting is allowable because volume has the effect of decreasing the cost of a unit of product or service. It should be stated that this approach assumes that the provider's cost is lower than its charges for products and services. This, and other concepts of cost management, will be discussed later in this chapter.

PAYMENT BASIS

Measurement of Products and Services For Sale

To assign a consistent price, a unit measurement must be associated with each discrete in-

Do It All Therapy, Incorporated Payer Mix and Schedule of Deductions September 30, 2005				
Payer Type	**Percent Revenue**	**Percent Discount**	**Revenue**	**Discount**
Medicare	33%	30%	$294,630	$88,389
Medicaid	8%	50%	$71,425	35,713
Manage Care	30%	15%	$267,845	40,177
Commercial	20%	5%	$178,564	8,928
Charity Care	1%	100%	$8,928	8,928
Self Pay	8%	30%	$71,425	21,428
Total	100%		$892,818	$203,563

FIGURE 7.7. Calculation of deductions from revenue.

crement of service or product for sale. A unit measure for service can be based on time or activity. A time-based unit could be a minute, an hour, a month or any other specific increment of time. An activity measure could be a visit, a modality, a treatment, or a procedure composed of several discrete procedures. It could be an entire course of care. Products are measured by the amount of product sold. A dose, a pair, one, a package, an ounce are all measures of amount. Even a small business like *Do It All Therapy, Inc.* will use several different types of measurements to define its services and products. In the case of *Do It All Therapy, Inc.,* measurements are required to define increments of service, supplies, and equipment to be rented and sold. Units of measure will vary between organizations. There is no one right way to select the units of measure a business will use. Some factors that should influence the selection process (3) include:

- The unit of measure used should be a logical choice for the product or service. If a product is always used in pairs, it should be packaged and sold in pairs. If multiple discrete services are billed to the same customer, a common unit of measure will make more sense to the customer. For example, all fifteen minute units or all procedures.
- The unit of measure should allow for accurate cost allocation. If the largest expense of a service is related to staff costs that are paid based on time, then a time based unit of measure may make cost allocation easier and more accurate.
- Units of measure should be standardized within the same organization for the same products or services. If a service charge for therapy is based on 15-minute time increments in one department, they should be based on 15-minute time increments in all therapy areas.
- When selecting a unit of measure, it never hurts to consider what the customer is familiar with and what the competition is using. This is essential for price sensitive products and services.

Cost-Based Reimbursement

As noted previously, governmental payers, such as Medicare, pay for some services under a cost based methodology. Under cost-based reimbursement, the provider of services is paid the lesser of charges or full allowable cost plus an additional amount to cover the depreciation of facilities and capital equipment. Allowable costs are defined by the payer but are generally limited to costs that can be shown to contribute directly to patient care. Under some cost-based reimbursement programs, total allowable cost is capped. Under a capped program, the provider is paid the lesser of charges, allowable costs or capped costs (3).

Fee-For-Service Payment

Traditionally, health care providers have been paid on a fee-for-service basis. Under a fee-for-service system, the provider delivers, bills and is paid for each discrete increment of service or product provided to a patient. Fees might be discounted, but payment is calculated for each increment billed and combined to create a total billed amount. Fee-for-service payment methodology means that health care businesses must define measurements for each discrete increment of service or product. The more diverse the care provided, the more extensive the charge master (fee schedule). Under fee-for-service payment, the care provided to a back strain patient would be billed for each specific unit of evaluation, exercise, and modality provided. A single visit might result in several billed charges.

Case Rate Payment

Competitive changes in the health care environment have lead to the use of a more comprehensive case rate as the basis for measurement and payment. Under the case rate payment method, the health care business offers to provide 1) all of some product or service or 2) all products and services required for the management of a specific patient's case at a pre-set charge. If the cost of providing the required products and services is less than the case payment rate, the provider makes money. If the average case costs more than the case payment rate, the provider loses money.

The broader the scope of services included under the case rate, the greater the potential variability in cost and the greater the provider risk of incurring unexpected cost. To protect the provider and payer under case rate payment, both parties must agree to the definition of case.

There should be mutual understanding about what is and what is not included under the case rate. This understanding should be supported by a written definition of the case and included services. When does service under the case start and stop? What products are included as a part of the case? Because case rates cover larger increments of product and/or service, accurate definition and pricing are essential. Per case pricing is referred to as a risk arrangement. The risk occurs because the provider is responsible for the delivery of care even if the case cost exceeds the case price.

The importance of accurate definition and pricing can be demonstrated by returning to the *Do It All Therapy, Inc.*, example and the 100 patients with back strain. As you will recall, *Do It All Therapy, Inc.* has determined that it is currently paid an average of $446.25 for services per case after deductions. If asked to provide services to adults with back strain on a case-rate basis, would $500 be a reasonable payment? The answer depends on the definition of what is covered. For the sake of discussion, let's assume that the case rate covers only required physical therapy services. Under that definition, a case rate of $500 may sound reasonable. But, what if 1 patient out of 100, who comes in with a diagnosis of back strain, does not respond to the usual treatment? Instead, the patient requires extensive modalities and manual therapy over a period of several months for a total of 36 treatments of 60 minutes each. The charges for this one case would be $5040. If the average charge for all other 99 cases was at the expected $525, this one outlier would raise the average charge to $565. At $565 per case, the $500 discount increases from the planned $2500 to an unplanned $6500 discount from charges. Such outlier cases have the potential to harm a small health care provider business.

What could have prevented this situation was a clearer definition of when the case coverage starts and stops. A major deviation from the routine course of care could have been defined as being outside of the case rate. Products that are to be included in the case rate should also be clearly defined.

The Medicare program reimburses hospitals for inpatient care using a case-rate payment system. Hospitals receive a pre-set payment for providing inpatient care to a Medicare covered patient. Each Medicare inpatient is assigned by diagnosis to a diagnostically related group (DRG). The payment rate is determined by the patient's DRG.

Per Diem Rate Payment

Applicable to inpatient and daily outpatient services, per diem pricing has more risk than fee-for-service, but less risk than a case-rate payment. Per diem payment uses a day as the increment of time for service delivery. Usually, the per diem rate stays the same through the course of the patient's care. This is important because the initial days of the patient's treatment are generally more service intense and costly than are later days (1). Day therapy programs have been known to use a per diem rate charge structure.

Capitated Payments

Capitated payment methodology is relatively new to health care. It is a payment method that is utilized by managed care insurance plans. Capitation methodology can only be used by managed care plans that have by plan design the right to direct all patients to the selected provider for the capitated service. Capitated payment allows the managed care insurer to shift some of the financial risk of care delivery from themselves to the health care provider. Under capitation arrangements, the provider agrees to accept a set fee in return for the delivery of specified health care services to a specified group of managed care plan enrollees. An enrollee is an individual who has paid a premium for coverage under a health insurance plan. Theoretically, provider payment under capitation should be based on historical utilization of services by the enrollee group and provider cost for care delivery. The utilization data is used to project the future volume and cost of service utilization. The provider then negotiates a set fee at a level that represents projected cost plus a reasonable profit margin. Fees are generally structured as a set fee per enrollee per month.

Under capitation payment arrangements, a provider will make money if the cost of providing services is lower than their capitation payment. The provider will lose money if the cost of providing care exceeds the total capitation payment. In practice, providers have experienced difficulty obtaining accurate utilization data and making accurate cost projections. If either volume or cost are underestimated, the provider is likely to lose money. The managed care plan pays only the agreed upon per enrollee rate. This allows the insurer to do accurate financial planning and set premium rates at a level that covers their committed cost and provides for a profit margin. The provider takes the risk of loss in return for the potential of a profit and the guarantee of a larger market share.

Third Party Payments Practices

There are other payment practices that impact provider revenue. Acceptance of assignment and application of usual and customary standards are two of importance. Frequently, nongovernmental commercial third party payers use a preset payment schedule, called a UCR schedule. Patients may be asked by providers to sign an agreement that they will pay the difference between charges and the UCR payment made by their insurance carrier.

Assignment is a term associated with charge reimbursement. When a health care business has agreed to accept assignment, it means that it has agreed to accept as full payment the UCR for that third party payer. In that case, the health care business will not bill that patient for the difference between the UCR and their charge. The patient may still be billed for co-payments. A co-payment refers to that part of the health care charge that is the responsibility of the enrollee. The amount of co-payment is determined by the insurance coverage plan purchased by the enrollee. Chapter 8 provides additional information regarding health care insurance and provider reimbursement.

Non-Operating Revenue

Non-operating revenue refers to incoming money that adds to the value of the business but does not result directly from the sale of product and/or services. Two possible sources of non-operating revenue are investment income and gifts. Investment income might come from an interest bearing savings account or other investment instruments. Health care organizations are often the recipients of philanthropic gifts. Such gifts are classified as non-operating income.

ACCOUNTS PAYABLE MANAGEMENT

The accounts payable function of the financial management system is involved in the recording and payment of money owed by the business to its creditors. Management of the accounts payable function comes through control of the process by which the business can incur debt. To maintain accounts payable within acceptable limits, a business must have adequate control of the purchasing process. Elements of an effective accounts payable function include:

- Inventory management policies and procedures
- Purchasing policies and procedures
- Policies on expense authorization
- Internal audit

EXPENSE MANAGEMENT

Managing expenses effectively requires a knowledge of types of expenses, what expenses can be controlled, how expenses are controlled and how expenses behave in relation to volume of goods and/or services produced. With this knowledge, expenses can be projected for any future volume of sales. The ability to project volume and related expenses is the foundation for financial planning and for creating an operating budget.

Types of Expenses

There are two types of expenses a business can incur: operating and capital. Both types of expenses are related to the production of goods and services. Operating expenses are associated with the cost of resources that are used in the production of goods and services within a specific period of time. Capital expenses are associated with the purchase of equipment, facilities and other high-priced items that will contribute to the production of goods and services over an extended period of time. Salary expense is an example of an operating expense. An hour worked in 1 week will have no value for the organization in future weeks. The purchase of a clinic building is an example of a capital expense. A building purchased in one time period will continue to contribute to the production of goods and services over many years.

A business will often use a dollar threshold such as $500 to differentiate operating from capital expenditures. Equipment with an extended life with a value equal to or greater than the threshold will be classified as a capital expense. The classification of expenses can impact reimbursement under Medicare and Medicaid cost based payment programs.

Calculation of Operating Expenses

There are many types of operating expenses. Figure 7.2B lists several types of expenses. These expenses are associated with the time period covered by the income statement. All of the expenses listed in Figure 7.2B are operating expenses that are common to therapy practice. For financial planning and budgeting, some expenses must be calculated. Others are recorded over time and then transferred to the income statement. Some key categories are labor, supply and accrued expenses.

LABOR EXPENSES

Labor expenses include costs related to personnel employment and compensation, including salary, insurance programs, recruitment, development, health and safety.

Salary Expense Calculation

Salary expense is a function of work hours paid times the hourly rate of pay.

Salary Expense

Salary Expense = Labor hours paid × Rate of pay

Salary expense management uses both the hours paid and expense dollars to track labor productivity. Hours paid are commonly expressed in terms of a Full Time Equivalent (FTE). A FTE represents the work hour equivalent to one full-time employee whose compensation is based on a 40-hour work week. It should be noted that an FTE does not always mean one full-time employee. An FTE can be filled by one full-time employee or two or more part-time employees.

Full Time Equivalent(FTE)

FTE = 40 worked hours per week × 52 weeks per year
also
FTE = 2080 paid hours per employment year

Hours paid can be categorized into productive and non-productive. Productive hours are those hours an employee spends performing work that contributes directly to the production of services or products. The organization defines productive and non-productive hours. For example, a physical therapy practice might define productive hours as direct care hours or billable service hours. Non-productive hours might include vacation time, education time, travel time, sick time, and holidays. These all represent time for which an employee may be paid, but which is not available to perform productive work. Productivity standards are projections of the amount of work that can be performed by a worker within a specific time period.

Productivity standards are used to project the work hours and related salary expense required to perform the volume of work to be done. The projection of work hours paid starts with the prediction of the demand for service or product volume for a period of time. A productivity standard is used to project the number of FTEs that will be required to fill the projected demand for services. Paid hours needed to fill the projected demand can then be multiplied by the rate of pay to reach an estimated salary expense. Management can then compare actual salary expense, FTEs and volume of work produced to evaluate worker and organizational performance.

Figure 7.8 demonstrates how productivity standards and the number of FTEs are used to determine the volume of work and related revenue that can be produced by *Do It All Therapy, Inc.,* employees. Figure 7.9A–C are FTE, Salary Rate and Annual Salary Schedules for *Do It All Therapy, Inc.,* for the fiscal year ending September 30, 2005. These schedules demonstrate how FTEs and salary expense are estimated during the budgeting process.

Other labor related expenses that must be incurred by most businesses are related employee benefits, employment payroll tax (FICA), recruitment, orientation, ongoing training and development, bonus and incentive pay. Employee benefits includes such things as vacation and sick pay, health, life and disability insurance, tuition reimbursement, membership in health and wellness programs, retirement plans, matching programs for employee savings and child care. The size and financial condition of a company will largely determine the benefits it can offer to employees. Generally, the larger the company, the greater the value of the benefits offered employees. *Do It All Therapy, Inc.,* spends an amount equal to 18% of salary on employee benefits. Many companies are moving away from offering a standard benefit package. Instead, employees are given a dollar amount to spend and may select the benefits they want from a benefits menu. These are commonly referred to as flexible benefits plans.

SUPPLY EXPENSES

Supply expenses vary greatly between organizations. In therapy practice, supplies are typically divided into four categories.

1. Office supplies
2. Medical supplies
3. Minor equipment
4. Supplies to be sold

Office and medical supplies are consumed during the delivery of care. Minor equipment may be used over a short period of time but has both a low cost and a short useful life. Supplies to be sold are purchased and placed into inventory until they are resold to customers. The inventory entry under the assets section of the balance sheet represents the value of supplies in inventory as of the balance sheet date.

PURCHASED AND PROFESSIONAL SERVICES

This expense category is used to account for services purchased to support the work of the organization. Purchased services can be clinical or support services. Fees paid for legal services, financial management and accounting services, consulting services, contract clinical staff, or educators would be accounted for under purchased or professional service.

ACCRUED EXPENSES

Accrued expenses are incurred, but not paid, over a period time. Accrued expenses are paid either on a regular schedule or as requested by the creditor. Accrued paid sick time is an example of an accrued expense. Sick time may be earned by an employee each pay period. Sick time is paid when as employee is ill. It may also be paid when an employee retires, leaves the organization or at the end of an absence free time period. Alternately, the accrued expense might never be paid. Responsibility for payment is based on the terms of the accrual. The concept of accrual would also apply to an arrangement in which consulting services are provided over a period of time with payment to be made after a satisfactory conclusion to the project. An accrued expense must be kept on the books as a liability until it is paid or the business is certain it will never need to be paid. If this is not done, expenses will be understated in the accrual period and overstated in the period they are paid.

Capital Expenses

Capital expenses are associated with the purchase of equipment, buildings, land and large pieces of equipment. Most expenses directly related to the start-up of a new business or business component may also be capitalized. Capital expenses are purchases that are expected to have an extended useful life. Useful life is the period of time over which a item will continue to be used in the production of goods or service. The definition of capital expenses may vary somewhat between organizations, as the acquisition value of the item

Do It All Therapy, Inc.
Productivity Schedule
Fiscal Year 2005

Position Category	UOS per Day	FTEs @ 2080 Hours	UOS per FTE per Year	Annual UOS per FTE Type	Average UOS Charge	Potential Revenue Per FTE	Potential Revenue per FTE Type
Manager/Owner	0	1.00	0	0	$35	$0	$0
Physical Therapist	24	1.60	5,688	9,101	$35	$199,080	$318,528
Occupational Therapist	24	1.00	5,688	5,688	$35	$199,080	$199,080
Speech Language Path	24	0.50	5,688	2,844	$35	$199,080	$99,540
PTA/COTA	26	1.00	6,162	6,162	$35	$215,670	$215,670
Billing Clerk	0	1.00	0	0	0	0	0
Rehab Aide	0	2.00	0	0	0	0	0
Secretary	0	3.00	0	0	0	0	0
Total		11.10		23,795	$35		$832,818

Assumptions:
1. Days worked per FTE = 260 - (6 Holidays, 3 education days, 14 vacation and sick days) = 237 days per year.
2. UOS per FTE per year = 237 days X UOS per FTE per Day.
3. Annual UOS per Position Type = Total FTE's per position category X UOS per FTE .
4. Annual Revenue per FTE = Annual UOS X Average UOS Charge.

FIGURE 7.8. Sample productivity schedule.

Do It All Therapy, Inc.
Fiscal Year 2005
FTE and Salary Schedule

FTE Per Position Type	Oct	Nov	Dec	Jan	Feb	Mar	Apr	May	Jun	Jul	Aug	Sep	Annual
Manager/Owner	1.00	1.00	1.00	1.00	1.00	1.00	1.00	1.00	1.00	1.00	1.00	1.00	1.00
PT	1.60	1.60	1.60	1.60	1.60	1.60	1.60	1.60	1.60	1.60	1.60	1.60	1.60
OT	1.00	1.00	1.00	1.00	1.00	1.00	1.00	1.00	1.00	1.00	1.00	1.00	1.00
Speech	0.50	0.50	0.50	0.50	0.50	0.50	0.50	0.50	0.50	0.50	0.50	0.50	0.50
PTA/COTA	1.00	1.00	1.00	1.00	1.00	1.00	1.00	1.00	1.00	1.00	1.00	1.00	1.00
Billing Clerk	1.00	1.00	1.00	1.00	1.00	1.00	1.00	1.00	1.00	1.00	1.00	1.00	1.00
Rehab Aide	2.00	2.00	2.00	2.00	2.00	2.00	2.00	2.00	2.00	2.00	2.00	2.00	2.00
Secretary	3.00	3.00	3.00	3.00	3.00	3.00	3.00	3.00	3.00	3.00	3.00	3.00	3.00
Total	11.10	11.10	11.10	11.10	11.10	11.10	11.10	11.10	11.10	11.10	11.10	11.10	11.10

FIGURE 7.9A. Schedule of full time equivalents (FTE).

Do It All Therapy, Inc.

Fiscal Year 2005

FTE and Salary Schedule

FTE Per Position Type	Rate/ltr
Manager/Owner	33.7
PT	22.60
OT	22.60
Speech	22.60
PTA/COTA	16.00
Billing Clerk	8.00
Rehab Aide	8.00
Secretary	10.00

FIGURE 7.9B. Salary rate schedule.

is considered. Each business has to set a minimum acquisition value for capital expenditures. For example, *Do It All Therapy, Inc.,* will capitalize any extended life purchase or business start-up with a value equal to or greater than $400.

CALCULATION OF A CAPITAL EXPENSE

Capital expense should reflect all expenses related to the acquisition of a capital asset and all expenses that are incurred to get the equipment ready to use. Expenses which should be considered for inclusion are listed below:

- Capital Equipment
  - Shipping
  - Site preparation
  - Installation
  - Required staff training
  - Consulting or legal services
  - Interest, if money was borrowed to make the purchase
- Land and Buildings
  - Real estate commissions
  - Escrow and legal fees
  - Titling costs
  - Accrued property taxes
  - Land preparation
  - Surveys
  - Clearing and landscaping
  - Capital improvements such as sewer and roads
  - Removal of existing structures

Do It All Therapy, Inc.
Fiscal Year 2005
Salary Schedule

Salary Per Month Per Position Type	Oct	Nov	Dec	Jan	Feb	Mar	Apr	May	Jun	Jul	Aug	Sep	Annual
Manager/Owner	5,841	5,841	5,841	5,841	5,841	5,841	5,841	5,841	5,841	5,841	5,841	5,841	70,096
PT	6,268	6,268	6,268	6,268	6,268	6,268	6,268	6,268	6,268	6,268	6,268	6,268	75,213
OT	3,917	3,917	3,917	3,917	3,917	3,917	3,917	3,917	3,917	3,917	3,917	3,917	47,008
Speech	1,959	1,959	1,959	1,959	1,959	1,959	1,959	1,959	1,959	1,959	1,959	1,959	23,504
PTA/COTA	2,773	2,773	2,773	2,773	2,773	2,773	2,773	2,773	2,773	2,773	2,773	2,773	33,280
Billing Clerk	1,387	1,387	1,387	1,387	1,387	1,387	1,387	1,387	1,387	1,387	1,387	1,387	16,640
Rehab Aide	2,773	2,773	2,773	2,773	2,773	2,773	2,773	2,773	2,773	2,773	2,773	2,773	33,280
Secretary	5,200	5,200	5,200	5,200	5,200	5,200	5,200	5,200	5,200	5,200	5,200	5,200	62,400
Total Salary Expense	30,118	30,118	30,118	30,118	30,118	30,118	30,118	30,118	30,118	30,118	30,118	30,118	361,421

FIGURE 7.9C. Salary schedule.

- Building renovations
- Architectural and design fees
- Insurance during the renovation or construction phase

All of these expenses may be capitalized as part of the acquisition value. If a business chooses to lease rather than buy a capital asset, it may enter into a capital lease. If the lease covers the projected life of the asset, then the lease costs may qualify as a capital expense. Lease arrangements should be evaluated on an individual basis.

DEPRECIATION OF CAPITAL ASSETS

Capital expenses are treated differently than are operating expenses. The matching principle requires that the capital asset value consumed during a time period be reflected as an offset to revenue from the same period. To maintain the matching principle, capital expenses must to spread across an asset's useful life. The value consumed during a specific period is reflected in operating expenses as depreciation.

Depreciation

$$\text{Annual Depreciation} = \frac{\text{Capital Expense}}{\text{Useful Life (Years)}}$$

Land is an exception because it has an unlimited useful life. Land is not subject to depreciation (9). Figure 7.1 indicates that *Do It All Therapy, Inc.* has $330,000 invested in capital assets, $40,000 in land, $90,000 in buildings and $200,000 in equipment. Under liabilities, you will note that $225,000 of this asset value is financed through long-term notes payable. Figure 7.2B shows an annual depreciation expense of $26,264. Figure 7.10 is the Depreciation Schedule for *Do It All Therapy, Inc.* for FY 2005. Note that land holdings are excluded.

As assets are added at various times and have different useful life estimates, depreciation should be calculated on an item specific or grouped basis. Many businesses will apply a first year convention. When this is done, only half of the annual depreciation is an expense the first year. Following years are at the annual rate until the full depreciation value.

EVALUATION OF CAPITAL EXPENDITURES

Because resources are limited, management should determine the potential contribution of a proposed capital purchase. Sometimes called a cost/benefit analysis, this is done to determine the short- and long-term financial impact of the purchase. The results of the cost/benefit analysis can help management make better purchasing decisions and/or better prioritize multiple capital purchase requests. Calculation of the payback period and the expected return on investment are two methods used to assess the impact of capital purchases.

Payback period is the length of time it will take to recover the entire cost of a capital investment from the annual net cash flow that results from the investment. A shorter payback period means a better investment. Payback is calculated by dividing the capital investment by the projected annual net cash flow. Net cash flow equals revenue less deductions and related operating expenses for the business or business unit using the asset.

Payback Period (Years)

$$\text{Payback Period} = \frac{\text{Amount To Be Invested}}{\text{Projected Annual Net Cash Flow}}$$

Return on invested funds is the ratio of the average projected net income from the investment divided by average investment. Average investment is calculated by dividing the total amount invested by two. The average projected net income is calculated for the life of the asset (9).

Return On Investment (ROI)

$$\text{ROI (\%)} = \frac{\text{Average Projected Net Income}}{\text{Average Investment}}$$

A higher ROI means a better investment. A look at personal finance will help to understand how ROI is used. If you were asked to choose between two savings accounts, one offering an interest rate (rate of return) of 5.0% and the other offering a 6.5% interest rate, and, all other factors being equal, you are likely to pick the account that offers the higher 6.5% rate of return. Use of the ROI ratio allows management to make the same type of decision about a proposed capital expenditure (9).

Do It All Therapy, Incorporated
Depreciation Schedule
Fiscal Year 2005

Asset	Booked Value	Useful Life (Years)	Annual Depreciation	Monthly Depreciation
Equipment:				
Clinic Furniture	$7,000	12	$583	$49
Office Furniture	13,000	12.5	1,040	86.67
Tx Equipment	110,000	11.75	9,362	780.14
Computer System	16,742	4	4,186	348.79
Billing Software	25,000	5	5,000	416.67
Transcription Equip	7,000	6	1,167	97.22
Car	21,258	7	3,037	253.07
Equipment Total	200,000		24,374	2,031.17
Buildings:				
1st Street Clinic	90,000	40	2250	187.50
Total	**$290,000**		**$26,624**	**$2,219**

FIGURE 7.10. Schedule of depreciation expense.

CONTROL OF EXPENSES

Direct And Indirect Expenses

Expenses that can be directly associated with the production of goods and services are called direct expenses. Costs that are incurred by the organization but can not be directly associated with the production of any specific good or service are called indirect expenses. Direct expenses are generally easier for management to identify. Indirect expenses are sometimes less so.

For a therapy department or clinic that is part of a larger organization, salaries, benefits, supplies, depreciation of equipment and staff education are examples of direct expenses. Indirect expenses would include expenses such as administrative salaries, financial services, information service, grounds and building services or the cafeteria.

Indirect expenses are not listed as department expenses, but are allocated to all departments as shared overhead expense. Indirect expense allocation is determined by use of a meaningful basis such as square footage, revenues, expenses, number of employees, volume of service. A department is allocated a percentage of overhead expense equal to their utilization percentage of the resource. For example, if a department occupies 15% of the total building square footage, it will be allocated 15% of the expense of building services. A manager can control the direct expenses related to their area of responsibility. The same manager may have some influence but will have no direct control over indirect expenses.

In the case of a small independent therapy practice such as *Do It All Therapy, Inc.,* all of the expenses can be directly associated with the productions of services. All of the expenses are under the control of the Manager/Owner.

Expense Classification

Every manager with responsibility for cost control will need to understand how expenses change in response to changes in production or service volume. Expenses are classified by their relationship to volume. There are three classifications, referred to as fixed costs, variable costs and semi-variable costs.

Fixed Cost

Fixed costs remain unchanged despite changes in service volume. For example, Figure 7.2B shows that the property and casualty insurance paid by *Do It All Therapy, Inc.,* is $1500. Insurance is paid in advance for the upcoming year. Assuming there are no coverage changes, insurance is fixed at $1500 for that period. It will stay at $1500 whether the company treats 0 patients or 1000 patients. Fixed costs may be committed for several years or as a discretionary cost on an annual basis. Figure 7.11 provides a graphic representation of fixed cost in relationship to volume changes. As you can see, the total fixed cost remains flat as the volume of sales increases. Of key importance is what happens to the cost per UOS. Because the total fixed cost remains unchanged by volume, the fixed cost per UOS will decrease as volume increases. Referring back to the *Do It All Therapy, Inc's.,* property and casualty insurance cost of $1500, if *Do It All Therapy, Inc.,* serves just one patient for UOS, then the insurance cost per UOS is $1500. In contrast, if *Do It All Therapy, Inc.,* serves 1000 patients for one UOS each, the insurance cost per UOS drops to $1.50 ($1500/ 1000).

Variable Cost

Variable costs increase or decrease in direct proportion to the sales volume. For example, the cost of direct treatment salaries, linen, medical supplies are variable. Consumption of these resources will increase and decrease as volume of UOS change. If the average cost of linen equals $0.42 per UOS, the total cost of linen will be $420 at 1,000 UOS and $1,000 at 2,381 UOS. In the case of variable costs, the cost per unit stays the same, while total costs

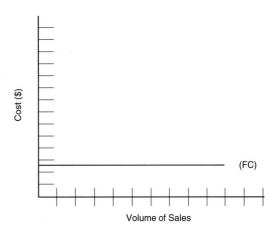

FIGURE 7.11. Fixed costs (FC).

will increase or decrease as sales volume (UOS) changes. Figure 7.12 provides a graphical representation of the variable cost to volume relationship.

Semi-Variable Cost

Semi-variable costs have both fixed and variable elements. These costs must be evaluated so that the fixed and variable components can be addressed separately. Otherwise, total and per UOS cost projections will be inaccurate. Business telephone service is an example of a semi-variable cost. The equipment and basic service are a fixed cost. Once the service is available, the business is charged an additional fee for each local and long-distance call. This usage fee is variable because use will increase as the volume of service increases. When a cost is semi-variable, the total fixed portions remain constant and the total fixed cost per UOS will decrease as volume increases and increase as volume decreases. The total variable portion will increase or decrease in proportion to the change in sales volume. Figure 7.13 provides a graphical representation of this semi-variable cost to volume relationship.

Total Cost

Total cost is the sum of fixed costs, variable cost and semi-variable costs. Figure 7.14 provides a graphic representation of fixed, variable and semi-variable cost combined to equal total

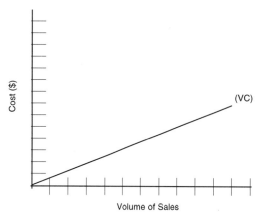

FIGURE 7.12. Variable costs (VC).

will increase at a rate equal to price per UOS times volume of UOS sold. At Point A, total revenue equals total cost. This is the break-even point where net income equals 0. Until break-even, the company is operating at a loss. After break-even, the company is operating at a profit. If a company understands its current position, proposed changes in volume, charges or costs can be inserted into the model to determine impact on total revenue. Break-even point can be calculated without charting using the break-even formula as demonstrated in Table 7.1. Using the same formula, the revenue impact of changes in price, volume or cost can be calculated.

cost. The graph demonstrates how total cost changes in relationship to volume.

COST-VOLUME-PROFIT ANALYSIS

The key to successfully managing financial performance is a working knowledge of the mathematical relationship between:

- Fixed, variable and semi-variable costs
- Cost per UOS
- Sales Volume
- Profit(Loss)

Use of cost-volume-profit analysis will allow managers to predict the overall financial impact of cost or volume changes. The goal is to minimize total expense by matching capacity for production to the demand for production.

The cost-volume-profit analysis relates cost to revenue. In doing this, cost-volume-profit analysis can be used to determine revenue and expenses at any sales volume. This can be useful for assessment of past performance, current position, and future performance. It can also be used to model the impacts of proposed expenditures with or without volume change. Figure 7.15 is a graphic representation of this cost-volume-profit relationship. It depicts total costs and total revenue from sales. Note that at zero volume, total cost would equal total fixed costs. As sales volume increases, total revenue

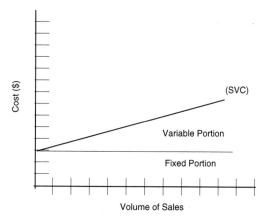

FIGURE 7.13. Semi-variable costs (SVC).

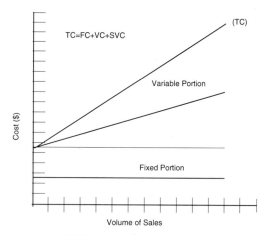

FIGURE 7.14. Total costs (TC).

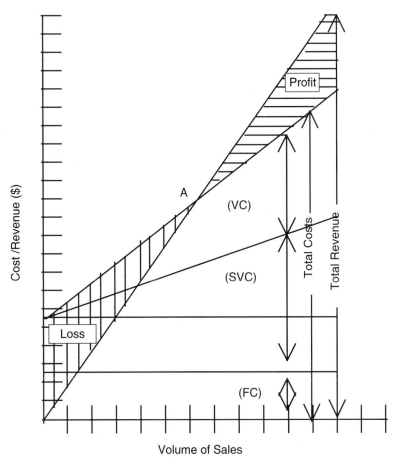

FIGURE 7.15. Cost-volume-profit analysis.

 TABLE 7.1
Breakeven Point Calculation

Where,
X = Volume of sales
P = Price
FC = Fixed costs
VC = Variable cost per UOS

GENERAL FORMULA	DO IT ALL THERAPY, INC. BREAK-EVEN, FY 2005
Total Revenue = Total Cost	
P (X) = FC + VC(X)	35(X) = 79,882 + 22.69(X)
Rearranging:	Rearranging:
X = FC/(P − VC)	X = 79,882 / (35.00 − 22.69)
	X = 6,489
	R = 227,115 = TC = 227,117
	(Difference due to rounding)

Cost-Volume-Profit Analysis Under Variable Reimbursement Methods

The application of cost-volume-profit analysis is straight forward under a fee-for-service payment methodology. Revenue may require some adjustment for allowances, discounts and deductions by payer type. Otherwise, the incremental UOS is discrete and consistent so cost analysis is reliable.

Under a per diem or capitated methodology, in which the unit of measure encompasses such a wide range of services and revenue that may be fixed, it becomes difficult to estimate or calculate average variable cost and break even. Projections of total cost are less reliable. Without accurate cost information, the provider is at risk of under pricing or over pricing. Under pricing could lead to a financial loss. Over pricing could as easily lead to the loss of business in a competitive environment. There are no easy solutions to these situations. The best protec-tion a provider can have is reliable data about service utilization by patient type. Data base development will be covered in more detail in Chapters 10 and 11, Information Management and Outcomes Measurement. Figure 7.16 presents a cost-volume-profit analysis under capitated payment. As volume rises, revenue per unit of volume will decline. Revenue is maximized at zero volume. This is in contrast to the same analysis under fee-for-service reimbursement in which revenue is maximized as volume increases.

SUMMARY

Financial management has become a critical job skill for today's health care managers. Industry-wide pressure to reduce costs while maintaining current levels of service often seems an impossible goal. Only managers who understand financial management, who can use financial information, who determine resource needs in relationship to volume demand and who predict the financial impact of incurring or cutting cost will feel confident in a leadership role. In times of change, employee performance and job satisfaction are dependent on confident and competent leadership to support them and meet their resource needs.

The concepts presented in this, and other chapters, may be explored more fully through the use of a continuous case study, a role play, presented in Appendix A. The role play has been designed to demonstrate how management concepts may impact the clinical setting on a daily basis. The intent of the role play is to provoke thought and build a connection between financial principles and the practice of physical therapy in today's health care environment.

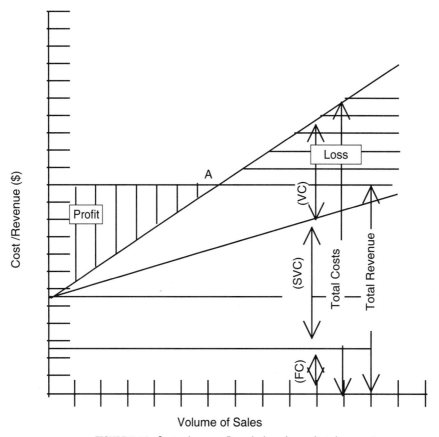

FIGURE 7.16. Cost-volume-profit analysis under capitated payment.

REFERENCES

1. Berman HJ, Kukla SF, Weeks LE. The Financial Management of Hospitals. 8th ed. Ann Arbor, MI:Health Administration Press, 1994:7–10,156, 642–665.
2. Case J. Open Book Management, the Coming Business Revolution. New York, NY:Harper Business, 1995:19–36.
3. Nosse LJ, Friberg DG. Management Principles for Physical Therapists. Baltimore, MD:Williams & Wilkins, 1992:95–125.
4. Financial Accounting Standards Board. Statements of financial accounting concepts. No. 1.
5. Weltman B. The Big Idea Book for New Business Owners. New York, NY:Macmillian Spectrum, 1997:14–25.
6. Meigs WB, Johnson CE, Meigs RF. Accounting, the Basis of Business Decisions. New York, NY:McGraw-Hill, 1977:15,102–103,13,400,48.
7. Dillon RD, LaMont RR. Financial statement analysis, A key to practice diagnosis and prognosis. Clin Manage 1983;35(4):36–39.
8. Skula RK, Psetian J. A comparative analysis of revenues and cost-management strategies for not-for-profit and for-profit hospitals. Hosp and Health Serv Adm 1997; 42(1):117–134.
9. Pyle WW, White JA. Fundamental Accounting Principles. 7th ed. Homewood:Richard D. Irwin, 1975:308.

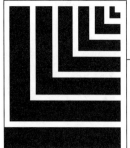

8

MONEY MATTERS: MAXIMIZING FINANCIAL PERFORMANCE

PREVIEW

Chapter 8 will build on the financial management concepts introduced in Chapter 7, taking the reader from concept to practical application. Financial management principles are standardized guidelines for the recording of a business' financial activity. Use of financial management principles allows multiple internal and external users to interpret the financial information produced by any organization.

In practice, the use of financial information varies widely among organizations. An organization's size, structure, management autonomy, as well as the quantity and the quality of information available, are some of the factors that influence day-to-day business practices.

Such topics as profitability, financial modeling, performance evaluation, who pays for health care, what they pay for and when they pay for it will be discussed. Practical issues related to pricing, maximizing reimbursement and making the most of the available resources through enhanced productivity will be introduced.

A full appreciation for these topics will require a knowledge of the information provided in Chapter 7. Concepts introduced in Chapter 7 will be referenced in this Chapter, but not routinely covered in-depth. For this reason, the reader is encouraged to review Chapter 7 before proceeding with Chapter 8.

KEY WORDS

Accounts Receivable: monies owed to a business.

Allocation Basis: the common measure used to divide allocated cost among unit level budgets. For example, the cost of an employee picnic is divided among departments based on the number of employees assigned to that department. If physical therapy has 50% of the employees, it will be allocated 50% of the cost of the picnic.

Beneficiary: an individual who is enrolled and eligible to receive health care insurance coverage under the Medicare and/or Medicaid programs.

Case Mix: the percentage of total patient services by diagnostic category.

Closed Panel Managed Health Care Plan: a health insurance plan that restricts enrollee choice of health care providers to those who have participation agreements with the plan. The group of participating providers is sometimes referred to as a panel.

Cost Allocation: the process of dividing, distributing or assigning indirect or general costs to revenue center level budgets.

Coverage Guidelines: a written description of the type and terms under which health care services are covered for payment under a health insurance plan.

Co-payments: an amount or percentage of the service cost a patient and/or family must pay after the deductible has been satisfied.

Deductible: an amount that the patient or family has agreed to pay out of pocket for covered health care services before the insurer must pay any part of the bill.

Enrollee: an individual who is enrolled in a health care plan and is entitled to receive health care payment coverage under an individual or group insurance plan for a specific period of time.

Ethical: a descriptor of behaviors that is in keeping with accepted standards of conduct. Additional information may be found in Chapter 2.

Financial (Budget) Variance: the difference between planned and actual performance.

Full-Time Equivalent (FTE): represents 52 weeks of full-time employment at 40 hours per week. It is equal to 2080 hours of paid time per year. The 2080 hours represents time when the employee is available to work (productive time) as well as time when the employee is paid but not available (non-productive time).

Loss: denotes a negative financial margin.

Margin: in relation to financial performance, this term is used to describe the difference between total revenue and total expenses. The terms net income, net revenue, profit and loss are also used to describe this difference.

Operating Margin: the ratio of net income to total revenue. See Chapter 7 for the formula to calculate margin.

Outlier: a patient case that falls well outside the norm for cost and/or service utilization.

Payer Mix: percentage breakdown of total patient service revenue by payer type.

Participation Agreement: a contract between an insurance plan and a provider that allows a health care provider to participate in the care of the plans enrollees.

Participating Provider: a health care practioner or organization who has applied, met criteria for participation and has a signed agreement with a government or private health care insurance plan for the provision of specific health care services to the plan's enrollees (beneficiaries).

Profit: denotes a positive margin.

Subscribers: individuals who hold or join a group that holds or subscribes to an insurance policy for health care coverage. A subscriber may enroll others under the policy or into the group that holds the policy. An employee who signs up for insurance as an employment bene-fit is the subscriber. All of the employer's employees and those they enroll will be part of the employer's group of insured individuals.

INTRODUCTION

Financial information is a management tool of incomparable value. To use this tool effectively, managers at all levels of an organization need to have a working knowledge of financial management principles. Application of financial management principles will allow therapy managers to relate the delivery of patient care to the revenues and expenses of operating a health care business. Decisions about services, staffing, and purchases that would otherwise be based on a manager's best guess, will seem clearer. Application of objective information about the performance of a business as compared to either what was planned and/or what others are doing will help the manager stay on target with performance objectives. The management of health care is too important and too complex to perform without good information.

No Margin, No Mission

Margin is the difference between total revenue and total expenses. Profit margin is a term that denotes a positive margin. Loss is a term used to denote a negative margin. Mission is the purpose of the organization. The reader is referred to Chapter 2 for a more specific discussion of organizational mission. The meaning of this statement is clear: without a profit margin, the purpose of the organization cannot be fulfilled. When an organization operates at a loss, it consumes existing assets to fund operations. A business producing a net loss from operations may be able to continue operations for a short period. Continued operations at a loss will eventually deplete the organization's assets. When its assets have been depleted, the business will cease to operate.

Operating at break-even, i.e., total revenue equals total expenses, may sustain an organization in the short run. Unfortunately, a business must have some level of profit even to maintain its current financial position over time. Addi-tional resources will be required for the future replacement of buildings, equipment and other capital assets. It is unlikely that the investment income from cash and other liquid assets will keep up with the devaluation resulting from inflation. As the value of its assets decreases, the break-even company will lack the buying power to replace assets that have exhausted their useful life. Break-even does not allow long-term survival. As the value of current assets decreases over time, the organization will be unable to sustain operations. Therefore, to exist into the future, an organization must bring in more money than it spends.

Should Businesses Profit From Health Care Delivery?

Having spent many years in health care management, it is the authors' observation that some people are bothered by the thought of making a profit from health care delivery. This concern is not limited to health care customers but is shared by many health care practitioners as well. The authors have heard many such concerns expressed by practicing physical therapists.

Why do they charge so much for my services?
I did not charge the patient because it only took a few minutes for me to review the exercises.
I know the patient does not have insurance to pay their bill.

These are statements heard time and again. These statements may represent advocacy for patients and criticism of the system. Most therapists have the good sense to address their concerns by working through the system. On occasion, some therapists may unwisely express these feelings through inappropriate action such as selectively undercharging patients for services provided.

Large physician practices, hospitals, long-term care facilities and insurers are all targets for this type of concern. When it comes to health care, the normal business practice of making a profit is viewed negatively. This sentiment indicates a general lack of appreciation for the fact that all health care businesses, large or small, must make a profit today to provide health care in the future.

We contend that, when any other alternative is available, it would be unethical to operate a health care business in a manner that does not have the potential to result in a profit. This holds true for both not-for-profit and for-profit businesses alike. Not-for-profit health care providers benefit from the use of community services, money from deferred taxes and the personal contributions of community members. These resources are provided with the expectation that the organization will contribute to the current and future well being of community members. The community has a reasonable expectation that health care services will be available when, and if, needed.

The owners and operators of not-for-profit health care businesses are the stewards of community resources. It is their responsibility to manage these community resources in a way that causes the business to grow and prosper. In addition, many health care organizations have financial obligations such as outstanding loans that are owed to other community businesses and/or governing bodies. Poor profitability could result in an inability to meet financial obligations. That would do harm to other community businesses. It is not within the standards of acceptable business behavior to act in a manner that will result in an inability to meet business obligations. To do so would be unethical. Knowing that a health care business needs to make a profit to survive supports the conclusion that the health care manager who deliberately continues to operate without producing a profit would be acting in an unethical manner (1).

Separating Ethical From Legal Issues

Managers and consultants are often asked to respond to questions about patient billing. Questions about billing practices may come from customers, staff members, the media or the community. These questions are commonly related to price, what was billed or how it was billed. It is a

customer's right to question their bill. It is the health care provider's obligation to evaluate all of the practices that an employer may ask them to follow. In our experience, the concepts of ethics and legality can be sometimes confused when staff has questions about billing practices. From our point of view, this is a critical distinction.

The American Physical Therapy Association (APTA) and many other professional organizations offer guidance to health care practioners through their member-adopted statements on ethical behavior (2). Specific to billing practices, there are also payer coverage guidelines that outline the accepted conditions for billing services provided to their enrollees. Coverage guidelines also specify when coverage is available and the terms of payment for services provided. For government-sponsored health insurance plans such as Medicaid or Medicare, the rules of participation are, in fact, legal requirements. The legal penalties for failure to follow Medicare billing regulations can be severe.

Undoubtedly, some health care providers are concerned about patient billing because they are advocates for the patient and hold a belief that no person should be denied, or put at undue financial risk, to receive health care services. Having explored billing concerns with therapists over time, we have concluded that patient advocacy motivates many therapist's concerns about patient billing practices. Knowledge about the relationship of charges to payments and accepted practices for managing the accounts of individuals who may lack insurance and other financial resources may help dispel the concerns of many practitioners who question patient billing practices. Armed with this knowledge, the care provider will be able to separate ethical from legal concerns. If a practitioner believes that they are being directed to follow an illegal practice, they have the right to refuse. It is the responsibility of every health care professional to review the applicable law and respond accordingly. If a practice is legal, but the practitioner remains uncomfortable, they may choose to leave the organization. If they stay, they should follow the practices of organization.

Selective charging of patients without an objective assessment and decision-making processes is a risky practice. For the business owner, it could result in charges of billing discrimination. This risk can be addressed through the use of specific criteria for provision of care to those in financial need. For the employed therapist, selective charging is unethical (1). The employer pays the cost related to the delivery of the service provided and has a legal right to the revenue from the services when sold. The therapist who gives away services without the permission of the employer is giving away something of value that does not belong to them. In fact, they are stealing revenue from their employer.

MANAGING FINANCIAL PERFORMANCE

A Four-Part Process

The goal of financial management is to maximize profit from operations. Financial management can be viewed as a four-step process. First, a business needs to establish a financial management plan. To do this, a business uses information about past performance and current market trends to set targets for future financial performance (profitability) (See Chapters 3, 7, 10 and 14.) Frequently covering a 3- to 5-year time span, this is often referred to as a long range financial plan.

Second, annual financial performance targets are set for each operating unit of the business.

This short-term financial plan is the annual operating budget.

Third, management prepares financial reports to compare actual performance to budgeted performance targets. When performance deviates from what has been planned, it is called a variance. A variance may be positive or negative. A positive variance means that actual performance has exceeded the target. A negative variance means actual performance was less than the target. Whether a variance is favorable or unfavorable depends on the performance targeted and the cause of the variance.

Fourth, management performs a variance analysis and takes corrective action as needed. Variance analysis should determine what factors lead to a specific variance and what resulted from the variance. Whether a variance is good for the company is determined by looking at the whole picture. Figure 8.1 depicts financial planning as a continuous management process.

Long-range Financial Plan

Profit is determined by the relative proportion of operating costs to revenues. Profitability can be influenced by management of revenue or expenses (3). When management undertakes efforts to influence financial performance through operations, it will involve some form of revenue and/or expense management strategy. The long-range financial plan represents a business'

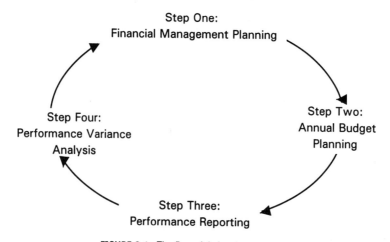

FIGURE 8.1. The financial planning process.

efforts to translate strategic directions into financial performance projections. Just as strategic directions should be based on a sound knowledge of the business, customers, competitors and other external factors, so too should the long-range financial plan.

The number of years covered by a long-range strategic and financial plan is determined by each individual business. Typically, health care organizations use a 3 to 5 year time period.

The accuracy of any long-range plan is dependent upon a company's ability to predict the future. The rate of change in the health care industry will impact the accuracy of long-range plans. The more distant the planning period, the less accurate the financial performance projections.

The Use Of Financial Modeling

Financial modeling is the application of financial principles to develop financial projections that can be used by management to assess business strategies. Financial modeling is an essential part of the business plan. If a business decides to move forward with a strategy, then projections from the financial model would be incorporated into its financial plan. Financial modeling can also be used to evaluate expense reduction strategies. Chapter 14, Entrepreneurship, will provide the reader with a business planning format that is applicable to either a new start-up business or business development projects.

Revenue Management

Revenue management refers to actions taken to enhance total revenue and improve the collection of accounts receivable. Most of the approaches to managing revenue are directly related to the marketing process. These approaches take into consideration such things as product, place, price and promotion (see Chapter 3). Revenue can be enhanced by increasing revenue from current services or expanding service volume. Revenue from current services can be increased by raising prices and/or improving collection of accounts receivable. Pricing and service volume expansion strategies will be used to demonstrate financial forecasting. Accounts receivable collection will be discussed later in this chapter.

FORECASTING THE FINANCIAL IMPACT OF PRICE CHANGES

Under the current health care reimbursement system, a price increase may have a limited effect on net income. In a price-sensitive market, over pricing may result in a loss of business volume and decrease in revenues. In a price-insensitive market, raising prices may increase revenue only if actual reimbursement increases in proportion to the price increase. A detailed review of price setting strategy can be found in Chapter 3.

Payer mix should be used to determine the relationship between price and reimbursement. Price increases will impact revenues only under fee-for-service or discounted fee-for-service payment methodology. Under cost reimbursement, fixed case rate payment, fixed per diem payment and capitated payment methodology, price increases have little to no impact on revenues. Cost-based reimbursement pays the provider the lower of cost or charges. A price increase will result in a reimbursement increase only if current charges are less than the providers cost. Case rate, per diem and capitated payments are generally fixed by contract terms for payment rates. An increase in prices will not result in an increase in payment unless the increase is recognized under the terms of the provider contract. Provider payment methods are discussed in Chapter 7.

Figure 8.2 demonstrates the impact of a 10% price increase in the reimbursement for *Do It All Therapy, Inc.* Using a baseline of fiscal year (FY) 2005, a 10% price increase will result in a $89,282 increase in gross revenue (charges). However, when adjusted for impact of payment method by payer type, the reimbursement impact of the price increase is reduced to $21,963. The actual reimbursement increase resulting from a 10% price increase was 2.5%.

ASSESSING THE REVENUE AND COST IMPACTS OF SERVICE VOLUME EXPANSION STRATEGIES

Strategies that seek to increase the number of customers are a common and often successful revenue-enhancement strategy used by health care providers. Service volume can be increased in two ways: the number of customers served can increase, or the amount of service provided to each customer can increase. Chapters 3 and 14 provide

Do It All Therapy, Incorporated
Revenue Impact Following 10% Price Increase
October 1, 2006

Payer Type	Percent Of Revenue	Percent Deduction	Gross Revenue Before Price Increase	Deductions Before Price Increase	Revenue After Deductions	Gross Revenue Following 10% Price Increase	Deductions Following 10% Price Increase	Revenue After Deductions	Revenue Impact Following 10% Price Increase
Medicare	33%	30%	$294,630.	$88,389.	$206,241.	$324,093.	$117,852.	$206,241.	$0.
Medicaid	8%	50%	$71,425.	$35,713.	$35,713.	$78,568.	$42,855.	$35,713.	$0.
Manage Care	30%	15%	$267,845.	$40,177.	$227,669.	$294,630.	$66,961.	$227,669.	$0.
Commercial	20%	5%	$178,564.	$8,928.	$169,635.	$196,420.	$9,821.	$186,599.	$16,964.
Charity Care	1%	100%	$8,928.	$8,928.	$0.	$9,821.	$9,821.	$0.	$0.
Self Pay	8%	30%	$71,425.	$21,428.	$49,998.	$78,568.	$23,570.	$54,998.	$5,000.
Total	100%		$892,818.	$203,563.	$689,255.	$982,100.	$270,881.	$711,219.	$21,963.

Assumptions:
1. Price increase of 10% of FY 2005 prices produces a $89,282 increase ($982,100 - $892,818) in gross revenue.
2. FY 2005 revenues are used as a base line to calculate the impact.
3. Medicare payment methodology for outpatient services is cost based and not affected by provider price changes (until the Balanced Budget Act of 1997 takes effect).
4. Medicaid payment based on a fixed fee schedule and not affected by provider price changes unless previous pricing was below current Medicaid payment rates.
5. Managed care payment rate is fixed by contract and not affected by provider price changes.
6. Commercial payments are fee-for-service and will be affected by price increases. Patient may pay more out of pocket.
7. Charity care deduction will remain equal to gross revenue.
8. Self pay is based on fee-for-service and will change with provider price changes.

FIGURE 8.2. Assessing the impact of payer mix on revenue less deductions following a price increase.

additional information about planning for volume expansion. To determine if a specific strategy will produce the desired financial results, the business should ask the following questions.

What are the clinical and payment characteristics of the customers the strategy targets?
What is the total and per unit of service incremental operating costs required to provide services to the target group?
Will strategy implementation require new capital expenditures?
Will the projected revenue after deductions cover the incremental costs?
Will the new services be profitable?

The impacts of service volume, payer mix and case mix on revenue are interdependent. When evaluating strategies for revenue enhancement, a review of the impact each of these factors has on the others is a good place to start. Using *Do It All Therapy, Inc.* as our model, strategy assessment and development of a 3-year financial plan will be demonstrated. Figure 8.3 demonstrates how *Do It All Therapy, Inc.* assessed two alternative service expansion strategies. The first strategy, is to enter into an exclusive provider agreement with a health maintenance organization (HMO) who subcontracts with the state Medicaid program. The second strategy, is to open a new clinic in a growing suburb. In order to begin the analysis of these expansion options, *Do It All Therapy, Inc.* had to project new service volume, patient type, case mix and payer mix. With this information in hand, *Do It All Therapy, Inc.* management could predict:

- What services are needed
- What equipment is needed
- How much of each service is needed
- How much equipment is needed
- What would be paid for the services delivered
- Incremental revenue from new services
- Incremental expenses related to the delivery of new services

Referring again to Figure 8.3, the incremental overall organizational impact on performance has been projected for each option. Before the financial assessment, *Do It All Therapy, Inc.* believed that the HMO contract was the best opportunity, as it was the less expensive option to implement and future expansion of the HMO would result in continued expansion. However,

once payer mix, services capacity and incremental costs were assessed, it became evident that the HMO contract would operate at a $12,021 loss and would have a negative impact on the company's overall financial performance. This assessment showed regional expansion to be the better opportunity. Of course, the reliability of both financial assessments is dependent upon the accuracy of the market assumptions.

Cost Management

Cost management involves the control of operating and capital costs. Managing operating cost generally requires different strategies for managing labor and nonlabor costs. Strategies for labor cost management are of particular importance for service organizations in which labor costs account for a high percentage of total cost. Capital cost management focuses on controlling total fixed costs, interest expense and on maximizing the return on investment of capital assets. Cost management strategies can be modeled using the same incremental approach used to model revenue. The process starts with a strategy for cost reduction. The cost decrease is projected and the impact incorporated into a financial model to determine the impact of the change on overall financial performance.

A Multi-Year Financial Plan

Long-range financial plans are projected from current revenues and expenses adjusted for projected changes in the base business and future strategies targeted for implementation. For example, nonlabor expenses will increase with inflation. Labor costs will rise due to annual wage adjustments and increased benefits costs. The cost of money will continue to increase. Additional support staff may be needed due to business expansion. The rate of reimbursement may be projected to decline over time. The long-range financial plan must account for these impacts as accurately as possible. Often there are published indexes that can be used to assist in making future projections. Support from financial management professionals is often necessary to develop a reliable long-range financial plan. The reader is referred to Chapter 13, Getting Advice: Using Consultants.

Figure 8.4 is a 3-year financial plan developed for *Do It All Therapy, Inc.* The assumptions used

Do It All Therapy, Incorporated
Financial Impact Analysis: Medicaid HMO Contract VS. Geographical Expansion
October 1, 2006

	FY 2005	Medicaid HMO		Regional Expansion	
		Projected Incremental Impact	Revised Income Statement	Projected Incremental Impact	Revised Income Statement
Work Statistics	23,795	10,000	33,795	10,000	33,795
REVENUE:					
Gross Revenue					
Services	$832,818	$350,000	$1,182,818	$350,000	$1,182,818
Equipment	60,000	0	60,000	25,000	85,000
Total Operating Revenue	$892,818	$350,000	$1,242,818	$375,000	$1,267,818
Less:					
Deductions	203,563	192,500	396,063	63,000	266,563
Gross Rev Net Deductions	$689,255	$157,500	$846,755	$312,000	$1,001,255
Non Operating Revenue	23,000	0	23,000	0	23,000
Total Revenue	$712,255	$157,500	$869,755	$312,000	$1,024,255

EXPENSES:					
Salaries	$361,421	$112,819	$474,240	$133,619	$495,040
Benefits	65,056	20,307	85,363	24,051	89,107
FICA	28,191	8,800	36,991	10,422	38,613
Education	6,300	1,935	8,235	1,935	8,235
Recruitment	5,000	0	5,000	500	5,500
Professional Services	11,000	0	11,000	2,160	13,160
Purchased Services	600	0	600	15,000	15,600
Supplies	51,095	21,514	72,609	21,514	72,609
Travel	4,000	300	4,300	600	4,600
Dues	2,000	0	2,000	0	2,000
Equipment	1,200	5,000	6,200	15,000	16,200
Rent/Lease	20,000	0	20,000	36,000	56,000
Utilities	9,000	500	9,500	6,000	15,000
Communication	3,375	650	4,025	2,500	5,875
Environmental Services	5,300	0	5,300	5,200	10,500
Accrued Expenses	40,083	3,616	43,699	3,616	43,699
Insurance	6,100	0	6,100	3,500	9,600
Total Expenses	**$619,721**	**$175,441**	**$795,162**	**$281,618**	**$901,339**
Net Income(Loss)	92,534	(17,941)	74,593	30,382	$122,916
Taxes	30,536	(5,921)	24,615	10,026	40,562
Net Income After Taxes	**$61,998**	**($12,021)**	**$49,977**	**$20,356**	**$82,354**

FIGURE 8.3. Assessing the financial impact of alternative business development strategies.

Do It All Therapy, Incorporated
Three Year Financial Plan
FY 2006 to FY 2008

	FY 2005 Actual	FY 2006 Projected	FY 2007 Projected	FY 2008 Projected
Work Statistics	23,795	34,985	48,483	54,301
REVENUE:				
Gross Revenue				
Services	$832,818	$1,224,459	$1,696,905	$1,900,533
Equipment	60,000	85,000	110,000	110,000
Total Operating Revenue	$892,818	$1,309,459	$1,806,905	$2,010,533
Less:				
Deductions	203563	302,732	408,772	434,388
Gross Rev Net Deductions	$689,255	$1,006,727	$1,398,133	$1,576,145
			0	0
Non Operating Revenue	23000	23000	23,000	23,000
			$0	$0
Total Revenue	$712,255	$1,029,727	$1,421,133	$1,599,145
EXPENSES:				
Salaries	$361,421	$534,600	$740,095	$844,124
Benefits	65,056	96,228	133,217	151,942
FICA	28,191	41,699	57,727	65,842
Education	6,300	8,672	11,995	13,490
Recruitment	5,000	5,638	6,803	6,974
Professional Services	11,000	13,489	13,040	10,000
Purchased Services	600	15,990	16,000	1,000
Supplies	51,095	77,043	108,888	125,003
Travel	4,000	4,715	5,448	6,199
Dues	2,000	2,050	2,101	2,200
Equipment	1,200	16,500	17,000	2,000
Rent/Lease	20,000	57,680	98,550	101,507
Utilities	9,000	15,375	21,909	22,457
Communication	3,375	6,042	6,304	6,611
Environmental Services	5,300	10,763	14,230	14,585
Accrued Expenses	40,083	44,791	53,513	58,928
Insurance	6,100	9,840	13,674	14,015
Total Expenses	$619,721	$961,115	$1,320,495	$1,446,877
Net Income(Loss)	$92,534	$68,612	$100,638	$152,268
Taxes	$30,536	$22,642	$33,191	$50,218
Net Income After Taxes	$61,998	$45,970	$67,448	$102,050

Assumptions:

The addition of one new suburban clinic location in FY 2006 and FY 2007
  (See Financial Impact Analyses).
A volume increase of 5% in 2006, 10% in 2007 and 12% in 2008.
A 5% increase in all salary rates per year.
A 3% increase in existing rental expense per year.
A 2.5% increase in all other expense categories per year.
A 5% decrease in the commercial payment rate for FY 2006 and FY 2007.
A 3% decrease in the commercial reimbursement rate for FY 2008.
A 1.5% increase in payment for Medicare and Medicaid payments per year.
A 5% payer mix shift from commercial to managed care for 2006 and 2007.
Prices will remain unchanged.

FIGURE 8.4. *Do It All Therapy, Inc's.* three-year financial plan.

to develop the plan are listed under the plan. The financial projections follow side by side.

Other reports that should be prepared include projected balance statements and cash flow statements to insure that cash flow requirements created by such a high growth rate can be met. As plans and circumstances change over time, the long-range financial plan should be adjusted accordingly. See Chapter 7 for an example of a balance statement and cash flow statement for *Do It All Therapy, Inc.*

The Annual Budget: Setting Performance Targets

In creating the annual budget, the financial performance target for the current year is broken down into a more detailed financial plan that can be used to direct day-to-day activity. First, the overall financial plan is broken down by division, operating unit, department, service program or any other subunit that the organization designates. The allocation of budgeted revenue and expenses should reflect the organization's structure and information needs. Operating units (departments) should be recognizable as distinct operating units. Organizational units should be designated as revenue or cost centers. A revenue center has a budget that includes both direct revenue and direct expense. A cost center budget includes only direct expense. Answers to the following questions will help determine if an organizational division should be designated as a revenue or cost center.

- Can the work of the unit be clearly separated from that of other units?
- Do the employees assigned to the unit share common knowledge and skills that distinguish them and their work from others?
- Is there an individual or team that has the authority and responsibility for the unit's performance?
- Is there sufficient and reliable information that can be used to separate the revenue and/or costs of the unit from the rest of the organization?
- Will separation of the revenue and/or costs of the unit increase management's ability to plan?
- Will separation of the unit make it easier to evaluate and improve its performance?

If the answers to these questions are yes, an operating unit should have its own budget. If the answer to one or more of these questions is no, the work of creating a budget is likely to outweigh any potential benefit. In fact, resources spent developing and maintaining a budget may decrease the performance of the company.

The owner of *Do It All Therapy, Inc.* requires information about the total cost per UOS for each revenue department. This information will improve the accuracy of cost projections for additional service volume and for price setting during managed care contract negotiations. Without this detailed information, *Do It All Therapy, Inc.* would have to use the average cost for all visits. Using average cost would place the company at risk of setting a price that is below actual cost for the service(s) to be provided. To make a profit, revenue after deductions must be greater than total cost. The reader should refer to the cost-volume-profit analysis presented in Chapter 7.

To provide needed information, the financial information system must collect the right data in the right way. How data is collected is tied to the way revenues and costs are budgeted and recorded throughout the year. In this case, the owner of *Do It All Therapy, Inc.* has divided total revenue and expense between the clinics. Within each clinic, the budgeted revenue and/or costs will be divided between general administration, office functions, physical therapy, occupational therapy and speech therapy. Department level budgets include all of the direct revenue and cost related to the department's operation. This budget structure will provide specific performance information for each clinic and each department within each clinic.

Projected work statistics, revenue and expenses are used to determine the portion of direct revenue and expense that is distributed to each clinic and department. This flow is depicted in Figure 8.5.

Projected expense and revenue are divided among the clinics based on total clinic work statistic projections. Revenue and expenses are divided among clinic departments in the same way. At the department level, revenues and expenses are allocated to the subaccounts based on projected utilization. An accurate division of resources is dependent on the availability of accurate performance history adjusted for any anticipated change.

Indirect costs are allocated to departments. Indirect costs are incurred by the organization but cannot be directly associated with the production of any specific good or service. Administrative salaries, financial services, information service, grounds care, building services or em-

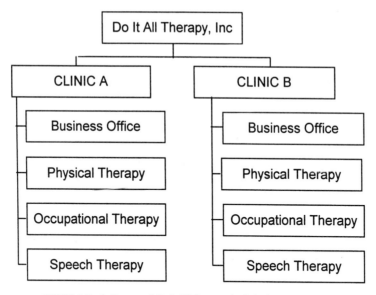

FIGURE 8.5. A diagram of *Do It All Therapy, Inc.*'s budget structure.

ployee food service related costs, for example, cannot be directly associated with the delivery of patient services but many are necessary to the operation of a health care business.

Shared indirect costs are referred to as allocated costs. Allocated costs are not listed as department expenses, but are allocated to departments as shared overhead expense. Indirect expense allocation uses a meaningful basis such as square footage, revenues, expenses, number of employees or volume of service. A department is allocated a percentage of overhead expense equal to their determined percentage of the basis. A department that occupies 5% of the square footage of a building, for example, would be allocated 5% of the building utility cost. Indirect costs should be included in the calculation of the total cost of a unit of service (UOS).

In review, information needed for accurate budgeting of revenue and expenses at the department level includes:

- Charges per UOS
- Equipment charges
- Volume of services and equipment to be sold
- Payer mix
- Case mix
- Percent of deductions from revenue by payer type
- Amount of anticipated non-operating revenue

- Salary increase planned for the FY
- Average hourly rates by job category adjusted by the anticipated salary increase
- Work statistic projections for each organizational division and department
- Productivity standard per full-time equivalent (FTE) employee by job category
- Variable cost per unit of service
- Direct and indirect fixed cost

Admittedly, few organizations are able to provide all of this information with complete confidence. Cost information is typically the most difficult to obtain. The larger and more complex the organization, the more difficult it will be to determine the cost of services. Our experience suggests that poorly designed data collection systems and lack of automation frequently cause most of this inadequate determination. The topic of information management is covered in Chapter 10.

Unit level budgets are presented in an income statement (profit and loss) format. Preparation of both monthly and annual budgets is common, although any time frame can be used. Monthly budgets provide periodic performance targets that are important for performance monitoring. Once set, the annual budget becomes a financial performance target for each operating unit of the organization.

Using Outcome Targets To Monitor Financial Performance

Organizational performance can be evaluated in many ways. Three techniques common to health care are quality control, outcome assessment and performance improvement.

QUALITY CONTROL

Quality control techniques are focused on standards compliance. Standards are set by the organization through use of job descriptions, competency requirements, performance standards, policies, procedures, formal and informal protocols, standardized care plans, company values and behavioral norms. Standards are also set by external parties such as government and professional organizations.

Any time an organization uses supervision, inspection, activity tracking or performance checks to insure compliance with standards, it is engaged in quality control. Employee observation, chart reviews for documentation and billing verification, inventory counts, usage and productivity tracking, and response time monitoring are all examples of quality control activities.

Quality control focuses on task performance. Quality control activities are nonproductive. They do not contribute to the productivity or add value to the organization. Quality control does not address the efficacy or the effectiveness of organizational standards in producing desired outcomes.

Outcome Assessment

Health care providers are under increasing pressure to demonstrate the cost effectiveness of services provided. They are challenged to demonstrate to customers that they provide a better value than the competition. Value is the measure of cost for the outcome. Providers who produce good outcomes at a lower cost are positioned to get the business of customers looking for value.

Outcome assessment techniques look at the result of health care services, rather than the clinical care process. Using internal and/or external industry outcome benchmarks, the health care provider compares its financial and clinical outcomes (performance) to the external, bench-mark, outcome targets. This comparison is called a variance analysis. Chapter 11, Outcomes, will provide an in-depth review of the clinical outcomes measurement process. Financial variance analysis will be discussed in more detail later in this chapter.

Performance Improvement

Performance improvement, also referred to as Total Quality Management (TQM) or Continuous Quality Improvement (CQI), is a performance monitoring and enhancement process. Performance improvement starts with the selection of key indicators, which can be process or outcome measures. Performance improvement indicators are selected for their relationship to high-volume, high-risk or high-value activities that have the potential to impact the success of a company. Key indicators are monitored and compared to performance benchmarks. Monitoring allows identification of performance variation that may represent opportunities for improvement. Performance for improvement incorporates quality control and outcome assessment techniques. But, where quality control and outcome assessment activities are reactive to customer demands, a performance improvement approach proactively seeks input from customers. Improvement efforts are attempts to proactively meet customer needs.

Financial Variance Analysis

Performance monitoring techniques all have one thing in common: they look for deviations from what was planned to identify potential problems. When a company identifies such a variation, it has the opportunity to take action. Performance variation should be seen as a signal for management attention. As stated earlier, variation can be positive or negative. If gross revenue and profit are above the target, then that could be favorable. But, until management knows the causal factors of the variation, the impact of the variance cannot be fully assessed. An assumption that a variation is understood without an analysis could cause management to miss future opportunities. If the variance is positive, then management needs to know what the company is doing correct so they can keep doing it.

If the variance is unfavorable, then management needs to know where change is needed.

DATA PRESENTATION FOR EASIER ANALYSIS

A key to effective variance analysis is information presentation. Management time is limited. If financial information is difficult to obtain or presented in a format that requires extensive rework, management is less likely to identify performance variances. Variance analysis can also be complicated by lack of detail in the information presented. Financial information systems should be flexible enough to provide more or less detail depending on the needs of management. General reports help identify variances. More detailed information is often necessary to determine causal factors.

COMPARATIVE AND COMMON-SIZE FINANCIAL REPORTS

In Chapter 7, the use of financial reports and financial ratios was introduced. Comparative and common-size reports are specifically designed to support variance analysis. Comparative reports present financial information from different sources or time periods. A comparative report can be used to present budget and actual, budget to budget or actual to actual from one or more comparative time periods (4). Figure 8.4, *Do It All Therapy, Inc.'s* Three Year Financial Plan is a comparative report that presents actual FY 2005 and budgeted for FY 2006–2008 income statements. Common-size reports provide information in dollars and as a percentage of the total category. For example, salary expense would be presented as a dollar amount and as a percentage of total expense. Figure 7.4 presents a combined comparative and common-size financial report.

FINANCIAL RATIOS

A technique that can be used to compare financial performance over time, between elements or between similar businesses involves the use of financial ratios. Financial ratio analysis refers to the use of the relationships between two mathematical quantities that have management significance. Financial ratios are used to summarize key financial data in a format that is easy to understand and evaluate (5). The use of financial ratios is well accepted. This makes it very easy for management and external parties to use ratios to evaluate business performance. Industry standards may be available for comparative analysis. Ratios can be used to assess change in performance over time or as performance benchmarks to compare a company's performance to the industry norm. In either case, the use of ratios is a form of variance analysis. The reader should refer to Chapter 7 for a review of capital, liquidity and activity ratios.

BEYOND FINANCIAL STATEMENTS: OPERATING INDICATORS FOR A THERAPY PRACTICE

There are other operating indicators that are not included in standard financial statements but that could be useful to a therapy manager's efforts to monitor and improve performance. Examples of operating indicators are listed in Chapter 7. Because these operating indicators are not routinely recorded as part of the accounts payable or accounts receivable processes, management must actively identify which operating indicators are important as well as how data on selected operating indicators will be captured, recorded and reported. Operating indicators that a therapy manager may wish to consider are listed in Table 8.1.

Operating indicators can be used to support both management and staff activities. They can be used by management and staff in several ways.

- To set and validate attainment of performance targets
- Provide an objective basis for assessment of day to day operations
- Evaluate variances between actual and planned performance
- Support process analysis activities
- Provide factual information in support of problem solving activities

Careful selection of operating indicators will help management set practical and meaningful performance expectations for all company operating units. Operating performance outcomes can be shared with every employee who plays a role in meeting performance targets (6).

Management should use only those operating indicators that are meaningful to the company's

TABLE 8.1
Risk Related To Type Of Payment Method

PAYMENT METHOD	PAYMENT RISKS FACTORS	LEVEL OF RISK
Cost Based	• Charges set below costs • Costs exceed cost caps • Non-payment of co-payments and deductibles	Low
Fee-For-Service	• Charges set below costs • Costs exceed cost caps • Non-payment of co-payments and deductibles	Low
Per Diem	• Per diem rate set below costs • Services included under the per diem rate are not specifically defined • High potential for variation in case required • Length of service too short • Providers inability to control daily service utilization	Medium
Case Rate	• Case rate set below costs • Services included under the case rate are not specifically defined • High potential for variation in case required • Length of service too long • Providers inability to control service utilization • Lack of an outlier provision	Medium to High
Capitation	• Capitation rate is set below costs • Service utilization projections are lower than actual utilization • Providers lack complete control over the delivery of services. • Providers inability to control service utilization	High

success. Data collection and analysis activities are expensive (7). Labor, equipment, information systems and consulting costs will increase with the amount of information collected. Careful planning and design of the information system is essential. Whenever possible, the need for manual recording and analysis should be minimized.

GETTING PAID FOR WHAT YOU DO

Without additional experience or training, the expertise of most therapy managers lies in the provision of quality therapy services. Therapy managers are often torn between the unfamiliar role of business manager and the familiar role of clinical manager and expert. Given that both roles are likely to feel like full-time responsibilities, many clinical managers find it easier to spend a disproportionate amount of their time on the service delivery aspects of their job. Perhaps unfortunately, to manage effectively, managers must be equally attentive to the business aspects of health care delivery. One of the most important

functions of the business manager is to ensure that the business is paid for services it provides.

Health care sales transactions are complex (5). Because of the cost of health care, the industry is unable to rely on the direct consumer, i.e., the first party patient, to pay the bills. Neither is it possible for the second party, the provider, to cover the remaining cost. As a result, the patient and provider must rely on a third party for payment. In most cases, multiple parties are involved and specific rules and procedures must be followed to get paid (5). When dealing with multiple third party payers, health care managers are challenged to accommodate significant variation in the coverage provided and in the requirements for provider reimbursement among insurance plans. Variation may exist in any aspect of a health care insurance plan.

- Coverage and payment criteria
- Coverage and payment limits
- Service and documentation requirements
- Bill processing procedures
- Payment limits, discounts and incentives

In addition, health care sales involve large numbers of low-price transactions purchased on credit. Managing health care billing and collections takes time, knowledge and effective accounts receivable function to get the job done. Without effective billing and collections, a therapy business that provides exceptional service, has a tremendous customer base, and enjoys a favorable payer mix may still not have the cash necessary to pay the bills.

Note: The who, what, when and how of third party payment will vary greatly among payers, geographical regions and over time. Any information provided here should be viewed as a discussion of the possibilities. The who, what, when and how of third party payment should be investigated for each payer in each therapy setting. Managers should expect to see variability between payer and settings. Change in payment practices will be rapid and continuous. To keep up, health care managers will need to continuously update their knowledge and skills.

Who Pays For Health Care Services?

Payment for health care services comes from many sources. Payment may come from:

- Patients
- Patient families
- Health care providers
- Charitable groups and individuals
- Employers
- Insurance companies
- Government

Each of the above payment sources has its own set of payment criteria that need to be met before a bill is paid.

Patients and Their Families

Patients and/or their families may be responsible for the payment of a bill for several reasons. These include (5):

- Insurance plan deductibles and co-payments
- Insurance coverage limits
- Insurance payment limits
- Lack of health insurance
- Patient election

Patients are commonly responsible for payment of all or part of their health care costs because of insurance deductibles and co-payments. An insurance deductible is an amount that the patient or family has agreed to pay out of pocket for covered health care services before the insurer must pay any part of the bill. Deductibles are often set at a per person and/or per family amount per calendar year. Co-payments refer to an amount or percentage of the service cost a patient and/or family must pay after the deductible has been satisfied. Co-payments may be limited to a total dollar amount per person and/or per family per year. Co-payments are made by the patient directly to the service provider. Some insurers require providers to collect the co-payment at the time of service.

Coverage guidelines are established by insurance plans to identify which health care services are or are not covered by the plan. Specific services, the amount of a specific service, preapproval requirements, payment limits or the source of service may be used to limit coverage. There are different types of coverage limits. Coverage limits may be applied to elective, experimental, and cosmetic procedures. Payment for outpatient therapy visits might be limited to a fixed number per policy year. Coverage may only be available for services received from specific providers. Payment may be denied or limited for any services received by the patient without prior approval. Services excluded from coverage are called non-covered services. Patients and their families are responsible for payment of non-covered services unless an insurer-to-provider agreement limits the patient's financial responsibility in some manner.

Payment limits are related to the amount the insurer will pay for a specific service. Often, indemnity insurers (private insurers) pay a fixed amount for services. According to Berman (5), what is paid is "based on the insurers definition of reasonable and allowable costs." While this may sound fair, it actually places an extra burden on the patient and their families who are responsible for payment of the difference between charges and insurer payment.

Payment may be the responsibility of a patient and/or family if they are uninsured for health care services or if they elect to receive a non-covered service. This payment category is referred to as self-payment. Because the self-pay patient is unable to negotiate special rates based on volume or other considerations, they ultimately pay more for health care than most third party payers.

Health Care Providers

Health care providers fund a portion of the health care service they provide. The provision of charity care, care that is funded below the cost of services and provisions for bad debt, are ways in which provider payment occurs. Not-for-profit teaching organizations commonly provide more unfunded care than their counterparts. It is this community service that qualifies health care providers for a tax exempt status.

Charitable Groups And Individuals

Once a major source of health care funding, charitable contributions still pay for health care services. Before the development of today's third party payer system, not-for-profit community health care institutions relied on individuals and philanthropic foundations to fund capital equipment and facilities investments. As government funding of health and social service programs has declined, the need for alternative funding sources has increased. Once again, health care providers are turning to individuals and philanthropic foundations for funding. This is evidenced by the increased resources being devoted to formal fund raising activities. Moneys received from individuals and philanthropic foundations to fund health care may be targeted for a donor specified use or given as a general contribution to a health care provider for the purpose of funding health care related expenses.

Employers

Berman (5) estimates that employers and their employees pay the greatest amount, about 32%, of national health care costs. Employers may pay health care costs through the purchase of employee health care insurance. Alternately, an employer may choose to self-insure. A self-insured employer is directly responsible for its employee's health care costs. Self-insured employers have the option of managing their self-insured program or outsourcing. Either an insurance carrier or third party administrator (TPA) may be contracted to perform utilization management and/or claims processing functions for self-insured plans. Traditional insurance companies also offer the self-insured employer the option of purchasing stop-loss insurance. Stop-loss insurance limits the employer's financial risk to a dollar amount per case. The stop-loss insurer pays costs above the stop-loss limit. For example, the employer may be responsible for all of an employee's health care expense up to $30,000. Any costs in excess of $30,000 become the responsibility of the stop-loss insurer.

Insurance Companies

Payment for health care services may come from a variety of insurance plans. Health, malpractice, personal liability, property and casualty, disability and workers compensation insurance all provide some level of payment for health care services. Health insurance plans are, of course, the primary source of health care payments.

INDEMNITY HEALTH INSURANCE PLANS

Traditional indemnity health insurance provides comprehensive coverage for medical and hospital service. To enroll in an indemnity insurance plan the employer and/or subscriber pays a premium, and the subscriber agrees to pay any required deductible, co-payments and amounts over the insurers usual and customary rate for specific services. In return, the subscriber may receive medical and hospital services from the physician, hospital or other qualified provider of their choice. The subscriber can choose a level of coverage from a package that may include (5):

- Hospital care benefits
- Outpatient care benefits
- Medical benefits
- Major medical (benefits paid after deductible is satisfied)
- Dental care

Coverage is usually restricted to services that are covered under the insurance plan, have been determined to be medically necessary and meet accepted standards of medical practice. Prior approval for coverage may be required. Experimental or other non-covered services may be negotiable under certain circumstances.

MANAGED HEALTH CARE INSURANCE PLANS

In the early 1980s, the federal government and other employers began to look for ways to control the costs of providing health care insurance for their employees. The cost of insurance premiums had escalated to the point in which the cost was threatening the financial health of businesses and the government-sponsored insurance plans. Many employers looked to the growing number of managed care organizations (MCOs) for relief.

MCOs offer an identified set of medical and/or hospital care for a predetermined, fixed premium (5). In return for this premium, the MCO is required to deliver all needed services within the cost limits of the fixed premium rate. To meet this requirement, MCOs restrict the subscriber's choice of providers and control subscriber access to health care through various forms of utilization management. A common method of control is the exclusive use of an employed or contracted panel of primary care physicians. Each enrollee chooses or is assigned a primary care physician (PCP) who acts as a gate keeper for all other medical and hospital services. Services may be provided directly by the MCO or provided under contract with a limited number of contracted providers.

Contracted providers may be required to accept significant discounts or capitated payment for the opportunity to get an increased volume of business. MCOs need contracted providers who will support their cost containment efforts. Payment reduction and utilization management, made possible by limiting enrollee choice of providers, are the foundation of managed care cost reduction strategies. Contract specifications, case and capitated payments are all elements of this strategy.

MCOs continue to evolve in an effort to gain an increased share of the health insurance market. The introduction of plan options that offer the subscriber greater choice of providers has become increasingly popular. Use of a Preferred Provider Organization (PPO), a network of affiliated providers who contract with a MCO to provide care to the MCO enrollees, is one approach. Use of a provider network broadens the enrollee's choice of providers but still allows the managed care insurer to operate at a cost less than an open-choice indemnity insurer. Under a network model, the insurer contracts with a panel of service providers in a specific geographical area. Contracted providers are preferred providers. Enrollees pay less when they choose to receive care from a PPO member; they pay more out of pocket when they choose to receive care from a non-PPO provider. Managed care plans that offer enrollees access to a broad choice of providers at different co-payment rates are commonly referred to as a point-of-service plan.

From the provider perspective, contracting with a MCO provides the opportunity to maintain and/or increase market share. When considering such a contract, a provider must weigh the potential value of holding or gaining market share against the terms and conditions of the managed care agreement. A provider considering a managed care contract must be able to determine the financial impact of the agreement. We are familiar with more than a few providers who entered into managed care contracts to capture the market only to face a financial loss on the business gained.

OTHER INSURANCE PLANS THAT PAY FOR HEALTH CARE SERVICES

Personal liability, malpractice, property and casualty, disability and workers' compensation insurance plans are also sources of health care payment. Coverage under these types of insurance is limited to services provided for the treatment of an injury or illness related to the specific circumstances. Workers' compensation insurance provides payment for medical services necessitated by a work-related injury or illness. Workers' compensation insurance plans vary greatly and are under the regulatory control of the state insurance commissions. Disability insurance may pay for medical services that have the potential to decrease insurance plan costs related to disability payments. Providers often must pursue and negotiate with the insurer for this type of service payment. Disability insurance plans may pay for extended rehabilitation services that are not covered under a patient's health insurance plan. Personal liability, malpractice, property and casualty insurance provide payment for services that are needed for the treatment of injury or illness which result from the circumstance that are subject to insurance coverage. An auto accident, slip and fall injury in a store, or an injury resulting from medical malpractice may all be subject to coverage under these types of insurance. Workers' compensation insurance provides payment for medical care that is related to job related injury or illness.

Government Programs

It is estimated that the federal government pays for 29% of national health care costs while state and local governments pay for an additional 15% (5). Government programs that provide payment for health care services include Medicare, Medicaid, CHAMPUS, Veterans Administration Health Facilities as well as health services provided by state and local government programs. The largest of these government payment sources are the Medicare and Medicaid programs. Medicare and Medicaid were enacted in 1965 as Title XVIII and Title XIX of the Social Security Act. It is estimated there are now 35 million people eligible for benefits under Medicare and another 25 million who are covered by Medicaid (5).

MEDICARE

The Medicare program provides services to persons 65 years of age or over as well as persons who meet special eligibility requirements. Special eligibility is provided for persons under 65 with longterm disabilities or chronic renal disease and widows, 50 or over, who are eligible for disability payments. There has been some indication that the Medicare program's age of eligibility will increase from the current 65 years of age in the near future. Medicare funding comes from a variety of sources, among them:

- Social Security payroll deductions of employees
- Social Security Act contributions of the employer
- Social Security Act contributions of the self-employed
- Federal Medicare Trust Fund

Medicare beneficiary deductible and co-payment amounts are set on an annual basis. The beneficiary deductible and co-payment under Medicare are structured in two parts: Medicare Part A and Part B. Each part provides coverage for a specific set of services under specified conditions and cost sharing (co-payment) requirements. Limits to coverage and the duration of coverage are also defined.

For Part A, the Medicare program uses contracted intermediaries to administer program services for defined geographical areas called regions. Intermediaries may administer the entire program for a region or only specific services. A large health care business providing several types of services such as hospital, home care and hospice may work with three different intermediaries. Intermediaries perform a variety of administrative functions including, claims processing, review and investigation, provider education, provider financial review, audit and provider certification review, and regulatory compliance functions. Periodic changes in the beneficiary payment levels, as well as the official interpretation of service coverage and benefits regulations, make it necessary for health care providers to frequently obtain updated information. Medicare program information can be obtained from industry publications, consultants, and industry representatives, such as professional organizations. Participating providers can obtain this information from their Medicare intermediary through periodic Medicare Advisory notices or direct contact with the intermediary provider services department. Medicare Part A helps pay for hospital care, services at a skilled nursing facility after a hospital stay, intermittent services from a home health agency for homebound patients, and hospice care.

For Part B, the Medicare program uses contracted fiscal agents who are referred to as carriers. A typical carrier is a large insurance company who is already doing business covering a large geographical area. Providers work directly with their assigned carriers to obtain information and for claims processing (5).

Part B is the medical insurance section of Medicare. It helps pay for physician services, outpatient services, medical, some home health services and supplies not covered under Part A. Part B is funded through beneficiary-paid monthly insurance premiums and co-payments. The premium rate is set each year to be effective in January. Annual premium increases must be at or under the annual percentage increase in Social Security payments (5).

MEDICAID

The Medicaid program was established to provide for the health care needs of the poor. This program provides services to people who are blind, disabled, families with dependent children, and elderly who are poor. Responsibility for funding the Medicaid program is shared between state and federal governments. Each pays a percentage of the total cost.

State participation in the Medicaid program is voluntary. Participating states are not required to implement the program with a standard set of benefits. States enter into an agreement with the Federal Government to furnish a minimum set of mandated health services to qualified persons described above. To qualify as financially needy, a family's income level must be below the state-set poverty level. Berman indicates that the poverty level set by states varies greatly with a 100% spread from lowest to highest (5). The percentage of federal funding received by a state is based on per capita income. A lower per capita income results in a higher percentage of federal payment of Medicaid costs.

What Do Third Party Payers Pay For?

Insurance Plan Coverage Guidelines

Employer self-funded plans, indemnity, managed care and government-sponsored insurance plans all have established coverage guidelines. These guidelines specify which health care services are and are not covered by the plan. They also specify administrative requirements that must be met before payment will be made. Coverage guidelines vary greatly between payers, geographical regions and over time. Coverage guidelines should be used by the enrollee (patient) and the health provider to determine what, when and how services are covered. These guidelines should either provide or direct the

subscriber and provider to detailed information on the following topics.

1. Health care services covered, partially covered and excluded from coverage under the plan.
2. Coverage limits by amount, type or source of service.
3. Source of care, defined by care giver qualifications, provider type, as well as authorized service locations.
4. Service preauthorization requirements.
5. Service and charge documentation requirements including, required forms and submission requirements.
6. Directions for obtaining preauthorization for covered services.
7. Procedures for addressing any disputed preauthorization decision made by the payer.
8. Responsibilities of patient, provider and insurer in the event that non-covered or unauthorized services are provided.
9. Payment limits, discounts and incentives that apply to the enrollee and/or payer.
10. Bill processing procedures and contacts.
11. Administrative responsibilities of the subscriber, the provider and, sometimes, the payer.

Coverage guidelines should be available from the enrollee or the insurance plan. Some health insurance plans have provider information departments that provide information by telephone. Coverage guidelines need to be met before a bill is paid.

Coverage Guidelines For Government-Sponsored Health Insurance Programs

The Medicare and Medicaid program coverage guidelines can be found in Title XVIII and Title XIX of the Social Security Act of 1965. Any modifications since its enactment are recorded in the Federal Register. A complete set of coverage guidelines and all subsequent updates both in the law or law interpretation are available to participating providers.

Providers who wish to provide services under government-sponsored plans must apply and meet requirements and program criteria for participation. If these requirements are met, the provider must enter into a participation agreement with the government health care insurance plan. The agreement will specify the health care services a provider may provide to the plan's beneficiaries. Providers participating in government-sponsored health plans are certified to provide services to its beneficiaries.

Providers may be certified for participation in the Medicare program, Part A, under the following classifications.

- Acute care hospital
- Long-term care hospital
- Rehabilitation hospital
- Skilled nursing facility
- Home health agency
- Hospice program

Providers can be certified for participation in the Medicare program, for Part B services, under the following classifications.

- Chiropractor
- Physical therapist
- Acute care hospital
- Skilled nursing facility
- Out patient clinic
- Rehabilitation agency
- Public health department
- Comprehensive outpatient rehabilitation facility
- Durable medical equipment dealer
- Independent laboratory

Providers who meet Medicare requirements can receive payment from the Medicare program, for Part B services, under the following classifications.

- Licensed doctor or medicine or osteopathy
- Licensed doctor of dentistry
- Licensed podiatrist
- Ambulance service

A specific set of coverage guidelines are available for each type of certified provider.

Medicare Coverage Of Physical Therapy Services

Physical therapy services are covered under Part A of the Medicare program under the following four conditions.

1. Services are provided to an inpatient of a participating hospital.
2. Services are provided to an inpatient of a participating skilled nursing facility. The patient's stay must be eligible for Part A coverage under Medicare.

3. Services are provided by a participating home health agency to a patient following a hospital or skilled nursing facility inpatient stay.
4. Services are provided by a participating hospice.

Physical therapy services are covered under Part B of the Medicare program under the following conditions.

1. Services are provided to an inpatient without Part A benefits or an outpatient by a participating hospital or a skilled nursing facility.
2. Services are provided to outpatients of a participating hospital, skilled nursing facility, home health agency, clinic, rehabilitation agency, comprehensive outpatient rehabilitation facility or public health agency.
3. Services are provided in the office of a licensed physician.
4. Services are provided by a participating physical therapist to patients in the office or in the home.

All physical therapy services must be provided under a written plan of care established and periodically reviewed by a referring physician. All changes in a patient's plan of care must be approved by the physician. The participation of the physician must be evidenced by documentation in the medical record. The requirements related to physician referral are not altered by state level direct access licensure laws.

Responsibilities of The Health Care Provider Operating Under Contract with a Health Care Insurance Plan

In the absence of a provider agreement, coverage compliance and financial responsibility for coverage compliance falls to the patient or their guardian. If the service received is not covered, the patient is responsible for provider payment. Under provider agreements, coverage compliance and financial responsibility for coverage compliance usually falls to the provider.

In practice, the risk of non-payment for services provided on credit often falls to the health care provider. It is common for patients to be unfamiliar with or confused by their insurance coverage guidelines. To minimize this risk, providers should be proactive in determining a patient's insurance coverage for the services in question. Providers should follow consistent admission, insurance verification, credit and collections policy and procedures. In addition, the patient or their guardian should be asked to sign a statement of financial responsibility for all services provided on credit during the admission process. Alternatively, payment can be obtained in advance or at the time of service.

Coverage guidelines for government programs are specified in the legislation that authorized the development of and the expenditure for the program. As such, these guidelines are legal requirements that beneficiaries and participating providers are required to follow. Failure to comply with coverage guidelines, even if unintentionally, is a violation of the law. In the case of Medicare and Medicaid, this would be a federal violation. Providers found to be in violation are subject to loss of their license to practice, loss of certification, fines and imprisonment. Compliance with Medicare and Medicaid coverage guidelines should be a priority for any qualified provider.

Third Party Payment For Administrative Services

Under some provider agreements, the payer may provide compensation to the provider for administrative services. Utilization management, participation in the payers outcomes management program, data collection, participation in meetings and training sessions or consulting services may all warrant additional compensation. Payment for administrative services would be negotiated as part of the provider agreement.

Performance Incentive Payments

As health care service utilization and cost information become more available, payer interest in payment for performance has increased. Cost per case, days of service, ongoing care requirement, and days lost from work are all examples of performance measures that are of interest to payers. They are of interest because they relate in some way to the cost of current and/or future care. Currently, payers offer incentive payments to providers who can produce outcomes that help them control their costs. Per diem, per case and capitated payment methodologies all offer financial incentives to providers who can continue to reduce the cost of care. The incentive is improved

net income. Control of resource utilization (products and services) is the performance to be rewarded. Cost control is the goal. If the provider is successful, patient care costs less because it takes less time, supplies, et al, to produce the desired patient outcome. Under incentive payment arrangements, the provider is accountable for maintaining the quality of the patient's care and outcomes.

Maximizing Net Income Under Third Party Payment Methods

Maximizing net income requires a working knowledge of the various third party payment methods. It also requires the ability and willingness to manage the resources used in the care of the patient. The following discussion will focus on the relationships among payment methods, volume of services, cost and net income. Under any payment method, there exists the potential for provider abuse. Providers must be cautious and apply their knowledge of the third party payment system in an ethical and legal manner. As providers assume more financial risk for the delivery of health care services, they must be increasingly mindful that any and all efforts to maximize reimbursement are guided by applicable standards of practice.

Managing Under A Cost-Based Payment Method

Under cost-based methods, the service provider is paid the lesser of charges or full allowable cost plus an additional amount to cover the investment in facilities and capital equipment. Allowable costs are defined by the payer but are generally limited to costs that can be shown to contribute directly to patient care. Under some cost-based reimbursement programs, total allowable cost is paid up to a pre-set maximum amount. Costs in excess of the maximum are not covered by the payment. The maximum is called a cost cap.

Cost-based payment methods encourage increased service utilization and cost. As discussed in Chapter 1, without a limit to allowable cost, there are no provider incentives to control cost. The use of cost reimbursement is limited at this time but it remains a significant payment method for outpatient rehabilitation services, inpatient rehabilitation units and freestanding rehabilitation, children's and long-term care hospitals under the Medicare program. Government and private health insurance plans have been and will continue to make changes that eliminate the use of cost-based methodology. The Balanced Budget Act of 1997 does this for many types of health care facilities.

Assuming that a provider's charges are set reasonably above their cost, net income is maximized under cost-based payment methods when:

- More patients receive service
- Individual patients receive more service
- Increments of service cost more to provide

When allowable costs to provide services are capped, net income is maximized under the same conditions as long as costs are kept under the cost cap. Some capped-payment programs offer providers an incentive payment when their costs are kept significantly below the cost cap. Under cost-based reimbursement, the provider has limited financial risk (5).

Managing Under Fee-For-Service and Discounted Fee-For-Service Payment Method

Under a fee-for-service system, the provider delivers, bills and is paid for each discrete increment of service or product provided to a patient. Payment is calculated for each increment billed and combined to create a total billed amount. Assuming the provider's charges are set reasonably above the provider's cost, net income is maximized when:

- More patients receive service
- Individual patients receive more services
- Increments of service are provided in the least expensive manner.

Actual payment under fee-for-service may be less than charges due to the application of a payers' usual and customary rate (UCR) schedule (See Chapter 7, Charge And Payment Methodology). If the health care provider has agreed to accept the UCR payment as payment in full, payment will usually be less than charges. Under Medicare and Medicaid, this is called accepting assignment. If the patient becomes responsible for the difference between UCR and charges, payment may be delayed and/or the cost of collecting

money owed to the provider may increase. As the Balanced Budget Act is fully implemented, fee-for-service payment will be eliminated for Medicare patients.

A health care business may desire to enter into discounted arrangements for two reasons: to keep current market share controlled by third party payers or to increase market share. Provider risk is minimal under fee-for-service. Provider risk under discounted fee-for-service payment method is minimal if discounts are based on good cost and utilization information. Cost and utilization information is required to set appropriate percentage discount rates. The provider must set a rate that keeps the total payment above total cost for services provided under the discount arrangement.

Managing Under Per Diem Payment Method

Under the per diem payment method, the health care provider is paid a set amount per patient per day. The amount paid covers all specified services provided in the care of the patient for the day. This method of payment can be applied to inpatient and outpatient care settings. It is usual for the per diem rate to stay the same throughout the course of the patient's care. This is important because the initial days of the patient's treatment are generally more service intense and costly than later days (5). The length of treatment is also an important factor when evaluating per diem payment arrangements. The financial contribution from services provided under per diem methods may be calculated on a case or contract basis. Total payments for the case or contract less total costs for the case or contract equal net income (loss). Under the per diem method, net income is maximized when:

- More patients receive service
- Average patient length of service is longer
- The health care provider(s) who is at financial risk has control over service utilization
- Individual patients receive only the services they require
- Required services are provided in the least expensive manner
- Care is coordinated between providers (as applicable)
- Provider incentives are aligned to minimize per day service utilization and cost
- Care plans are standardized to minimize variations in care for similar patients
- Common complications are managed proactively

Note: Collective efforts to manage resource utilization is often referred to as case management.

Accurate definition of covered services included under the per diem rate is key to minimizing provider risk. Both parties must agree to the covered service definition. The covered services should be specifically documented and acknowledged in writing by all parties. The health care provider does share in the financial risk under the per diem method. The degree of risk depends on the setting, services to be provided and the potential for expensive variation from the standard plan of care. Anything that results in an increased need for services on a per day basis will decrease net income.

Managing Under Case Rate Payment Method

Under the case rate payment method, the health care business offers to provide 1) all of some product or service or 2) all products and services required for the management of a specific patient case at a pre-set charge. For example, if a provider agreed to provide all health care services related to a knee joint arthroplasty procedure for one inclusive price, that would be a case rate.

The provider's goal is to set the case payment rate at a level that exceeds the average case cost. Net income (loss) equals the difference between case rate and average cost per case. The average case cost is used because some variation in service utilization (high and low) is expected. The greater the number of cases, the greater the potential net income (loss). Using the average case cost gives a better performance picture. Once the case rate is set, the health care provider is responsible for any cost related to the provision of covered care. This is a risk agreement because the provider is responsible for the delivery of care, even if the costs for the case exceed the case rate. The broader the scope of the case, the greater the potential variability and provider risk of incurring unexpected cost. Assuming the case rate covers the average cost of providing the specified care (case cost), net income is maximized when:

- More patients receive service
- The health care provider(s) at financial risk also controls service utilization
- Individual patients receive only the services they require

- Required services are provided in the least expensive manner
- Care is coordinated between providers and settings (as applicable)
- Provider incentives are aligned to minimize service utilization and cost
- Care plans are standardized to minimize variations in care for similar patients
- Common complications are managed proactively

Accurate definition of the case, including covered services and pricing, is essential to minimizing provider risk. Both the provider and the payer must agree on the definition of the case. The definition should include what is and what is not covered under the case rate. A description of covered services should be written and accepted in writing by all parties. When do services under the case start and stop? How and by whom is the care plan determined? What products are included under the case rate? Is there a point at which the high cost of an individual case will trigger extra payment?

A case that falls well outside the norm for cost and service utilization is called an outlier. Outlier payment provisions are often included in case rate agreements. Outlier provisions act as stop-loss insurance. The outlier provision comes into play when the cost of a case exceeds a pre-set dollar amount. Outlier provisions limit a providers financial risk.

Managing Under Capitation Payment Method

Capitated agreements are full-risk payment arrangements. Under a capitated payment arrangement, the provider agrees to accept a pre-set dollar amount in return for accepting full financial responsibility for the delivery of specified health care services to a specified group of managed care enrollees during the effective period of the arrangement. Capitation is unique to managed health care insurance plans.

Capitated payment rates are not based on the actual amount and cost of services used. Rather, capitated rates are based on estimated utilization of service and the expected cost of utilized service for the enrollee population (members) to be covered. Utilization projections are usually expressed in terms of the amount of service used by the members in a given time period. For example, utilization projections for outpatient therapy services might be expressed as the number of visits or procedures per 1000 plan members per month. The cost of service is based on the average use and cost of services delivered under a managed care approach (5).

The capitation method offers many technical challenges. In our experience, one of the greatest challenges is the accurate projection of service utilization and related cost when applied to small, self-selected populations of enrollees. Without adequate correction for costly outliers, adverse population selection and unreliable utilization and cost data increase the financial risk assumed by the health care provider to an extreme (5). If the payment rate is inadequate, a capitated agreement could jeopardize the financial viability of the health care provider. Payment under capitation can be based on a set amount of payment per enrollee per month or as a percentage of the monthly premium (8). Assuming that the payment rate is appropriate for the patient population, net income is maximized when:

- Less patients receive service
- Access to and utilization of service is controlled by the at risk provider
- Individual patients receive only the services they require
- Required services are provided in the least expensive manner
- Care is coordinated between providers and settings (as applicable)
- Provider incentives are aligned to minimize service utilization and cost
- Care plans are standardized to minimize variations in care for similar patients
- Common complications are managed proactively

Under capitation payment, the provider benefits when patients covered under the plan receive less care and/or services are provided more efficiently (9).

Payment Related Practices That May Impact Net Income

There are additional payment practices that have the potential to impact net income. These include quick pay discounts, payer audits and pre-authorization requirements.

Quick payment discounts are offered by providers who do a large volume of business with a specific payer. The provider offers the payer a discount off billed charges in return for quick payment and an agreement that there will be no post-payment audit of charges. This practice minimizes the cost of dollars sitting in non-interest bearing accounts receivable and payer bad debt. It also improves cash flow.

Payers may audit patient medical records to determine if charges can be verified by matching billed items against medical record documentation. They may review documentation to determine if services provided were medically necessary based on the practice norms, that services provided were covered under the plan, and that all services were based on a physician-approved plan of care. Charges that cannot be verified or justified are not paid.

Many health insurance plans require the provider, the enrollee or their representative to obtain prior authorization for services. Payment is denied for services that were not authorized in advance of service delivery. Under this situation, the patient or the provider may be financially responsible for the charges. Responsibility for charges may be determined by a payment agreement signed by the patient, the patient's insurance plan coverage guidelines, and/or a provider participation agreement.

Getting Paid: Things To Do

If service delivery is the top priority of the health care manager, then getting paid for services provided should be a close second. In fact, getting paid may have everything to do with the a business' ability to deliver service. Owners and managers of small, independent health care practices may recognize the need to focus on getting paid more readily than their colleagues working in large multi-faceted health care organizations. This may be because larger organizations have more support functions to assist with the business aspects of service delivery (See Chapter 10). No matter, large or small, getting paid is becoming almost as complex as service delivery. Third party payer demands for service and outcome documentation, prior authorization requirements, complicated coverage guidelines, service type and location restrictions, as well as care management have placed the responsibility for getting paid in the hands of clinical managers and their staff. Unless the front line and support services coordinate efforts, no one gets paid. The following is a list of the common things all health care businesses must have to get paid.

1. Insurance plan participation agreements.
2. A descriptive list of services and products to sell.
3. A price list for the services and products to be sold.
4. A process for patient registration, payer verification and coverage verification.
5. A credit policy.
6. A process for recording charges, billing and tracking payment.
7. Accounting procedures for the intake and posting of cash receipts.
8. A process for collection and write-off of delinquent accounts.

Participation Agreements

Participation agreements are also referred to as managed care contracts, preferred provider contracts, and service agreements. As noted earlier in this chapter, a participation agreement is a contract between an insurance plan and a provider that allows a health care provider to participate in the care of the plan's enrollees. Third party payers may require health care businesses to have provider participation agreements before they will pay the provider for services provided to the plan's enrollees. Participation agreements set out the terms and conditions under which a health care business must operate if they wish to provide services under the plan. Participation agreements are not required by all payers under all circumstances. For example, Medicare pays for physical therapy provided by a participating hospital, skilled nursing facility, home health care agency, rehabilitation agency, outpatient clinic, public health agency, CORF, and physical therapist. Medicare also pays for physical therapy services provided in the office of a licensed physician. A participation agreement is not required for the physician to bill for these services. Provider participation agreements are usually required if a provider wishes to provide services to its enrollees. A few managed health plans will allow enrollees to receive service from nonparticipating providers if the enrollee is willing to pay a greater portion of the service charge.

A health plan may take an open or restrictive approach to provider participation agreements. The least restrictive allows participation by any willing and qualified provider. Medicare, Medicaid and most traditional indemnity health insurance plans take an any willing provider approach.

Managed health plans want to limit the number of providers in return for provider discounts. These plans will take a competitive approach to awarding limited term participation agreements. The competitive selection process may be by invitation only or open to any qualified provider. During a competitive selection process, interested providers receive and respond to a Request For Proposal (RFP) to provide the RFP specified services. The RFP should provide information regarding the services needed and delineate the information required from the provider if they wish to be considered for participation. The RFP may specify minimum requirements for participation. For example, a payer seeking to limit the number of providers may have requirements related to the provider's service capacity and geographical coverage area (9,10). If selected for participation, providers sign an agreement and become part of the plan's preferred provider panel.

The most restrictive approach to provider participation is an exclusive participation agreement. Using a competitive selection process, as described above, the health care plan chooses one provider to deliver the specified care to an identified group of its enrollees. This approach guarantees the provider a higher volume of patients. In return, the health plan will expect to pay less for the services.

A participation agreement provides access to the market of patients requiring services. As managed care plans gain a greater share of the health insurance market, including Medicare and Medicaid beneficiaries, participation agreements become more important to both large and small providers. If 40% of the population in a market area is enrolled in a single managed care plan, the provider without a participation agreement lacks access to 40% of the market. Unfortunately, this is the type of market pressure that may cause a health care business to accept unreasonable financial risk.

Access to the market should be a strategic direction for any provider facing an increase in the use of restrictive provider contracting. Chapter 3 provides the reader with a market-oriented approach to business development. The marketing process starts with an assessment of customer needs. The successful health care business is one that can offer the customer a service that can meet their needs. Industry experts agree with this approach (9,10). Gill states that managed care plans are looking for three elements in contracting for rehabilitation services (9):

1. A reduction in cost.
2. Geographical coverage.
3. Quality service that satisfies enrollees.

Proactive strategic and financial planning will help minimize the risks inherent in manage care contracting. As noted previously, to plan effectively, the health care provider must have access to reliable financial and outcome information.

Services and Equipment For Sale

All businesses must identify the services and/or products it has available to sell. Decisions regarding a product come from the assessment of customer needs. Catalogs, menus and price tags are all ways of telling potential customers what is for sale. Health care businesses must do the same. Although this may sound simple, the health care provider's information needs, coupled with the multiple customer transaction characteristic of health care, make this somewhat of a challenge. As you might suspect, everyone would like to receive this information in a different way. Fortunately, third party payers have told us what information they need to pay the bill.

SERVICE AND PRODUCT DESCRIPTIONS

Potential customers need a list and description of the services and products for sale. The name and description of each item should be user friendly. Accepted industry terminology should be used whenever possible. For example, the term physical therapy evaluation would be more easily understood than a name like neurodevel-

opmental assessment. Descriptions should be understandable to individuals lacking knowledge of medical terminology. These are tools meant to educate the customer. If desired, a technical description can be used internally. The description should also define the incremental units by which the service or product is sold. For example, *Do It All Therapy, Inc.* sells therapy services in 15 minute increments with partial increments rounded up to the nearest whole number. A customer who receives a 25 minute treatment would be billed for two units, i.e., 30 minutes, of service.

The number of listed services and products will vary based on the size and complexity of the business as well as management and customer information needs. The greater the information needs, the greater the number of items on the list. The challenge is to limit the list to only those items that will provide useful information. The list of items for sale delineates the information contained in the billing data base. Many of the operating indicators listed in Table 8.2 that may be useful to management, use information from the billing data base. Billing records will be the primary source of service utilization information. In the absence of a fully integrated information system, the billing data base may be structured to provide utilization information by patient type, product line, customer type, etc. It may also be used as a staff, equipment, and facility productivity tracking system. See Chapter 10, Information Management, for an expanded discussion on data base management.

Procedure Codes

In addition to a name, description of the service, and increment of product or service to be sold, each item on the list must be assigned a unique internal numeric code. The numeric code is used to classify and to differentiate one revenue subaccount from the others. The numeric code assigned is determined by the structure of the organization's chart of accounts. Please refer to Chapter 7, Chart Of Accounts, for a more complete discussion of this topic. It is the numeric coding that facilitates billing automation.

There are also external service codes that need to be incorporated into the service and product

TABLE 8.2
Operating Indicators For Therapy Practice

INDICATOR TYPE	OPERATING INDICATOR
Referrals Admissions Visits	• Referral date, day and time • How was your clinic selected • Source by payer • Source by physician • Source by geography • Case mix • Type of service per admission • Percentage of referrals admitted • Appointments per admission • Treatment visits per admission • Appointment cancellation rate • Cancellation rate by payer type • UOS per admission • UOS per visit

Revenue	• Gross and net revenue per:
	  • Admission
	  • Visit
	  • UOS
	  • Equipment type
	• Gross revenue per FTE by category
	• Patients required to pay on-site co-payments

Cost	• Fixed and variable cost per:
	  • UOS
	  • Piece of equipment
	• Labor cost per UOS
	• Non-labor cost per UOS
	• Cost of a cancellation
	• Benefits cost as a percentage of salary
	• Allocated indirect cost per UOS
	• Cost per case by patient type
	• Cost per case by payer type

Efficiency	• Annual and monthly break-even point • Time to schedule new referral • Time from referral to appointment • Direct work hour paid per UOS • Indirect work hours paid per UOS • Direct hours worked per UOS • Indirect hours worked per UOS • UOS per clinic hour (outpatient) • UOS per square foot clinical space • Rates for clinical equipment use • Productivity per measure for support functions
Service Utilization	• Visits per patient type • UOS per patient type • Referrals by contract • Visits/UOS by contract • Patient type by contract

descriptions. There are two standardized external service coding systems that are used to identify physical therapy services on health insurance claim forms. The first system is the Current Procedural Terminology (CPT) procedure codes (8). This coding system was developed and is updated annually by the American Medical Association (AMA). The CPT coding system was developed to meet the needs of physicians for standardized procedure codes. An updated CPT coding manual is published annually. A second coding system is the Common Procedural Coding System of the Health Care Financing Administration (HCFA). HCFA is the administrative arm of The Department of Health, Education and Welfare, which has responsibility for operation of the Medicare program. Medicare, Medicaid and many other third party payers require providers to use the appropriate CPT and Common Procedural Coding System procedure codes when billing. An insurance plan may require the use of a specific coding system as part of the conditions of payment. Information regarding coding requirements could be found in the participation agreement, the coverage guidelines or by calling the insurance plan's provider service department.

Price Setting

Each service or product for sale needs a standard price. In Chapter 3, basic price setting strategies were reviewed. Earlier in this chapter, a model for predicting the change in net income resulting from a price increase and the concept of price setting to maximize revenue less than third party reimbursement were reviewed. Price is a management decision. Decisions about price setting need to balance the desire to maximize net income against business development strategies and market sensitivity to price. All businesses must be mindful of laws that govern pricing. The Robinson-Patman Act prohibits businesses from charging similar customers different prices unless the differences are based on " . . . differences in the cost of manufacture, sale or delivery resulting from the differing methods or quantities in which commodities are to such persons sold or delivered" (11). Differential pricing must be based on real cost differences.

Credit Policy

A high percentage of health care services are provided on credit. Credit purchasing occurs when the customer is billed through the use of an invoice for money owed after the services or products are provided. When this is the case, it is advisable to establish clear policies and practices regarding the extension of credit. Policies on charity care and discounts, financial counseling, patient self-pay obligations, coordination of third party benefits, billing procedures, and cash receipts management should be considered.

The Patient Registration Process

Effective management of accounts receivable starts before admission or at the point of patient registration (5). Ideally, the source of payment should be established before service is provided. Patient self-pay obligations should be identified. Payment terms and conditions should be discussed in advance of patient receipt of services. Of course, urgent and emergency services should be delivered upon patient presentation. The routine payment screening process should be initiated as soon as possible thereafter. When third party payment benefits are available, the patient or their representative should be asked to sign a statement of assignment. This will allow insurance payments to go directly to the provider. If the patient is unwilling to assign benefits, self-pay policies would be applied.

THIRD PARTY BENEFITS VERIFICATION AND PRE-AUTHORIZATION FOR SERVICES

When necessary, services should be preauthorized with the payer. Pre-authorization does not guarantee payment, though it may limit loss of payment due to technical issues. Usually, it is the responsibility of the enrollee to understand and comply with the terms of their insurance plan. In practice, it is in the provider's best interest to assist the patient with benefit verification and pre-authorization compliance. Not only is it good customer service, pre-authorization of service coverage has the potential to increase the speed and rate of payment.

ROLE OF THE CLINICIAN IN MAKING COVERAGE DECISIONS

There are insurance plans that hold the provider responsible for compliance with the plans' coverage guidelines. Charges for services provided or products given to enrollees that are not covered under the plan are not paid. Neither is the provider allowed to bill the enrollee directly. Notably, the Medicaid and Medicare programs operate in this manner. It is the responsibility of the provider to know and apply coverage guidelines and limits. A coverage determination for physical therapy service requires the treating therapist to have a working knowledge of the coverage guidelines. Using the Medicare program as an example, the treating therapist is largely responsible for insuring coverage of services provided.

First, the therapist must know what services and products are covered under the Medicare program.
Second, the therapist must know the conditions under which coverage is available (coverage restrictions).
Third, therapists must determine through clinical assessment, what specific services and equipment are needed. Then they must determine if what is needed is considered to be reasonable and necessary for a specific beneficiary. Under Medicare, to be reasonable and necessary, services and equipment must be expected to result in a reasonable level of improvement in a reasonable and generally predictable period of time.
Last, therapists must document information in support of their clinical decision, including patient history, current status and progress toward improvement over time. Should Medicare dispute the therapist's decision and deny coverage, the therapist must be prepared to defend their decision through an appeal process.

A full review of insurance coverage requirements is beyond the scope of this section. Our intent here is to demonstrate the impact front-line therapists have on a business' ability to get paid.

The Billing Process

The billing process is a multi-step process that starts with the delivery of service or sale of a product. Delivery of the product or service triggers the creation of a transaction record. This transaction record may double as the customer's invoice. In the case of a credit transaction, the transaction record is used to create an invoice (bill) at a later date. Invoices are sent and used to track payment. When payment is received, the customer's account is credited, and cash receipts are deposited in the bank. On the surface this is a relatively simple process.

However, when a business has a high percentage of credit sales, the billing process can become complex. This is especially true for health care in which multiple parties may be billed for a portion of the charges from the same transaction. When a high percentage of sales involve credit, an effective billing process can financially make or break the company. There are performance measures that may be used to evaluate the effectiveness of the billing and collections process (5,12). For example:

Days in accounts receivable. The amount of money held in accounts receivable is divided by the average amount of sales per day. This measures the average number of days it takes to collect payment on credit sales.

Average age of accounts receivable. The older the account, the greater the probability the account will not be paid. Unpaid accounts must be written off as a bad-debt expense.

Rate of collections. The percentage of accounts receivable that get paid. Dollars obtained through improved collections minus the cost of collecting the money goes directly to net income.

Accounts receivable carrying costs. There are three types of costs associated with accounts receivable. First, carrying cost is the opportunity cost of having money tied up in accounts receivable rather than another revenue producing investment. Second, credit and collection costs represent all of the business' operating costs related to the credit and collections function. Third, the cost of delinquent accounts (bad debt) is a cost to the company.

CHARGE RECORDING

The mechanics of setting up and operating an effective accounts receivable function, including billing, is business specific. We recommend that this be done in collaboration with a financial management professional. The financial management specialist understands billing systems and can provide expert assistance. The reader is referred to Chapter 13, Getting Advice. The therapy manager understands clinical operating issues that should influence the design of the billing function. Some examples of operating is-

sues that may have an impact on design are provided below.

The delivery of physical therapy is dynamic. Time, type, and resources used during the course of a treatment visit can easily vary from what was planned. As a result, the care provider is the only person who can accurately record charges.

Therapists' time is an expensive resource. An approach that minimizes time spent in billing-related activities will save money.

Billed charges must be verifiable through a medical record audit. If charge recording can be combined with medical record documentation, duplication of effort may be avoided.

Demands for high productivity during peak business hours lends itself to an end of day (next morning) billing process. This approach may result in higher therapist productivity but the time lapse between delivery and charge recording may jeopardize billing accuracy.

Manual activity logs have been used to improve the accuracy of an end-of-day billing. When used appropriately, activity logs allow therapists to record charges right after service delivery with minimal impact on time. But if the information from the activity log must be manually transcribed to a second form, transcription error rates may be a factor to consider.

Billing accuracy is of great concern. If the customer is under charged, the fixed and variable cost of that customer's service will be shifted to remaining customers. If the customer is over or incorrectly charged, the business loses credibility and risks decreased customer satisfaction, accusations of fraudulent billing and possible legal sanctions. Billing errors often delay payment for services provided. Everyone involved in the billing process needs to be committed to getting it right, the first time.

Invoicing, Payment Tracking And Collections

For cash sales, including the collection of co-payments, the invoice is presented and paid at the time of service or sale of equipment. For credit sales, the charge record is transferred to an invoice that is sent to the customer. It is customary to send the invoice to both the patient and the third party payer for traditional insurance plans. When the patient has no financial responsibility for payment, double invoicing may not be necessary.

To create an invoice, the health care organization must combine elements of the patients demographic and clinical record with charge information. Elements of information that should be available for completion of health care services invoice are listed below.

Many large insurance plans are promoting or mandating the use of electronic invoicing. Electronic invoicing can save time and money on both sides of the transaction. Often there is a substantial capital expense that may delay provider use of on-line billing.

Once invoiced, the remaining steps include accounting for incoming cash receipts, tracking payments, the identification of delinquent accounts and the application of more direct collection efforts as appropriate. A financial management professional is the best resource for system design. An information systems specialist may be needed to set up an electronic data transfer system to support electronic invoicing. In large organizations, most of the mechanics of the accounts receivable function will be the responsibility of the financial services and information systems departments. In a small business, owners may need to perform every step of the process themselves. In either case, the clinical manager should have input and an understanding of how to bill and get paid.

MAKING THE MOST OF WHAT YOU GET PAID

The goal of financial management is to maximize net income. To reach that goal, the spread between gross revenue and total cost must become wider. Armed with a working knowledge of cost characteristics and cost-volume-profit analysis, managers should be able to predict the impacts of their decisions regarding the purchase and use of resources on net income. The importance of efficiently managing resources has increased as payment cuts reduce the net income of most health care businesses. Health care payment rates, even when maximized, are expected to decline over the next several years. For more specific information, see Chapter 15, Futures. As payment rates decline, health care companies will need to continuously improve revenue and/or decrease cost. It should be no surprise that cost management has become a priority for health care businesses (3).

Managing Operating Expenses

Cost management should start with a clear understanding of what the business wants to accomplish.

What is the goal of the cost reduction effort?
Does the company want to reduce total cost?
How about cost per unit?
Is the goal to manage cost in response to volume fluctuations?

A clear definition of the goal guides management decisions about resource selection, acquisition, and utilization. Targeted time frame is another important aspect of cost management. Is there a need to control expenses for a short or long period of time? Cost management efforts that are meant to produce a long-term or progressive decrease in operating expenses will require fundamental and sustainable changes in the operating processes.

For example, *Do It All Therapy, Inc.* anticipated a cash shortfall for the first 3 months related to the opening of a new clinic. The shortfall is due to the large number of incremental expenses incurred due to the new clinic opening. To cover the payroll without taking out a high-priced, short-term loan, the owner-manager has put a hold on all nonessential expenditures for a period of 4 months. For example, instead of using temporary staffing, the manager personally filled staff absences on two occasions. The strategy was to reduce total current expense for a short period. The goal was to preserve the company's short-term cash position. The strategies selected would be difficult for a company to sustain over time.

Resource Productivity

Resource productivity refers to the amount of a resource consumed in the production of an increment of output. For example, if a physical therapist routinely provides and bills for 6.5 hours of service per 8-hour work day, then productivity per man hour worked would be at 81.2% (6.5 hours of service divided by 8 hour work day). Productivity could also be expressed as the number of hours worked to produce an hour of patient care (output). In this example, it takes 1.23 hours worked (8 hours worked divided by 6.5 hours of output) to produce 1 hour of output. The above calculation represents a performance standard for operations, but it does not give an accurate representation of the financial productivity of this resource.

Financial productivity measures the total cost of the resource against the value of the output. Figure 8.6 demonstrates how the financial productivity of a therapist's time would be calculated. The productivity per man hour paid for both the physical therapist and the physical ther-

apist assistant is 72%. It takes 1.44 hours paid to produce 1 hour of output.

Financial productivity can be calculated for any resource used in the production of services and products for sale. Financial productivity must be known before the production cost of a distinct unit of service or product can be calculated.

PRODUCTIVITY STANDARDS AND MEASUREMENT

As with any other aspect of organizational performance, an objective performance target

Resource Cost Element	Physical Therapist	Physical Therapist Assistant
Amount	1.0 FTE	1.0 FTE
Hours Paid	2080	2080
Non-Productive Hours:		
Vacation	120	120
Holiday	56	56
Education	40	40
Sick/Personal	24	24
Total Non-Productive	240	240
Productive Hours	1840	1840
Billed Hours		
(6.5 Billed Hrs/8 Wrkd Hrs)	1495	1495
UOS (15 Min)	5980	5980
Resource Cost:		
Compensation	$47,008	$37,918
Benefits	8,461	6,825
FICA	3,596	2,901
Education	750	500
Human Resource	200	100
Employee Recognition	100	100
Total Annual Cost	$60,116	$48,344
Position Cost Per UOS	10.05	8.08
Productivity Per Hour Paid	0.72	0.72
Hours Paid Per Hour Billed	1.4	1.4

FIGURE 8.6. Calculation of *Do It All Therapy, Inc.* financial productivity for FTE physical therapist and physical therapist assistant positions.

will help direct management and staff efforts in the right direction. Productivity standards are performance targets. To be of maximum benefit, productivity standards should be:

- Based on the work statistic of the organization or department
- Objectively measured
- Readily available
- Understandable
- Achievable

Management is responsible for setting productivity standards (performance expectations) for resources consumed. Where productivity standards do not exist or are out of date, new standards should be set using internal and, whenever possible, external utilization data. Internal data will demonstrate how well the organization is performing in comparison to historical performance. Comparison of external benchmarks to internal performance measurements will show how the organization is performing in comparison to other similar organizations. External benchmarks may be available through professional organizations, business associations, consultants, proprietary data bases or directly from similar business. Even if the organization exceeds external benchmarks, management may still find opportunities to improve performance.

Labor Costs

Typically, labor expenses represent a high percentage of the total operating expense of a health care organization. Control of labor expenses can be approached in many ways because there are so many types of labor related expenses. Compensation, benefits, recruitment, staff training and development, and employee recognition are the major labor expense categories. Examples of labor related costs that may be found in those categories are listed in Table 8.3.

Expenses associated with personnel recruitment, hiring and benefits administration may also be included under the heading of labor related expenses.

Labor costs are determined by management decisions. Examples of management decisions that impact labor related costs include the following.

- How to obtain needed human resources
- Number of FTE employees to hire
- Type of FTE employees (skill mix)
- How to recruit for employees
- Who to hire
- Level and method of compensation offered
- Benefit package offered
- The amount of investment in staff training and development
- The type of staff training and development
- Funding available for employee recognition

The first decision management must make is whether to hire or contract for needed services. This is a decision that needs to weigh both cost and performance impacts. The cost impacts can be calculated using the comparative model presented earlier in this chapter. The incremental

TABLE 8.3
Categories And Types Of Labor-Related Expenses

COMPENSATION	BENEFITS	TRAINING AND DEVELOPMENT	EMPLOYEE RECOGNITION
Regular Compensation	Auto Allowance	Paid Education Time	Subsidized Meals
Overtime	Club Membership	Paid Registration	Employee Recognition Events
Holiday Differential	Subsidized Child Care	Travel Expenses	Performance Awards
Shift Differentials	On-site Health Facilities	Tuition Reimbursement	
Recruitment Bonus	Employee Discounts	Continuing Education	
Retention Bonus	Stock Purchase Plans	Professional Dues	
Incentive Bonus	Employee Assistance Programs		
Tuition Repayment			
Profit Sharing			
Early Retirement Pay			
Severance Pay			

cost of hiring an employee is compared to the incremental cost of contracting for services required. The performance impacts are likely to be more complex. Performance of contract labor is situational. The performance of staff brought into a company under contract can be affected by their qualifications, familiarity with the work of the company, the company's ability to orient contract staff to the new environment, contract period, receptivity of employees, and the contracted employee's satisfaction with the arrangement. The therapy manager should keep in mind that contracted employees require the same orientation and training as any regular employee if they are to be maximally effective.

Management must also decide the number of FTE employees to hire. Ideally, these decisions should be based on the projected utilization of the department's products or service and the productivity standards set for each budget center. A full-time equivalent represents 2080 hours of paid time per year. The 2080 hours represents time when the employee is available to work (productive time) as well as time when the employee is paid but not available (nonproductive time). In calculating the amount of staff required to get the work completed, the nonproductive time must be included into the equation. This process is demonstrated in Figure 8.6. Using this example, if *Do It All Therapy, Inc.* had projected the demand for 3500 units of physical therapy service, the owner would want to employ or contract for 0.60 FTE (3500 UOS/ 5980 UOS Per PT Per Year) of physical therapy time.

Skill mix is another area in which the manager will need to balance cost and performance demands. Skill mix refers to the types and combination of positions hired. Going back to the example in Figure 8.6, if a physical therapist assistant (PTA) were hired instead of a physical therapist, the lower compensation rate for the PTA would reduce the cost per unit of service. The therapy manager needs to weigh the cost savings that result from lowering the skill mix to the clinical performance requirements of the practice.

How employees are recruited and who is recruited will impact labor cost. Advertising, mailing, exhibiting at conferences, attending career days or the use of recruitment agencies are all options open for the recruitment new staff. Some practices rely on student training programs to provide candidates for future positions. Each of these methods has an associated direct cost. Unmet demand for service due to staff vacancies can be associated with the opportunity cost of lost revenue. Management decisions regarding recruitment should weigh the direct cost to the opportunity cost. The goal is to minimize both lost revenues and direct recruitment costs. Who is recruited has an impact on both the recruitment cost and the compensation-related costs. The more experienced and/or specialized the employee sought, the more likely the recruitment and ongoing compensation costs will be high.

Level and methods of compensation are management decisions that are often driven by market practices and going rates. Management really needs to decide if the organization should lead, keep up or follow the market going rate for employees. Leading the market generally makes it easier to recruit and may reduce the opportunity cost related to vacant productive positions. Keeping up with the market makes compensation a neutral issue in the recruitment process. If the market for employees is competitive, other job elements take on a more important role in getting a candidate to accept a position. When management chooses to lag behind the market, recruitment will become difficult if the market is competitive. In this case, the therapy practice must rely on other employment incentives such as significant staff development opportunities.

Benefits account for an increasing percentage of labor related costs. As you can see in Table 8.3, there are many varied benefits that can be offered to entice employees to join and remain with an organization. The makeup of the benefit package determines its cost. Again. the makeup of the benefits package is a management decision. Benefits can also be used to attract employees. Benefits offered are often driven by market practices.

Other discretionary labor-related expenditures include the amount and type of investment in staff training and development and funding for employee recognition. For therapists, funding of continuing education remains a standard benefit. Availability of continuing education funds may not cause a candidate to accept a job offer. Lack of education funding may cause a candidate to decline a job offer. Employee recognition can take the form of an awards dinner or a performance bonus. Employee recognition is for the most part discretionary and varies widely among health care businesses.

NonLabor Operating Costs

Although labor related costs account for a large percentage of health care business costs, control of nonlabor related costs is of equal importance. Watching what the company spends on nonlabor related resources is the most obvious approach to controlling both fixed and variable costs. Using financial modeling, management can and should project the impact of decisions that will change the amount of short-term or long-term fixed costs. Day-to-day decisions about the purchase of resources that comprise the variable operating costs should be guided by the budget and volume of services.

The budget provides management with two performance measures to gauge spending patterns. The first is the total budgeted amount of resource for the period under consideration. Any difference between budgeted and actual resource use will manifest as a budget variance. The second performance measure is the expense per increment of service or product. Expense per increment can be viewed in total or broken down into fixed and variable components. In situations in which workloads fluctuate, expense per increment may be the only effective way to monitor operating expense levels. When budgeted expense per increment is multiplied by the volume of service and product sold, it provides a volume adjusted total expense performance target. Flexible budgeting refers to the use of updated budget expense targets to account for volume fluctuations.

In addition to controlling the utilization of resources, there are some other opportunities for cost reduction that the health care manager should consider. Group purchasing discounts, inventory reduction plans, service and product outsourcing, and workload balancing may all represent cost reduction opportunities.

Group purchasing discounts may be available to high-volume buyers or buyer groups. Identification of opportunities for volume discounts should begin with a review of accounts payable. Management should investigate any expenditures or category of expenditures that show high numbers of purchases or high dollar expenditures on a regular basis. For example, the purchase of all types of office supplies, if purchased from one source, could amount to a considerable annual expense. A volume discount may be available if the purchase of office supplies was consolidated with one vendor. In the case in which a single small business has insufficient purchasing power to warrant a discount, a buying group may be able to obtain a discount for group members.

Inventory control is another opportunity for cost reduction that should not be overlooked. There is an expense associated with stocking an inventory of supplies or products for sale. Every dollar in inventory is a dollar unavailable for productive investment in other activities of the business.

The utilization of resources might also be reduced through the application of proactive workload balancing efforts. Workload balancing occurs when the organization has systems in place to match capacity with demand. For example, a therapy practice that directs referral to one of two clinic locations based on availability of schedule openings is engaged in workload balancing. By decreasing the down time of available resources, cost is minimized as productivity is maximized.

Outsourcing also offers opportunities for cost reduction. If some aspect of the work of the organization can be performed at a lower cost by an external contractor, outsourcing represents an opportunity to cost reduction. Factors such as quality, customer perception, and management control of service all need to be considered in the decision to outsource.

SUMMARY

Financial management principles are constant, which allows multiple internal and external users to interpret the financial information produced by an organization. The application of financial information and accounting principles will allow management to plan and implement strategies to insure the success of the organization. In addition, management will be able to use the information produced by a well-designed financial information system. This information can be used to evaluate actual performance against planned performance as well as the performance of others. A company's size, structure, culture, management autonomy, and the quality of information available are some of the factors that will influence day-to-day business practices. Profitability is the goal. Financial planning and good management are the strategy for success.

The concepts presented here and in other chapters may be explored more fully through the use of a continuous case study, a role play, presented in Appendix A. The role play has been designed to demonstrate how management concepts may impact the clinical setting on a daily basis. The intent of the role play is to provoke thought and build a connection between theory and prac-tice of physical therapy in today's health care environment.

REFERENCES

1. Cava A, West J, Berman E. Ethical decision making in business and government:An analysis of formal and informal strategies. Spectrum:The Journal of State Government, 1995;Spring:28–36.
2. American Physical Therapy, Association. Guide for professional conduct. APTA core documents. PT Magazine 1996a; 4(1):2–5.
3. Shukla, RK. A comparative analysis of revenue and cost-management strategies of not-for-profit and for-profit hospitals. Health & Hospital Services Administration 42:1 Spring 1997:117–134.
4. Dillon RD, LaMont RR. Financial statement analysis, A key to practice diagnosis and prognosis. Clin Manage 1983;35(4):36–39.
5. Berman HJ, Kukla SF, Weeks LE. The Financial Management of Hospitals. 8th ed. Ann Arbor, MI:Health Administration Press, 1994:71–85,97, 142–163.
6. Case J. Open Book Management, the Coming Business Revolution. New York, NY:Harper Business, 1995: 19–36.
7. Hudson T. The cost of keeping up. Hospital & Health Networks 1996; Dec:54–60.
8. Kirschner CG, Davis SJ, Duffy C, Evans D, Hayden D, Jackson JA, et al. Physician's Current Procedural Terminology CPT '98. 4th ed. Chicago, IL: American Medical Association, 1997.
9. Gill HS. The changing nature of ambulatory rehabilitation programs and services in a managed care environment. Arch Phys Med Rehabil 1995; 76:SC-10–15.
10. Beckley NJ. Reviewing contracts. Rehab 1997; April/ May:128–129.
11. Garrison RH. Managerial accounting: Concepts for planning, control, decision making. Revised ed. Dallas, TX:Business Publications, 1979:505,640–646.
12. Van Horne JC. Financial management and policy. 5th ed. Englewood Cliffs, NJ:Prentice-Hall, 1980:711–730.

9

FACILITY PLANNING

PREVIEW

In this chapter, we address the planning and development of an effective and efficient work space for physical therapy service delivery. This will include planning stages and processes, work space design, and introduction of the language of health care facility construction. Special emphasis will be placed on the critical steps in planning the construction and occupancy of a new physical plant.

KEY WORDS

Basis: book value of any asset.

Blue Print: architect's planning document that graphically represents the layout of a facility.

Building Codes: rules and regulations that govern the methods, materials and designs used in construction.

Building Permits: legal record that construction has been approved according to the local building codes. Permits may require the contractor to have inspections at various stages of the work.

Closing: when a contract is transacted and each person fulfills his or her role under the terms and conditions of the agreement. In a sale, it is the moment when the title is deeded to the buyer and the seller gets the proceeds of the sale.

Closing Costs: broker fees and the cost of preparation of all the documents between the buyer and seller to effect a transfer between the two parties.

Code Violation: breach of a current local building code that must be corrected before successful completion of a building inspection.

Communications Systems: systems related to the efficient flow of communication through a facility including, telephone, intercom, background music, mail delivery, signal lights, and data transmission.

Contingency Plan: alternative plan prepared and used in case initial assumptions are not accurate.

Easement: an interest in land that gives another public or private entity the right to either use another person's land for a limited and specific purpose, or to prevent other persons from using their land in a specified way. The most common easements are rights of way, which give people the legal right to pass over or under another's land, such as driveways, roads, sidewalks, and footpaths.

Escrow Deposit: the amount of deposit held by another party. In buying or leasing property, the owner or their agent usually holds a deposit (escrow deposit) from the buyer or tenant.

Facility Plan: a comprehensive plan of the construction project.

Floor Plan: detailed, graphical representation of the layout of a facility that is used to construct the facility.

Gantt Chart: a horizontal bar chart that graphically displays the time relationship of steps in a project. Also known as a time line chart.

HVAC: heating, ventilation, and air conditioning systems.

Market Value: presumed value for which a specific property will sell in any given market condition.

Master Plan: overall comprehensive plan for the development or redevelopment of a community. Master plans indicate the zoning that is allowed for each area of a community.

Ordinances: laws within a community that govern many aspects of construction.

Physical Plant: buildings, equipment, and fixtures of a business establishment.

Punch List: a document that lists all the changes and incomplete items in a construction project.

Safety Systems: systems within a building that address occupant and general community safety, including fire, disaster, weather, and security.

Sound Abatement: processes and structures to reduce excess noise and noise pollution inside a facility.

Structural Systems: structural components of a facility, including wall, ceilings, floors, floor coverings, windows, window coverings and doors.

Title Insurance: insurance designed to protect the buyer against problems following the acquisition of a property.

Work Flow Chart: graphic representation of the progression of the work in a project.

Zoning: process by which a municipality regulates the use of property, including the development of land within its jurisdiction.

Zoning Ordinance: a law that establishes the parameters of use of any property.

INTRODUCTION

The space in which we work and the tools we use within that space in many ways define the quality and quantity of work that we can accomplish. Although some people can produce fine work in an inefficient or poorly designed work space, most people find that a well-designed work space can contribute significantly to individual and collective productivity. A well-designed clinic will allow clinicians to focus on clinical care, not on overcoming physical obstacles or searching for equipment and materials. This chapter will help the reader understand some of the issues that must be addressed when designing work spaces, both clinical and nonclinical.

Designing Values Based Facility

The organization's values, vision and mission statements should guide actions and deeds in interpersonal relationships. Who will use the facility? Will clients' needs be served? Will clients be better served at a reasonable price to payers?

What is the motivation for producing this facility? Is the motivation to be better than the competition? Is the facility a monument to the owner, board of directors or chief executive? Will the community be enhanced?

In the greater scheme of things, is a bigger, newer facility needed or is it a marketing tool to attract clients from competitors and drive them out of business? What is the driving force? Money? Power? Pursuit of excellence?

Consider the mission. Is there a profit motive? Is there a service motive? What does a wide sample of potential clients feel and think about this project?

Chapter 2 discussed how the values, vision and mission statements of an organization guide work related actions. It is also true in decisions related to the structure and potential functions of a proposed work space.

Value and motive considerations are important in facility planning. For example, if there is a question of renovation of existing or construction of new facilities, it will help to consider the preferred course in the moral context of duty and responsibility (Chapter 2). Understanding the motives driving the choice will clarify the thought processes and may re-affirm the decision. If the motivation is to gain a larger market share of clients with high-paying health insurance (see Chapters 3, 8, 14), what will happen to those clients who do not have insurance? Will they still have good access to services? Will clients who have traditionally been served at the facility be harmed in any way by the proposed changes? This relates to the question of duty. If these clients will be harmed in any way by the proposed actions, what course of action will the organization take? This may raise a question of responsibility.

If the underlying motive for upgrading the physical plant is to generate more income so that clients who are unable to pay for services can continue to be served, the motive may be benevolence. If the motivation is to gain power and that motive is sustained by placing great value on the acquisition of wealth, the answers to the client-related questions are less likely to be favorable for uninsured or under insured clients. Conducting a moral assessment should be part of the facility planning process.

Facility Planning As a Marketing Task

The facility in which we work is just another tool used to serve customers, albeit a very expensive one. Planning a new department or renovating your existing work space must be driven by many market, as well as facility, considerations. Table 9.1 lists market and facility considerations in planning a new facility.

All of these issues must be addressed from the perspective of the clients and care partners within the context of the overall project objectives.

Facility Planning as a Project Management Task

Planning a new department or renovating the existing space in which clinical activities occur can be a very complex and sometimes a daunting task. However, by using the appropriate management and project planning tools, the many facets of a construction project can be managed. Fortunately, there are excellent tools available to help organize the tasks that need attention in the planning and implementation of facility planning projects.

To successfully plan for a new or renovated space, it is necessary to use project management tools such as project time line charts, Gantt charts, work flow diagrams, and other useful tools. These management instruments will assist in designing and revising a space plan, planning the project tasks, developing a project budget, tracking the progress of multiple simultaneous tasks, monitoring expenditures and adherence to budget, and comparing overall progress to the anticipated time lines developed. Most importantly, a plan can be used to communicate with staff, the work crew, administration, and other interested parties and stakeholders.

PLANNING: THE KEY TO DEVELOPING A USABLE ECONOMIC FACILITY

It is necessary to clearly identify the objectives of the construction project before investing any significant resources in the implementation of the project. This process should include a review

TABLE 9.1

Market and Facility Considerations In Planning a New Facility

TYPE OF CLINIC
- Hospital-based department
- Sub acute rehabilitation center
- Free standing outpatient center
- Home care center
- Extended care facility

CHARACTERISTICS OF THE CLIENT
POPULATIONS SERVED
- Age of clients and care partners
- Type of disabilities clients are likely to have
- Method of transportation to the center and within the center
- Typical amount of time a client and/or care partner is likely to be in clinic
- Volume of clients to be served
- Number, type and intensity of clinical services
- Major equipment to be housed
- Amount and type of non clinical services
  - Educational activities
  - Business functions
  - Other services

ANTICIPATED CHANGES IN SERVICE DELIVERY AND PRACTICE ACTIVITIES INCLUDING GROWTH
SERVICES CURRENTLY BEING DELIVERED TO VARIOUS CLIENT POPULATIONS
FLOW OF TRAFFIC TO THE LOCATIONS OF THE VARIOUS SERVICES
RENOVATION OF EXISTING STRUCTURE OR NEW BUILD
EXTENT OF DEMOLITION OF EXISTING STRUCTURES NEEDED
NEED TO MAINTAIN CLINICAL AND BUSINESS OPERATIONS DURING CONSTRUCTION
ABILITY TO EXPAND OR CHANGE THE FACILITY TO MEET CHANGING NEEDS
BUDGET FOR CONSTRUCTION OR RENOVATION
- Construction costs
- Future expansion costs
- Utility costs-both initially and over time
- Electrical, heating, cooling, ventilation, telephones, intercoms, cable TV, background music, computer network, message conveyance systems

OVERALL SAFETY ISSUES
- Fire, theft, protection from the elements
- Flooring safety
- Furniture and equipment safety

COSMETIC CONSIDERATIONS
- Visual attractiveness
- Colors
- Decorating
- Fabrics

AUDITORY ATTRACTIVENESS
- Sound control and abatement

CONFIDENTIALITY IN SPECIFIED AREAS
ATTRACTIVENESS TO REFERRAL SOURCES AND OTHER STAKEHOLDERS

of the organization's fundamental documents. Early in the project, the goal is to clearly articulate criteria for success of the project. This should happen BEFORE undertaking the actual detailed planning or construction.

There Are No Boundless Projects

Every project has an initial set of basic facts that must be taken into consideration as the project develops. These facts are often real world constraints that define the limits imposed on the project.

Fiscal constraints are always present. A planner will need to have clear answers to the following questions before proceeding.

- What is the overall purpose of the construction project? Is it to expand replace, or relocate services?
- What is the budget? How much of the budget is for construction? How much for equipment?
- What is an acceptable payback period on the construction or expansion?
- How quickly must the increased revenue (if any) that will be derived from the new facility surpass the expenses that were incurred to develop the physical plant, i.e., how quickly must the project break even?
- What are the financial incentives in moving or building?
- Will there be a change in the scope of the services that are offered?
- What is the projected scope of practice and services for the new space?
- Have non clinical uses and potential future changes and responses to market trends been considered?

The initial task in developing a construction project is to complete a full statement of objectives and to clearly state how it will be known that these objectives are met. Table 9.2 is a sample of an area-by-area objective success criteria statement.

Table 9.2 details only a few of the clinic areas that are needed. A grid similar to this table should be completed for all clinical areas. Other clinic areas and functions are listed below:

Storage: General
- General storage: clean and dirty
- Linen storage: clean and dirty
- Coat closet: staff and clients and visitors
- Small supply storage
- Ambulation device storage
- Casting and splinting supply storage
Treatment
- Booths
- Gym
- Hydrotherapy
- Hand therapy areas
- Private treatment rooms
- Private consultation rooms
- Pool or other special construction areas
- ADL areas
Office
- Clerical staff
- Clinical staff
- Management office(s)
- Medical Director

- Other personnel using facility may also need office space
Waiting Space
- Clients
- Care partners
- Others
Staff room
- All disciplines
- Each discipline
Other spaces
- Lunchroom
- Rest rooms
- Staff lounge

In completing this information, consider the following additional questions.

What will be the intensity of speciality services such as wound care, mat activities, ventilators, prone carts, pediatrics or other clients with limited mobility or special needs be in the new clinic?

Who are current and future staff and what do/will they do? Refer to the job descriptions that have been prepared to help answer this question.

What is anticipated for staff case loads and staffing levels? (It will be necessary to refer to productivity expectations and staffing projections over time to adequately formulate this answer. Review Chapter 8).

What else is known from market analysis that should be considered?

Although Table 9.2 contains only a few examples of areas in a rehabilitation-oriented clinic, it demonstrates the level of detail to be specified at the outset of the facility planning project. There is no replacement for good planning in a facility planning project. In the carpentry field, there is an old saying, "Measure twice, cut once". This philosophy allows the carpenter to be sure that his resources are not wasted. In facility planning, similar to carpentry, it might be stated, "Plan thrice, build once".

There are tremendous economies that will be realized when a concise plan is followed as opposed to discovering the best configuration as it is built. Fully understanding the scope of the project will prevent re-work or acceptance of a less than ideal facility.

Room Space Requirements

Table 9.3 details the major data that must be collected early in the layout planning process to

TABLE 9.2

Samples of Selected Clinic Functions and Facility Objectives

SELECTED CLINICAL FUNCTION	OBJECTIVE	EXAMPLES OF CRITERIA FOR SUCCESS
Confidential storage of records	There will be adequate space on site to store clients' medical records for 2 years.	Records are accessible in a timely and geographically expedient manner. The storage area is secure from unauthorized access.
Reception of clients and care partners	There will be areas available for clients and their care partners to be comfortable while they wait for care. These areas will be conveniently located to minimize the distance that staff and clients have to travel within the clinic.	Clients will be able to wait in a waiting area that is visually and auditorily attractive. These areas will be able to be monitored by staff for the safety of clients.
Treatment of pediatric clients	Treatment areas will be available that allow therapists to control visual and auditory stimulation of clients. Treatment areas and treatment equipment will be appropriate to the age and abilities of the clients and care partners served.	There will be quiet treatment rooms equipped with materials specific to pediatric clients and their care partners. Supervised space will also be available for siblings to safely wait during client care where they will not be disruptive to others.
Treatment of clients with open wounds	Treatment areas will be available for the private, efficient and safe treatment of clients with open lesions, burns and infected open wounds.	There will be isolated, private treatment areas located adjacent to the hydrotherapy area for wound care. These areas will have doors that can be closed. These areas will have ready access to storage areas for sterile and clean wound care supplies and to clean and dirty linen. A separate ventilation system will be in place in these areas. Water and waste drainage will be available in these areas. Structural support for a large whirlpool will be present. Because clients may sometimes be involved in extremely painful treatments in these areas, extra sound insulation will be installed.
Billing, intake and reimbursement activities	Business office space will be available for staff to efficiently prepare client bills and to meet with clients privately to discuss financial matters concerning their care in the clinic.	The business office area is separate and distinct from clinical areas. There is adequate filing space near the business office area. Each staff member in the business office has a work space and access to computerized billing and scheduling systems. There is at least one private consultation area in close proximity to the business area where staff can meet with clients and their care partners to discretely discuss confidential matters. Noise from thebusiness area, client care areas and client waiting areas is controlled and does not interfere with ongoing operations.

continued

TABLE 9.2 *Continued*
Samples of Selected Clinic Functions and Facility Objectives

SELECTED CLINICAL FUNCTION	OBJECTIVE	EXAMPLES OF CRITERIA FOR SUCCESS
Management Functions	There is adequate work space for the management to confidentially interact with staff and control access to private files and materials.	There will be a separate manager's office that will seat at least 3 people comfortably. This office will be separate and distanced from the staff lounge or lunchroom. There will be a locked door and secured files within the manager's office. There will be additional sound insulation installed in this area. There will be adequate floor space to allow two distinct work areas in the manager office: a desk for ongoing work and a small conference table to facilitate small meetings.

TABLE 9.3
Sample Individual Work Space Requirements

ROOM	FUNCTIONS	MINIMAL MAXIMAL DIMENSIONS	SQUARE FEET	NUMBER NEEDED	TOTAL SQUARE FOOTAGE	SPECIAL COMMENTS
Manager Office	Work space for manager; storage of confidential personnel records; private meetings with staff and visitors	8′ × 8′ min 12′ × 16′ max 10′ × 10′*	64–192 100*	1	100	Isolate from general staff activities for privacy; unique key lock; extra sound abatement measures for privacy with staff.
Treatment Booths	Treatment of client with various modalities and therapeutic procedures	7′ × 8′ min 8′ × 10′ max 8′ × 9′*	56–80 72*	8 Depends on volume projection	576	Ground fault electrical outlets in each; individual lighting adjustments in each; outlets at 36″ height; not all need to be exact same size and shape; linen and modality prep in close proximity; space for patient clothing hooks; room for chair or stool in each.

* Preferred

assure adequate availability of individual work stations and space. Here we will discuss samples of individual clinical work space requirements (Table 9.3) and nonclinical work space requirements, including equipment and furniture requirements (Table 9.4), checklists for work space for clinical areas (Table 9.5), and nonclinical areas (Table 9.6); space needs for individual pieces of clinical equipment (Table 9.7) and office equipment and furniture (Table 9.8).

Refer to the samples as guides to use as worksheets. Use the worksheets throughout the early stages of the facility planning process.

For each step of the facility planning project, it is necessary to prepare projections. To prepare projections, first identify which factors that are expected to occur in the future will have an impact on the outcome of the project. This will come from marketing information and environmental scanning activities as discussed in Chapter 3. Then

TABLE 9.4
Sample Worksheet: Equipment and Furniture Requirements

AREA	FURNITURE (QUANTITY)	EQUIPMENT (QUANTITY)	COMMENTS
Manager Office	Executive desk with chair (2) Side chairs Small conference table (3) Conference table chairs Executive credenza Locking 4 drawer lateral file Cabinet	Personal computer Printer Telephone/voice mail (2) Pieces artwork Carpeting Horizontal blinds on windows and door	
Traction Booth	Side chair with arms Coat hook on wall Storage cabinet for linens and supplies Adjustable height rolling stool Curtains	Pelvic traction unit Ultrasound unit on cart Client call system	

TABLE 9.5
Worksheet for Individual Work Space Requirements: Clinical Areas

ROOM	FUNCTION	MINIMAL MAXIMAL DIMENSIONS	SQUARE FEET	NUMBER NEEDED	TOTAL SQUARE FOOTAGE	SPECIAL COMMENTS
Gym-General						
Treatment Booths						
Private Rooms						
Occupational Therapy						
Hand Therapy						
Speech-Language Pathology						
Pediatric Gym						
Biofeedback						
Hydrotherapy						
Therapeutic Pool						
IsoKinetic Area						
Work Hardening						
Functional Capacity Evaluation						
Computer Room						
Modality Prep						
ADL area						
Driver Educ. Area						
Other						

TABLE 9.6
Worksheet for Individual Work Space Requirements: Non Clinical Areas

ROOM	FUNCTION	MINIMAL MAXIMAL DIMENSIONS	SQUARE FEET	NUMBER NEEDED	TOTAL SQUARE FOOTAGE	SPECIAL COMMENTS
Waiting Room						
Business Office						
Staff Office						
Storage						
Linen Storage Clean						
Linen Storage Dirty						
Medical Records						
Client Bathroom						
Staff Bathroom						
Staff Lounge						
Manager Office						
Physician Office						
Conference Room						

prepare a set of conclusions about these factors. This can be done using the standard business process of establishing multiple possible scenarios. To create a best case scenario, assume that all of the factors identified that will affect the project will occur in the most favorable manner for the project. To create a worst case scenario, assume that all of the factors identified that will affect the project will occur in the most unfavorable manner. Then create a most likely scenario, using what is considered to be the most likely set of assumptions. This will provide a projection of the relative success of the project should all factors occur as projected.

It is also necessary to decide if the project will proceed should the worst case occur. This is often a tough decision. If best and worst case comparison still does not clarify the decision, it is sometimes best to configure construction with an option to expand or contract the project in the future. This could be the best option but it is not always possible.

Contingency Planning

Contingency planning provides options should the original plan be found inadequate. All construction or renovation projects need alternate plans to be considered throughout the project. Contingency plans take into account options that may be needed as the project progresses. Because the project is occurring in real time, the environment or some of the earlierst assumptions may change. Contingency planning takes new information into account.

Design Decisions

There will be many seemingly insignificant details that must be determined early in the planning process. However, many of the special details that must be addressed are either required by building regulations for the safety of the public or will impact the overall usability of the facility. A typical objective is to develop a new or improved clinical facility to enhance client comfort and staff efficiency. The initial step of defining values, vision and project mission is one component of developing project objectives.

Areas of special consideration include the following:

- Structural systems including walls, ceilings, windows, doors

TABLE 9.7

Worksheet for Space Requirements: Clinical Equipment

EQUIPMENT	NUMBER	SIZE	PERIMETER CLEARANCE SPACE	MOVABLE OR FIXED	SPECIAL NEEDS	TOTAL SQUARE FOOTAGE
Mat Table						
Treatment Table						
Hi-Low Table						
Isokinetic Equipment						
Free Weight Equipment						
Exercise Bike						
Treadmill						
Parallel Bars						
Balance Beam						
Ballet Bar						
Stairs/Ramp						
Portable Mirror						
Circuit Training Stations						
Rowing Machine						
Pulley System						
Therapeutic Ball						
Balance Equipment						
Tilt Table						
Whirlpool						
Moist Heat Unit						
Cold Pack Unit						
Traction Unit						
Fluidotherapy Unit						
Electrical Stimulator Unit						
Ultrasound Iontophoresis						
Utility Cart						
Other						
				Total Square Footage Required		

- Communications systems, including phone systems, intercom, background music and mailboxes
- Lighting
- Electrical
- Safety requirements, including fire and security alarms, smoke detectors, fire exits and safety equipment
- Plumbing, water supply and drainage, including floor drains, location and quantity of bathrooms, drinking fountains, hand sinks and hot water supply
- Sound abatement measures for control of noise
- Heating, ventilation and air conditioning
- Storage of clinical, clerical and used supplies, including linen, waste and hazardous materials, and staff and client clothing and coats
- Regulatory considerations, including zoning, pub-

TABLE 9.8
Worksheet for Equipment and Furniture Requirements

AREA	FURNITURE (QUANTITY)	EQUIPMENT (QUANTITY)	COMMENTS

lic health codes, municipal, county, state and federal governance
• Interior design
• Cosmetics

Structural Systems

Basic components such as wall, ceiling, and floor coverings are important considerations for your clinic. Beside the obvious cosmetic factors such as color, texture and overall appearance, there are functional considerations.

The walls, ceilings and floors of your clinic must be sturdy enough to support the clinical functions that will occur within your clinic. For example, should exercise equipment suspended from the ceiling be needed, the ceiling support structures must be designed to hold the excess weight. The height of the ceiling should be considered. If clients will be using sports equipment such as golf clubs or mini-trampolines, the ceiling should be higher than the typical 9-foot level. Walls also need special preparation for wall mounted devices such as pulley systems and weight racks. Placement of excessively heavy equipment such as Hubbard tanks and walking tanks may require additional floor support.

Communications Systems

Chapter 10 will deal with communications in general. In this section, an infrastructure for internal communications will be reviewed.

One of the most important decisions for clinic efficiency is the communication systems technology that is designed into the clinic. Phone system outlets should be liberally spread throughout the clinic. The initial tendency is to identify how the clinic will function as originally designed and place phone outlets in the most obvious locations. However, the daily use of the clinic is likely to change over time. Sometimes the clinic use will evolve well past anything anticipated in the design phase. Because the cost of installing phone outlets is significantly less during the construction phase while the wall studs are still accessible, it is usually prudent to install an excessive number of outlets rather than an inadequate number. The less often staff need to leave treatment areas, the more time they can devote to care of clients. This can enhance productivity significantly.

The same argument can be made for computer connections. Clearly, the trend is toward the networking of computers. While computer wiring may not be needed today in the existing clinic, the cost of installing the wiring during construction is minimal compared to installation after the walls are finished. This may mean the installation of computer network connections within each individual treatment area, or even in each booth, so that a portable computer can be moved from area to area.

A key communication system is the intercom. Because clinicians are often unable to leave their clients to answer a phone call at their location, it is necessary to use overhead paging in almost all clinical settings. Because overhead paging and announcements can be very disruptive to the clinical activities, it is necessary to purchase intercom systems that allow broadcasting of messages to individual locations. It is also critical that the staff be able to respond to the page without having to leave their clients. Voice activated intercom systems, also referred to as hands free operation, are needed.

Intercom technology is changing rapidly. Internal mobile phone links, such as a mini phone with pager that operate via wireless ceiling antennae using internal broadcast networks, are rapidly being adopted in new facilities.

Overhead or background music is often a pleasant way to help reduce noise pollution from one clinical area to another. Although some people compare background music to elevator music (though some simply find both distracting or annoying), many businesses and clinics have found it to be a calming influence for both clients and staff. Custom programming, based on client preference, is available.

Staff mailboxes are also an important means of communication between staff members. A place for messages, mail and other announcements should be located where staff can review this material at their convenience. A convenient, yet private, location is needed. The staff mailboxes should not be located in client treatment or traffic areas.

Lighting

Few systems will affect the overall atmosphere of the clinic as much as the manner in which it is illuminated. An appropriate lighting system will provide a comfortable, yet professional, atmosphere for clients and visitors while helping the clinicians provide appropriate treatments. Often, building code will specify the type and amount of light required. However, most people prefer natural light to artificial, whether incandescent or flourescent.

An additional lighting consideration is the projected expense to light and maintain the lighting system in the facility. Although individual lighting controls and dimmer switches in each booth and treatment area can become rather expensive, the ability to control the amount and type of light within the treatment area may be very desirable for the types of clients to be treated. At a minimum, there should be a high degree of location specificity in the lighting schema so that specific zones of the clinic can be controlled by individual switches.

Electrical

Of all the systems within the clinic, the electrical system, if well thought out, should be quite invisible in daily operations. The electrical supply should have an adequate capacity for future expansion and there should be an ample supply of strategically located outlets. With the rapid increase in electrical demand seen with the increasing use of computers and other technology in physical therapy clinics, it is best to overestimate the electrical need. This will preclude needing expensive electrical work done after the initial construction period is over and the walls are finished.

Within each clinical treatment area, there should be sufficient numbers of electrical outlets located at easy-to-reach heights. Each booth and private treatment area needs at least a four-outlet fixture (usually called a quad outlet). Outlets intended for clinical equipment, such as that in booths, should be placed at 36 inches in height so that staff is not required to bend and reach behind sometimes heavy and awkward equipment.

In open clinical areas, such as gyms, regularly placed quad outlets should be spread throughout the space. Every effort should be made to avoid floor outlets in favor of wall outlets. A typical distance between outlets in a busy gym is 6 to 12 feet. In many building codes, the use of extension cords is prohibited. The height of the outlets should also be 36 inches, unless there is reason to place them at another height. Special care should be taken with special client populations, such as children and clients with impaired judgement, so that safety measures, such as outlet covers, are employed to avoid injury or accident. Chapter 12 details other aspects of reducing client safety risks.

Safety Systems

Because the business of operating a clinic serves the public, there is a responsibility to assure that the facility is safe for those served (See Chapter 12). This responsibility includes meeting the appropriate safety codes such as fire, disaster and security. This usually is well defined in the locality's safety code and varies from location to location. However, the placement of fire extinguishers, emergency exits with exit lights and emergency backup systems, and posting clearly marked exit plans is a bare minimum. Special care should be taken when the clinic is located on the second floor, or above, which would necessitate the use of elevators or escalators not available during fire or electrical outage. Because many clients have limited mobility, managers must take special care to address safety issues in these situations.

Another important area that is best addressed during planning and construction is the use of a security system to limit unauthorized access to the facility and to reduce theft and vandalism risks. Use of appropriate security systems with a central monitoring service often allows a reduction in insurance costs to the clinic that may, over time, actually pay for the cost of the security system.

Plumbing Systems

One of the most expensive and necessary systems that must be addressed in facility planning is plumbing. This includes the intake of fresh water and the drainage of used water and waste material into the municipal sewer system.

As plumbing installation can be very expensive, care must be taken to concentrate as many water-supplied functions in as few areas as possible. This will reduce plumbing costs. This also explains why it is common to see hydrotherapy areas located near client showers and rest rooms. Each share the plumbing.

Hydrotherapy water supply usually requires special plumbing accommodations. Larger than usual piping (at least 3/4-inch rather than 1/2-inch diameter pipe) is needed to provide an adequate flow of water to fill a large hydrotherapy tank quickly so that the water will remain warm. Additionally, large capacity hot water heaters with quick recovery times are needed to handle the large volume of hot water needed in hydrotherapy.

Plumbing systems for therapeutic pools or walking tanks are even more complicated. An architect well versed in pool design and construction should be consulted should your plans include a therapeutic or recreational pool or a walking tank.

Sound Abatement Systems

Excessive noise is not only irritating within an enclosed space such as a physical therapy clinic, it can also interfere with clinical operations by preventing clinicians from communicating properly with their clients. Additionally, excessive noise has been shown to contribute to several work site maladies that may harm employees and expose the organization to unnecessary workers compensation costs or even lead to employee litigation. For more on risk management see Chapter 12.

A therapy clinic can be a noisy place. There can be overhead announcements blaring from loudspeakers throughout the clinic. Staff talk to clients, often encouraging them to try their best at louder-than-average volumes. Phones ring. Equipment alarms go off. Clients use noisy exercise equipment like treadmills, bikes and weight equipment.

Knowing that every clinic will produce a significant noise level, the design should allow effective noise abatement measures. These include the use of sound absorbing materials on large surface areas like walls, window coverings and floors. The use of carpeting instead of vinyl flooring often will dramatically reduce the ambient noise in a clinic. Special acoustic ceiling materials can also be used to control noise.

The isolation of particularly noisy activities can reduce noise levels in other areas of the clinic. As shown in Figure 9.1, this can be accomplished by putting loud activities and noisy equipment beyond turns in a hallway which cuts noise pollution to other clinic areas.

Heating, Ventilation, and Air Conditioning Systems (HVAC)

Heating, ventilation and air conditioning are systems frequently referred to together as HVAC. These systems deal with the quality, temperature and flow of the air throughout the facility. The quality of the insulation, the relationship of the facility to the sun, the prevailing wind, and the number and direction of windows can impact heating and cooling costs significantly.

There may be special areas of the clinic, such as hydrotherapy, that have special HVAC needs. For example, the hydrotherapy area may need to be warmer than the gym. It may be necessary to vent the exhaust air from the hydrotherapy area directly to the outside rather than to circulate it throughout the clinic. Separate ventilation is particularly important if hydrotherapy will frequently be used to care for clients with open and infected wounds or if strong odors are present.

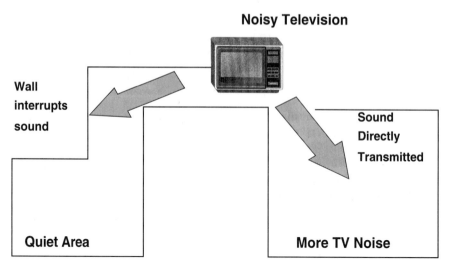

FIGURE 9.1. Effect of a wall on sound transmission.

Like lighting, HVAC zones can be established in the facility plan to provide maximal flexibility and economy for the clinic.

Storage Systems

The key to storage systems, whether rooms or cabinets, custom or stock, is to have an adequate availability of the right supplies in the right place in a manner that is easy to find and use. Access to waste storage should also be efficiently located and of adequate size.

One can never be too rich, too attractive, or have enough storage in a clinical setting. Although it is unclear if all three of these situations are actually true, there are those who have designed, built and now occupy clinics with inadequate storage space who would not argue against the statement. Determining storage needs should include input from the entire staff.

Several types of storage should be considered. It will be necessary to store inventory, supplies, equipment and records safely and efficiently. Storage rooms are usually used for large volumes of linen, equipment or waste products. Storage cabinets and storage areas are used for smaller quantities of materials and rarely used for waste products.

Storage rooms should be located as close to the functional area that they support. If the room stores supplies or waste for several areas, it should be as centrally located to those areas as possible. Never mix supplies (clean items) with waste products (dirty items). The specific design of the storage room will, like everything else in the clinic, depend on its use. It can be helpful to construct special storage bins or racks for items such as crutches, wheel chair parts, or free weights. Storage rooms are an opportunity to be creative in design. If a mistake is made in the design of a storage room, it can be hidden behind a closed door.

Storage cabinets can be built as custom cabinets or purchased in standard sizes as freestanding cabinets. Custom, built-in cabinets are known as case work. Case work can be very expensive, but few construction features confer a more professional look to clients. Custom case work will also be built to your specific needs and the size and shape of your clinic. Stock cabinets are not always available to meet specific clinic needs; however, with the newer materials and products available on the market today, stock cabinets can be very economical, functional and attractive.

Regulatory Compliance

It will be necessary to consult an experienced architect or engineer to help identify which regulatory agencies and codes will need to be addressed in preparing for construction. This will vary from locality to locality. Check with a professional who is experienced in these matters early in the facility design process.

Interior Design

There are many factors that determine if a facility has the right look and feel. Interior decorating involves all aspects of that look and feel, including the floor, wall and window coverings, their color, quality and function. Furniture, doors, doorways and floor moldings will also portray a specific look to clients and visitors (see Chapter 14). The interior and exterior signs are referred to as signage. Signage should also be considered a design factor.

The decision to use an interior designer is an important one to make early on in the planning process, before purchase decisions are made for furniture, carpeting, and wall covering. Although interior designers can be expensive, they may be necessary to help achieve the end result desired in the clinic. Chapter 14 expands on this concept.

Having reviewed the specific decisions that must be made to move the project of construction forward, let's now review the process that should be used to manage and control the overall facility design process.

PLANNING STEPS

There are nine steps (Table 9.9) that comprise five stages in the process of designing and constructing a therapy facility. The following outline will assist the reader to follow these steps.

Throughout the planning process, when there are decisions to be made, the fundamental documents of the organization (See Chapter 2) should be consulted. There also needs to be a detailed outline for designing and constructing a therapy facility.

DETAILED PLANNING PROCESS FOR PHYSICAL PLANT DEVELOPMENT AND ALTERATION

Stage 1: Pre-Design

Step 1: Planning Team Selection

The selection of the team to plan the facility and the initial planning steps are often the most important steps in determining the quality of the final physical plant.

To determine the members of the planning team, it will be necessary to consider what expertise is available within the organization and what skills will be required of outside consultants.

The role of each selected member must be clearly defined.

Define and communicate the role of staff and clients in the design of the facility.

Step 2: Pre-planning

Evaluate existing services critically.

Review service area data available from marketing sources and environmental scanning.

Review historical performance data such as productivity, referral and financial. Give special consideration of geographic issues such as location of referrers and home and business addresses of current and potential clients.

Review projections of client and service volume for facility.

 TABLE 9.9
Overview of the Planning Stages and Steps

STAGE	STEP
Pre Design	1. Planning team selection
	2. Pre planning
Design Development	3. Detailed planning
	4. Final planning
	5. Keeping track of the project
Construction	6. Construction and equipment procurement
Pre Operations	7. Final check out
Occupancy/Start Up	8. Occupancy
	9. Revisions and critique

Define financial constraints for the project. Use Table 9.10, The Preliminary Construction Budget Worksheet (below) to develop a working budget. To determine preliminary space calculations refer to Tables 9.5 and 9.6. Decide if there will be a change in the scope of services offered to clients. If necessary, define the new scope of services. Review new scope of services in light of philosophy and service objectives (See Chapter 2). Develop a Pro Forma analysis of new service area (Refer to Chapter 7). Review alternatives and select site for construction/renovation.

Stage 2: Construction Design

Step 3: Detailed Planning

At this step, the construction project becomes more tangible. For areas that are to be renovated, it is often helpful to use tape on existing walls and floors to demarcate the proposed location of walk ways, doors, equipment and other major objects. Taking a walk through the tape-designated space can provide a more realistic impression of traffic patterns, adequacy of work space and other practical features of the space. Many of these issues are often difficult to visualize or anticipate from a blue print or construction plan. This is particularly true for health care personnel who are typically novice facility planners. There are several additional tasks in this step.

Define operational interdepartmental relationships in proposed space. Develop an initial flow diagram of typical services such as that shown in Figure 9.2.

Develop an initial traffic flow diagram for client care service activities for movement within space and to external departments or locations. Develop an initial traffic flow diagram for staff movement within the space and to external departments or locations (Fig. 9.2). Identify equipment needs by developing a detailed listing with fixed and movable equipment. Identify any special wiring or electrical considerations for equipment. Identify any other special needs such as the special plumbing required by hydrotherapy tanks or the special storage and accessibility required for emergency equipment. Review all planning to-date considering philosophy, vision, mission and project objectives.

Step 4: Final Planning and Checks

This step is often completed by architects, designers, and contractors who may be external to the organization or, in large organizations, internal employees of the organization. These consultants should provide final floor plans and review all planning for completeness and compliance with external regulatory agencies.

There will need to be a major emphasis on communication of the construction activities and timetable and the expectations of staff in this changing physical space. Use of a Gantt chart, such as illustrated in Figure 9.3, is an excellent way to track and communicate progress of the project.

Figure 9.3 shows the general steps of the construction project over time. Much greater detail will need to be communicated to staff and other interested parties. Listed below are some of the key components of the final planning process.

Development of final floor plan and construction blue prints.
Development and approval of final construction budget and time tables. Refer to Chapter 7 for budgeting information.
Development and approval of final capital budget.

TABLE 9.10
Preliminary Construction Budget Worksheet

AREA	SIZE	FURNITURE AND EQUIPMENT COSTS	CONSTRUCTION COSTS	TOTAL COSTS	TOTAL

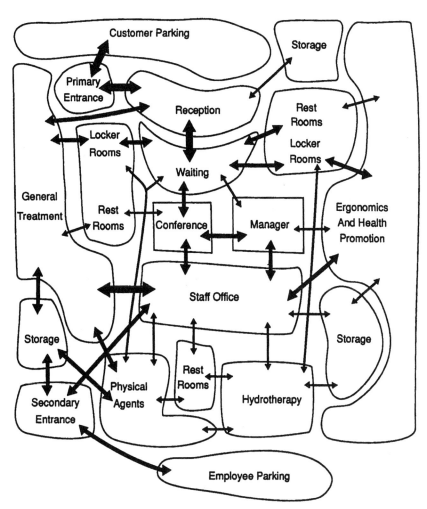

FIGURE 9.2. Activity flow and volume bubble diagram. Arrow heads indicate direction of human traffic flow. Arrow width represents the relative volume of traffic. The thicker the arrow shaft, the greater the traffic volume. Modified from Magistro CM. Department planning, design, and construction. In Hickok RJ, ed. Physical Therapy Administration and Management. Baltimore, MD: Williams and Wilkins, 1974:154.

Development and approval of final supply budget.
Development and approval for personnel budget for transition period. Budgeting information is in Chapter 7.
Development and approval of final plan for transition to new space and exodus from previous space, if applicable.

Step 5: Keeping Track of the Project and Adjusting the Work in Progress

A professional who is experienced in construction management should supervise the actual construction. Most often, this is a general

contractor who coordinates the activities of many different sub-contractors, such as painters, plumbers and carpenters. A general contractor works closely with the existing facility staff and management. An important component of managing the project will be to monitor budget and time constraints.

Projects often exceed budget, run into delays or both. Sometimes these situations are unavoidable. Sometimes they are the result of poor planning. As soon as it is determined that there will be an unanticipated delay or expense, it is the re-

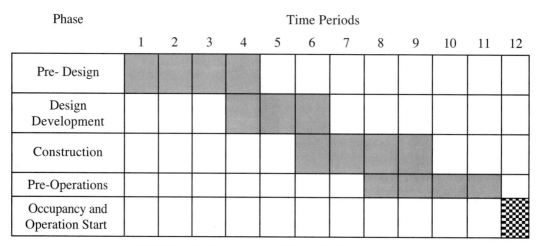

FIGURE 9.3. Gantt chart example of the facility design process.

sponsibility of the project manager or general contractor to notify those whose work will be affected. This allows implementation of contingency plans that were developed earlier.

Stage 3: Construction

Step 6: Construction and Equipment Procurement

Because of the noise and dirt of construction projects, it may be challenging to continue to offer clinical services in an area near construction. In renovation projects, it is often necessary to occupy clinical space very close to construction activities. As construction continues, it is very important for staff to develop workable relationships with the construction crew. Close friendships are not required, although they do sometimes develop. At the minimum, a peaceful co-existence and tolerance is needed. At this stage in the project, there is real progress with some parts of the physical plant starting to take shape as equipment is delivered and installed. This is an exciting and very busy time in any construction project.

- Order equipment and track receipt and installation of the equipment as it becomes available
- Regular inspection of the work and progress by general contractor and staff
- Supervision of the construction without obstruction of progress
- Consideration of what to do when changes become apparent mid construction

Stage 4: Preoperations

Step 7: Final Check Out

The final step before occupying the new or renovated space is final inspection. A list of items to be revised, corrected or completed is compiled. This list is called the punch list. Once the project manager is informed of the items on the punch list, it is the responsibility of the project manager to complete or correct those items in a timely manner. It may be necessary to occupy the space and begin operations before completion of the punch list items; however, final payment to the project manager should not be made until all work is complete and satisfactory.

Stage 5: Occupancy and Operations Startup

Step 8: Occupancy

Moving in to a new space is a complex task. It must be well planned and coordinated. Once moved in, it will be important to get operations underway as quickly as can be safely accomplished. Listed below are some of the key actions to accomplish the move in an efficient manner.

Develop and implement a plan to move equipment, personnel and operations into new facility.
Communicate occupancy plan to staff, other stakeholders and clients.

Train staff on new equipment and operating procedures. Begin operations within the new facility.

Step 9: Revision and Critique

Upon successfully initiating operations in the new facility, a discerning retrospective evaluation of the facility and project plan and process should be undertaken. It will be necessary to compare the actual outcome of the project to the projects' objectives. Several key questions should be asked:

Did the project team keep everything and everyone informed, coordinated and on schedule?
How could the use of project management tools have improved the process?
Does the new physical plant meet our needs?
Did the project meet its objectives?

Mistakes Happen

Facility plans are based on the best information available at a particular point in time. The operations of a clinic are ongoing. Information changes as the project planning progresses. Prices change, competitors respond to each other's actions and market conditions evolve.

Facility planning, like a budget, is a best guess. There is a margin of error in any guess, however informed those guesses are. Table 9.11 lists facility design mistakes. This list is offered to help those involved in the planning process minimize mistakes. These mistakes are based on our practical experiences in designing facilities.

SUMMARY

A physical structure has to have a purpose. The purpose comes from values that serve motivations and are expressed in an organization's fundamental documents. Motivation to meet patients' and other shareholders' needs can be achieved through a well-conceived physical

TABLE 9.11
Common Facility Design Mistakes to Avoid

MISTAKE	REMEDY
Inefficient traffic flow	Keep hallways and intersections to a minimum.
	Keep related functions in close proximity.
	Keep clients in wheel chair near entrance.
	Provide separate entrance for pool.
Inappropriate placement of clinical areas	Keep hydro areas together.
	Keep sterile areas together.
	Centralize staff office for efficiency of movement.
	Provide separate entrance for deliveries and waste removal.
Inadequate flexibility in functional uses	Choose curtains rather than walls when possible.
	Consider folding walls and multipurpose spaces.
	Avoid signage that claims areas for one group.
Inadequate storage space	Anticipate needing more storage than expected.
	Allow separate space for various types of storage, clean and dirty, disposable and reusable.
Inadequate quiet work space for staff and managers	Provide offices for key personnel.
	Provide areas dedicated to documentation completion.
	Allow staff access to computers and other technology.
Excessive noise and difficulty in cleaning	Consider various noise abatement measures such as ceiling tiles, carpeting and soft wall hangings.
	Consider carpet tiles instead of vinyl floor covering, at least in parts of the treatment area.
Inadequate staff and equipment	Estimate early in the planning process if the new facility will require more or less staff to handle the existing level of work.
	Project changes in work load that may occur because of the physical plant changes.
	Determine if basic equipment needs will be increased if square footage in the new space is changed.

plant design. A well-designed physical plant allows staff to focus on delivering services rather than overcoming physical obstacles. A good design leads to efficiency. The appearance of the structure, equipment, furniture and its amenities can enhance patient attendance and participation in therapeutic programs. To accomplish such goals, five-stage, 9-step planning process was presented along with a summary of responsibilities of the various participants in the process. Specific suggestions were offered for enhancing the utility of work areas common to physical therapy physical environments. To help the reader put the information from this chapter into practice, Role-Play 9 in Appendix A was developed. This role-play will allow the reader to put their

new knowledge about the facility design process to use.

SUGGESTED READINGS

Lord PJ, Johnson BE. Your Private Practice. Planning and Organization. Lake City, FL: Peter J. Lord and Associates, 1984:91–160.

Magistro CM. Department planning, design, and construction. In Hickok RJ, ed. Physical Therapy Administration and Management. Baltimore, MD: Williams and Wilkins, 1974:143–183.

Nosse LJ, Friberg DG. Management Principles for Physical Therapists. Baltimore, MD: Williams and Wilkins, 1992: 167–175.

Quinn P. APTA Resource Guide. Design and Planning of Physical Therapy and Rehabilitation Departments. Alexandria, VA: American Physical Therapy Association, undated, unpaginated.

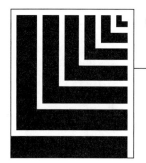

10

INFORMATION MANAGEMENT

PREVIEW

This chapter will help the reader understand the critical role that the management of information and automated systems play in the everyday operation of a typical physical therapy department, clinic or practice. This chapter reviews the most typical types of data that need to be collected and managed, discusses appropriate and inappropriate uses of these data in everyday operations, investigates the options available for automation and addresses differences in these systems among private clinics and departments that are part of an integrated health care system.

KEY WORDS

Application: a computer program designed to help people perform a certain type of work. An application thus differs from an operating system (which runs a computer), a utility (which performs maintenance or general-purpose chores), and a programming language (with which computer programs are created). Depending on the work for which it was designed, an application can manipulate text, numbers, graphics, or a combination of these elements. Some application packages offer considerable computing power by focusing on a single task, such as word processing; others, called integrated software, offer somewhat less power but include several applications, such as a word processor, a spreadsheet, and a database program.

Automated Medical Record: system of data collection, storage, protection, verification of accuracy, and retrieval of medical information concerning a single individual or group of individuals in an electronic format.

Browser: software programs used on an Internet or intranet network to retrieve information in the form of text, graphics and other data formats.

Data: information in its most basic form.

Data Aggregation: the process of collecting and analyzing data as a collective or data grouping.

Data Base: any collection of data organized for storage in an electronic format and designed for easy access by authorized users. The data may be in the form of text, numbers, or encoded graphics.

Electronic Data Transfer: movement of information from one location to another, either within a computer (as from a disk drive to random access memory) or between a computer and an external device (as between two computers or a file server and a computer on a network).

Fire Wall: systems, including hardware and software, designed to prevent unauthorized access to information systems within an organization.

Hardware: physical components of a computer system, including any peripheral equipment such as printers, modems and mice.

Health Information System: electronic medical record.

Hospital Information System: the system of data collection, storage, protection, verification of accuracy, and retrieval of medical and financial and other types of performance information concerning a hospital system, its employees, medical staff and patients in an electronic format.

Information: data that has been manipulated into a useful form, i.e., the knowledge that resides in the human brain, in all written and electronic records.

Information Flow: passage of information and communication through an organization. The system of data collection, storage, protection, verification of accuracy, and retrieval of medical information concerning the health status, history, potential risks and behaviors of a defined population in an electronic format.

Information Superhighway: terms popularly used to refer to the availability and use of advanced information services by means of a variety of high-capacity data transport facilities, especially computers and computer networks. Often confused with Internet (see below) or World Wide Web (see below).

Internet: an open interconnection of networks that enables connected computers to communicate directly. There is a global, public Internet and many smaller-scale, controlled-access internets, known as enterprise internets or intranets.

Local Area Network (LAN): a group of computers and other devices dispersed over a relatively limited geographic area and connected by a communications link that enables any device to interact with any other on the network. LANs may include microcomputers and shared resources such as laser printers and large hard disks. Most LANs can support a wide variety of computers and other devices. Each device must use the proper physical and data-link protocols for the particular LAN, and all devices that want to communicate with each other on the LAN must use the same communications protocol. Although single LANs are geographically limited (to a department or an office building, for example), separate LANs can be connected to form larger networks (See WAN).

Management Information System: the system of data collection, storage, protection, verification of accuracy, and retrieval of financial performance information concerning an organization, its employees and customers in an electronic format.

Operating System: software responsible for controlling the allocation and usage of hardware resources such as memory, central processing unit (CPU) time, disk space and peripheral devices. The operating system is the foundation upon which applications, such as word-processing and spreadsheet programs, are built. Popular operating systems include MS-DOS, Windows-NT, the Macintosh OS, OS/2, and UNIX.

Personal Information Manager: software programs used to store information typically used by a single individual about that individual's schedule, personal contacts and projects, similar to a personal organizer.

Security: processes involved in protecting an information systems from unauthorized access, damage or misuse.

Software: computer programs; instructions that cause the hardware to do work. Software as a whole can be divided into a number of categories based on the types of work done by programs. The two primary software categories are operating systems (system software), which control the workings of the computer, and application software, which addresses the multitude of tasks for which people use computers.

Spreadsheet: type of computer software program in which numerical or text data or formulas are displayed in rows and columns.

System Administrator: the person responsible for administering use of a multiuser computer system, communications system or both. A system administrator performs such duties as assigning user accounts and passwords, establishing security access levels, and allocating storage space, as well as being responsible for other tasks such as watching for unauthorized access and preventing virus programs from entering the system.

Tele Medicine: use of electronic, computerized remote communications and teleconferencing tools to practice medicine from a geographically distant location.

Wide Area Network (WAN): a group of computers or computer networks and other devices dispersed over a large geographic area and connected by a communications link that enables devices to interact with each other. Similar to a local area network except that it covers a much larger geographic area.

Word Processing Program: an application program for manipulating text-based documents. All word processors offer at least limited facilities for document formatting, such as font changes, page layout, paragraph indentation, etc. Some word processors can also check spelling, find synonyms, check grammar, incorporate graphics created with another program, correctly align tables, charts, and mathematical formulas, create and print form letters and perform calculations. Examples of word processing programs are Microsoft Word and WordPerfect.

World Wide Web: a system of resources available to computer users who are connected to an Internet. It is accessed primarily through the public Internet and enables users to view and interact with a variety of information sources, including magazine archives, public and university library resources, professional organization home pages, current world and business news, and programs.

INTRODUCTION

The U.S. health care system is undergoing an historic shift from a conceptual view that concentrates on individual care to one that focuses on the health of populations and the care of individuals across a health care continuum. To understand and, eventually, manage the health of a population requires managing massive amounts of integrated data. This shift has added stress to many of our existing systems, some of which are outdated or inadequate to meet increasingly vigorous data requirements. The new information demand will become more evident as we shift toward outcomes analysis and management (Chapter 11), the development of automated documentation, scheduling and billing systems, and integrated, automated management information systems (MIS's) and health information systems (HIS's). The design and implementation of MIS's and HIS's will have a significant impact on the completion of work within organizations. This will be especially true for large organizations. Because of the complexity of large organizations, systems that are intended to bring order and efficiency to daily processes, can, if poorly designed, actually interfere with the performance of meaningful work and deter real progress.

Clinical, marketing and financial decisions need to be based on information and assumptions that are timely, accurate and understandable. These trends encourage the therapy manager and the therapist to manage information in a way that will optimize its usage and usefulness.

Although there have been tremendous advances in the management of information within health care organizations, it is imperative to remember that information systems are merely tools. They are tools that are used as an adjunct to the primary work that therapists perform—the effective and compassionate therapeutic care of the patients served. The tools of information management should be used as efficiently as possible to help care for patients and manage clinics successfully.

VALUES

In accord with the ethical principle of confidentiality, as progress is made toward having increasingly faster and easier ways of accessing information and data, there must be assurance that the information and data that is collected, accessed and managed, is restricted to those who are privileged to have such information. The patient's basic right to privacy does not change in an electronic environment. It simply becomes more difficult to accomplish. The simple rule to share information only with those who are related to the care of the patient or authorized by the patient to have such information still remains. Additionally, the principle of truth telling obligates health care professionals to assure that the data collected is accurate and useable. The principle of veracity suggests that data be used or shared with others when it benefits a mutually cared for patient. The principle of loyalty requires assuring that the information is used to benefit patients and the organization. In cases in which this causes a dilemma, one of the analysis processes suggested in Chapter 2 may provide a viable solution. In general, do what favors the patient whenever possible. Finally, the driving force to automation and more sophisticated information systems should be the ability to improve, refine or enhance the services that are offered to patients and other customers. Information systems with more options are not necessarily more beneficial to patients.

Meeting the training needs of staff is essential to the successful and efficient utilization of information systems. Staff must be adequately trained

and allowed adequate time to become comfortable with any system that is introduced if the system is to optimally contribute to better care of patients. Patience is necessary. Each person has their own learning rate when trying to integrate new technology into their work life. It takes time to get accustomed to new systems and there are inevitably unanticipated transitional difficulties no matter how judicious the planning may have been. Adopting the principle of beneficence suggests over estimating the time it will take for users to become efficient with the system rather than pushing quick deadlines for total changeovers. Finally, the time lag between system selection and installation can be considerable. A system considered good at selection time may be less than good when it is put into operation.

THE INFORMATION CRUNCH

The amount of information that crosses the typical health care clinician or manager's desk is increasing each year. As more sophisticated automated systems become available, there is the opportunity to try to record, monitor and analyze many more things than was possible in the past. Although attempting to manage a department, practice or clinic without adequate information is very difficult and risky, the opposite is also true: managing with too much information is also difficult and risky. Finding balance is a challenge to the manager. As more and more information becomes available, the prudent manager must ask the question: What information is most important, given limited resource availability?

Automated information systems are very expensive to purchase and operate. Necessary resources include the hardware and software to develop and produce the informational reports. Also, the human resources of time and energy to collect data, review and interpret the information, and develop and implement actions based on the information are also critical.

The greatest demand on physical therapy managers and practitioners is the time spent interacting with information that could be spent taking actions to improve the lives of patients. There is a constant competition for the attention and focus of managers and clinicians at work. Clearly, there is great potential for automation and information systems to help improve efficiency. But efficiency alone is not enough. How the manager or clinician chooses to devote time and energy will determine how effective they are in their role.

With so many opportunities for distraction, there will be an increased emphasis on effectiveness concurrent to the continued focus on the efficient performance of tasks.

THE MANAGEMENT AND FLOW OF INFORMATION IN AN ORGANIZATION

In most, if not all, organizations, control of and access to organizational data and information is a source of power. It is often also a source of competition within an organization. How internal information is accessed and by whom is very important within any organization.

Historically, information has been protected as a resource within organizations. Frequently, it was available only on an as needed basis. Access to information was only granted to those who could demonstrate a need to know. This sort of approach leads to a hierarchy of information access. There are those with access to the information (and subsequent power) who are the haves and others who are the information have nots. See Chapter 2 for a related discussion on the issue of power differences.

The flow of information has changed over time in organizations. Historically, information was collected both centrally and locally (Fig. 10.1). Locally gathered information was then dispersed to a central depository of data. There it was aggregated and finally shared with a limited number of selected individuals by overt action of leaders who saw their role including the protection of the corporate data.

More recently (Fig. 10.2), information continued to be collected locally, but began to be aggregated and interpreted locally before it was then sent to a central repository. There it was re-aggregated and then dispersed in aggregate by actions of leaders who continued to control access.

Currently (Fig. 10.3), information is often collected and aggregated locally. It is then available to be retrieved from a local depository by a centralized communication center where it can be retrieved on demand by local users and management.

In the future (Fig. 10.4), data will be collected locally and then be dispersed to the entire organizational community. Data will be aggregated as needed and retrieved on demand by the entire community as needed.

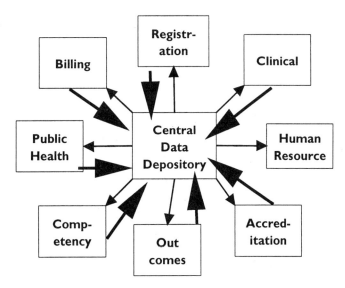

FIGURE 10.1. Historical information flow.

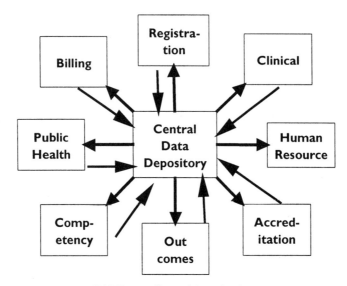

FIGURE 10.2. Recent information flow.

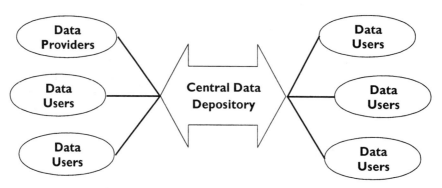

FIGURE 10.3. Current information flow.

This is a dramatic change in the manner in which data is accessed and controlled. It represents a democratization of data and information within organizations.

Decentralization of information systems also carries with it some increased expenses and challenges. Included among these are the demands for protection of the organizational data from corruption, destruction or misuse. Confidentiality also becomes much more difficult when a larger population has access to the data. There is the increased potential for inappropriate release of organizational data to parties who may use the data against the organization (see related discussion in Chpapter 12). Finally, in a disseminated information system, there will be increased time and expense related to the education and training that will involve many more of the personnel in the organization compared to systems in which only a few highly skilled personnel interact with a centralized system.

In most cases, solutions have been, or are being developed, to address these problems associated with the decentralization of information systems. Six factors to consider in information system development are shown in Table 10.1.

Traditional Areas of Information Management

In addition to the typical internal data that health care organizations collect and manage in the course of clinical and managerial operations,

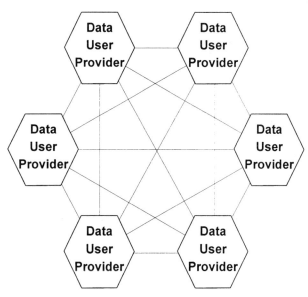

FIGURE 10.4. Future information flow.

such as those listed in Table 10.2, there are several additional types of information that must be managed. Information management also includes data that is generated external to the organization.

Differences in Typical Information Needs in Private Practice Compared To Organization-Based Clinical Services

There are many information management similarities in small compared to large organizations. There are also differences. These differences are often related to the size of the physical spaces and the complexity of the organizations. This section will describe the typical information systems from the perspective of the therapy leadership in a medium-sized community hospital, *ABC Community Hospital* and in a medium-sized private practice, *XYZ Rehab, Inc.* Please note that the authors are not intending to describe the most or least advanced information systems, but rather to present a picture of how these functions may be organized in hospital and private practice-based organizations.

TABLE 10.1
Factors to Consider in Information System Development

1. Confidentiality
2. Access
3. Efficiency
4. Cost
5. Usability
6. Learnability

Information Systems at a Community Hospital

Organization

ABC Community Hospital is a 350-bed acute hospital in a medium-sized city. There are approximately 2,000 employees who work at *ABC Community Hospital.* Only 50 employees work in therapy. Therapy services are provided to patients who are acutely ill, including those in the emergency room and intensive care units of the hospital. Services are also provided to patients in the 15-bed inpatient medical rehabilitation unit and in the 35-bed skilled nursing facility located on the campus of *ABC Community Hospital.*

TABLE 10.2
Typical Information Managed in Health Care Organizations' Information Systems

Demographic data
Patient clinical data
Patient financial data
• Billing data
• Accounts receivable data
Scheduling data
Human resource information
• Staff demographic data
• Staff payroll and benefit records
• Staff medical records
• Staff performance, disciplinary and employment records
• Staff clinical efficacy data
Organizational information
• Accounts payable data
• Corporate confidential records
• Real estate records
• Records and information required by external agencies, e.g., accreditation, governance and legislative bodies.
• Trade secrets
• Contracts and other legal records
• Performance data
• Internal communication records such as meeting minutes and memos
• Asset tracking inventory, etc.

Outpatients are also treated at *ABC Community Hospital;* however, these services are housed in a separate building from the main hospital. Home care patients are also served by the therapy staff.

Management Structure

A single therapy manager supervises physical therapy, occupational therapy, speech-language pathology, rehabilitation nursing, rehabilitation psychology and therapeutic recreation in all locations. The therapy manager reports to the vice president of patient care services, who reports to the president of the hospital.

Information Systems

We will now examine how the typical information systems work at *ABC Community Hospital.*

Patient Information Systems at *ABC Community Hospital*

Demographic data on patients is collected in the admitting and registration department. The data is entered into the hospital-wide admitting, discharge and transfer system (ADT). When any department of the hospital needs demographic data on any patient, that department uses data terminals located in the local department to access this data. Many, but not all departments, can change demographic data on patients. Access to the system is by password and user identification code. The mainframe computer keeps a record of who accesses the system and what activities they perform.

Patient clinical data is collected on paper in each individual clinical area and compiled into a centralized medical record. Each patient has only one medical record, but components of that record may be kept in many different locations. For patients who receive outpatient therapy, a unique therapy chart is kept for each episode of care that the patient receives. For inpatient care, the therapists keep the therapy record in the patient record that is maintained in the nursing station or at bedside for each patient. It is very difficult to coordinate multiple disciplinary charts such as those from radiology and therapy.

Patient financial data is coordinated in a centralized database that is maintained in the finance department. This information is based on a unique patient identification number that is given at the time of patient admission.

This information is also coordinated with credit checks and insurance verifications that are performed to determine the patient's ability to pay. It is also used to identify the viability of health insurance coverage and past financial performance for patients who have previously been cared for at *ABC Community Hospital.* Included in the financial system is a method to track the patient's insurance company and to indicate if it is required to have payment approved before treatment. Except for the data on prior approval of care, the therapy manager does not routinely access this data.

Billing data is closely coordinated with the other financial data. All departments, including therapy, enter daily billing data into the same terminals that are used for the ADT system. This information is then aggregated into a bill that is mailed to the patient or to the patient's insurance company. The therapy manager routinely reviews reports showing the amount of billing that has occurred in his or her area of responsibility.

Accounts receivable data represents those bills that the hospital has issued to patients and insurance companies that have not yet been paid. This data is closely coordinated with the billing data. The therapy manager does not routinely access this data.

Scheduling data is not centralized at *ABC Community Hospital.* However, in many hospitals, scheduling is centralized. Data related to the times patients are to receive care and when additional patients could be scheduled is maintained separately in each department. Conflicts between staff for access to patients occur on a regular basis. The only exception to lack of centralization of scheduling is on the Medical Rehabilitation Unit where all services and care are scheduled on a scheduling board that is coordinated by the nursing staff.

For outpatients receiving therapy, the schedule is kept in a departmental personal computer that is part of a local area network. Clerical personnel are very active in trying to match staff availability with patient appointment preference. All staff within the department can access the scheduling data. In addition to clerical personnel, therapists and therapist assistants can also change patient times and days from any of the seven nodes on the local area network that are distributed throughout the outpatient department.

The therapy manager reviews the scheduling data on a daily basis, often runs reports on the staff's productivity levels, and frequently uses this system to try to accommodate high-priority patients who need therapy immediately. Reports from this system are also sent to the vice president of patient care and the president of the hospital. Additional information that is available to the therapy manager is the frequency with which referrers sent patients to therapy and attendance history of individual patients.

Human Resource Information at ABC Community Hospital

Staff demographic data and performance, payroll and benefits, and disciplinary and employment records are centralized in the human resource department of the hospital. This information is closely held in confidence and requires password and identification codes for access. Much of this information is automated but some of it exists only in paper format. See Chapter 12 for additional information. Performance and disciplinary records are initiated at the department level but stored as redundant systems in the individual department by the department therapy manager and the human resources department. The therapy manager regularly receives and reviews reports from human resources. These written reports are then filed in the department records. Payroll data for the therapy department is routinely reviewed and approved by the therapy manager.

Staff medical records, including employment physical examination data, are maintained in the employee health department of the hospital. This area has restricted access for all employees. Both the entire employee health department and the file area are under tight security. There is very little automation in the employee health department.

Staff clinical efficacy data, including individual and collective productivity and clinical outcomes, is collected and maintained in the departmental personal computer that is part of a local area network. Clerical personnel enter this data once it is supplied to them by the supervisor or clinician involved. All supervisory staff within the department can access the productivity and outcome data.

The therapy manager reviews this data on a regular basis, often runs reports, and frequently uses this system in the performance appraisal process. Reports from this system are also sent to the vice president of patient care and the president of the hospital.

Organizational Information at ABC Community Hospital

Accounts payable data are maintained in the purchasing and finance departments. This information is part of the same automated financial system that includes patient finance and billing. Individual departments can use this system from the terminals in all departments. The therapy staff use this system to place orders for supplies and equipment. Reports on the expenses associated with these purchases are routinely reviewed by the therapy manager.

Corporate confidential records are key documents such as real estate records, trade secrets, internal communication records such as meeting minutes and memos, contracts, records and information required by external agencies, such as accreditation, governance and legislative bodies, endowment, physician credentials, quality improvement activities and other records needed to establish and maintain the organization. With the exception of medical staff credentials, most of these documents are filed as paper copies rather than being electronically stored. This information is kept in the administrative department and in the legal department. The therapy manager rarely, if ever, accesses these records.

Performance data of the entire organization is also maintained in the administrative and financial departments. This data is part of the financial information system and is the source of reports on the performance of the entire organization and the individual departments within. The therapy manager receives regular performance reports on the therapy department and can, to a limited basis, review some of this information on the terminals located within the therapy department.

Typically, each of the various information systems is maintained by personnel in the department in which the system is housed. There is a substantial information systems department to assist hospital personnel in the maintenance and use of these systems. All other departments are thought of as users of the system, rather than owners of the system.

Information Systems at a Private Therapy Practice

Organization and Management Structure

XYZ Rehab, Inc. is a single site private rehabilitation agency located in the same medium sized city as *ABC Community Hospital.* Chapter 14 explores entrepreneurial physical therapy

more fully. There are approximately 20 employees who work at *XYZ Rehab, Inc.* The owner of the practice, who is a physical therapist, is the manager of the clinic. As the only shareholder in the corporation, the owner is also the board of directors. Fifteen employees work directly with patients and 5 work in the billing and collections department. Only outpatient physical therapy and social work services are provided.

Information Systems

Patient Information at XYZ Rehab, Inc.

Demographic data is collected and entered into an automated practice management software program by the receptionist who is the same person who contacted the patient to schedule the appointment. This information is available, via password and identification code access, at all five of the nodes of the local area network that runs throughout the clinic. An external consultant administers the system in case of trouble or problems with the software.

Patient clinical data is collected on paper in a folder that comprises the patient's medical record. Each patient has only one medical record that includes all the records for each past episode of care that the patient has received. Open records (records for patients currently receiving care) are stored in a file in the business office. Closed records (records for patients who have completed therapy) are stored in a file in the finance area located in the basement of the clinic.

Patient financial data is entered into the automated practice management software program by the receptionist at the time of the patient's first appointment. This database is coordinated by the finance staff. This information is based on a unique patient identification number that is given at the time of patient admission.

Patient financial information is coordinated with credit checks and insurance verification, which are performed by the finance staff to determine the patients' ability to pay for therapy. Historical financial information for patients who have been cared for at *ABC Community Hospital* in the past is also part of this system. Included in the financial system is a method to track the patient's insurance company and to indicate if it is required to have payment approved before treatment. The owner reviews this data on a regular basis.

Billing data is closely coordinated with the other financial data. The clerical staff enter daily billing data into the same practice management software program that is used for financial data. This billing data is provided by the clinical staff to the clerical staff at the end of each patient treatment day. This information is then aggregated into a bill that is reviewed by the owner and then sent to the patient or to the patient's insurance company. The owner reviews individual bills daily and aggregate reports for monthly and quarterly summaries.

Accounts receivable data represents those bills that the practice has issued to patients and insurance companies that have not yet been paid. This data is closely coordinated with the billing data. Because the speed with which a bill is paid is closely related to cash flow, and hence the ability of the practice to pay its bills, accounts receivable data are closely monitored by the owner. Much like the hospital's outpatient area, scheduling data at *XYZ Rehab, Inc.* is kept in a personal computer that is part of the local area network. Clerical personnel are very active in trying to match staff availability with patient appointment preference. All staff within the department can access the scheduling data. In addition to clerical personnel, therapists and therapist assistants can also change patient times and days from any of the five nodes on the local area network that are distributed throughout the clinic.

The owner of the practice reviews the scheduling data on at least a daily basis, often runs reports on the staff's productivity levels, and frequently uses this system to try to "fit in" high-priority patients who need therapy immediately. Additional information that is available to the owner is the frequency with which referrers send patients to the clinic and attendance history of individual patients. The owner also previews the patient load over the next few days and weeks to determine if staffing changes are needed.

Human Resource Information

Staff demographic data and performance, disciplinary and employment records are maintained in the owner's office. This information is main-

tained as a collection of forms and files that are kept in locked files. Only the owner has access to these files. None of this information is automated, it exists only in paper format. Performance and disciplinary records are also kept in the personnel record in the owner's office. The owner reviews these files when performance reviews are needed or when a problem with an employee's performance arises. Payroll is outsourced to a local company that provides payroll services to many companies in the community. The payroll company performs all payroll functions for a fee that is based on a percentage of the total payroll expense.

Staff medical records, including employment physical examination data, are maintained by an external company that provides employee health services to small businesses. This data is stored offsite and therefore not available to any staff in the clinic, including the owner.

Staff clinical efficacy data, including individual and collective productivity and clinical outcomes, is collected and maintained in a personal computer that is part of a local area network. Clerical personnel enter this data once it is supplied to them by the owner or clinician involved. Only the owner can access this data. The owner reviews this data on a regular basis, often runs reports, and frequently uses this system in marketing activities and in the performance appraisal of staff.

Access to the many types of data that are stored offsite or locked in the owner's office is sometimes difficult or cumbersome for staff who may need to use these records.

Organizational Information

A local certified public accountant provides consultation to the practice on financial and tax-related matters.

Accounts payable data are maintained by the finance staff. This information is part of the same automated practice management system that includes patient finance and billing. Staff can use this system from any of the five computers connected to the local area network, but password and identification codes are required. The owner, clerical staff and finance staff use this system to place orders for supplies and equipment. Reports on the expenses associated with these purchases are routinely reviewed by the owner at the time bills for the practice are paid. The owner personally signs all checks issued by the clinic. Finance staff, in cooperation with the owner, monitor all practice bank accounts to assure there are adequate funds available to pay payroll and other expenses.

Corporate confidential records such as real estate records, trade secrets, internal communication minutes and memos, contracts, records and information required by external agencies, and other records needed to establish and maintain the organization are filed as paper copies in the owner's office or in the office of the clinic's corporate legal counsel. Legal counsel is provided by a local attorney who is experienced in health care and small business matters. The owner and corporate legal counsel frequently review these records.

Performance data of the clinic is also maintained in the owner's office. This data is part of the financial information system. The owner reviews the clinic's financial performance reports regularly.

Typically, all of the information systems are maintained by the owner with the assistance of the information systems consultant.

Information Systems in Large and Small Organizations

As the examples of the various systems in *ABC Community Hospital* and *XYZ Rehab, Inc.* show, there are many similarities and many differences in how information is managed. Although the same basic information systems must be addressed in each setting, the manner in which the organization structures itself to address these systems is dramatically different. Each structure presents certain advantages and specific challenges.

In the larger setting of the hospital, many specialized departments assist and support the therapy manager in the daily operations of the department. These support departments, such as finance, admissions and information systems, act as internal consultants to the patient care areas. By allowing these support departments to monitor and handle some of the functions of the business, the therapy department manager is able to focus attention more intensely on those aspects of the business that are unique to therapy—especially clinical care and referral development. However, the therapy manager may become too focused on the clinical aspects of the department and become isolated from many of the critical functions that occur out of the therapy manager's typical areas of focus. The therapy manager in the larger organization must be willing to make the extra effort to establish strong relationships with all the support departments to assure that they are kept aware of any potential problems as early as possible. Additional concerns for larger, more bureaucratic organizations are the potential for systems and communication to require substantial resources to support the corporate overhead of the system itself, and the potential for the decision-making time to become excessively long due to the larger number of individuals who will need to be consulted about the decision.

In the smaller setting of the private practice, it is often not possible to employ a staff of professionals to function as internal consultants in the areas of finance, accounting, legal affairs, etc. This expertise is no less needed in a small organization than in a larger one. To provide this expertise, the owner must either develop those skills internally or contract with external professionals to provide the services as needed. An advantage of this arrangement is that the owner continues to be involved in all aspects of the business. However, the potential for the owner to be distracted from the clinical development of the practice by all the business and finance activities is substantial. The owner of a small practice must learn to balance the finance and clinical leadership of management. Chapter 12 deals further with this issue.

An advantage of a smaller, more compact information system is quicker decision time and less bureaucracy. However, quicker decisions are not always better decisions and the quality of the information provided to support the decision process is critical to optimal decision-making.

USE OF DATA

Collection of data for its own sake is of minimal value. How the data is incorporated into the daily operations of the organization is much more important.

There are appropriate uses and inappropriate uses for all the data types listed above. There are some individuals who should have access to each of the data types listed, and some who should not. Employees, for example, will need to have access to patient medical records to effectively treat the patient. However, if a staff nurse is also the neighbor of a person who is admitted as a patient to your hospital, there may be some concerns when discussing what information the nurse/neighbor really needs.

Every organization should have clearly defined rules of access to any data collected and maintained. These rules should define who can access what data and clearly state what they may do with that data. These rules should be universally applied across the organization and should be routinely monitored, reviewed and updated as needed.

The ability to use organizationally maintained data should be based on the real, working requirements of those who access the data. For example, clinical department requirements typically consist of access to past clinical information that is available on a patient. Most, but not all, of the patient's past medical history should be made available to the clinical team members that treat the patient. Particularly difficult questions arise when the patient has requested specific information be withheld from the care givers especially when the patient has exceptionally contagious pathology that may endanger the clinical team members. The requests of the patient will need to be weighed against the safety of the care team.

Information management requirements are also often conflicting. When an employee is injured in a work-related injury, for example, the employee has specific rights and privileges for workers' compensation healthcare and indemnity benefits. The employee should be offered the same level of confidentiality as any other person in need of health care. However, because there is a pre-existing personal relationship with the employee, there is potentially a conflict between the roles that the therapy manager may play—employer to an employee, care giver to a patient and friend to someone who is injured.

EXPERT SYSTEMS IN MEDICINE

Another use of automation in health care, both clinically and administratively, is expert systems. "Expert computer systems" or "knowledge-based systems" are computer programs (software) that analyze data in a way that, if performed by a human, would be considered intelligent. Three main characteristics of expert systems are (1):

1. Symbolic logic rather than just numerical calculations.
2. An explicit knowledge base that is understandable to an expert in that area of knowledge.
3. Ability to explain its conclusions with concepts that are meaningful to the user.

Expert systems can be useful in two different ways:

1. Decision support: to remind an experienced decision maker of options or issues to consider that he or she once knew but may have forgotten. This is the most common use in medicine.
2. Decision making: to allow an unqualified person to make a decision that is beyond his or her level of training and experience. This is the most common use in many industrial systems.

The future for the use of expert systems in healthcare is very positive, however, there are "obstacles to development of expert systems for medical applications:

1. Medical tasks are difficult because of differences among individual patients and the uncertainty of the available clinical data.
2. The range of acceptable error is small because of ethical concerns and malpractice risks.
3. There is no perceived shortage of human experts.
4. FDA requirements discourage vendor research and development.
5. Funding for capital expenses is in short supply" (1).

The main beneficial factors of expert system technology that would support further development include:

1. Cost effectiveness in capitated and rural systems.
2. Improved quality of patient care.
3. Diminishing technical barriers (widespread access to the Internet, increased computer literacy by end-users, and availability of cheap but powerful computer hardware and software (1).

Financial and reimbursement expert systems are very attractive to the therapy manager. These sorts of systems can be valuable in helping the therapist manager in assessing the relative value of alternate financial arrangements with third party payers or similar arrangement with alternate third party payers. For example, given alternate sets of assumptions on the demographics, therapy-seeking behaviors and anticipated utilization of therapy services by a given patient population, an expert system could be instrumental in helping the therapist manager consider alternative courses of action.

An additional clinical use of expert systems could be the development of clinical care plans based on key findings of physical examination and patient history. By referring to an outcomes database that has been built over time, the knowledge that is available about the relative value of alternate clinical courses can be identified and used by the clinician in the clinical decision-making process.

DOCUMENTATION AS AN EXAMPLE OF A COMPLEX INFORMATION SYSTEM

The manner in which staff record clinically relevant information is referred to as clinical documentation. Documentation systems may be automated or manual. Unfortunately, the style and format of documentation varies throughout the country and sometimes even within a single clinic. This variation may be due to many reasons including, requirements of third party payers, peculiarities of specific legal and legislative jurisdictions, varying requirements for interstaff communication, and clinician experience, skill and preference.

In general, there are four major purposes of clinical documentation:

1. To communicate patient-specific information to various interested parties, including other clinicians, referral sources, the patient themself, employers, third party payers and sometimes, even to remind the clinician of the patient's condition at a future time.
2. To document the status of the patient, the procedures that are used with the patient, and the pa-

tient's response to the treatment. This would also include the ability to use this documentation to analyze the effects of clinical intervention on similar future patients, i.e. to learn about the impact of therapeutic intervention and refine the skill and judgement of the clinician.
3. To minimize the potential for a negative outcome of any future litigation for the clinician and or patient.
4. To comply with requirements of internal and external interested parties such as regulatory or reimbursement agencies.

Documentation is a very important function of all professional members of a therapy department. Decisions on the structure and processes of producing documentation will influence reimbursement, legal liability, productivity, teamwork and, to a significant extent, the structure of clinical care. Because of its importance to the department, special care should be taken in considering alternative methods of producing and managing documentation. It will be necessary to consider many aspects of this decision, including personnel considerations, technology considerations, financial considerations, and realistic expectations of success.

Personnel Considerations in Documentation Management Systems

Foremost among the factors to be considered in implementing a documentation system should be the impact that it will have on the staff. As is the case with any significant change, acceptance or rejection of the plan by staff will be critical to the overall success of the project. To effectively develop a documentation management system of any type, it will be necessary to develop a significant degree of standardization of content and format of the documentation. Willingness of the staff to follow the standard procedures is essential. Without standardization, it is unlikely that the new system will be an improvement over an existing system.

Also important to the success of the project, and a factor to consider in the documentation system development, is the degree of sophistication, experience and familiarity of the staff with automated systems and processes. This will include the staff's prior experience with computerized systems and general computer skills such as keyboard and data entry skills.

The geographic dispersion of personnel within the department or clinic will also be important to consider in the design of the documentation system. Staff members distributed throughout a large physical space may require the utilization of satellite filing stations or additional computer network nodes. If staff are located in multiple locations in disparate physical locations, it may be necessary to incorporate not just a LAN, but also a WAN that connects facilities throughout a geographic region. Obviously, additional cost and training will be required.

A final consideration in system design will be the ability of the staff to support automation and to problem solve the inevitable glitches that will accompany any implementation of new processes and technology. All of these must be considered during the planning and design phase for the documentation system.

Technology Considerations in Documentation Management Systems

There are many technologies that can be used to meet the preceding purposes. Among the technologies available are to have notes:

- Hand written using paper and pen in an unstructured narrative format
- Hand written using paper and pen in a structured, forms-based format
- Hand written using paper and pen using checklists and flow sheets
- Dictated, then transcribed using an unstructured narrative format
- Dictated, then transcribed using a structured, forms-based format
- Dictated, then transcribed using automated data entry forms
- Computer entered into an automated format by clinician in an unstructured narrative format (word processed)
- Computer entered into an automated format by clinician in a structured, checklist and flow sheet format
- Computer entered into an automated format by clinician in a data based format using keyboard, bar code, voice recognized, or electronic scanning technology

In each of the hand written methodologies listed above, the documentation is created by the clinician themselves. The outcome is a hard copy paper document. The advantages to these methods is the ease of use of paper and pen, the relative low cost of these materials, timeliness, and familiarity of staff with this sort of record. The disadvantages include the difficulty in analysis of aggregate data that paper presents, ease of loss of records, difficulty tracking progress in record completion, and inconsistency in methodology between different staff members, including illegibility.

In each of the dictation methodologies listed above, the documentation is created by the clinician and then handled again by a clerical staff member. The advantages of these methods include legibility and standardization of formatting appearance. The disadvantages include a higher cost to produce the documentation (due to payroll costs for the transcriptionist and higher equipment purchase and maintenance costs), lost clinical time for the clinician to proof the completed transcription, redundancy of handling the documentation multiple times, the difficulty in analysis of aggregate data that paper presents, ease of loss of records, and difficulty tracking progress in record completion.

In each of the computer entered methodologies listed above, the documentation is created by a clinician entering data in various formats into a personal computer. No clerical staff member is involved. The advantages of these methods are the lower payroll cost due to no clerical staff being involved, the ability to aggregate the data into searchable electronic formats, immediate availability of reports in a legible and highly consistent format, and the ability to retrieve the data in real time at many locations, including those distant from the clinic. The disadvantages include the need for clinicians to become computer literate and skilled, the increased cost of computer equipment and training, and reliance on a potentially unreliable technology for a very important departmental function.

Financial Considerations in Documentation Management Systems

Numerous costs must be considered in the financial analysis of a documentation system. Among these are the following:

- Development and design costs for the system including staff time and lost revenue from staff involved in decision processes rather than clinical, revenue producing activities
- Space renovations and furniture for equipment and storage of records
- Hardware and software capital and operating expenses to initiate the system
- Hardware and software capital and operating expenses involved in the ongoing support and operation of the system
- Training cost for staff
- Lost revenue due to staff inefficiencies during the period of transition to the new system
- Improved or worsened reimbursements during and after the period of system transition
- Staff time for system evaluation and revision on an ongoing basis

All of these costs must be weighed against the potential benefits of the new system and the likely benefits and risks of taking no action.

Realistic Expectations in Documentation Management Systems

Documentation is frequently a major source of complaints by staff. Even in the most efficient documentation systems, it is unlikely that staff will derive much satisfaction from this aspect of their job. Understanding that documentation systems are viewed by staff as what Herzberg might call hygiene factors (2), will be important to developing realistic expectations concerning the impact of the new system on the daily operations of the clinic. Clearly, documentation system management is not likely to be a motivator according to Herzberg (2). It will also be helpful to remember as these systems become more efficient, that streamlining is not likely to mean elimination of documentation activities by clinical staff. Because documentation is often the only tangible source of credibility to many external agencies including in the courtroom, therapy services will continue to emphasize the importance of these systems as a means to differentiate a clinic in what is frequently a crowded market.

NONTRADITIONAL AREAS OF INFORMATION MANAGEMENT

Information management can also be thought of as including several nontraditional data systems. Examples of these nontraditional systems include, telephone, closed circuit and cable television, voice mail, pager, fax, email, teleconferencing, and remote communication and computing systems. As automation becomes more widely available and increases in sophistication, additional methods of communicating within an organization will become available.

An exciting area of information management that is rapidly developing is convergence of different types of communications systems into new systems composed of previously dissimilar parts, such as interactive television, two-way, computerized alphanumeric paging, distance learning, telecommuting and telemedicine.

SUMMARY

Information management is necessary for effective health care management. This chapter has examined some of the critical components of successful data management systems. As the health care system continues to shift toward the management of the health of populations, additional emphasis on information management will be needed. Physical therapists need the skill, hardware and software to enter and access the kinds of data that can improve the quality and management of physical therapy services.

REFERENCES

1. Widman LE, Loparo KA. Artificial intelligence, simulation and modeling. Interfaces 1990;20:48–66.
2. Herzberg F. One more time: How do you motivate employees? Harvard Business Review 1968;Jan-Feb: 53–62.

SUGGESTED RESOURCES

American Physical Therapy Association: www.apta.org
The FOCUS group: www.TheFOCUSGroup.net
Healthcare Finance Administration: www.hcfa.gov
National Committee on Quality Assurance: www.ncqa.org
Special Interest Group on Technology in Physical Therapy, Section on Administration, APTA: www.APTA. org\SOA

11

OUTCOMES: WHAT TO COLLECT AND WHAT DOES THE INFORMATION MEAN

PREVIEW

This chapter addresses the measurement and management of performance outcomes in clinical care. Satisfaction outcomes, cost outcomes and technical or functional outcomes will be considered. Issues related to defining an acceptable quality and quantity of services and measures, along with the concept of health care provider accountability will be explored. Performance improvement methods, including commonly used continuous quality improvement (CQI) measures and outcomes systems, are reviewed.

Use of performance outcome information within the clinic setting is critical to a health care service organization's success. This chapter provides the reader with a foundation for understanding why and how to incorporate outcome information into daily decision-making processes. The role of a manager in interpreting data and the role of the entire staff in using the data to change practice behaviors is discussed.

KEY WORDS

Appropriateness: degree to which care provided is relevant to a patient's clinical care needs, given the current state of knowledge.

Cause and Effect Diagram: a problem-solving statistical tool that indicates effects and causes and how they interrelate. Also known as a fish bone diagram.

CARF, The Rehabilitation Commission (CARF): Non-profit organization for the promotion of quality services for people in need of rehabilitation. Formerly known as the Commission on Accreditation of Rehabilitation Facilities (CARF). CARF accreditation is voluntary.

Common Cause Variation: normal variation in the number of undesirable outcomes, errors and deviations from standards.

Continuous Quality Improvement (CQI): a system in which individuals in an organization look for ways to do things better, usually based on understanding of processes, process improvement, and control of variation.

Control Chart: a graphic method for evaluating whether a process is or is not in a state of statistical control.

Efficacy: the degree to which the care of a patient has been shown to accomplish the desired or projected outcome.

Flow Chart: a problem-solving statistical tool that shows the way things go through the organization (the current process), the way they should go (the improved process) or the difference between the two. Also known as a work flow diagram.

Health Plan Employer Data and Information Set (HEDIS): the HEDIS tool is a set of standardized performance measures designed to ensure that purchasers and consumers have the information they need to reliably compare the performance of managed health care plans.

Joint Commission on Accreditation of Healthcare Organizations (JCAHO): Non-profit accrediting body covering seven types of health care, i.e., ambulatory care, home care and hospice care, long-term care, psychiatric facilities, hospital care and managed care. JCAHO accreditation is voluntary.

National Committee for Quality Assurance (NCQA): an accrediting body for managed care organizations. NCQA accreditation is voluntary.

Pareto Chart: bar graph that helps focus the user's attention on the few most important factors rather than on many less important factors.

Performance Standard: the expectation of how a job or task should be done according to objective requirements and specifications.

Program Evaluation and Review Technique (PERT) Chart: graphic representation of a project, its tasks and deadlines. Performance standards can also be used to plot and communicate the progress of a project. Also known as a time plot.

Scatter Diagram: diagram that shows the relationship between two variables with data plotted in two dimensions.

Special Cause Variation: unexpected variation in the number of undesirable outcomes, errors, and deviations from standards due to an event that can be identified and, hopefully, rectified.

Stratification: breakdown of information into meaningful categories or classifications to better develop an interpretation and action plan.

INTRODUCTION

Outcomes management in health care is broadly defined as the process of data collection, analysis and interpretation of the effectiveness and efficiency of patient treatment. Outcomes management has been defined as "the determination of the results of the health care intervention through a reliable measurement methodology, ascertaining the most efficient manner in which to achieve the desired result an improving results over time" (1). The general purposes of outcomes management include measurement of the:

Effectiveness (assessment of the impact of treatment on a population)
Efficiency (assessment of the outcomes in conjunction with the resources used) of health care (1).

THE OUTCOMES IMPERATIVE: VALUES

In the United States today, there are relatively few health care markets "where the measurement of outcomes remains an option; rather, it is an essential part of clinical practice and survival" (1). Even in environments in which outcome data are not demanded, it is the responsibility of the professional to provide the highest quality of care feasible. Although the Code of Ethics of the American Physical Therapy Association (APTA) does not clearly identify its core value base, it does contain ethical principals that are identifiable. Principle 3 of the Code states that "physical therapists accept responsibility for the exercise of sound judgement" (2). This principle assumes that the exercise of sound judgement is predicated on appropriate knowledge and training. Values that support these motives are to do no harm and pursue excellence and competence. Clearly, a key component of outcome management is developing a system to constantly monitor the efficacy of treatment and then to revise future treatment based on past experience, to pursue excellence and competence.

Principle 8 states that "physical therapists participate in efforts to address the health needs of the public" (2). Values that support these motives are to enhance the profession, beneficence, service to the community and social justice. This principle assumes that physical therapists are able to evaluate the results of clinical intervention from the perspective of the public and know what is in the public's best interest.

Outcomes analysis and management should play a central role to meet patients' needs in the professional development of all physical therapy personnel. Figure 11.1 illustrates the scope of clinical practice of a therapist. This scope of practice represents all of the different types of patients and conditions that the therapist may treat throughout the course of their professional career. Some of the patients within this universe are patients with conditions that are very familiar to the clinician. There is, however, a second group of patients within this universe. This second group represents those patients with conditions that the clinician is not familiar with or

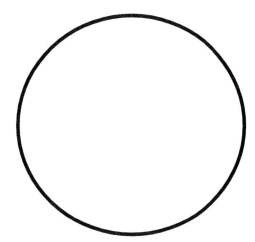

FIGURE 11.1. Scope of clinical practice universe.

comfortable treating. Throughout the course of a professional's career, as the professional develops experience and skill, the size of the second group, patients with conditions unfamiliar to the clinician, generally becomes smaller.

Figure 11.2 illustrates the scope of clinical practice for a typical novice clinician. This clinician may be a recent graduate or even a student. Clearly, those conditions with which the clinician is familiar or comfortable are in the minority.

Figure 11.3 illustrates the scope of clinical practice for a typical experienced clinician. Notice that the area representing patients with unfamiliar conditions has grown smaller. Conversely, the area representing familiar patients or conditions has grown larger. This represents professional growth and increased experience in the therapist.

Figure 11.4 illustrates the scope of clinical practice for an expert or master clinician. Notice how small the unfamiliar or uncomfortable zone has become. This represents a very high level of knowledge, skill, experience and expertise.

A question that should be asked here is: what will facilitate the transition from a novice clinician (Fig. 11.2) to experienced clinician (Fig. 11.3) to expert clinician (Fig. 11.4)?

For a specific patient type to move from the zone of unfamiliar to the zone of familiar patients, a clinician must interact with patients in that population. This comes only with experience, strong

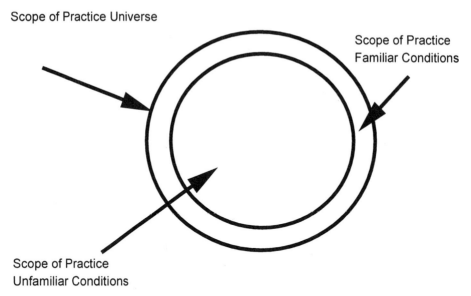

FIGURE 11.2. Scope of clinical practice: Novice.

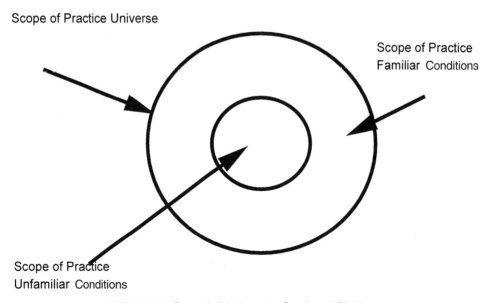

FIGURE 11.3. Scope of clinical practice: Experienced Clinician.

supervision, appropriate mentoring (see Chapter 4), quality continuing education and sufficient self-education. However, merely having contact with these patients will not assure that the care rendered will be effective or meaningful. Professional expertise develops from intense analysis of the type of care provided, the results of that care, and the implications of replicating desir-

able results in future patients in this category. This is the analysis and management of outcomes.

To develop adequately as a professional, each clinician should analyze their practice, the techniques used in clinical care and patient interaction, the outcomes achieved and the implications of past experience on future patients. Figure 11.5

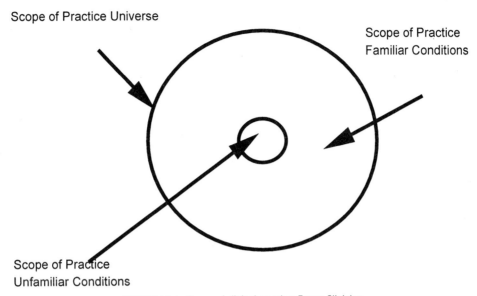

FIGURE 11.4. Scope of clinical practice: Expert Clinician.

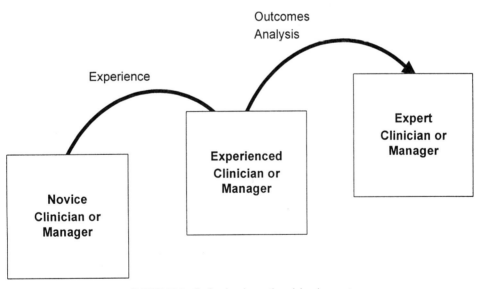

FIGURE 11.5. Professional growth and development.

illustrates this relationship. To grow from novice to an experienced clinician, it is necessary to invest adequate time becoming exposed to a variety of patients and situations. However, to move to the expert or master clinician status, analysis and management of outcomes is needed.

DEFINING ACCEPTABLE QUALITY AND QUANTITY OF SERVICES

The goals of outcome management are very basic to clinical care. They are shown in Table 11.1.

TABLE 11.1
Goals of Outcome Management

1. To document the results of clinical intervention
2. To examine and document practice patterns
3. To identify the most effective and cost efficient practice patterns
4. To gain a better understanding of practice
5. To use the outcome information in daily clinical and business decision making
6. To improve practice

Modified from Kovacek P. Improving Productivity without Sacrificing Quality. Harper Woods, MI: Kovacek Management Services, Inc., 1995:121.

USES OF OUTCOME MANAGEMENT

There are many potential uses of outcome data. Foremost of these is the ability to improve practice because of what is learned from the process. Second is the ability to use the data in marketing efforts with referral sources, payers and other communities of interest.

"Outcome measurement and management and the utilization of outcome information in planning should reflect the organization's ability to achieve outcomes that meet the identified needs of past, current and prospective consumers" (3).

Measuring Performance To Develop And Maintain Accountability

To develop the accountability of clinicians for the results of their work, it is necessary that "outcome indicators reflect the important health care goals" (4). It is also important that these indicators allow determining when and to what extent these goals have been achieved (4). In a typical rehabilitation center, there are three key areas from which to sample outcome information.

1. Clinical outcomes. These are often referred to as functional outcomes. The goal of clinical outcome management is to improve clinical care.
2. Financial outcomes. The goal of financial outcome management is profitability and cost effectiveness.
3. Satisfaction outcomes. The goal of satisfaction outcome management is to understand customer perception and to identify actions to improve customer satisfaction.

Each of the three areas above must be assessed in an outcome management program.

Clinical Performance

The measurement of clinical outcomes is often the area of performance measurement that is most difficult for the clinical manager. However, the importance of this measure cannot be over emphasized. Clinical physical therapy performance is the single thing that truly and uniquely differentiates physical therapy within the health care delivery system. If physical therapists are to continue to be important within health care organizations, it will be necessary to clearly define the clinical scope and limitations of the profession and of individual clinicians within the profession.

Clinical outcomes are the results, in terms of the patient's level of recovery and function, that are achieved as a result of clinical intervention. They are sometimes referred to as functional outcomes or technical outcomes. There are three prerequisites to effectively capture the essence of clinical outcome management:

1. Adequate measurement, description and documentation of the clinical and functional condition of the patient before intervention.
2. Adequate measurement, description and documentation of the clinical intervention.
3. Adequate measurement, description and documentation of the clinical condition of the patient after intervention.

To appropriately interpret these prerequisites, it is necessary to collect and analyze outcome data on relatively large numbers of patients in each category of diagnosis so that patterns of outcomes can be identified.

Choices regarding data to be collected, data collection methods and data analysis methods will be addressed later in this chapter. What will be addressed here is the second prerequisite: the ability to adequately measure, describe and document clinical intervention.

As previously stated, there are several excellent reasons to undertake outcome management programs. In our opinion, the most significant reason to proceed with outcome management programs is to learn the most effective clinical behaviors and to improve clinical practice, i.e., to improve patient care. To do this, it is necessary to accurately define existing practice. This requires a significant level of standardization of care. Without this standardization, it will be very difficult to improve the practice. Without standardization of clinical care, there are too many variables that can affect patient outcomes that may be attributed to clinical care. If there is interest in making adjustments to improve practice, the baseline practices must be defined, documented and consistently performed as documented.

Such standardization of practice is often difficult for physical therapists to accept. Often, as highly trained professionals, there is the misconception that with training, education and a certain level of autonomy, come the right to deviate from the discipline that is needed to provide high quality care in a structured and scientific manner. A research frame of mind is crucial. There is also an ethical obligation to provide the best possible care.

Many clinical practices are developing formal mechanisms to standardize care. These include critical pathways (often referred to as clinical pathways or care maps), protocols, clinical decision algorithms, and treatment guidelines. All of these mechanisms serve to reduce variation in the care delivery process. Adoption of standardized clinical programs is advantageous to the provision of high quality clinical care. Standardization is also critical to understanding practice patterns and fully describing the therapeutic interventions as required in prerequisite two above. Standardization supports adequate measurement, description and documentation of the clinical intervention.

Financial Performance

Chapters 7 and 8 review the measurement and management of financial performance on a macro level. Concerning cost outcomes, it is necessary to assess financial performance on a much smaller scale, at a micro level. Typical financial outcome measurements include:

- Average cost, revenue or margin per case
- Average cost, revenue or margin per visit
- Average cost, revenue or margin per unit of service
- Average revenue collected per case, visit or unit of service

Each of these financial outcomes is related to the financial resources devoted to the delivery of patient care. See Chapters 7 and 8 to review these components. Each may be further analyzed for specific staff members, types of patients, clinical sites or venues in the continuum of care.

In some clinical practices, personnel costs may represent as much as 80% of the ongoing operational expenses. Because of this, it may be helpful to develop systems to analyze and manage personnel productivity as an indicator of costs involved and overall financial success.

Customer Satisfaction

As care givers who frequently spend a significant amount of time in very intimate physical and emotional contact with patients, physical therapists should be very concerned about their customers' perception of physical therapy services. Given that physical therapists often function within a health care system which patients can easily perceive as less than friendly and accessible, one would expect that patients perceive physical therapists as warm, kind and talented professionals. Experience indicates that this is frequently the case.

Patient satisfaction is the relationship between patient expectations and their perception of the organization's success in fulfilling those expectations. To achieve higher levels of patient satisfaction, it is necessary to either lower patient expectations or raise the patient's perception of performance in relation to those expectations. Clearly, there are ethical considerations in inappropriately lowering or raising patient expectations. There is the potential to violate the ethical rules of truth telling, patient autonomy and veracity (giving information that is needed to make informed decisions). However, appropriate expectations and perceptions, especially when high quality care is being delivered, are in the patient's best interest.

Patient satisfaction studies can assist clinicians in several ways. They can:

1. Provide a better understanding of the patient's frame of reference.

2. Add an important component of a comprehensive outcomes measurement system.
3. Assist in predicting health-related behaviors and health care utilization.
4. Determine a patient's compliance to his or her treatment program.
5. Provide data for continuous process improvement.
6. Aid in developing a service oriented culture (5).

In a large study of 19,834 physical therapy patients in more than 120 centers in 12 states, key factors related to overall patient satisfaction were identified (5). The five areas that were found to most frequently drive overall patient satisfaction were:

1. Communication. The clinician's ability to communicate the treatment plan, from the patient's perspective.
2. Respectful, professional attention. The quality of time the clinician spent with the patient.
3. Consistency of clinician and other service providers.
4. Personally relevant knowledge of the patient's case by the service provider.
5. Respect for patient autonomy. The amount of patient input in treatment goal setting.

There are many methods to measure satisfaction. The APTA has produced a compendium of satisfaction instruments from clinics in diverse geographic and clinical settings that demonstrate the variety of tools that could be used to collect patient satisfaction data (6).

USING OUTCOME INFORMATION

There are some questions that may help management establish a patient satisfaction outcomes management system, including the following:

*   What is your place in the delivery system? (Who are we?)
*   What are the most common diagnoses? (Who are our clients?)
*   Who are the customers seeking outcome information? (Who wants information?)
*   What are the typical questions being asked? (What do they want to know?)
*   Which outcomes do you wish to measure? (What will be measured?)
*   What outcome measures or systems are (already) available? (What do we already know?)

*   What is the data collection protocol? (How should we handle the data?)
*   How will you train the staff? (How can we be sure we are good at this?)
*   How will you process the data? (Will we handle the data correctly?)
*   How will you analyze and interpret the results? (How do we make sense of the data?) (1)

Each of these questions must be answered to establish a successful patient satisfaction outcome management program.

HOW TO MEASURE AND MANAGE OUTCOMES

There are nine key steps to measuring and managing outcomes. Figure 11.6 illustrates the outcome management process.

Nine Steps To Outcome Management

The nine steps to outcome management are as follows:

1. Identify the population to be studied.
2. Choose an outcome tool.
3. Collect admission data.
4. Clinical intervention.
5. Collect discharge data.
6. Collect follow up data.
7. Analyze the collected data.
8. Develop actions based on data analysis.
9. Evaluate the outcomes program.

A more detailed examination of the nine steps is required.

Step One: Identify The Population To Be Studied

The most likely patient population to study is the current patient population served by the clinical practice. Not all tools or processes will work well with every population. It may be necessary to identify a subset of the entire patient population to get started. In the early stages of outcomes management program development, it may be best to limit the scope of the project to patients in the most frequently treated diagnostic

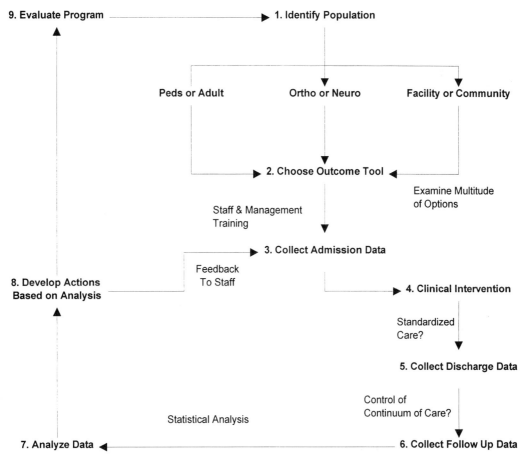

FIGURE 11.6. Outcome management steps.

groups. Starting on a smaller scale could increase the likelihood of success.

Step Two: Choose An Outcome Measurement Tool

There are a wide variety of tools available from which to choose. Each has its advantages and disadvantages with regard to the specific population to be studied and project limitations. Tools can, and should, be combined if necessary.

A specific outcome measurement tool must be selected. The tool evaluation process must address several difficult issues. One issue is whether the chosen instrument should use clinician measured or patient measured data. There are several advantages to clinician measured functional data.

- Greater reliability
- More sensitivity to change
- Excellent for showing validity of task being performed
- Measured usual activity vs. maximal activity (3)

The disadvantages of clinician measured functional data compared to patient report are:

- Poor for cognitively impaired patients
- Influenced by language, culture, and education
- More time consuming
- May need special training of examiners
- May need modification for different settings (i.e., the home)
- Performance on standardized tests may not represent performance in real life
- Potential injuries (3)

CLINICAL APPLICATIONS: INTERPRETING OUTCOMES DATA

To make valid measurements, and then valid comparisons across institutions and locations, it is essential to take into account the differences in types, severity, and complexities of illnesses among the patients treated at various institutions and locations. A process called risk adjustment (7) does this by accounting for factors beyond the control of the clinician that can influence outcomes (1). Risk adjustment includes identification of confounding variables including:

- Patient's age
- Source of insurance
- Insurance type
- Ethnicity
- Income
- Level of education
- Gender
- Number of prior episodes of care
- Co-morbidity
- Severity of the patient's condition
- Patient acuity level

To interpret correctly the data that is collected in an outcomes management program, it will be necessary to include and consider these and other confounding variables.

To effectively use any outcome measurement tool, it is necessary to identify confounding factors and understand the appropriate use of the tool. As with any standardized instrument, each outcome tool should define the following items:

Population. The specific type of person for which the tool applies.
Mode of Administration. How the tool is completed. For example, will the tool be completed by the patient with paper and pencil and self-administered or will the therapist ask the questions or grade the activities?
Completion. How long the test takes to complete and score.
Interpretation. What do the scores mean? How will the scores be used by the examiner?
Reliability. The degree to which the instrument produces consistent results when reproduced under similar circumstances.
Validity. The extent to which a test measures what it was designed to measure. Validity can not be directly assessed but must be evaluated through the use of the operational definition of the measure or through comparison to similar or dissimilar measures (3).

There are several key questions to ask at this stage of the outcomes management development process. "How much time does the practitioner have available to devote to a functional measure? Can the practitioner set aside time to administer a performance based measure" (3)? These are difficult questions and their answers can have a significant impact on staff productivity and morale.

Step Three: Collect Admission Data

To begin the data collection process, it will be necessary to assure that the participating staff are competent in the process. This will require substantial orientation and training. This should include a full explanation of the purpose and limitations of the study. The staff should also recognize the scope and limitations of outcome management before undertaking what can be a substantial amount of extra work. Staff will also need to understand that there will be delay periods between process steps. Delays can be expected between data collection and data analysis, between data analysis and the implementation of action plans. It may be necessary to view the staff as one of the customers of the outcome management system.

At the time of initial data collection, the procedures to gather, validate, store and access the data should have been established. All issues of information management discussed in Chapter 10 apply to outcomes data management.

Step Four: Clinical Intervention

At this stage, the actual treatment of the patients is not uniquely a part of the outcomes management system development. Treatment was ongoing before the clinic became interested in managing outcomes and treatment will continue even if efforts at outcomes management fail. However, several key issues often arise at this stage of the outcomes management program, among them, the realization by the staff and management that it will be very difficult to interpret the outcomes of treatment when it is not possible to clearly define a standardized treatment. During the later stages of the outcome management development process, discussions related to treatment standardization are likely to arise. These discussions are very important to the outcomes

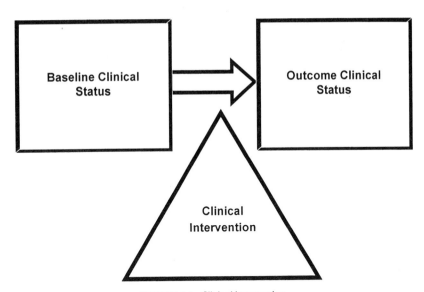

FIGURE 11.7. Clinical intervention.

management educational process for clinicians. Figure 11.7 illustrates the relationship between the patient's baseline status compared to the clinical intervention and eventual outcome status.

As the development process continues, it will be important to define each of the three components identified in Figure 11.7. Inability to clearly define the initial status of the patient (baseline clinical status), the final status of the patient (outcome clinical status) or the treatment provided to the patient (clinical intervention) invalidates the outcomes data collected.

The three components (Fig. 11.7) will be especially important if internal outcome comparisons are desired. The physical therapist chooses an intervention, and the data is collected and pooled with similar information. The pooled data is analyzed and feedback is given regarding the most effective intervention. One therapist, for example, may choose to use electric stimulation and ultrasound to treat a neck condition, while another may choose a hands-on approach and exercise. Patients in both groups are given a functional outcome evaluation initially and at discharge. If it is determined that the hands-on treatment and exercise group realized significantly more improvement on the measures of interest compared to the electric stimulation and

ultrasound group, the therapist should be informed about the outcome of their treatments and encouraged to modify their treatment strategies and programs appropriately.

As an example, consider the hands-on techniques and respond to these questions:

- Which are most helpful?
- Which practitioners are most successful?
- How does treatment frequency and duration affect clinical success? (3)

Discussions among the staff on topics such as those identified above are very valuable and should be encouraged throughout the outcomes management process.

Step Five: Collect Discharge Data

Step Five is a repetition of Step Three, except that it is done postinterventionally. For a valid comparison of data, similar data collection procedures should exist. As in the initial data collection step, appropriate processes of information management (Chapter 10) apply to outcomes data management.

Step Six: Collect Followup Data

Although it may be tempting to try to analyze data after admission and discharge collection, it will be best to consider the sustainable effects of therapeutic interventions. This requires the collection of data at a point significantly after discharge from treatment. Ninety days after discharge has been suggested (1).

There are many reasons to collect postdischarge data, including the evaluation of sustainable effects of interventions, reduction of bias that person-to-person interaction between patients and staff may encourage, and assessment of the entire continuum of therapeutic care as opposed to a single venue in the continuum.

Step Seven: Analyze The Collected Data

Earlier it was recommended that outcomes management be performed by individuals with expertise in statistics and computer science (1). This step may intimidate some managers and staff members. Use of a statistician as a consultant (See Chapter 13 for more information on the use of many types of consultants) is a well-established practice in outcomes management. A statistical consultant can be helpful in setting up the data collection process, analyzing the data and overall program design.

The potential for misinterpretation of statistical data is significant. The data that is being collected is very personal to both patients and staff. Clinicians may fear or believe that the outcomes evaluation process is an attempt to determine who are the best clinicians and who are the worst. Although this is often an inappropriate use of the data, staff will frequently have that impression. Training and orientation to the limitations of outcome management should help alleviate these concerns. However, extreme care should be taken not to overextend the use of the collected data.

An additional area of concern regarding data analysis is the potential for high levels of energy and resources to be devoted to analysis with commensurately lower levels devoted to action plans to address identified problems or opportunities.

Step Eight: Develop Actions Based On Data Analysis

Considering all the steps in the outcome management process, this step is the most crucial. It asks the question, So what?

The collection and analysis of data is of little value if nothing further occurs. Opportunities and problems may be identified during the interpretation of the data. A definitive plan to address these must be developed and implemented.

The most basic of action plans should include developing a mechanism to report summarized data to the clinicians and customers. Emphasis on the educational value of the outcome information may reduce concerns. This will be especially beneficial should there be opportunities to learn through continuing education or from others who are achieving better outcomes.

Hopefully, outcome data is incorporated into some, diverse activities of the clinic. Table 11.2 shows some of the activities that should consider outcome data.

Step Nine: Evaluate The Outcomes Program

To adequately close the outcomes management loop (Fig. 11.6), it is necessary to periodically and formally evaluate the success of the program. If the organization is to improve clinical care, then management must critically examine all programs in relation to the specific care improvement objectives. Because to develop an outcomes management program is evolutionary, the more experience the managers and staff develop evaluating and using outcome in-formation, the more they will be able to refine the processes to meet the needs of their service environment.

In evaluating an outcomes management program, it is necessary to consider the feedback available from many different sources, includ-

TABLE 11.2

Using Outcome Data in Daily Practice

Performance appraisal of staff
Cost/value decisions for managed care
Clinical research on treatment efficacy
Data-based decisions in a changing environment
Program development decisions
Program termination decisions
Staff assignment to specific programs

Modified from Kovacek P. Improving Productivity without Sacrificing Quality, Harper Woods, MI: Kovacek Management Services, Inc., 1995:123.

ing, patients, staff, referring groups, payers and other stakeholders.

This model is consistent with what has been identified as essential strategies for the successful collection and management of outcomes (1). The model in summary suggests:

1. At the onset of the management process, identify the most prevalent diagnoses.
2. Select a minimum number of measures.
3. The three main data collection points should be at admission, at discharge, and at 90 days postdischarge.
4. Consider the data collection interface for customers entering data, and minimize data gathering redundancy when feasible.
5. Train those involved in the outcomes management process.
6. Data processing and analysis of outcomes data demand statistics and computer programming support and expertise.
7. To include usual variations, a minimum of 1 year should be spent examining and monitoring outcomes information before making major changes in the delivery of the services being monitored.

QUALITY IMPROVEMENT

A key aspect of clinical improvement has been programs within health care institutions generally referred to as quality improvement programs.

According to the Joint Commission on Accreditation of Healthcare Organizations (JC-AHO), an organization's performance of important functions significantly affects its patient outcomes, the cost to achieve these outcomes, and the perception of its patients and their families about the quality and value of its services. This general area is referred to as quality improvement (QI), continuous quality improvement (CQI) or total quality management (TQM). The goal of improving organizational performance is, ultimately, to continuously improve patient health outcomes (8). A key to achieving desirable outcomes is process improvement through continuous quality improvement.

This sentiment is mirrored throughout health care as evidenced by the large number of health care organizations engaged in continuous improvement initiatives. Because of the emphasis on CQI and its purported impact on outcomes, this section will review the movement toward quality improvement in health care, key concepts of QI, and applications of QI for the physical therapist.

The process of improving organizational processes consists of several specific activities. Figure 11.8 is a process chart that illustrates these activities.

Measurement of quality can be very difficult. The most effective method of measuring quality in complex organizations is to consider what JC-AHO calls the dimensions of performance in the context of the most important functions of the organization. Table 11.3 illustrates the relationship of functions and dimensions of quality for any given patient population.

Improving quality within an organization, even a simple organization, is complex and involves extensive examination of current processes. CQI involves defining and doing the right thing first and, second, doing the right thing well. To be successful and achieve the desirable performance outcomes, appropriate care must be provided. That care must also be well done to be successful. Although this concept sounds simple, it is the basis for efforts to improve performance. There are two simple questions that arise from this position:

What is the right thing to do?
What is the best way to do it?

CQI strives to answer both of these questions by developing a body of knowledge and procedure to help the clinician and manager examine internal procedures and daily activities in standardized ways so that performance can be improved efficiently.

Much of the body of knowledge collectively known as CQI was pioneered by W. Edwards Deming, who developed his philosophies in work in Japan after the devastation of World War II. After the war, the Japanese manufacturing industry had a reputation for producing poor-quality products. Reversing this situation, according to Deming's concepts, involved determining what customers wanted, studying and improving product design and production to a

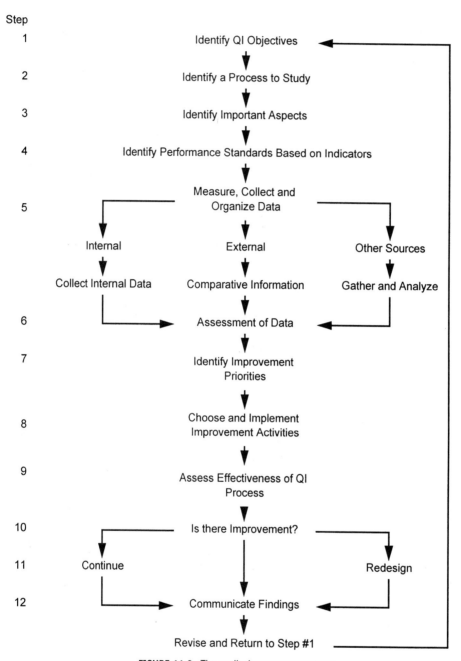

FIGURE 11.8. The quality improvement process.

point of excellence (9). The processes and procedures Deming put in place in Japan were later distilled into what are frequently referred to as Deming's 14 Principles (Table 11.4), which provide a blueprint for successful organizational improvement through CQI.

Deming describes what he calls a "chain reaction" in improvement (9). It includes both internal variables and external variables. Each step encourages and catalyzes the next. In the list below, internal variables are indicated by (I). External variables are indicated by (E).

TABLE 11.3
Relationship of Functions and Quality in a Health Care Organization

	DIMENSIONS OF PERFORMANCE								
Important Organizational Functions	EFFICACY	APPROPRIATENESS	AVAILABILITY	TIMELINESS	EFFECTIVENESS	CONTINUITY	SAFETY	EFFICIENCY	RESPECT AND CARING
Surveillance, Prevention & Control of Infection									
Management of Information									
Management of Human Resources									
Management of the Environment of Care									
Leadership									
Improving Organizational Performance									
Continuum of Care									
Education									
Care of Patients									
Assessment of Patients									
Patient Rights and Organizational Ethics									

Modified from JCAHO. 1996 Comprehensive Accreditation Manual for Hospitals. Oak Terrace, IL: Author, 1996.

TABLE 11.4
W.E. Demings' 14 Principles for Continuous Improvement

1. Create constancy of purpose for service improvement
2. Adopt the new philosophy
3. Cease dependence on inspection to achieve quality
4. End the practice of awarding business on price alone; make partners of vendors
5. Constantly improve every process for planning, production, and service
6. Institute training and retraining on the job
7. Institute leadership for system improvement
8. Drive out fear
9. Break down barriers between staff areas
10. Eliminate slogans, exhortations, and targets for the work force
11. Eliminate numerical quotas for the work force and numerical goals for the management
12. Remove barriers to pride of workmanship
13. Institute a vigorous program of education and self-improvement for everyone
14. Put everyone to work on the transformation

Modified from Deming WE. Out of Crisis. Cambridge, MA: Massachusetts Institute of Technology, 1986:23–24.

- Improve quality (I)
- Decrease costs(I & E)
- Improve productivity (I)
- Decrease price (I)
- Increase market share (E)
- Stay in business (I & E)
- Provide jobs and add more jobs (I & E)
- Increase return on investment and profit margin (I & E)

Clearly, each of these steps is desirable and should be pursued. As was stated in Chapter 8, without margin, there is no mission. Today, quality improvement should be a basic component of all physical therapy missions.

To accomplish this transformation, specific tools and techniques are required. CQI is a discipline. As such, it should be studied, practiced and perfected. Good CQI techniques should be employed in any CQI plan.

Figure 11.9 illustrates the steps to attain quality leadership. Note that this illustration is in the form called a fishbone chart. A fishbone chart is one of the tools of CQI.

CQI uses a scientific approach to the improvement of organizational processes as it seeks to identify problems at their root and then to develop solutions to eliminate the problems. To effectively identify problems in organizations, it is necessary to examine what causes process problems and to recognize them when they arise. Excessive process complexity is often the cause of problems. So are mistakes and defects, breakdowns and delays, inefficiencies and process variation.

Variation

Variation is a key focus of many CQI projects in health care. Variation in input leads to inconsistency in output or outcome. There are two types of variation. These are common cause variation and special cause variation. It is very important to recognize the difference between these two before taking action to correct variation problems.

Common cause variation is typically due to a large number of small sources of variation. Common cause variation is typically outside the control of the individual doing the work. Common cause variation is a part of the process itself and is typically thought of as a normal byproduct of the work process.

Special cause variations are not part of the process itself. Special cause variation is due to something out of the ordinary occurring that is having an impact, good or bad, on the work process.

Working to reduce variation in outcome is integral to the CQI concept. Once asked what he considered his greatest contribution to CQI, Deming indicated that he had worked to eliminate variation (9). The specific actions that are effective in resolving common cause and special cause variation are very different. To improve performance in common cause variation, it is necessary to actually redesign the process. Special cause variations are often resolved by identifying the condition outside of the process that needs to be addressed. This could include operator training or replacement of faulty equipment.

Tools of Continuous Quality Improvement

The tools of CQI are the steps of process improvement. CQI tools are primarily designed to help identify the root cause of the quality problem so that an appropriate and effective resolution can be planned. Several of the tools of CQI are already familiar to the reader. Additional tools include work flow or process charts, fishbone or cause and effect charts, Pareto charts,

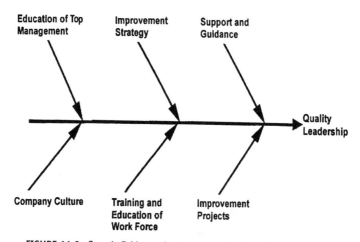

FIGURE 11.9. Sample fishbone chart: components of quality leadership.

spider charts, scatter diagrams, histograms, decision matrix charts, time plots, and control charts. Each of these tools will be examined.

Work flow or process charts detail the stages of a process. In the case of a work flow chart, it may also include the physical movement through space of the work or workers. Figures 11.6 and 11.8 are examples of process charts.

CAUSE AND EFFECT DIAGRAM

Cause and effect diagrams allow the listing of possible factors thought to affect a problem or desired outcome. Also known as fishbone diagrams, these diagrams can help focus attention on a desired result or problem. Figure 11.9 is a fishbone that illustrates the factors associated with the development of quality leadership. Review Chapter 4 for more on leadership. Figure 11.10 is a sample of a fishbone chart that illustrates the multitude of factors that contribute to accurate documentation. Note that this figure is not specific to medical documentation, but rather illustrates the generic concepts of contributing factors for documentation.

PARETO CHART

A Pareto chart is a horizontal or vertical bar graph with bars whose heighths or lengths reflect the frequency or impact of problems or conditions. Figure 11.11 is a Pareto chart that illustrates the use of wound care supplies in a hydrotherapy center. From this chart, it is easy to see that 45% of the supplies are not available for patient or staff use due to loss, theft, waste or unknown reasons. Appropriate followup action to determine the extent of the loss attributable to each of the identified sources is required.

SCATTER DIAGRAM

Scatter diagrams represent two variables on separate axes to allow the relationship between the two to be easily seen. Figure 11.12 illustrates a scatter diagram showing the relationship that was found between the number of physical therapy visits and the percent of patient improvement in one clinic. From this diagram it is easy to see that there was a general relationship between number of visits and percent of improvement.

HISTOGRAM

Histograms represent the frequency of occurrence of an event. Figure 11.13 shows the responses of patients to a satisfaction questionnaire in a histogram form.

SPIDER DIAGRAM

Spider diagrams represent multiple characteristics in a graphic form. By plotting the scores for various indicators on a single graph, the observer can recognize certain patterns or combinations in multiple axes or indicators. Figure 11.14 shows a spider diagram that illustrates the average functional score for a group of patients with anterior cruciate ligament repairs on seven different characteristics: range of motion of the knee, strength of the knee, overall balance, safety in ambulation, judgement regarding abilities, speed of locomotion, and lower extremity coordination.

It is also possible to use spider diagrams in much the same way as histograms. Figure 11.15 shows the same data as Figure 11.13.

DECISION MATRIX

A decision matrix is a chart that compares potential actions with key factors and the likely outcomes of choosing that action. Figure 11.16 is a decision chart that examines the cost, ease of implementation and return on investment factors of four options: expanding the existing clinic, developing a new clinic in the same town, developing a new clinic in a new town, and doing nothing. The key to a decision chart is the discussion and background information that is gathered to develop the assessments of the various factors. The better the assessment of each factor, the more likely the eventual decision will be the most beneficial one.

Figure 11.17 is also a decision chart. It illustrates the assessments of one practice labeled Us and six competing clinical operations in terms of quality and cost. Note that this chart subdivides the major factors of quality and cost into subfactors. Each subfactor is individually assessed. In

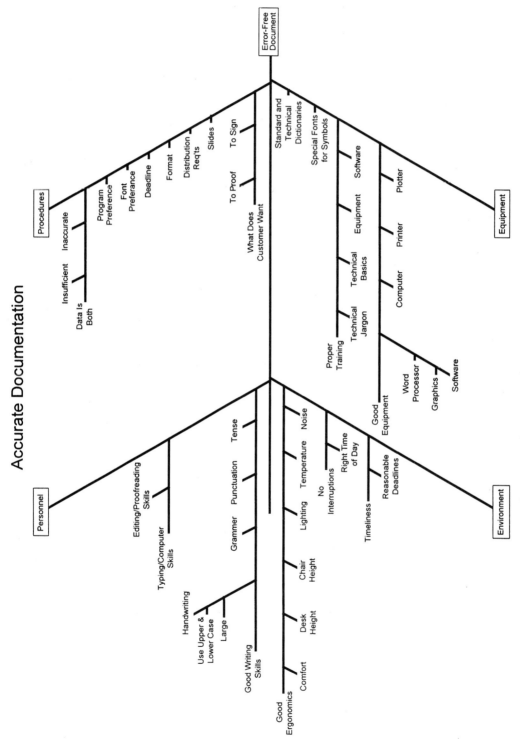

FIGURE 11.10. Sample fishbone chart: accurate documentation.

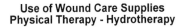

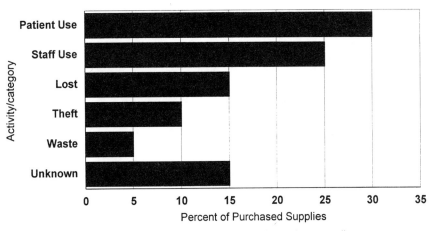

FIGURE 11.11. Sample Pareto chart: use of wound care supplies.

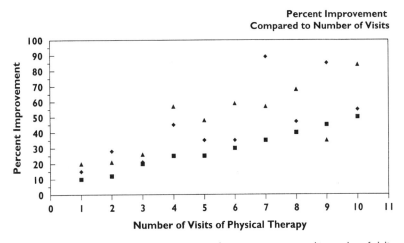

FIGURE 11.12. Sample scatter diagram: percent improvement compared to number of visits.

this case, each factor is ranked according to a scale of good, satisfactory and poor.

TIME PLOT

Time plots show the relationship of events to specific time frames. Times can be absolute, such as January 1, 2004 or relative, such as 60 days from actual start of the project. Time plots are excellent ways to study the flow of information across time through an organization in identification of where there are delays or lags. Time plots are also excellent tools to use to describe specific projects that are unique or not typical within an organization. Time plots for projects can be thought of as time budgets for project completion. Because time is a critical and scarce resource within any organization, the use of time plots to budget time is very appropriate. Figure 11.18 shows a time plot for the development of a new product or service.

Time plots can also be used to measure events within specific time frames to identify patterns or relationships. Figure 11.19 shows the relationship of days lost to absenteeism and number of incidents of absenteeism within monthly

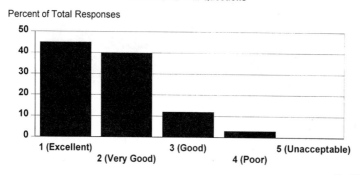

FIGURE 11.13. Sample histogram: patient satisfaction.

FIGURE 11.14. Sample spider diagram: average discharge ability for patients with anterior cruciate ligament repairs.

FIGURE 11.15. Sample spider diagram as replacement for histogram.

Problem: Outgrowing Existing Facility

	Cost	Implementation	ROI
Expand	4	2	1
New - Same Town	2	3	3
New - New Town	3	4	2
Do Nothing	1	1	4

Score: 1= best; 4 = Worst

FIGURE 11.16. Sample decision matrix: outgrowing existing facility.

Comparative Features of Physical Therapy Clinics

		Quality			**Cost**			
Vendor:	Scope of Care	Clinical Quality	Access	Satisfaction	Cost per Case	Unit Charges	Risk Ability	Info Systems
Us	Satisfactory	Satisfactory	Poor	Poor	Good	Satisfactory	Good	Satisfactory
Clinic A	Good	Satisfactory	Satisfactory	Poor	Good	Satisfactory	Good	Satisfactory
Clinic B	Satisfactory	Satisfactory	Satisfactory	Poor	Good	Satisfactory	Satisfactory	Satisfactory
ECF A	Good	Good	Satisfactory	Satisfactory	Poor	Satisfactory	Satisfactory	Satisfactory
ECF B	Poor	Satisfactory	Satisfactory	Satisfactory	Poor	Satisfactory	Satisfactory	Satisfactory
Hospital A	Satisfactory	Satisfactory	Satisfactory	Satisfactory	Poor	Satisfactory	Satisfactory	Poor
Hospital B	Satisfactory	Satisfactory	Poor	Good	Satisfactory	Poor	Good	Poor

Good **Satisfactory** **Poor**

FIGURE 11.17. Sample decision chart: comparative features of physical therapy clinics.

periods. This plot allows a comparison of the individual factors of days lost and episodes to monthly periods and to each other.

CONTROL CHART

A control chart is a time plot that includes the acceptable or typical range of variation within the chart. Figure 11.20 shows the absenteeism data from Figure 11.19 and the acceptable range for days lost. The range of acceptable variation is bounded by an upper control level and a lower control level. It is assumed that variation within these boundaries is primarily due to common cause variation and that deviation outside of these boundaries is due to special cause variation. These assumptions may or may not be accurate.

Tools Are Just Tools

The tools of CQI that have been described above are just that, tools that should be used to study and learn about the practice of physical therapy within an organization. Neither individually nor collectively can these tools replace good man-

Development Schedule   Timeline

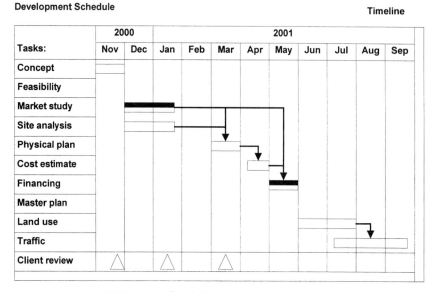

FIGURE 11.18. Sample time plot: development schedule.

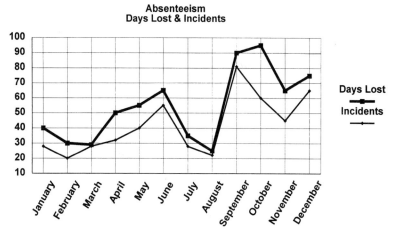

FIGURE 11.19. Sample time plot: absenteeism.

agerial judgement or rational analysis of practice. These tools will, however, aid management in making effective, accurate and complete problem analysis that leads to making good decisions.

REGULATORY COMPLIANCE

Accreditation is a rigorous and comprehensive evaluation process used by external organizations to assess how well a health care organiza-

tion manages all parts of its care delivery system. This section will review several of the most important regulatory agencies that affect physical therapy services.

CARF, The Rehabilitation Commission (CARF)

CARF is a private, not-for-profit rehabilitation accreditation commission whose mission is

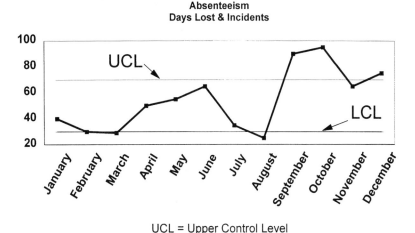

UCL = Upper Control Level
LCL = Lower Control Level

FIGURE 11.20. Sample control chart: absenteeism.

to promote quality programs and services for people with disabilities and others in need of rehabilitation. It does so by establishing and using standards of quality for rehabilitation services to determine how well an organization is serving its consumers and how it can improve.

Standards developed by CARF are developed with input from consumers, rehabilitation professionals, state and national organizations, and third-party payers. The standards guide an organization to capably and competently serve its consumers and address their needs.

The purposes of CARF include:

1. Improve the quality of health care delivered to people in need of rehabilitation programs and services.
2. Identify those organizations that meet nationally recognized standards for rehabilitation programs and services.
3. Develop and maintain current standards that health care providers can use to assess and improve the quality of their programs and services.
4. Provide an independent, unbiased and objective system of organizational review and assessment based on a peer review approach.
5. Conduct accreditation research on outcomes measurement and management, and to share relevant information on programs and services strengths and areas determined to need improvement.
6. Provide education and training that lead to enhanced performance of programs and services to constituencies.

7. Provide a forum for stakeholders for participation in standards setting to improve program and service quality.
8. Provide advice and consultation on the development of public policy related to the delivery of rehabilitation programs and services (10).

The programs and services accredited by CARF have demonstrated that they substantially meet nationally recognized standards. The basis for meeting standards is an on-site survey conducted by knowledgeable, trained surveyors who are professionals in rehabilitation. The survey offers the organization's personnel an opportunity to consult with CARF surveyors to enhance the delivery of quality services. Input from consumers is obtained during the on-site survey process. CARF accreditation acknowledges that an organization has made a major commitment to enhance the quality of its programs and services that focus on positive outcomes.

According to CARF, there are significant benefits to the consumer in using accredited organizations. These benefits are assurance that:

1. Consumers participated in the development of the accreditation standards.
2. The facility's programs and services met consumer-focused, national standards of performance.
3. The facility is focused on obtaining the optimum outcome for each person served.

4. The accredited program actively involved stakeholders in decision making related to the planning and implementation of the services they received (10, 11).

CARF guidelines direct health care organizations to demonstrate:

That systems are present to measure outcomes, e.g., effectiveness, efficiency and satisfaction of those served, and their status after discharge.
The outcomes of all programs are measured.
Outcome information is used throughout its planning processes.
Outcome information is shared with stakeholders (8).

CARF has as its fundamental purpose the preservation and improvement of programs provided by organizations serving those with disabilities and others in need of rehabilitation. It provides organizations with an accepted blueprint for operations, a guide to organizational development, and an internal tool to evaluate and improve their programs on an ongoing basis.

The Joint Commission on Accreditation of Healthcare Organizations (JCAHO)

The mission of JCAHO is to improve the quality of care provided to the public by offering health care accreditation and related services that support performance improvement in health care organizations.

JCAHO evaluates and accredits more than 15,000 health care organizations in the United States including more than 5200 hospitals and nearly 10,000 other health care organizations (8). A sample of JCAHO's Accreditation Grid is shown in Figure 11.21.

National Committee For Quality Assurance

The National Committee for Quality Assurance (NCQA) began accrediting managed care organizations (MCOs) in 1991 in response to the need for standardized, objective information about the quality of these organizations. The NCQA accreditation program is voluntary, and

has been recognized by purchasers, consumers and health plans as an objective measure of the quality of MCOs. Since the inception of the managed care organization accreditation program, NCQA has continued to revise its standards to ensure the program's currency and relevance, and to maintain its rigor. As part of that effort, NCQA has recently begun expanding the scope of its accreditation programs to include other managed delivery systems. NCQA strives to establish a comprehensive evaluation process, one that is flexible enough to adapt to changes within the health care marketplace and rigorous enough to establish a continuum of accountability.

Health Plan Employer Data and Information Set

One of the key components of NCQA is its development of the Health Plan Employer Data and Information Set (HEDIS). The HEDIS tool is a set of standardized performance measures designed to ensure that purchasers and consumers have the information they need to reliably compare the performance of managed health care plans. In combination with information from NCQA's accreditation program, HEDIS provides a view of health plan quality that can be used to guide choice among competing health plans. HEDIS 3.0, which will be widely implemented across the country in 1998 (11), is intended to provide purchasers and consumers with an ability to both evaluate the quality of different health plans along a variety of important dimensions and to make their plan decisions based upon demonstrated value rather than simply on cost.

HEDIS has eight performance domains for which measures are in place:

1. Effectiveness of care. These are measures that assess how well the care delivered by a managed care plan is achieving the clinical results that it should.
2. Access/availability of care. These are measures that permit assessment of whether care is available to members, and when they need it, in a timely and convenient manner.
3. Satisfaction with the experience of care. These measures provide information about whether a health plan is able to satisfy the diverse needs of its members.

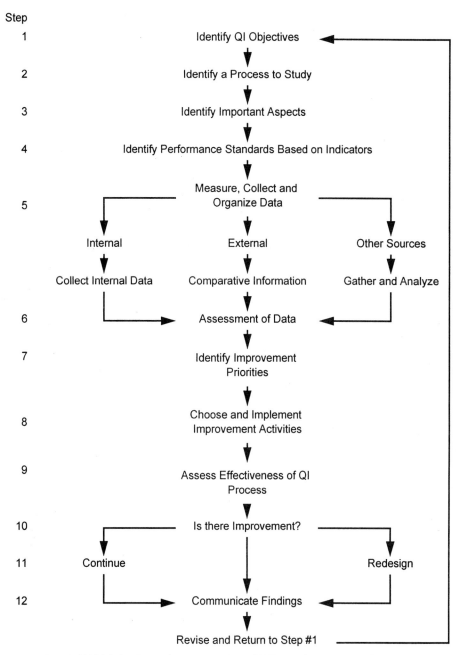

FIGURE 11.21. Sample JCAHO Accreditation Grid. Adapted from JCAHO, 1996. Comprehensive Accreditation Manual for Hospitals. Oakbrook Terrace, IL: Author, 1996.

4. Cost of care. These are measures that compare health plans based on the economic value of the services they deliver.
5. Stability of the health plan. Health plan stability is important because consumers make enrollment decisions that generally bind them for a year. Should the plan's network of providers change significantly or should the plan become insolvent, the member's health care could be severely disrupted. The measures are to help consumers estimate how likely these problems might occur.

6. Informed health care choices. These are measures to assess how a managed care plan helps members become active partners in their health care decisions. To do so means that the health plan must equip members to make informed choices about their care.

7. Use of services. How a health plan uses its resources is a signal of how efficiently care is managed and whether or not needed services are being delivered; it may also provide some information about where there are opportunities to improve both the effectiveness and efficiency of care. These measures assess patterns of service use across different health plans.

8. Health plan descriptive information. These measures are a variety of elements of interest to consumers regarding plan management (including a description of selected network, clinical, utilization and risk management activities).

While items 6 through 8 above are not performance measures per se, they are information of consistent interest to purchasers and consumers.

HEDIS and NCQA are used primarily in the accreditation of health plans, but they also affect health care providers, such as physical therapists. Because providers are interested in attaining NCQA accreditation, they are required to collect information in the HEDIS data set. A substantial component of the HEDIS data is clinical data that can best be collected at the provider (physical therapy department or clinic) level. Health plans frequently require contracted providers, including physical therapists, to assist in such data collection efforts. Therefore, it is necessary for the physical therapy manager and clinicians to become familiar with these tools and organizations.

In this section, essential information on the emphasis of CARF, JCAHO and NCQA on the collection and use of outcome data and outcome management has been reviewed. It should be clear to the reader that the management of outcomes is a high priority of clinical accreditation agencies. As such, outcomes management will be a part of the daily responsibilities of every manager and clinician who is involved in the delivery of health care programs and services.

SUMMARY

This chapter has reviewed the role of outcome management, quality improvement and external accrediting agencies in the processes of delivering physical therapy services. The three major accrediting bodies were discussed as they relate to stakeholders, insurance providers and health care providers. Within this discussion, the implications of accreditation requirements for the manager of physical therapy services and clinical staff were presented. For additional experience in dealing with outcomes issues, the reader should see the role-play for Chapter 11 in Appendix A.

REFERENCES

1. Dobrzykowski, Edward A. The methodology of outcomes measurement. Journal of Rehabilitation Outcomes Measures 1997; 1(1):8–17.
2. American Physical Therapy Association. Code of ethics. Physical Therapy 1997;77:1628.
3. Lewis, CB and McKerney, T. The Functional Toolbox: Clinical Measures of Functional Outcomes. Washington, DC: Learn Publications, 1994.
4. Goldfred, N, Pine, M, Pine, J. Measuring and Managing Health Care Quality: Procedures, Techniques and Protocols. Rockville, MD: Aspen Publishers 1993.
5. Elliot-Burke, TL , Pothast, L. Measuring patient satisfaction in an outpatient orthopedic setting. Part 1: key drivers and results. Journal of Rehabilitation Outcomes Measures 1997;1(1):18–25.
6. American Physical Therapy Association. Patient Satisfaction Instruments: a Compendium. Alexandria, VA: Author 1996.
7. McLaughlin, CP and Kaluzny, AD. Continuous Quality Improvement in Health Care. Rockville, MD: Aspen Publishers, 1994.
8. Joint Commission on the Accreditation of Healthcare Organizations. 1996 Comprehensive Accreditation Manual For Hospitals. Oak Brook Terrace, IL: Author, 1996.
9. Deming WE. Out of Crisis. Cambridge, MA: Massachusetts Institute of Technology, 1986.
10. Commission for the Accreditation of Rehabilitation Facilities. 1996 Accreditation Manual. Tucson, AZ: Author, 1996.
11. www.ncqa.org

ADDITIONAL RESOURCES

www.carf.org
www.TheFOCUSgroup.net
www.jcaho.org

 **12**

PLAYING IT SAFE:
MANAGING RISK

PREVIEW

Risk is something we all deal with on a daily basis. For example, there is the possibility or risk of an auto accident when we travel by car. To protect our passengers and ourselves, we reduce risk of injury by driving cautiously under poor-weather conditions like darkness and heavy traffic. When we make protective adjustments, we are managing risk.

Health care businesses and other organizations are also interested in managing risk. In doing this, the quality of patient care is enhanced.

This chapter will familiarize the reader with a formal process and tools for managing risk in health care organizations. By becoming familiar with the process, it is hoped that the reader will be able to participate in and effectively contribute to departmental and organizational risk management efforts, which ultimately benefit patients.

Risk management has several goals. The most basic goal is to protect from harm or loss. In health care, this involves protecting patients from harm as well as protecting both organizational and individual members' assets.

A five-step process for protecting patients and the organization from loss is discussed. This process is then applied to organizational, departmental and individual risk-related situations of interest to physical therapists.

This chapter includes some legal information. The reader should use this general information to familiarize themselves with the concepts of managing risks and the consequences of not managing them. This material is not intended for use, nor should it be used, as a substitute for legal or other professional advice.

KEY TERMS

Abuse: neglect or harm of a minor or vulnerable adult.

Adverse Patient Outcomes (APO's): undesirable results of care such as death, infection, over-medication, or fracture.

Assault: any threat made by another that a person fears or expects to cause them immediate harm.

Battery: unjustified, offensive, unwanted intentional contact.

Breach: violation of a law or legal obligation.

Civil Law: involves legal actions brought about by private citizens (plaintiffs) against a person (defendant) or group (defendants) deemed liable (see below). To correct civil wrongs, the remedy in civil cases is monetary.

Claim: demand based on a right to payment or right to an equitable remedy for breach of performance.

Fiduciary Duty: requirement to act primarily for another's benefit in a professional relationship. This requirement is based on trust, confidence or responsibility wherein fairness is required in dealing with the other party.

Incident: also called an occurrence, is an event that could lead to a liability or legal claim for damages.

Incident Report: also called an occurrence report, is a factual written summary of an unusual event.

Liable: obliged, compelled or bound in law or equity to make good.

Liability: the state of being bound by law or justice to do, pay or make good.

Occurrence Screening: identifying variances from what is expected through the inspection of multiple reports and interviews.

Malpractice: professional negligence or misconduct, i.e., unreasonable lack of skill or knowledge, fidelity or fiduciary responsibility that results in injury, loss or damage to a recipient of services.

Negligence: failure to exercise ordinary care, i.e., failure to do or refrain from doing what a competent, careful person would do or not do.

Potentially Compensable Events (PCO's): situations that may lead to legal actions.

Risk: possibility of suffering harm or loss.

Risk Management: in a health care entity this involves coordinated efforts to identify, assess and minimize, where possible, the risk of suffering harm or loss to patients, visitors, staff and the organization.

Sexual Harassment: a form of sex discrimination in the workplace involving unwelcome sexual advances or demands or other verbal or physical conduct of a sexual nature.

Suit: court proceeding by a person or group against a person or group in which a legal remedy is pursued. A suit is often called an action.

INTRODUCTION

In the 1970s and through the 1980s, there were increasing numbers of suits against physicians, nonphysician health care workers and health care organizations (1). Anyone who has watched any of the weekly television hospital drama programs has seen some of the situations that can increase risk in a hospital, e.g., violence in the emergency room, impaired professionals, administration of the wrong medication, equipment failure, misdiagnosis and patient falls.

In the 1970s, because of increasing frequency of suits and amount of awards, hospitals and other health care providers began risk management programs (2). These programs, intended to prevent, control and monitor risk exposures, were desired to improve quality of care and to protect the organization's assets.

GENERAL CONCEPTS

The goal of every health care provider should be to provide the highest possible quality of care. This goal is attainable if there is coordination, cooperation and integration of clinical, service and administrative departments. An essential component of this collaborative process is managing risk.

Organizations are made up of many people. These people deal directly and indirectly with multiple types of other employees, customers, venders, visitors, interested parties and stakeholders. In the course of these interactions, there is potential risk that mistakes or perceived mistakes will be made by members of the organization. Like many organizations, health care organizations often own large buildings, many vehicles, and expensive equipment inventories of supplies that are used to provide services. Buildings, vehicles, equipment and supplies can deteriorate and pose risks to employees and customers.

Responsibilities

A health care organization's board of directors and the chief executive officer are responsible for high-quality care being delivered in a safe and satisfactory manner. To deal with actual and potential risks, large health care organizations have risk management programs, which involve risk management personnel and other individuals from a variety of clinical and administrative disciplines. A risk manager or coordinator is responsible for implementing a coordinated process that minimizes the likelihood of the organization being harmed due to someone involved with the organization being injured. To facilitate coordinated efforts, there is often a risk management committee. The makeup of such committees varies, but typically includes representatives of segments of the organization that have been or are most likely to be at risk for claims. This membership helps assure organization-wide perspectives on risks and risk management opportunities.

Ideally, risk management is an organization-wide endeavor. The risk management process itself begins with the identification of situations that have resulted in harm to someone or financial loss to the organization. These risk situations are analyzed by the risk management team for level of severity, frequency of occurrence, and level of loss that might result should the situation became a reality. Solutions are posed and the most appropriate implemented. Finally, the results of risk management activities are monitored. This process and the tools used to manage

risk are discussed more thoroughly in the following sections.

Risk Management Process in Health Care Organizations

Effective risk management protects assets from loss. Organizational assets include property, money, human resources (employees) and intangible items such as public opinion (3). To manage risks that may result in the loss of any of these assets, a traditional problem-solving process should be used. One version of this process involving five overlapping steps (4) is shown in Figure 12.1.

Identification of Exposure to Risk

Risk is often viewed in terms of certainty and uncertainty. In a health care organization, as in other types of organizations, risks can be real in that they have occurred, or probable in that they may occur. There are several areas of uncertainty associated with making decisions about risks. For example, there is uncertainty estimating:

- If harm will occur
- How severely someone will be harmed
- If the organization will be harmed
- If someone will sue
- Which course of action should be followed

Looking for exposure to risk should not be limited to occurrences associated with patient care. Every segment of the organization, from administration to the maintenance department, is a potential source of risk. Table 12.1 lists some

FIGURE 12.1. Process model for risk management.

TABLE 12.1

Examples of Areas of Interest to Risk Managers in Health Care[a]

- Abuse (child, elder, physical, sexual)
- Noncompliance With Americans With Disabilities Act (1990)
- Antitrust Violations
- Assault and Battery (staff, patients, visitors and others)
- Breach of Contract
- Credentials of Medical Staff
- Discrimination (age, race, religion, sex)
- Embezzlement
- Equipment Risks, Damage, Loss, Maintenance
- Fraud
- Informed Consent
- Incident Reports
- Infection Rates
- Insurance Against All Types of Liability, Damage & Loss
- Professional Malpractice
- Property Risks, Damage, Loss, Maintenance
- Quality Assurance
- Recruitment and Hiring Practices
- Safety and Security
- Sexual Harassment
- Theft
- Workers' Compensation

[a]Adopted from Kavaler F, Spiegel AD. Risk management dynamics. In: Kavaler F, Spiegel AD eds. Risk Management in Health Care Institutions. A Strategic Approach. Sudbury, MA: Jones and Bartlett, 1997:5, 53–55 and Scott RW. Promoting Legal Awareness In Physical and Occupational Therapy. Saint Louis, MO: Mosby, 1997: 85–105.

general areas of interest to risk managers. Several of these areas will be discussed later in this chapter.

The broad scope of the areas of concern in risk management requires that managers have access to records from all areas of operation. The authority to have such access comes directly from the highest levels of administration (Fig. 12.2).

Anything that hinders or potentially hinders the delivery of quality care, diminishes customer satisfaction or has the potential to harm the organization financially, is considered a risk. It is logical that risk consciousness should be a priority in an organization. This logic is reflected in the upper portion of Figure 12.2. With administrative support, is it more likely that risk management will become part of the organization's culture (see Chapter 4).

Another means of stimulating risk consciousness is through an interdisciplinary risk management committee that is represented near the middle of Figure 12.2. Representation on the risk management committee typically includes individuals from organizational units in which there is the potential for incidents that can result in harm. The major focuses of the risk management committee are to manage risks and assure that quality care is delivered. These two purposes can put the risk management and quality assurance functions in somewhat overlapping yet complementary roles. Risk managers typically are more often concerned with the financial aspects of risk, while quality assurance managers are often more concerned with standards of care (5). Major accrediting bodies require that risk management and quality assurance functions work collaboratively (4) to protect the organization and its patients.

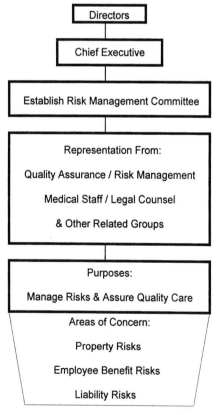

FIGURE 12.2. Example of a general structure of a risk management system in a large health care organization.

The categories of risk listed at the bottom of Figure 12.2 are general and need further explanation.

- Property risks include structural damage like a broken or uneven sidewalk. In physical therapy, this could be a rough edge on a mat table.
- Employee benefit risks relate to long-term disability and retirement costs.
- Liability risks or casualty risks are related to workers' compensation (e.g., an injury occurring on the job), directors and officers liability (e.g., theft) and professional negligence (malpractice) (4). Liability risks are probably the best known type of risk. See Figure 12.2 for further examples.

These three classifications of risk are helpful in grouping events, and there are many common risks in health care organizations; however, each organization also has its own unique set of risks to fit into the classification system.

Identifying risks has a subjective aspect. What is considered a risk is partly influenced by the organization's fundamental documents (see Chapter 2). The values of the organization, particularly the values of those involved in risk management, influence determining what a risk is as well as its significance to the organization (6). For example, if the organization deeply believes in the importance of patient autonomy and dignity, then it is likely to support a restraint-free environment and accept some risk that slips and falls will occur. To counter this, however, staff might be added to better supervise patients, to respond more quickly, and training programs could be implemented to assure that staff meet patients' needs without restraints. In a different environment, say in a long-term care facility, honoring the values of autonomy and dignity while maintaining a restraint-free environment may present some unique challenges, solutions and accompanying risks (7). For example, hand rails could be placed on all patient room walls. Circular walk ways could be developed to allow long duration walks (7). Floors at selected doorways could be painted to look like deep holes. This may stop patients from wandering in less supervised areas.

Increased risks that might occur include falls due to fatigue, patients bumping into one another or staff, and patients wandering out of the designated safe areas. Architectural changes and new equipment add risk because of unpredictability of patient and staff responses to novel situations (3). From the preceding examples, it can be seen that each environment has idiosyncratic risks. The interpretation of the importance of these risks varies.

Information Is Needed To Manage Risk

The risk manager has numerous sources of information to consult (see Chapter 10 for more examples). Some data come from historical sources such as previous claims against the organization, information from insurance company representatives, incident reports and other records. Other sources of information require more investigation but may be helpful in anticipating incidents before they occur. These additional resources are presented in Tables 12.2 and 12.3. Table 12.2 identifies resources that assist with identifying occurrences that have occurred in the past. Table 12.3 lists resources that may be useful in gathering information about potential risks.

PREVIOUS CLAIMS

A claim is a demand for something that is alleged to be rightfully due. When a claim has been made against an organization or individual and the organization or person has been found liable, there may be an out of court or court mandated financial settlement. Typically, some form

TABLE 12.2

Examples of Important Sources of Historical Information About Health Care Organization Risks

INTERNAL RESOURCES
- Previous Claims
- Incident Reports
- Patients Records
- Committee Reports
- Quality Assurance
  - Safety
  - Medical Staff
  - Others

EXTERNAL RESOURCES
- Insurance Company Representatives
- Industry Publications
- Expert Consultants

TABLE 12.3

Examples of Additional Sources of Information About Potential Risks in a Health Care Organization

- Administration/Department Managers
- Quality Assurance, Safety & Other Committee Members
- Financial Services Managers
- Medical Records Manager
- Social Services Manager
- Public Relations/Marketing Directors
- Chaplain Services Director
- Case Managers
- Admissions Clerks
- Aides/Orderlies/Certified Nursing Assistants
- Patient Escorts
- Security Officers
- Maintenance Personnel
- Students
- Volunteers
- Venders
- Discharge Clerks
- Employees Voluntarily Terminating Employment

of liability insurance covers legal and settlement costs. For now, the main point is that all information related to settled claims is available to risk management personnel and committee members for review. If there was more than one incident or claim related to the same cause, data on the frequency of occurrence in the industry can be consulted to see if this is a common or uncommon problem. Experts may be required to clarify the information.

INCIDENT REPORTS

Most health care organizations have a system for reporting nonroutine events. A report is required whenever something unusual occurs in the care of a patient, operation of equipment, interaction with visitors and other areas. The system is activated by the occurrence of an incident. It is reported on a written form called an occurrence or incident report (Fig. 12.3). The system is based on trust, i.e., the belief that employees will report unusual occurrences that they have been personally involved in or have witnessed.

For systemization purposes, an incident needs to be clearly defined so everyone in the organization recognizes when one occurs. It should be clear that anyone involved in or knowing of an incident is required to report it. Once completed, reports should be signed by the person making the report and given to a designated person within the specified time frame. Typically, the incident report form would be sent to quality assurance or risk management personnel (4). Legal experts recommend that incident report forms be kept separate from patients' records. Organizations should take steps to protect the information contained in incident reports from disclosure in case of litigation. How this information can be protected will vary between states. Incidents that are likely to result in suits should be forwarded to the organization's legal counsel. Once in their possession, the information may be considered privileged communication between lawyer and client and kept from a plaintiff's lawyer (3). This is to the named defendant's (an individual or organization) advantage should a claim be made (8). There are at least 10 states (AR, CO, FL, KS, MD, MA, NY, NC, RI, and WA) that have mandated reporting of incidents (9). Even if a claim is not made against an organization by a patient, these states may require corrective actions to protect future patients.

For ease of tracking, as suggested in Chapter 10, an incident report form may be part of the organizations' computer system. However, internal access to the report must be strictly limited to those associated with managing risk. The system must be secure from outsider's access. If security is in doubt, one hard copy should be kept in a locked location with access limited to the organization's risk managers and legal staff. Whether a computer-based reporting form (Fig. 12.3) or a hand written form is used, forms need to be readily accessible for staff to complete. Regardless of format, the basic information requested on an incident report is similar.

The usual information included on an incident report form is the name of those involved, including witnesses, what occurred, when it occurred and where it occurred. The report should avoid interpretive information such as the cause of the occurrence or corrective actions that were taken (8). The person who responded to an adverse patient occurrence should follow established emergency procedures. Reiteration of this

ABC HOSPITAL   (Automatic date and time of entry)

ABC Hospital System Log ID:_____

PATIENT INCIDENT - OCCURRENCE REPORT   (Form=RM1)

PERSON(s) INVOLVED:_____LOCATION:_____

STREET:_____PHONE:_____

CITY/STATE:_____ ZIP: _____DEPT: _____

OCCURRENCE: DAY OF WEEK:_____ DATE:____TIME: _____

PATIENT/VISITOR CONDITION PRIOR TO OCCURRENCE: (01) ALERT
(02) AMBULATORY   (03) ORIENTED   (04) OTHER

AIDES:_____ OTHER:_____

PATIENT/VISITOR/EMPLOYEE ACCIDENT: (01) UNWITNESSED

DESC OF OCCURRENCE:_____ TYPE:_____

EXPOSURE TO:_____OTHER:_____

BED HT:_____ BED RAILS: U D RESTRAINT IN USE: Y N TYPE:_____
BED CHECK IN PLACE: Y N   SAFETY ALERT IN PLACE: Y N

BODY PART: (01) HEAD (02) NECK (03) SPINE (04) SHOULDER (ETC.)
EXTENT OF INJURY: (01) MINOR (02) MODERATE (03) OTHER

ADDITIONAL DETAILS:_____

PHYSICIAN:_____

PHYSICIAN NOTIFIED:_____

PATIENT SEEN BY MD _____

NAME, ADDRESS, PHONE # OF WITNESSES:_____

DATE:_____

SIGNATURE OF PERSON PREPARING REPORT:_____

MANAGER SIGNATURE:_____

**THIS INCIDENT REPORT IS TO BE COMPLETED AND ROUTED TO THE DIRECTOR OF
RISK MANAGEMENT AS SOON AS POSSIBLE.**

FIGURE 12.3. Example of a computerized incident report form.

procedure is not needed on the incident report form. Deviations from established procedures do require explanations.

Incident reports provide information on what occurred. What is done with this information will be discussed more fully in the next section. In general, incident reports can lead to activities to prevent, reduce or eliminate future occurrences of incidents. However, by themselves, incident reports are insufficient tools to reduce risks because they are dependent on employees complying with the requirement to complete and file reports. Compliance has been reported to be poor, as only an estimated 5% to 30% of adverse patient occurrences are actually reported in hospitals (4).

Reasons offered for failure to report incidents include a lack of understanding of what constitutes an incident, reluctance to implicate physicians and fear of personal liability (4). Some employees believe that filing an incident report puts their job in jeopardy. Department managers need to make clear that not filing an incident report reduces the organization's ability to defend the employee should a claim be made.

With a minority of incidents being reported, for risk management and quality of care purposes, it is necessary to consult additional records to identify actual or potential adverse patient occurrence information. This is called occurrence screening. This will be discussed further in an upcoming section.

TREATMENT RECORDS

In addition to what is recorded in a patient's chart, there are other records documenting what services were provided and other relevant information. The information in the patient's chart should match with all other records for that patient. It is the risk manager's responsibility to look for corresponding and discrepant information related to an adverse patient occurrence when a claim has been filed. As will be seen later, reviewing records can help prevent repeated occurrences as well as raise awareness (4). Some of the important records available to review for related information include:

- Patients' medical records
- Records of patient transfers to a higher level of care
- Transfer to another acute care facility
- Hospitalization for complications from prior care
- Nosocomial (infections occurring after admission) infection rates/infection control reports
- Unscheduled returns to surgery/surgical reports
- Records of emergency responses
- Hospital readmissions
- Return to emergency services within 48 hours
- Medication records
- Cancellations

COMMITTEE REPORTS

The members of risk management committees should include representatives of diverse, interested departments. The agenda of the committee should be based, in part, on what is of concern to the members. Familiarity with the contents of the reports of the various committees and departments represented by the members of risk management committee can help guide risk related discussions, planning and actions.

INSURANCE COMPANY REPRESENTATIVES

Insurance companies pay out money when they settle claims against insured parties. It is to an insurer's benefit to help their policyholders reduce the number of claims filed against them. Insurance representatives called loss control consultants help reduce risks by sharing relevant information and experience with their company's policyholders (10). These consultants have pooled data from similar organizations that help identify common trends, causes, successful remedies and other information useful in preventing, minimizing or eliminating compensable risks. Other information on claims can be obtained from organizations like the National Association of Insurance Commissioners, National Health Lawyers, American Academy of Hospital Attorneys, state hospital associations and expert consultants. See Chapter 13 for more information on consultants.

Occurrence Screening

An incident report is filed after the occurrence of an unusual event. It is a retrospective document. Occurrence screening has not only a reactive purpose, it also has a proactive focus. There are three differences between incident reports and occurrence screening.

First, occurrences have not already been identified as unusual events as they are in incident reports. In occurrence screening, the event has to be discovered by piecing together information from many sources. This will be discussed shortly.

Second, when occurrences are identified, corrective actions are initiated to stop, remedy or minimize further complications. This can take place for patients still in the hospital. This is a combined proactive and reactive position. The proactive part is looking for potential risks before an incident occurs. The reactive part is taking actions to minimize harm to the patient and the organization or others that might result if no remedial action were taken. By taking both types of actions, it is assumed that patients will be less likely to sue (3).

The third difference between an incident report and occurrence screening is in the proactive focus of occurrence screening. Risk managers look for signs of potential trouble for the organization. Purposely looking for risks within the organization can lead to the discovery of potential risks before harm occurs and before there is a lawsuit initiated. Having foreknowledge of a potential claim allows the risk manager time to prepare to manage the suit and work with those likely to be named in the suit should a claim be made (3). Identifying occurrences while the patient is in the hospital and taking immediate corrective actions may minimize the likelihood of a lawsuit (3).

Occurrence screening information is not solely dependent on incident reports. It is information extracted from other routine records of patient care, emergencies, patient comments, repair orders, security calls and other activities reports. Occurrence screening involves more effort on the part of risk managers than is required in reviewing incident reports. This is because the information may not be previously identified as an incident.

A risk manager or department manager screens multiple documents to get a broad perspective on past and potential risks. Some of the important documents, such as patient treatment records and committee reports, have been mentioned earlier.

The basic question is, "Are there problems that should be considered further?" The focus is on looking for possible evidence of adverse patient outcomes. In physical therapy, for example, this might be a patient who has been using a cane with supervision for several days who now requires a walker and physical assistance. Why? What happened? Was there a fall? Is there increased pain? Was there an incident?

A result of consulting multiple sources of information is the compilation of a fairly compre-

hensive list of adverse patient occurrences (APOs) specific to the organization. Up to 85% of such occurrences can be expected to be identified through occurrence screening activities (4). In following up on APOs, risk management personnel may call upon representatives of departments identified in the occurrence screening to do a peer review of relevant cases to determine if standards were upheld and if changes need to be made (4). From this discussion, the reader should see that risk management involves all segments of an organization and that a close and coordinated working relationship between risk management and quality assurance managers (see Chapter 11) can protect the organization and its patients. The focus thus far has been on direct patient care occurrences and direct care providers on staff. There are other people who can provide useful risk management related data. Contacting these people may, however, be time consuming.

Walking the Beat

To assess potential risk organization wide, risk management should be a part of organizational thinking. This means that everyone from the board of directors and chief executive officer to student volunteers is a potential resource for identification of the organization's risks. For example, financial services may receive complaints written on bills. Financial personnel may not say anything to anyone except that the bill was paid. Volunteers may know patients personally and may be told things that were not expressed to employees. The potential value of interviewing various employees and others is that common concerns may be identified before an undesirable occurrence. This is information that may not be found in the more official data bases or reports because there may be no occurrence associated with them. Such informal information may alert the risk manager to risks before they materialize. The following list and comments identify additional resources for acquiring risk management information. The list and comments represent our thoughts and those of others (1, 3, 4, 11–14).

1. Administration and Department Managers: sometimes patients and others send complaints

directly to the top. It is possible that trivial concerns are dismissed and not passed on to the risk manager. A system for centralizing and reviewing all complaints can help assure a comprehensive view of the risks. In the case of department managers, the scope of the issue may be beyond that of the department manager's responsibility. In these cases, the manager should involve those who have wider authority. Inquiries made to other department managers may uncover the breath of the situation.

2. Quality Assurance, Utilization Review and Safety Committee Members: may be able to bring up situations that have not yet been addressed in interdisciplinary risk management committee meetings. There may be issues they would rather discuss on an informal or individual basis.

3. Financial Services Manager: when bills come due, complaints that were suppressed can surface. Such complaints may be made over the phone or in writing. Unless inquires are made, they may not be reported. If a patient or former patient gets no response from the organization, animosity may escalate and increase risk of a claim being made. There may be concerns about financial resource management. There may be questions about cash flow problems, large expense accounts, suspicions of fraud, theft or other serious matters that individual managers may bring up.

4. Medical Records Manager: may have received requests for patient information from unauthorized individuals. Knowing who is asking for the information may forewarn of a future claim.

5. Social Services Manager: is often involved with more people than just the patient, i.e., the family, third party payers, employer, etc. They may have an integrated view of a patient's environment and be able to pinpoint potential risks not obvious to others.

6. Public Relations/Marketing: involves dealing with many individuals external to the organization. Such interactions may provide perspectives on the organization that are unique. This is particularly important in terms of public opinion, perceptions and misperceptions. These departments may conduct customer satisfaction and visitor surveys. A visitor survey mailing list may be generated from visitor sign-in lists. These surveys may provide useful information regarding risks associated with specific departments and may alert staff concerning a future suit. Useful information may come from visitors because they may notice situations that patients do not. Visitors may be less stressed and more observant than patients and close family members.

7. Chaplain Service Director: may offer unique insights regarding risks that others may not have considered.

8. Case Managers: have frequent contact with patients and third party payers. They may have heard concerns raised during these contacts. Interviews with several case managers may lead to discovery of common impressions that suggest further investigation may be worth while.

9. Admission Clerks: are often the first contact the patient has with an organization. The impressions they get of patients and their families may forewarn of potential risks.

10. Aides, Orderlies, Certified Nursing Assistants: may spend more time with patients than some professional staff members. They may have useful information regarding a specific patient's level of expressed satisfaction. These individuals often do much of the physical labor involved in patient care. They may work with various pieces of equipment from pneumatic lifts to electric hospital beds. These front line employees are a valuable source of information about patient satisfaction, physical demands of work, and the condition and availability of equipment not obtained from other sources.

11. Patient Escorts: may hear comments of patients and family members relevant to their feelings about the care they received, accidents that occurred, and observations that they were concerned about

12. Security Officers: are often called in emergencies. Discussions and reviews of their records may show patterns, areas of increased activity and raise concern about many areas, including theft, assault and suspicious activities. Security records and records of emergency calls can be used for cross checking purposes.

13. Maintenance Personnel: respond to requests for repairs, new installations, remodeling and other services. They may see problems reoccurring, know of deteriorating conditions and have insight into potential problems.

14. Students: may have unique perspectives because they have not been fully acculturated into the organization. They may question why things are done as they are. They may raise issues based on experiences gained in other organizations or they may reflect on differences between what they have been taught and what they are doing or observe others doing.

15. Volunteers: patients may speak freely to non-employees. Volunteers overhear care-related comments from patients, family members and visitors, which may have risk implications.

16. Vendors: may have information about potential risks related to equipment or supplies they have sold the organization. They may also have published information about equipment or supplies from other manufacturers as well.

17. Discharge Clerks: comments regarding satisfaction may be directed toward discharge clerks

who may be among the last members of the organization to interact with patients.

18. Voluntarily Terminating Employees: are usually interviewed by their department managers and human resource representatives. Employees leaving on good terms may be willing to express risk-related concerns that they were reluctant to raise while they were employed. Following up on these employees may uncover new potential risks.

From the many sources listed and discussed, a representative list of APO's, as well as other types of risks, can be compiled. The APO's then need to be prioritized and possible solutions discussed. These activities are included in the second step in the risk management process (Fig. 12.1).

Analysis

Risks are often prioritized based on which risks have the most severe financial consequences for the organization (15). The judgment of many people is considered, i.e., risk management personnel and members of risk management, safety, utilization review and quality assurance committee members to name a few. Identified occurrences and potential risks need to be prioritized so they can be managed in order of perceived importance.

Asking and answering several questions can guide prioritizing. For occurrences, undesirable events that have happened, it is important to ask (3):

1. What was the frequency of each specific occurrence?
2. What was the severity of the loss(es)?
3. What is the possible severity of loss that could have occurred?
4. What was the effect of past occurrences of this type on the organization?
5. What is the likelihood of an occurrence happening again?
6. What effect would a reoccurrence likely have on the organization?

A form such as shown in Figure 12.4 may be helpful to organize the responses to these questions.

The analysis in Figure 12.4 requires the analyzers to integrate historical and potential risk information, compare occurrences and risks, use actual current data and estimate the relative importance of each of the listed criteria. The advantage of adopting a quantification method is that comparisons are easier to make. Among the disadvantages of such a method is that it may not account for some special issues associated with certain occurrences and risks. For potential risks, those that have been identified but have not yet occurred, the same questions and form can be used. The answers are necessarily more speculative.

Discussions of options for dealing with the risks may be carried on concurrent with the analysis of known risks. Once it is clear which occurrences and potential risks will be dealt with and what options are available (Table 12.1), the focus changes to selection of the most appropriate option.

General Risk Management Options

Selection of the most appropriate options for managing identified risks is the third step in the risk management process (Figure 12.1). The general options for dealing with risk are presented in Table 12.4 and discussed below.

LOSS PREVENTION

Ideally, risks are resolved so they no longer occur. Preventable risks are identified in the examination and analysis stage. Examples of corrective actions include educational programs, improved communication among involved parties, typed orders and preventative maintenance. All of these procedures can be useful in physical therapy environments.

LOSS REDUCTION

One way to describe loss reduction is to say it is a way to cover your back. It involves being prepared in case there is a claim. Among the means of managing claims effectively are: having all records completed in reasonable time frames, informing staff about claims that have been filed, educating staff for the possibility of legal action, and revising procedures that have lead to occurrences. Each of these loss-reduction suggestions is applicable to physical therapy departments.

CONTROLLING EXPOSURE

In situations in which repeated occurrences have taken place, one solution is to carry out a

OCCURRENCE ANALYSIS SHEET Date:_____

Occurrence: Name _____ Description_____

Comments:

Frequency Code # ____ x Weighted Value ____ = ____

Severity Code # ____ x Weighted Value ____ = ____

Est. Correction

Cost Code # ____ x Weighted Value ____ = ____

Est. Correction

Time Code # ____ x Weighted Value ____ = ____

External Interest/Intangibles

Code # ____ x Weighted Value ____ = ____

Sum of Weighted Values: [   ]

Priority Rating: [   ]

Instructions: Descriptor code #'s range from a minimum of .5/5 to a maximum of 5/5. Weighted values are determined by the Risk Management Committee.

Frequency # 5 = Daily

Severity # 5 = Catastrophic

Correction Cost # 5 = Under $1000

Correction Time # 5 = Under a day

External Interest # 5 = Widespread

FIGURE 12.4. Example of an occurrence analysis form for prioritizing risks. (Modified from Salmon SL. Risk management processes and functions. In: Troyer GT, Salman SL, eds. Handbook of Health Care Risk Management. Rockville, MD: Aspen Systems Corporation. 1986:171–174).

series of corrective actions. For example, one experiment could involve spreading the delivery of the service, say from a single physical therapy location, to several different areas and rotating personnel through the various locations to see where and who is involved in occurrences. Alternatively, an already decentralized area could be centralized to see what effect it has on frequency and severity of occurrences.

RISK ACCEPTANCE

Risk acceptance may occur by choice or oversight (16). A risk that would cost more to insure against than the probable loss might be accepted by the organization. This does not mean that nothing will be done to try to protect organizational assets from harm or loss. It does mean that the organization will limit investment of resources used to fully eliminate the risk. Risks accepted inadvertently are risks that were not considered. They are not deliberately covered by existing insurance policies (16). Although risk acceptance is a risk management decision, physical therapy managers should seek clarifications regarding who and what is and is not covered by institutional insurance policies and the limits of applicable policies.

TABLE 12.4
General Options for Managing Risk

- Prevention
- Reduction
- Controlling Exposure
- Risk Acceptance
- Risk Transfer
- Avoidance

Modified from Kavaler F, Spiegel AD. Risk management dynamics. In: Kavaler F, Spiegel AD eds. Risk Management in Health Care Institutions: A Strategic Approach. Sudbury, MA: Jones & Bartlett, 1997:5–6.

RISK TRANSFER

Risk can be shifted through contractual arrangements. This is frequently done for radiology services. The risk is transferred to the organization providing the service when the contract has a clause indicating that the contractor assumes responsibility for all risks. These clauses do not, however, eliminate the organization's risk entirely (4).

Another form of risk transfer is through insurance. The insurance company assumes the risk of a suit in exchange for a premium paid by the health care organization. Over a sufficient period of time, the premiums paid to the insurance company can increase to the point that the cost of insurance is greater than the risk being assumed by the insurer (4).

AVOIDANCE

Certain health care services are associated with greater frequency of legal actions and high dollar amount settlements. Neurosurgeons and obstetricians are notable examples. A health care organization may decide not to offer such services and thus avoid exposure to risks. In general, by concentrating on the services the organization is most proficient at providing, risk is reduced. A physical therapy example of exposure avoidance might involve not treating certain high-risk diagnoses such as premature infants.

The concepts of risk management have thus far been applied in an organizational context. These concepts, the five risk management options and suggestions for managing risk will now be directed specifically to physical therapy environments. The next sections deal with risks to

which departmental managers and individual practitioners are likely to be exposed. Included in the discussion are suggestions for self-protection against civil and criminal actions.

RISK MANAGEMENT CONCERNS IN PHYSICAL THERAPY

A comparison of Table 12.1 and Table 12.5 shows many similar topics. However, the scope of the two tables differs. Table 12.1 relates to an entire organization. It was constructed from a risk manager's viewpoint. Table 12.5 has a limited scope. It focuses on areas of risk directly related to physical therapy environments. There are physical therapy related resources on many of the topics listed in Tables 12.1 and 12.5 that can be consulted, e.g., references 11, 13, 17, 18.

Abuse, Assault and Harassment

The topic of abuse will be discussed because abuse, in some form or degree, is associated with ten of the topics listed in Table 12.5. Abuse means to misuse, hurt or injure. Abuse typically involves

TABLE 12.5
Some Important Areas of Risk In Physical Therapy Environments

Abuse (child, domestic, elder, sexual)
Assault (fear of impending sexual or other type of harm)
Battery (unjustified, offensive direct or indirect contact)
Discrimination (age, race, sex)
Defamation (false communication about a person)
False Imprisonment (a form of abuse)
Invasion of Privacy, Public Disclosure
Sexual Misconduct (related to sexual abuse)
Sexual Harassment (can be related to sexual assault or abuse)
Failure to Obtain Informed Consent
Theft/Burglary
Americans with Disabilities Act of 1990
Civil Rights Act of 1964 (Title VII)
Civil Rights Act of 1991
Equal Pay Act of 1963
Occupational Safety and Health Act of 1970
Pregnancy Discrimination Act of 1978
Recruitment and Selection
Employee Discipline and Termination
Restrictive Covenants in Employment Contracts

neglect or harm of minors or vulnerable adults (19). Because physical therapists treat all diagnoses and age groups, an awareness of the signs of abuse is important for the protection of patients. It is the moral, ethical (see Chapter 2) and legal obligation of a physical therapist to protect those who are defenseless. While abuse is abhorrent no matter who is abused, it is particularly disturbing when it occurs within the context of health care.

Abuse can cause emotional harm, physical harm or both. For example, sexual abuse may cause both physical and emotional consequences. Developing an awareness of physical and behavioral patterns associated with abuse may aid the therapist in recognizing abuse cases when patients are interviewed and examined (Table 12.6).

Abuse Considerations and Risk Management

The risk management connection to abuse has four parts: Situations involving individuals external to or outside of the institution and three types of situations involving individuals within the institution. The external individuals include

 TABLE 12.6
Example Physical and Behavioral Signs Associated with Abuse

PHYSICAL SIGNS
- Crying
- Unwillingness to make eye contact
- Easily startled
- Withdrawing from touch
- Flinching when therapist makes unexpected movements
- Bruises in unusual areas or in areas inconsistent with history
- Recurring abrasions, bruises, burns or cuts
- Sunken eyes, cheeks, thin (malnutrition? lack of sleep? ill?)
- Unexplained weight loss
- Poor hygiene
- Clothing dirty, torn, out of context
- Repeated touching of ones genital area

BEHAVIORAL SIGNS
- Anxious, nervous
- Signs of depression
- Hostility
- Lethargy
- Emotional lability (emotional responses unusual for circumstances)
- Refusal to respond to reasonable relevant questions

a patients' acquaintances, care givers, guardians, relatives, parents or spouse. Individuals internal or within the health care setting who might abuse patients include nonprofessional staff members, other patients and professional staff members.

EXTERNAL SOURCES OF ABUSE

A physical therapist may be the first person to suspect abuse of a patient. Listening to patient comments may be helpful in gaining insight into the source of unreported abuse. In addition to unconvincing explanations for physical injuries, a physical therapist should listen for comments that might indicate (19):

- Denial of basic essentials (clothing, food, medications, social contact, etc.)
- Exploitation (financial and other forms)
- Sexual abuse
- Unreasonable confinement (to room, restraints)

When abuse of a child is suspected, particularly sexual abuse, the physical therapist should be careful not to interrogate the child. Rather, write down what the child says using their words (20). Police or a child protective agency should be called. Until those called arrive, the therapist must assure that the child is safe from further abuse (20). The same general procedure should be followed should spousal abuse be discovered, though one must have the consent of the patient. Formal policies and procedures should be developed to authorize and guide staff actions in abuse situations. Assistance from legal staff may be required to assure the adequacy and legality of the adopted procedures.

Observations of interactions between the patient and others may also be informative. Watch how a patient reacts around certain family members or how a family member treats a patient when they are unaware that others are observing them. This may raise suspicions. This type of vigilance may be necessary because patients may be reluctant to implicate a family member on whom they depend for medications, toileting, food or other basic needs.

INTERNAL SOURCES OF ABUSE

One internal source of abuse occurs between patients. Patients are assigned to beds based on such criteria as surgical procedure, bed availability and services needed. The compatibility of patients in a room is not typically a major consideration. Patients under duress can get angry, may argue and harm each other. They can bring these ill feelings to the physical therapy area and squabble in wheel chairs or on adjacent mat tables. They can reach out and grab, swing or shout at one another. This can distract other patients who may become upset or lose balance and hurt themselves. When two or more patients do not get along, separate the individuals. Treat them in different areas or at different times. Discuss the situation with nursing personnel to be sure that everyone is aware of the potential risk of harm. Inquire if psychological or social services have been or will be requested.

Another internal source of abuse is from staff members. Use of controlled substances, personal problems and stress are reasons a staff member might be rough, discourteous, abrupt or rude in their treatment of a patient. If these undesirable patient care behaviors are intended to do harm and they do result in harm, this may be a criminal act. If these patient care behaviors are not intended to do harm, but they do have harmful consequences, professional staff such as physical therapists may be considered professionally negligent. This may be prosecuted as a civil wrongdoing rather than a criminal act. It is worth noting that personal professional liability insurance covers the insured person for professional negligence but not for criminal acts. An employer is responsible for the acts of its employees. Proven misconduct in the form of abuse should be subject to disciplinary action. Failure to take action may increase an employer's liability in an abuse situation.

A department manager needs to be aware of the level of care being provided by the professional staff and their extenders, e.g., aides. This involves more documentation review. Periodic observation of actual treatments being delivered is necessary to find out more than what has been written in reports or notes. Therapist extenders usually do not write reports. Observation of their performance is vital. For example, if behaviors become erratic, there are unexplained absences, tardiness and/or radical mood changes, then one might suspect illicit drug use. It is appropriate to request drug testing following an accident that results in serious injury to a patient or staff member to rule out impairment as a cause of the accident. If there is reasonable suspicion that an employee is using illicit drugs, to maintain a safe workplace, a manager may request that the employee submit to drug testing (13).

Assault Considerations and Risk Management

A distinction between abuse and assault is the status of the individual harmed. Abuse is related to individuals who are vulnerable or less able to fend for themselves then perhaps others. Assault is defined as "any willful attempt or threat to inflict injury on a person when coupled with an apparent ability to do so, and any intentional display of force such as would give the victim reason to fear or expect immediate bodily harm" (21). An assault can be committed with or without touching another person or doing bodily harm.

Assault and Battery

Assault is often coupled with the word battery, which means unjustified, offensive unwanted intentional contact (13). The key element of the action of battery is the lack of consent to physical contact on the part of the injured party (22). Together, assault (no physical contact) and battery (contact) means any unlawful touching of another without justification or excuse (21).

An understanding of assault and battery is very relevant to physical therapists. Physical therapy is a physical contact profession. Accusations of assault and battery may stem from the handling of a patient in the course of treatment. There are multiple possible situations in which a patient might claim that they feared they were going to be touched for sexual purposes. Such a fear of contact or injury, as discussed, is legally considered an assault. For example, asking a person of the opposite sex to expose their clavicle or sacrum might frighten some patients. Palpating the pubic ramus to identify its location and mobilizing it before other activities to relieve a sacroiliac problem may seem very unusual to a patient. This may be construed as sexual battery.

This is the nonconsensual touching of another's body parts. If pain increased with the maneuver, perhaps battery could be added to the picture. Patients may be concerned about unwanted touching or viewing of their genital area, breasts, thighs or buttocks (20). To protect the patient, departmental personnel and the institution, there is a need for departmental policies to manage these types of contact risks. Some policy suggestions are:

1. Requiring appropriate discussion be carried out before obtaining a written informed consent from each patient. This is especially needed from patients who will receive massage, manual therapy or other physical agents applied to areas with sexual connotations.
2. Requiring a staff member of the patient's sex to be present when a member of the opposite sex is treating a patient in the area(s) near their genitals or other areas usually considered private by the patient (22).
3. Requiring that patients be informed that they can request a same sex chaperone be present during treatment.
4. Requiring a knock and enter rule which allows a staff member to knock before entering and then to enter a private treatment area which is in use.
5. Requiring treatment room doors be left partially open whenever the therapist senses a concern on the part of the patient or administer the treatment in a less secluded area such as in a curtained booth (22).
6. Requiring draping of all patients.
7. Requiring patients to wear clothing appropriate for the activities in which they will participate.

Policies require procedures for their enactment. To assure that the above and other policies are carried out requires ongoing education and monitoring. The department manager must provide orientation and ongoing education to assure that new staff develops appropriate skills and experienced staff maintains their skills in carrying out procedures needed to enact policies.

ASSAULT BY A PHYSICAL THERAPIST

A final consideration is sexual assault of a patient by a physical therapist. A claim of assault may be the end result of a typical therapist-patient relationship. A professional who has sexual feelings for a patient under their care or who believes the patient has such feelings toward them, has a reasonable option to terminate the relationship.

The most convenient action often taken is to simply refer the patient to another therapist. However, this transfer may or may not alleviate the situation, especially if therapist and patient continue to be present in the same treatment environment.

The physical closeness inherent in the practice of physical therapy and the long duration of treatment are two elements that facilitate building rapport with patients. This rapport may lead to more substantive thoughts and feelings. There is a progression of actions that move from rapport building to sexual misconduct. This progression has been called boundary crossings, boundary violations and sexual misconduct (23). The concepts of boundary and progression are clarified in the following 11 criteria (24):

1. Role of the therapist: Does it change over time?
2. Time together: Do treatments get longer? Are there extra treatment sessions?
3. Place: Are treatments administered in view of others?
4. Space: Is there less space between patient and therapist than usual, i.e., what is needed, how similar patients are treated? Hugging? Touching in comforting ways? Hand holding?
5. Money: Are charges reduced or not made for treatment?
6. Gifts: Are gifts given or exchanged?
7. Services: Are additional services offered? Is nonphysical therapy assistance offered?
8. Clothing: Is the dress appropriate for the setting? Is clothing suggestive? Is the clothing noticeably different when patient X and therapist Y work together?
9. Language: Is the language and the content of the conversation appropriate for therapeutic needs? Is it personal? It is intended to be just between therapist and patient?
10. Self-disclosure: Does one party tell another very personal things? Is this a reciprocal self-disclosure?
11. Physical Contact: Is there touching that is not necessary for treatment? Is there touching for touching sake?

There can be no hard and fast rule regarding touching in physical therapy. Crossing boundaries is situational. If crossing one of the boundaries noted above has a therapeutic purpose, it should be clearly noted in the patient's record. If it can not be justified on a therapeutic basis, it is likely that a boundary has been crossed. What can be done? A guideline for psychiatric professionals can be followed. This guideline suggests that if a relationship is to occur, it would be judicious to wait at least 6 months after treating a patient before having intimate relations (25).

A manager must be aware of developing relationships that may have an impact on the organization. Relationships may be very public or they may be divulged in private discussions with a staff member. If there is reason to believe that a patient is being abused, assaulted or battered, for everyone's welfare, i.e., patient, therapist and organization, the therapist must be confronted and reported. If, after discussions, suspicion remains, the suspicion should be reported to the organization's risk manager or other official. Needless to say, illegal acts like abuse and assault are unethical acts. The Guide for Professional Conduct of the American Physical Therapy Association (APTA), (Appendix B), infers sexual misconduct in sections 1.1c and 5.4 while specifically prohibiting it in 1.3. Members who abuse patients must be reported by contacting the president or ethics committee of the states' chapter of the APTA and legal authorities.

Abuse and assault are criminal offenses punishable by jail time. Civil claims may also result from a sexual assault. The remedy for civil claims is payment of money. Because insurance policies exclude payment for criminal acts, the offender is obligated to pay the award from their personal resources. To complete the discussion of issues related in one way or another to sexual conduct, one additional topic needs to be discussed. This is sexual harassment.

Sexual Harassment and Risk Management in Physical Therapy

Sexual harassment is distinct from abuse and assault in three major ways. First, sexual harassment is prohibited by federal law, specifically Title VII of 1964 Civil Rights Act (26). Second, sexual harassment is an illegal type of sex discrimination. And third, sexual harassment is a civil wrong, not a crime. All members of an organization are affected by sexual harassment regulations. Sexual harassment may occur between:

- Supervisor and supervised
- Coworkers

- Employees and venders
- Employees and customers
- People of the same or opposite sex

The Equal Employment Opportunity Commission (EEOC) is the federal agency created by Congress in the 1964 Civil Rights Act. The EEOC enforces all federal regulations, policies and actions affecting equal employment opportunity. One of the work-related areas the EEOC deals with is sexual harassment. The EEOC's definition of sexual harassment includes the following unwelcome acts:

- Leering or ogling
- Sexist remarks
- Off-color jokes
- Verbal abuse
- Patting, pinching, brushing against the body
- Pressures for dates
- Demands for sexual favors in return for hiring, promotion or tenure
- Physical assault or rape

The 1990 EEOC guidelines made further clarifications regarding sexual harassment. "Harassment on the basis of sex is a violation of Sect. 703 of Title VII. Unwelcome sexual advances, requests for sexual favors, and other verbal or physical conduct of a sexual nature constitute sexual harassment" (27) under two conditions. The first is called quid pro quo (something for something). This means that granting sexual favors that are explicitly or implicitly a term or condition for initial or continued employment or to access other opportunities in the workplace. The second implication in the above guideline relates to the work environment itself. A hostile work environment is one in which conduct of the type noted above has the effect of unreasonably interfering with an individual's work performance or it presents an intimidating or offensive working environment. The guideline goes on to state that "the employer has an affirmative duty to maintain a workplace free from sexual harassment and intimidation" (27).

MANAGING THE RISK OF SEXUAL HARASSMENT

Sexual harassment can occur in stages or degrees of severity. A description of progressive sexually oriented behaviors is:

1. Invited and reciprocal (this is not harassment).
2. Uninvited but welcome (a light gray area).
3. Offensive but tolerated (this is legally actionable).
4. Flatly rejected (clearly actionable).

The preceding comments and criteria related to sexual harassment are gender neutral. However, they have been interpreted to apply to women being harassed by men. The Supreme Court has recently begun deliberating about same-sex harassment as may be covered by the Civil Rights Act of 1964.

These criteria above apply to all levels of personnel equally. This means an aide or executive officer of a health care organization may be involved in sexual harassment. There is no doubt that it is the employer who is liable for quid pro quo and hostile environment situations. Efforts by an employer to reduce the incidence of sexual harassment are called for by EEOC guidelines. For example, "to avoid liability, employers have to educate and sensitize their workforce." And, "an employer is liable when it knew, or upon reasonably diligent inquiry should have known of the harassment" (27).

Table 12.7 contains several suggestions for reducing the incidence of sexual harassment and the risk of claims against the employer.

An ideal process is one that provides anonymity to individuals making complaints of sexual harassment, is responsive to the complaint, and reflects concern for the person being harassed and earnestness in stopping sexual harassment. Risk to the organization due to sexual harassment cases is likely to be reduced when these actions are taken. However, not all complaint processes are considered ideal. Some individuals prefer to deal with such issues themselves. An individualized approach to dealing with sexual harassment involves saying no and putting it in writing. Clearly tell the person to stop the behavior soon after it has occurred. If it continues, write a letter to the harasser. In the letter, describe the offensive behavior, when it occurred and the circumstances, the negative reaction the behavior caused and request what should be done to rectify the situation in addition to ending the harassment. Deliver the letter in person in the company of a reliable witness.

 TABLE 12.7

Options for Managing the Issue of Sexual Harassment

1. Establish a strongly worded written policy based on current EEOC guidelines.
2. Establish a grievance procedure for sexual harassment complaints. The procedures must ensure confidentiality, be directed by two organizationally powerful managers, one of each sex, who have credibility. The person making the complaint should be allowed to complain to someone outside of their supervisors' chain of command.
3. Establish a management response program that immediately reacts by starting an investigation. The investigation should check for trends, job changes, go back to earlier records and contact past employees regarding sexual harassment.
4. Provide mediation between an employee and supervisor.
5. Educate all employees, especially managers, about sexual harassment as well as the organization's policy and procedures. This may be done by training programs to increase awareness of attitudes, behaviors, stereotyping and objectionable language.
6. Discipline offenders in accordance with the severity of the offense. To do this, solid evidence is necessary. Keeping records of complaints, investigations and actions develops an evidential database. It is important to conduct exit interviews with individuals who are terminating to clarify the reason for their leaving the organization.

Adapted from Wolkinsin BW, Block RN. Employment Law: The Workplace Rights of Employees and Employers. Cambridge, MA: Blackwell, 1996:74–75.

This individualized approach keeps the matter private and it may solve the immediate problem. However, it bypasses the data gathering process. If the person engaging in the harassment does it habitually, and complaints remain individualized, the problem is not solved; it is just passed on to the next person who is harassed.

SUMMARY

Risk management involves coordinated efforts to identify, assess and minimize, where possible, risks to patient, visitors, staff, and the organization. Risk management programs aim to protect the patient as well as the organization.

An occurrence is an unusual event that could lead to a lawsuit. Any occurrence needs to be reported in a standardized way and sent to a central location for analysis. Individualized occurrences or trends can lead to policies and procedures as well as other actions that will likely reduce the chance of similar untoward events happening in the future. Among the sources of risk are the environment, equipment, services offered and employees. A plan to reduce risks in each of these areas has been discussed. Of particular pertinence to physical therapy was a discussion on abuse, assault and sexual harassment. Recognition of the signs of abuse in vulnerable patients was also discussed. Legal distinctions were made between abuse, assault and sexual harassment. Suggestions for dealing with these situations were offered. To deepen thought about sexual issues in the workplace, the discussion included several perspectives. The focus was placed at different times on issues relating to a physical therapist examining and treating a patient, on a manager's responsibility for safeguarding patient and employee welfare, on the person being assaulted or harassed, and on the person committing the assault or harassment. Appendix A, Role-Play 12, deals with the sensitive issues covered in this chapter.

REFERENCES

1. Ashcroft C. Betting the odds: Risk management. Clinical Management, 1991;11:12–13.
2. Monagle JF. Risk Management: A Guide for Health Care Professionals. Rockville, MD: Aspen Systems Corporation, 1985:7.
3. Salman SL. Risk management processes and functions. In: Troyer GT, Salman SL, eds. Handbook of Health Care Risk Management. Rockville, MD: Aspen, 1986: 149–182.
4. Kavaler F, Spiegel AD. Risk management dynamics. In: Kavaler F, Spiegel AD, eds. Risk Management in Health Care Institutions: A Strategic Approach. Sudbury, MA: Jones & Bartlett, 1997:3–25.
5. Salman SL. Quality assurance and risk management. In: Troyer GT, Salman SL, eds. Handbook of Health Care Risk Management. Rockville, MD: Aspen, 1986: 411–419.
6. Troyer, G. (1986). The concept of risk. In: Troyer GT, Salman SL, eds. Handbook of Health Care Risk Management. Rockville, MD: Aspen, 1986:141–148.
7. Singleton JK. Identifying and controlling risks in long term care. Nursing homes and home health. In: Kavaler F, Spiegel AD, eds. Risk Management in Health Care Institutions: A Strategic Approach. Sudbury, MA: Jones & Bartlett, 1997:245–268.
8. Gaynor E. Policies and procedures. In: Managing Risk in Physical Therapy: A Guide to Issues in Liability. Alexandria, VA: American Physical Therapy Association, 1995:III.1–III.34.
9. Spiegel AD, Kavaler F. Regulatory environment. Standards and risk management. In: Kavaler F, Spiegel AD, eds. Risk Management in Health Care Institutions: A Strategic Approach. Sudbury, MA: Jones & Bartlett, 1997:26–46.
10. Kroft GG. Synopsis of an insurance company safety specialist. Preventing injury 1992;1:10–11.
11. Melzer BA. An introduction to risk management. In: Managing Risk in Physical Therapy: A Guide to Issues in Liability. Alexandria, VA: American Physical Therapy Association, 1995:I.1–I.11.
12. Mittermaier AJ. Organizing a risk management program: The smaller hospital. In: Troyer GT, Salman SL, eds. Handbook of Health Care Risk Management. Rockville, MD: Aspen, 1986:313–326.
13. Scott RW. Promoting Legal Awareness in Physical and Occupational Therapy. St. Louis, MO: Mosby, 1997: 185, 202, 285.
14. Young GJ. Home health: Special risks. PT Magazine, 1991 (Sept):63–64.
15. Rail R. Financial and risk management in hospitals. In: Troyer GT, Salman SL, eds. Handbook of Health Care Risk Management. Rockville, MD: Aspen, 1986:81–100.
16. Nelson RT, Gill WH. Alternative methods of risk financing. In: Troyer GT, Salman SL, eds. Handbook of Health Care Risk Management. Rockville, MD: Aspen, 1986:209–227.
17. American Physical Therapy Association. Risk Management. An APTA Malpractice Resource Guide. Alexandria, VA: Author, 1990.
18. American Physical Therapy Association. Managing Risk in Physical Therapy. A Guide to Issues in Liability. Alexandria, VA:Author, 1995.
19. Rohman LW, Huber PL. Health: Patient rights and policing the quality of health care. In: Hauser BR, ed. Women's Legal Guide. Golden, CO: Fulcrum Publishing, 1996:34–64.
20. Quaintance K. Sexual assault. In: Hauser BR, ed. Women's Legal Guide. Golden, CO: Fulcrum Publishing, 1996:85–98.
21. Nolan JR, Nolan-Haley JM. Black's Law Dictionary. 6th ed. St. Paul, MN: West Publishing, 1990:114–115, 247, 625, 914–915, 959, 1032, 1375, 1434.
22. Schunk C, Propas Parver C. Avoiding allegations of sexual misconduct. Clinical Management 1989;9(5):19–22.
23. Gutheil T, Gabbard GO. The concept of boundaries in clinical practice: Theoretical and risk management dimensions. American Journal of Psychiatry 150;2: 188–196.
24. Wysoker A. Risk management in psychiatry. In: Kavaler F, Spiegel AD, eds. Risk Management in

Health Care Institutions: A Strategic Approach. Sudbury, MA: Jones & Bartlett, 1997:225–244.

25. Stromber CD, Haggarty DJ, Leibenluft RF, et al. Physical contact and sexual relations with patients. The Psychologist's Legal Handbook. Washington, DC: Council for the National Register of Health Service Providers in Psychology, 1988:463.

26. Civil Rights Act of 1964, Title VII, 42 U.S.C., 29 CFR. § 1604.11(a–f).

27. Gimble BS ed. EEOC: Policy guide on employer liability for sexual favoritism under Title VII, January 12, 1990. In: Appendices, Sex Discrimination Handbook. Washington, DC: BNA Books, 1992: 349–353.

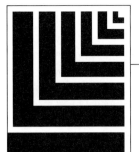

13

GETTING ADVICE: CONSULTANTS

PREVIEW

Today's health care managers face an unprecedented level of demand for diverse knowledge and expertise in management theory and practice. In reality, no one manager can be an expert in every aspect of management. To handle what can become a set of overwhelming expectations, the prudent manager quickly learns to focus energy on mastering those skills that they must use on a routine basis. For non-routine tasks, a general knowledge of a topic may be all that a manager will need if they can get help. When an unusual task or circumstance presents itself, a manager may need to consult with other internal or external experts. With a growing reliance on consultants, managers must become skilled at locating, selecting and evaluating the performance of the consultants they need to assist them. Research and planning are the keys to successful management of the consultation process. This chapter will provide general information on the types and sources of commonly available consultation services. A situational assessment approach to the use of consulting services will be provided. In addition, a process for consultant selection and contracting will be discussed.

KEY WORDS

Certified Public Accountant (CPA): an individual who has passed state licensure exams and meets continuing education requirements in finance and accounting.

Consultant: a person who gives professional or technical advice.

Consulting Engagement: the arrangement between the party or parties seeking consulting services and the party or parties providing consulting services for a particular project or scope of work to be completed.

Contractor: parties from outside of the organization used to augment existing resources to do specific tasks on a short or long-term basis. An independent contractor's involvement is generally temporary until the company can hire employees. The temporary need for contract service disappears or the companys' employees are trained to do the contracted work.

Public Accountant: an account who is not certified but frequently has received formal education in accounting and related subjects.

Temporary Employee: an individual hired for a limited period after which employment automatically terminates.

Vendor: an individual or company that offers a product or service for sale to others.

INTRODUCTION

As the role of manager and leader becomes increasingly complex, managers will need to turn to others for information, direction and support. Help may be found both inside and outside of an organization. Internal consulting support may come from individuals hired by the organization to consult with management on specific topics. For example, a company may have a computer technology expert on staff to support system selection, installation and operation. A physical therapy practice may have a billing expert on staff to assist management in maximizing revenue from services provided. Internal consulting support can also come from employees recognized for their expertise though consulting is not their formal role. For example, a therapist with work experience in pediatrics might be consulted on the selection of equipment for a new pediatric treatment room.

Expert advice is also available from sources external to the organization. Support through consultation can be obtained from a variety of outside sources, including professional colleagues, professional associations, and professional consultants. When seeking advice from outside of the organization, the best source should be determined by the specifics of the situation. Situational factors that should be considered include the type of assistance required, the availability of knowledgeable people and resources, the amount of assistance required, need for confidentiality and the cost. Under some circumstances, a professional colleague may be a good source for advice. Such advice may be readily available at little cost to the organization. If the engagement requires a significant amount of time over an extended period, a professional consultant may be a better choice. There may also be competitive reasons why a professional colleague should not be used as a resource.

The use of consultants does not release management from their accountability for organizational performance. A consultant is simply a tool that management may choose to employ to meet their performance objectives. When used, consultants and the consultation process are the responsibility of management. Therefore, managers must approach the use of consultants as they would any other management decision. Essential steps when considering the use of a consultant include:

- A situational analysis
- Identification of the performance variances
- Development of clear performance objectives
- Identification of situational barriers

The process used to identify and select the best possible consultant should be organized and objective. Consultant qualifications and the conditions of the engagement, such as references and project experience, should be defined.

The need for a formal consulting agreement will depend on the source of the consulting services and the complexity of the engagement. When the goal is to contract with an external professional consultant, additional issues such as liability and insurance requirements enter the picture. Good planning and follow through will improve the odds in favor of a successful consulting engagement. A written plan and consulting agreement are always advisable.

CONSULTANT, CONTRACTOR OR TEMPORARY EMPLOYEE?

A consultant may be defined simply as someone who gives professional or technical advice (1). Consultants can be used to provide expertise, provide an outside point of view and/or serve as an agent for change (2). Using the definition of advice giver and doer, most health care professionals and managers function in the role of consultant and/or use the services of consultants on a routine basis. The reasons are simple. No one can be the best at everything. On the other hand, someone will have developed a superior expertise in most things. There will be times also when every manager feels the need to tap into a greater level of expertise than they personally possess.

Independent contractors are outside parties used to augment existing resources to do specific tasks on a short or long-term basis. Independent contractors generally have a different role than consultants (2). They are brought in to fill a gap. The independent contractor's involvement is generally temporary until the company can hire employees, the temporary need for contract service disappears or the companys' employees can be trained to do the contracted work.

An independent contractor is self-employed or employed by another contracting company. Independent contractors are not considered employees of the contracting company for the purposes of benefits, liability, workers compensation, income or social security taxes. Independent contractors are differentiated from employees by their independence in performing the work to be done. They are generally provided with less orientation by the contracting company. An independent contractor would collaborate with management to decide how the work should be done and then, with management approval, do it.

When individuals are hired for short periods to augment the company's work force, they are temporary employees. A temporary employee is different from either a consultant or an independent contractor. A physical therapy department may hire temporary employees to cover during extended staff absences or during periods of high service demand. Temporary employees are hired by a company for a limited time to do a specific job. Their scope of decision making is different from an independent contractor or consultant. The company alone defines the work to be done and evaluates the temporary employee's ability to do the required tasks. A temporary employee does their work according to work rules and management direction of the company.

SERVICES AVAILABLE

The diversity of services available on a consultation basis is virtually unlimited. Consulting arrangements (engagements) vary greatly in scope and complexity. Consultants are available who can assume management responsibility of an entire corporation or simply assist with a particular aspect of a company's operation. Businesses, large and small, use consulting services. Consultants provide access to special expertise that many companies would be unable to afford if they had to hire experts on a full-time basis.

In Chapter 6, the structure of an organization was divided into three basic parts: management, the operating core and support services. Depending on the size of the organization, owners and employees may function within one or more of the organization's parts. The operating core is that part of the organization that actually does the work (3). Consulting services are available to support or replace functions within all three parts of an organization. Most commonly, consulting services are used to support management directly or through provision of support functions. Table 13.1 provides a listing of common consulting service areas.

Management must determine what skills and expertise are required to operate the organization. The decision to hire or buy needed services is a part of that decision-making process. If an internal source is unavailable or unable to meet all of a company's service requirements, external sources may be used. The relative cost of using internal versus external consulting services is one factor in the decision-making process. As with all other resource utilization decisions, a financial analysis should be used to determine the cost of alternative approaches. See Chapter 7 for the elements of this type of analysis.

Financial Services

Chapters 7 and 8 clearly outline the importance of financial management to the success of the organization. Depending on the size and complexity of the organization, the required financial expertise may be available through the support functions of the organization. If not, management may obtain the assistance of exter-

TABLE 13.1
Commonly Available Consulting Services

	CONSULTING SERVICES
Financial Services	Financial planning
	Audit services
	Financial systems design
	Financial systems
	Operations
	Investment management
	Billing and collections
	Taxes
Legal Services	Business organization
	Business incorporation
	Regulatory compliance
	Legal document
	preparation
	Legal document review
Human Resources	Benefits
	Wage and salary
	Recruitment
	Staff training and development
	Diversity training
	Legal and regulatory
	Compliance
	Employee satisfaction
	Communications
	Performance appraisal
Real Estate	Facilities location
	Lease negotiation
	Facilities management
Equipment and	Biomedical engineering
Technology	Telecommunications
	Information management
	technology
	Equipment evaluation
Operations	Business development
Management	Organization design
	Work and operations
	design
	Business practices
	Performance assessment
	Performance improvement
	Marketing and public
	relations
	Facilities design
	Facilities construction
	management
	Building services
	Fund raising
	Insurance

nal consultants for audit, financial information and accounting system design, as well as billing and collections. Other services that may be required at some point include financial planning, investment management, inventory management, cash flow management and tax planning.

Financial consulting services are available through large nationally known accounting firms known as the Big Six in reference to Arthur Andersen, Coopers & Lybrand, Deloitte Touche, Ernst & Young, KPMG Peat Marwick and Price Waterhouse. While the services of these accounting firms may be warranted, a decision to use one of the national firms should be based on need and cost. The higher fees charged by a larger firm may not be necessary for routine accounting services (4).

A Certified Public Accountant (CPA) is an individual who has passed state licensure exams and meets continuing education requirements. An account who is not certified is called a public accountant. A public accountant has generally completed some formal education in accounting and may have an accounting degree. Either CPA or a public accountant may be able to meet the consulting needs of a business. The best way to find any consultant is by word-of-mouth from other managers who have had a positive experience and are willing to recommend the use of a particular consulting firm or individual. The local phone directory, state CPA society or the National Society of Public Accounts may also be a source of information on financial consulting services.

Legal Services

The services of an attorney are typically needed to get started in business and for ongoing operations. For health care organizations, risk management related to regulatory compliance is a common reason for consulting a health care attorney. Another key reason for using the services of an attorney is contract preparation and review. Larger companies may have internal legal counsel.

There are software packages and books available to businesses that contain the basics for carrying out some business legal functions such as model lease agreements. Although these resources may meet some of a company's needs, these tools are standardized. They cannot meet the individual needs of a company without modification. It may be inadvisable to use these tools in place of the advice from a qualified attorney when such advice is needed (4).

As with financial services, the best way to find a qualified attorney is through the recommendations of business colleagues. Recommendations should be sought from individuals who have had direct experience with the consultant involving a similar situation. Like physical therapists, attorneys also specialize in different areas of the law. When seeking legal services, be sure that the attorney selected has the knowledge and expertise to handle the specific needs of the situation. More than one attorney may need to be used. Often the larger legal firms will have attorneys who specialize in different areas of law. Such a firm can probably meet a greater number of diverse needs. The county, state and national bar associations may also be a resource for locating attorneys who can provide needed consulting services.

Human Resources

There are many aspects of human resource management that require significant expertise. Set up and management of benefit plans, employee compensation programs, employee assistance programs and performance appraisal programs may require assistance from legal, financial, management and/or human resource consultants at some point in time. The smaller the business, the less likely that the skills and expertise to do all of the necessary human resource activities will be available within the organization. Should this be the case, then ongoing support from consultants may be required. Larger companies may only require the assistance of external consultants for special projects. Internal consultants would be available to help with routine situations.

Professional recruiters are another type of human resource consultant. They are used to locate key and/or hard-to-find employees. This is a service used extensively by health care organizations to fill physical therapist position vacancies. Typically, a professional recruiter will search for qualified applicants to interview for employment. Should the recruiter's candidate be hired, the recruiter is paid a percentage of the first year wages. This percentage varies but can be as high as 30% to 40%. Part of the recruitment fee may be refundable if the employee does not pass probation and/or complete a full year of employ-

ment. Arrangements with professional recruiters do vary and should be negotiated on a case-by-case basis.

Staff training and development activities are frequently supported by internal and external consultants. Consultation may be provided in a variety of ways, including lectures, the provision of training materials, off-site training and teleconferences. Reliance on other employees to provide inservice education is actually a form of internal consulting. Diversity training is one type of employee training and development that is often done by external consultants. Refer to Chapter 5 for more information on the topic of work place diversity.

Professional associations, referrals from other professionals or organizations, and personal experience are all good sources of information on human resource consultants. Human resource consultants have more diverse backgrounds and experiences than do financial or legal consultants. When an external consultant is not licensed or credentialed by a third party, management must rely on other sources to evaluate potential consultants. A demonstrated track record of success and references from reliable sources are used when evaluating the credentials of human resource consultants.

Real Estate

The services of a real estate agent, developer or attorney may be required to assist with real estate related activities. There are several areas for which they may be of help.

- Find office space for the operation of a business unit
- Negotiate terms for the lease of office space
- Prepare and/or review property lease agreements
- Manage facilities which the organization may own and operate
- Facility design and upfit

The relative value of services provided by a real estate consultant is determined by the needs of the organization. Health care organizations acquire property for a variety of reasons. However, with few exceptions, real estate management is not an area of expertise for health care managers. Where such specialized management expertise is required, it is the authors' opinion that lacking internal expertise, this is best handled by using a consultant or contractor.

In selecting a real estate consultant, a company can look for a track record of success in serving customers with similar needs. Local reputation is another indicator. References are very important. Potential consultants can be asked to provide several references. References should be checked. Again, referrals from other satisfied customers who have used a consultant for similar services are some good barometers of the consultants' potential to meet specific needs. For example, if a physical therapy practice owner wishes to sublet part of an owned office building to other medically oriented businesses, a commercial real estate broker who has a good track record for leasing medical office space would be a logical choice.

Equipment And Technology

The technologies used in health care delivery and information management continue to evolve at an unprecedented rate. It is incumbent upon health care managers to remain informed about technological advances. But it is unrealistic to expect managers to have the expertise needed to fully evaluate, select and place into operation all of the technology used in the operation of today's health care businesses. Whenever a manager lacks direct experience with a new technology, outside assistance should be sought. The size of the potential investment, along with the complexity of the technology, are two good reasons to seek expert assistance.

Equipment and technology vendors are often able and willing to provide assistance in support of management decision making. The use of the vendor as a consultant may be both beneficial and necessary. A vendor should know their product better than anyone else. If the technology is unique, the vendor may be the only source of information. Management should never forget that the vendor's goal is to sell their products and services. Whenever possible, information should be sought from multiple vendors. In this way, management will hear the pros and cons of the alternatives and be better positioned to select the best product. See Chapter 12 for a related risk management example. When large expenditures are involved, use of an independent consultant who will not benefit directly from the purchase may be the best strategy. The use of an internal product selection team may be considered if the use of an independent consultant is not possible or the purchase will affect multiple work areas. The use of a product selection team will improve the odds that all of the important questions are asked and answered.

Operations Management

Consulting support can be found for every aspect of the management role. Table 13.1 lists 12 key areas related to business operations and practice management. The listed areas are really broad categories covering hundreds of highly specialized consulting services. In fact, the entire operations management function of a health care company can be purchased as a consulting or contracted service. When this occurs, the responsibility for managing the consultation process falls to the owner or governing body. The use of consultants in the role of interim management may be considered for several reasons. First, the departure of key leaders may have left a critical void that cannot be left unfilled while new leaders are sought. Second, the owner and/or governing body may have identified the need for expertise which existing leadership does not possess. Finally, interim management may be brought in as a change agent to set a new direction for the organization.

Short of an interim management role, external consultants offer services that may be used to improve operations at all levels of the organization. Professional consultants have the opportunity to experience first hand the approaches used in many organizations. This first-hand knowledge along with the right experience places the professional consultant in a unique position to help management improve performance. For example, a physical therapy manager may recognize that both the costs per visit and number of visits per outpatient need to be reduced to stay competitive in a managed care market. Both support and clinical practices will need to change. A consultant may be beneficial to assess current practices, help set performance benchmarks, suggest opportunities for change and/or facilitate a team improvement process. If and how a consultant might be used is dependent on the situation and the people involved.

WHEN AND WHEN NOT TO USE A CONSULTANT

Managers should consider the use of consultants for a variety of reasons. The engagement of an external consultant represents an investment of company resources and, as such, should add value to the organization.

Ask The Right Questions

When confronted with a performance problem or an opportunity for improved performance, the following questions may help determine the need for and benefit of using an outside consultant.

1. Is there a need to take action?
   a. Will inaction increase the risk of a decline in performance?
   b. Will action offer the opportunity to improve performance?
   c. Do/will others assess the need for action the way I do?
   d. Is the situation time sensitive?
2. Has the situation been reviewed in the past?
   a. Was action taken?
   b. Was the action successful?
   d. If yes, has the situation changed?
   e. If no, why not?
3. Do I have the ability to take action?
   a. Do I have the knowledge to take action?
   b. Do I have the skill to do the needed work?
   c. Will others perceive my abilities the way I do?
4. Is it within the scope of my position to act?
   a. If yes, do I have the authority to take action?
   b. If no, do I have the credibility to convince others to act?
5. Do I have the resources to take action?
   a. Time?
   b. Information?
   c. Money?
6. Will my actions be supported by others?
   a. Subordinates?
   b. Superiors?
   c. Peers?
   d. Customers?

7. Does the organization have the resources to act?
   a. Internal expertise?
   b. Information?
   c. Equipment?
   d. Time?
   e. Funds to hire a consultant?
   f. Funds to support the solution?

When considering the use of an external consultant, the need to act is the obvious starting point. The use of any consultant should be triggered by an opportunity to improve company performance. Either the risk of declining performance or the opportunity to improve performance are reasons to take action. The degree of risk, the value of the opportunity and the urgency of a situation should dictate the resources management invests to improve a specific situation. When possible, the degree of risk or the potential benefit should be quantified. When this is not possible, the assessment of others may be the best benchmark.

The situational assessment should also look at past corrective actions. It is not unusual for a company to have repetitive or cyclic performance problems. Often, these problems have been addressed over time. If so, the history of past corrective actions, successful and unsuccessful, should be reviewed. It is possible that the true cause of the problem was missed in earlier reviews.

A manager must also assess his or her ability and authority to address identified problems. Does the manager and work group have the knowledge, skill and resources necessary to do the work required? Do they have the authority to make changes? Will others perceive their abilities and authority the same way? Will the solutions of the manager be supported by others in the organization? Use of an external consultant should be considered when:

- A manager perceives that the degree of risk is high. Is there is a significant, situational time-pressure to act?
- The company lacks internal resources with the skill or experience needed to lead the improvement effort and/or,
- The perception of other internal parties is significantly different from that of the manager.
- For repetitive problems, an external consultant may be able to look at the situation from a fresh and objective point of view.

SUPPORTING THE CONSULTATION PROCESS

Good solutions may be ineffective if others fail to cooperate. Lack of cooperation is often the outcome if people do not trust the judgment of the problem solver(s). Lack of cooperation can also occur if the problem solver lacks the organizational authority to make the desired changes. Under either of these circumstances, the use of external consultants may facilitate a problem solving and performance-improvement process. The simple fact that an individual is recognized by the organization as an expert worthy of hire may establish a consultant's credibility. In addition, the expenditure of resources for a consultant signals that a company is serious and has a commitment to evaluate some situation and/or make changes. The credibility and authority implicit in the engagement of a consultant will often garner support for the performance improvement process when other efforts could not.

HOW TO SELECT A CONSULTANT

To begin the consultant selection process, management needs to have three things in place.

1. Clearly stated goals and objectives for the engagement.
2. Ground rules regarding the role of the outside consultant within the organization and for getting the job done (2).
3. Objective consultant selection criteria.

With these elements in place, management is ready to begin the search for the right consultant.

The Goals And Objectives Of The Engagement

The goals and objectives for the engagement are used to set the performance expectations against which the success of the engagement will be evaluated. The company has the right to expect added value from consulting services. The consultant needs to understand what is expected to propose an effective plan and price for the desired consultation. Goals and objectives for any proposed consultation should be stated in a written form understood and agreed to by both the company and the consultant.

Ground Rules

It is important to establish ground rules for bringing outsiders into an organization (2). Ground rules are used to establish how the consultant(s) and members of the organization will work together. Such things as decision-making authority, reporting relationships, reporting schedules, lines of communication, interactions with staff, use of space, equipment and facilities and managing variances from the agreed upon plan are some things that need advanced agreement to ensure a smooth and effective consultation process.

Selection Criteria

Selection criteria should be established before the search for the best consultant. Selection criteria may include many factors such as:

* Consultant education, skill and experience
* Availability of consultant
* Accessibility of the consultant
* Proposed time frames to start and finish the engagement
* Consultant proposed action plans
* Cost of services
* Quality of consultant proposed action plans
* Fit with the organization
* References
* Track record

Using the engagement goals and objectives as a guide, application of selection criteria will help management find the consultant who can best meet the organization's needs. When multiple choices are available, objective criteria can be used to make the final selection. When multiple people are involved in the selection process, selection criteria can be used to minimize any potential conflicts.

The Request For Proposal (RFP)

The engagement goals and objectives, ground rules, consultant qualifications, supporting information and other requirements can be presented in a written request for proposal (RFP). The RFP can then be sent to potential consultants. A consultant, if interested, would submit a written response in the form of a proposal. The RFP is used as a guide for proposal development. The quality of a consultant's proposal is highly dependent on a well written RFP. To get the best outcome, a RFP should include all relevant information and provide complete instructions for completion of the requested proposal. The RFP can define the proposal format and content requirements.

Ideally, a company will receive several quality proposals from which to select the best consultant. The field of candidates can be narrowed based on the submitted proposals. Candidates can also be asked to meet with key company representatives to present their proposals and/or participate in an interview process. Consultants will generally have to incur the cost of proposal development and participation in an interview process. Their willingness to participate in this process may be based on the monetary value of the consulting engagement in relation to the cost of getting the job. The proposal and, potentially, an interview, are tools to be used to select the consultant who best fits the preestablished selection criteria.

Occasionally, there may be only one consultant able to meet a company's needs. This being the case, the process may be more focused. Goals, objectives and ground rules will still be needed. Selection criteria, as such, may not be needed. However, not all consulting engagements proceed as planned. Not all consultants perform as promised. To protect against unforeseen problems, a written statement of the consultant's qualifications and specifics of the engagement should still be developed.

General Guidelines

Locating and selecting a consultant is not an easy task. It takes time and effort. The following guidelines may help make the process easier and more successful.

1. Have clear and quantifiable performance expectations. If you do not know what you want, how will a consultant?

2. Do not feel obligated to use a familiar consultant for a specific engagement. Match each engagement with the right consultant. That's one of the best things about using a consultant: when the engagement is over, so is the obligation.
3. Take nothing for granted. Whenever possible, check everything for accuracy. For example, if response time to company calls needs to be 30 minutes or less, make sure that is what the consultant has done in the past. If not, what will change so it can be done in the future?
4. Do not be afraid to ask about qualifications. Ask for and use references. If you are not satisfied that you are getting a good picture, ask for more references. We like to ask for an expanded client list. If that is not available, ask for references from customers who had problems.
5. Do not be afraid to ask about cost. Make sure that the extent of your obligations, the type, terms and amount of charges are clearly defined in writing. Make sure allowable living and travel expenses are defined. Negotiate for the best deal possible. Identify in advance under which circumstances the financial terms may be extended or renegotiated.
6. Make sure that the company's strategic plan and the consultant's plan are integrated.
7. Include as many stakeholders as possible in the selection process to get the internal support required.

THE CONSULTATION AGREEMENT

When a formal arrangement is made for consultation services, there should be a written agreement between the company and the consultant. The agreement should describe the terms and conditions under which the engagement will occur. The written agreement should describe and/or define the following items.

- Involved parties
- Relationship of the parties
- Goals and objectives of the engagement
- Responsibilities of each party
- Joint responsibilities
- Agreed upon performance requirements
- Confidentiality requirements
- Conflict of interest, non-hire or non-compete terms
- Insurance coverage requirements, including general and professional liability
- Limits on liability and indemnification provisions
- Amount, terms and conditions for compensation
- Terms covering nonperformance
- Conditions for termination before the end of the agreement
- Conditions and terms for dispute arbitration

In addition, the agreement should meet all of the requirements of qualified legal counsel. We advise a review by legal counsel whenever a company enters into a legally binding arrangement. Be aware that legally binding agreements do not have to say contract at the top of the page. Letters of agreement and verbal agreements may also be legally binding. When entering into any agreement with any outside party, be cautious and make sure to get legal advice when it is needed.

THE POTENTIAL FOR INTERNAL CONTROVERSY AND RESISTANCE

The use of an outside consultant will sometimes create controversy within a company. The role of a consultant is to assess a situation and give advice. That means they must evaluate performance of at least some aspect of the organization. In doing so, the consultant has to evaluate the work of some of the company's management and employees. If the consultant is engaged by someone other than the manager(s) and work group(s) being reviewed, the situation can be very threatening. Affected members of the organization may fear that the consultant's findings will jeopardize their credibility or even their job. In fact, their concerns may be valid in some cases. Under these circumstances, the need for and work of a consultant may be challenged on several points. For example:

1. The need to take action
2. The type of action needed
2. The need to use an external consultant
3. The selection process
4. The value of the consultants findings and recommendations

In our experience, the willingness of staff to accept the role of the consultant is the single most important indicator of the consulting engagement's success. Management can influence the success of any consulting engagement through the inclusion of affected staff in the consultation process.

SUMMARY

As the complexities of health care management continue to increase, so will the demand for expert advice. Experts may be found within a company. When available, managers should welcome their assistance and support. When needed expertise is not available, managers may need to look outside of the organization. Several sources for professional advice are available to the health care manager. Professional organizations, such as the American Physical Therapy Association and its state affiliates, can provide both resources and referrals to other experts. Professional colleagues offer another source for advice. Their experience may be just what is needed. When the situation is more involved and time consuming, the manager may wish to use the services of a professional consultant or consulting firm.

Professional consultants are a great resource for companies of all sizes. They may be used on an ongoing basis or for a single, time-limited engagement. Consultants should be used as a management tool. They help managers meet their performance expectations. However, the use of consultants does not limit the responsibility of the manager. Management remains accountable for performance of the organization and the consultant.

There are consulting services available to meet almost any management need. The use of outside consultants, like any other expenditure of resources, should be approached from a cost-benefit perspective. The need for and goals of consulting services should be defined. Armed with a knowledge of what is needed and objective selection criteria, consultants should be sought who can add value to the organization.

Professional consultants can be located through many sources but referral from satisfied customers is a common method. For those so inclined, there is an increasing amount of information about consulting and consultants on the Internet. When in need of a consultant, never be afraid to shop around.

The concepts presented in this, and other Chapters, may be explored more fully through the use of a continuous case study, a role play, presented in Appendix A. The role play has been designed to demonstrate how management concepts may impact the clinical setting on a daily basis. The intent of the role play is to provoke thought and to build a connection between theory and practice of physical therapy in today's health care environment.

REFERENCES

1. Macmillian Contemporary Dictionary. New York, NY:Macmillian Publishing Co.,1979:217.

2. Meyeroff WJ, Meyeroff RE. Consultants or contractors? How to find the right help. info CARE 1997; Jul/Aug:66–68.

3. Mintzberg H. The Structuring of Organizations. Englewood Cliffs, NJ:Prentice-Hall, 1979:2,

4. Weltman B. The Big Idea Book For New Business Owners. New York, NY:Macmillian Spectrum, 1997.

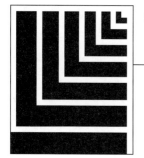

14

ENTREPRENEURSHIP: OWNERSHIP AND PRIVATE PRACTICE PHYSICAL THERAPY

DONALD OLSEN, MMSc, EdD, PT, OCS

PREVIEW

Many physical therapists graduate only to find that they have not been prepared by their ba-sic education to face the complexities of plan-ning and operating their own business (1). Much service business management material has already been well covered in preceding chapters of this text. Many of the key business concepts will be integrated throughout this chapter as they apply specifically to a small physical therapy practice owned by a physical therapist.

This chapter provides an overview of the planning process necessary to begin a physical therapy private practice. There are two main focuses of this chapter: first, on the characteristics of entrepreneurs and the opportunities and threats associated with ownership of a physical therapy practice; second, practical application of selected business principles and procedures to the entrepreneurial physical therapy environment.

KEY WORDS

Business plan: formatted explanation of the steps that will be taken to meet the objective of starting and running a business.

Entrepreneur: one who undertakes to start and conduct an enterprise or business, assuming full control and risk with the intent of making a profit.

Goal: statement of what is to be accomplished. The target toward which effort is directed.

Network: group of health care providers joining together under a common structure to better accomplish common goals such as negotiating contracts with managed care organizations.

Physical Therapist in Independent Practice (PTIP): according to the Health Care Financing Administration (HCFA), a PTIP is a physical therapist who (a) renders services on his or her own, free of the administrative and professional control of an employer; (b) treats his/her own pa-

tients; (c) collects a fee or other compensation for services rendered; (d) maintains at their own expense an office or office space and the necessary equipment to provide an adequate program of physical therapy (2).

Planning: forming a scheme or method of doing or an arrangement of means or steps for the attainment of a goal.

Private practice: providing services in an environment in which the practice owner(s) has/have taken the financial risk to develop the practice for which they have managerial responsibilities.

Private practitioner: a health care professional who has ownership in a private practice.

Self-Employed: working for oneself rather than being employed to work for someone else. A business owner is self-employed.

INTRODUCTION

Physical therapists have been described as bright and dedicated professionals who have endured the rigors of an intense formal education and clinical internships inspired by a desire to serve mankind by treating their injuries and diseases (3). Honorable intentions notwithstanding, physical therapy practice is a business. Therapists with an entrepreneurial spirit must consider it as such to survive financially.

ENTREPRENEURIAL CHARACTERISTICS

"Entrepreneurs are the aggressive catalysts for change in today's world of business" (4). Entre-

preneurs are often independent thinkers who dare to be different and assume the risks of creating new products and services. Given the changing environment of health care and the growth of the managed care payment system, physical therapists are being challenged to alter service delivery models to meet the needs of their patients while remaining financially viable. Private practice owners often have the opportunity to lead the way to new delivery models because they can respond to changing needs quickly.

While meeting the needs of patients is the core element of any physical therapy practice, developing and managing an environment within which a practice can function successfully requires significant organization of efforts. These organizational efforts are in addition to providing direct clinical care to patients. This wider scope of activity involvement extends to the salaried staff members who work in a private practice. Because there are fewer staff members and less access to specialized support personnel, e.g., marketing, therapists employed in private practice settings are likely to be involved in non-patient care activities such as developing new services, marketing and budgeting. These experiences increase staff members' breadth of knowledge. It may even lead them to managerial positions or practice ownership.

What it Takes

Every professional, regardless of their employment status, may at some time think about being his or her own boss. With or without the aspiration to be a business owner, having knowledge of the principles of management, marketing and finance is useful in many employment settings as well as in life outside the work place. Management principles have general applicability in the many roles we play as family members, community leaders and business owners. In addition to this type of knowledge, an entrepreneurial therapist must be willing to take some financial risks, have stamina to work long hours and be committed to being self-employed. As will be discussed in the next section, in return for hard work, there are financial and other rewards to be gained.

Tangible and Intangible Benefits

Financial

In return for taking the risk of losing money, owners have the potential to receive profit from operations. This profit may be taken in addition to a salary for his or her efforts. Based on gross earned income comparisons, physical therapists who are self-employed on a full time basis earn approximately twice as much as their full-time salaried colleagues (1,5).

Self-Expression

Private practice may take place in a variety of clinical settings and operate under legal structures ranging from solo practitioner to corporate practice with several shareholders (see Chapter

6) and many sites. See legal structures in Chapter 6 for the complete spectrum of types of arrangements one may consider when starting a private practice. Physical therapists who are owners of private practices typically seek autonomy and control over their professional practice. The wide variety of situations encompassed by the term "private practice" offers diverse opportunities for increasing numbers of physical therapists who want to gain professional independence. The percentage of American Physical Therapy Association (APTA) active members estimated to be working full-time and self-employed rose from 15.8% in 1987 to 17.0 % in 1993 (5). A more recent report indicates that the percentage of physical therapists in private practice has risen slightly (6).

Opportunities to Lead

Leadership, as discussed in Chapter 4, is often a compromise driven by a manager's leadership style, the situation and the characteristics of the personnel involved. Ownership of a private practice offers the owner the opportunity to develop a leadership style appropriate to their unique mix of circumstances and staff members. Ownership is an opportunity to become a leader of a staff. As a leader, the owner must facilitate interrelationships between people, identify opportunities that will benefit the practice and make decisions regarding these opportunities so the practice is advanced in some way (7). Owner-leaders are in a position to develop and enhance their leadership skills, their ability to apply business principles and their clinical skills in a unique way to promote the delivery of quality physical therapy services.

Community Contribution

A successful health care manager supports activities that increase the influence of their organization with the local community. The goal is to assure community involvement and support for the organization (7). Accordingly, the private practice physical therapist has the opportunity to be involved in efforts that address community health problems. This might be accomplished by being involved in community service organizations or working with community leaders to provide needed services. Common examples of this type of community involvement are scoliosis and posture screening clinics, providing pro bono care at athletic events, giving presentations at high school career days, and speaking to senior citizen and business-oriented groups. These activities provide support to the community while promoting the physical therapy practice.

CONTRIBUTIONS OF SMALL BUSINESSES

Many private physical therapy practices fall into the category of small businesses that employ under 20 people (8). Small businesses contribute to communities in several ways. First, they account for most of the new jobs created in this country. Second, small firms are likely to develop new ideas, test new products and services, and try new methods of doing business to get a foothold in a market and to grow. Regardless of size, to be profitable and successful, a business must provide something customers value and deliver it efficiently (see Chapter 3). The benefits attributed to small businesses are easily translatable to the private physical therapy practice environment.

Small businesses offer opportunities for potential innovations in management, service delivery, product development and other areas. The more people are free to innovate and profit from their efforts, the more likely innovations will occur. Successful innovations will improve the performance and profitability of a business. Successful innovations help a business become more competitive in retaining or increasing its market share. Innovation has the potential to improve the physical therapy service delivery process, increasing the value a private practice offers to its customers, e.g., effectiveness and efficiency.

Independent practices are important for several additional reasons. A private practice setting can offer cost-effective competition at a time when cost containment is the watchword. Costs may be kept down by offering incentives to employees for increased productivity and bringing in new customers, locating in moderate cost areas and employing staff part-time rather than full time. The independent practitioner has autonomy in his or her business. He or she is relatively

free to make clinical decisions based on professional judgment without the pressure of considering what is best for the parent company. However, the pressure is more personal, e.g., to meet payroll each month. Employees are dependent on the owner for their income.

The private practice owner has the freedom to make changes quickly without having to deal with multiple levels of managers. The pressure to make the right decision is again personal. Making the right decision can keep the business profitable. Make the wrong decision and employees may have to be let go.

The opportunities that have been available to the independent physical therapy practitioners of the past continue in new forms. As might be expected, challenges and threats to the independent practice of physical therapy have also evolved.

THREATS TO PRIVATE PRACTICE PHYSICAL THERAPY

Few Women

The most comprehensive demographic information about physical therapists comes from APTA studies. In 1992, the APTA reported that women comprised 74% of APTA membership (5). APTA also gathers demographic information about the employment status of its members. One category of employment is full-time self-employed, which includes individuals who work in private physical therapy practices. In the full-time self-employed category, men outnumber women three to one (1,5). A similar disparity is reflected in current membership statistics of the Private Practice Section of the APTA.

The question of why there are mostly men in private practice when women are the majority in the profession of physical therapy has received some recent attention. The main difficulties encountered by women starting a private practice are little different from the difficulties women face when starting any business (1). Some of the difficulties expressed by women physical therapists in private practice are (1):

- Making contacts with referral sources
- Obtaining financing
- Becoming part of local business organizations

- Networking opportunities
- Mentoring and role models
- Business knowledge
- Family commitments

The general experience of women who raise such issues as listed above is that it is more difficult for women to start a private practice because women may be perceived differently in business and banking than men (1). This perceived difference may hinder acceptance within some business groups. This can result in limiting the number of beneficial business contacts that can be made. With limited contacts, networking and mentoring opportunities may not materialize.

For private practice to grow and continue to be a viable form of delivery of physical therapy services these types of professional growth experiences must be facilitated. If they are not facilitated, the majority of physical therapists who are women may continue to discount private practice as a career path. The potential threat to private practice is the limited numbers of people contributing their talents to the development of innovative ways to deliver quality physical therapy services. In the changing health care environment, the more talented people there are involved in problem solving, the more likely problems will be solved and desirable outcomes achieved.

Large Versus Small Private Practice

Large national and regional corporations can offer many benefits that a small local practice owner may not be able to afford. These benefits include improved access to financial resources and a variety of internal support services such as legal staff, training and development personnel and technical expertise in many areas from computer networking to acquisition specialists. Acquisition specialists are individuals who identify other businesses worth purchasing.

In recent years, there has been a notable decline in the number of newly opened and surviving independently owned physical therapy practices. There are several reasons for this decline, which include retirements, closures, consolidations, and acquisitions by large national and regional corporations. We believe that this latter ac-

tivity has and will likely have the greatest negative impact on small, local, private practice owners. When large corporations purchase and absorb small locally owned physical therapy practices, fewer physical therapy service options are available to customers. Ultimately, large national and regional corporations may control local private practice physical therapy markets. This limits competition.

The goal of national publicly traded corporations is to increase the value of their stock for stockholders. One strategy to accomplish this is to strive for market dominance, i.e., get all of the referrals in a geographical area, and make a sizable profit. The outlook for small, local private practice owners within corporate targeted areas is often mixed. If the practice is sold for a profit, that is good for the owner. However, it is also possible that the value of the practice declines due to loss of market share.

Increasing Numbers of Physicians

There are many physicians who are self-employed private practice owners. They have their own offices and serve patients who are covered by many types of insurance plans. However, an oversupply of some types of physicians in some geographic areas has been reported (9). The result is an increasing competition for patients. Physicians are striving to retain market share of patients as well as entering into new markets to increase the numbers of patients they serve and to maintain or increase their income level.

Physical therapy has long been an added service some physicians have offered to their patients. This has been done under numerous types of arrangements ranging from the utilization of on-the-job trained staff providing care in their office to employing physical therapists to owning physical therapy services. One potential incentive for a physician to offer physical therapy services in which they have an ownership interest is to use the service to increase their revenue. This is a potential conflict of interest issue: physician financial benefit versus the patient's best interest.

The APTA has long been in opposition to arrangements in which professional autonomy may be limited and over utilization of physical therapy services occur (10). This can occur if a physician orders, and a physical therapist administers, unnecessary physical therapy services. For patients in federally subsidized programs such as Medicare and Medicaid, the federal government has passed protective legislation (Stark I, II) to limit physician involvement in many services, including physical therapy services (11).

Some physicians, under various guises, continue to promote referrals for physical therapy services for their own self-interest. The negative impact of such arrangements on private practice physical therapists is the loss of market share controlled by these physicians. The adage here is that he or she who has the referral wins. In these situations, the winner is not the local physical therapist practice owner. This situation is one example of why private practice physical therapists need to be politically aware and active.

Balancing Demands

In every facet of life, setting goals is important. With a goal in mind, a plan to achieve the goal can be established. However, the pursuit of goals can become ends in themselves. This can lead to the exclusion of wider interests and other responsibilities such as those to family members, the community and to professional associations. The number of hours full-time self-employed physical therapists work in a week is typically greater than the average number of hours worked by salaried physical therapists (5). Eighteen-hour days are not uncommon in the life of a new private practice owner (1). As pointed out in Chapter 2, personal values need to be understood because they are expressed in professional life. Values guide the many decisions that confront health care practitioners whether owner or employee. With the additional responsibility of managing a practice that one depends on for their livelihood, consideration of morality, professional ethics and personal values is all the more important. It is important to balance pursuit of all life goals and to do so in ways that reflect respect for moral and ethical principles.

Ideally, for the continued viability of private practice physical therapy, what is needed are:

- Capable clinicians;
- Who are technically skilled;
- Interested in management and skilled in applying business principles to deliver quality care efficiently;
- Able to manage multiple life roles;
- And adhere to professional ethical precepts

Technical skill comes from practice, continuing education, mentorship relationships as well as other formal and informal sources. Nominally, the private practice manager-owner requires knowledge of marketing, managing people, fiscal management, controlling growth, and, possibly, how to develop and participate in a network comprised of other physical therapists in private practice. The personal qualities of creativity, vision, responsibility, wisdom, enthusiasm, flexibility, perseverance and physical endurance complement good clinical and business skills. Physical therapists with entrepreneurial interests, who have the above characteristics and skills, are needed for private practice of physical therapy to survive and thrive in the future (12).

GETTING STARTED

Two attributes are needed to start a private practice. The first is a strong desire to be in control of one's future. The second is a clear vision of this future. Many direct and indirect learning experiences are available to stimulate both self-determination and vision. See Chapter 15 regarding developing a vision of the future.

Direct Experience

An invaluable source of stimulation can come from direct experience. Working in a private physical therapy practice gives a first hand picture of all aspects of private practice and self-employment. Being mentored by someone in this environment provides an additional opportunity from which to grow (see Chapter 4).

Other Experiences

There are additional experiences that can stimulate a desire for self-direction and help formulate a personal vision of the future. Some of these learning experiences are:

- Discussions with owners of private practices and consultants (see Chapter 13)
- Reading professional journals and books from many fields, materials of the APTA and the Private Practice Section of the APTA
- Consulting community business organizations such as the Chamber of Commerce and the Better Business Bureau
- Attending meetings of national associations, including the APTA and the National Foundation for Women Business Owners
- Soliciting advice from governmental sources like the Small Business Administration and Service Corps of Retired Executives (SCORE)
- Acquiring further education through continuing education courses or for credit courses offered by educational institutions
- Internet resources

In general, the above experiences provide a foundation to be used to assess personal strengths and weaknesses, set reasonable expectations, identify when and what assistance is needed and develop an organized planning process to make decisions and carry out actions.

Planning is a Must

Planning is an important aspect in many life roles. For example, planning vacations, social events, meeting personal financial goals, purchasing or building a home, changing jobs or moving are all important aspects. Planning for the start-up, operation and eventual disposition of a physical therapy practice will likely improve the probability that a physical therapist will be successful as a business owner.

In today's rapidly changing health care environment that includes high levels of uncertainty and strong competition for market share (see Chapters 1, 6), the process of starting a physical therapy practice demands a shift from informal planning to formal planning. Formal planning fosters strategic thinking (review Chapter 6) while synthesizing intuition and creativity into the future vision of the business (4). A good plan enhances the odds for success and is a sign of visionary management. While the development of a business plan is advisable, not everyone does it. In a recent survey of sports medicine centers, 44% of which physical therapists had some form of ownership interest, just over two-thirds had written business plans (8).

Historical records make it clear that planning is a necessity for survival (13). Yet, as thorough as a planning process may be, it is often difficult to control the environment and the actions of others. As noted in Chapters 1, 3 and 6, markets and competitors are constantly changing. For this reason, plans need to be dynamic and estimates of what is to be done flexible. Continual research and innovation are required to accommodate the demands of a changing business environment. The realization that the most diligently constructed plans are imperfect (14) encourages the adaptation of a continuous planning process. Doing so rewards planners with minimal surprises in market conditions and competitors' strategies.

Know Yourself: Self-Assessment

Education, personal traits and experience interact to give each of us an individualized perspective or frame of reference when encountering life's personal and professional tasks. Self-assessment is useful to anyone considering starting any major project. The key purpose of self-assessment is to gain insight into personal strengths and weaknesses relative to the project under consideration. Self-assessment will help the entrepreneur identify personal assets and deficits that can impact on goal achievement.

Self-understanding can be gained by completion of selected self-assessment instruments. One self-assessment method is a checklist. Table 14.1 contains an example checklist of questions that the Federal Governments' Small Business Administration suggests potential entrepreneurs ask themselves (15).

The information gained from this checklist includes identification of essential strengths, weaknesses, tendencies, preferences and, at a basic level, values. The overall picture allows exploration of feelings, of comfort and discomfort, and other feelings about moving forward to start a business. Identified weaknesses should be of particular interest. Are there personality characteristics that may interfere with the ability to make certain decisions like firing an employee? By learning of these potential limitations, consideration can be given to solutions. Three example solutions to consider are getting further relevant education, hiring an em-

TABLE 14.1

Example Self-Assessment Check List For A Prospective Entrepreneur

QUESTIONS	YES	NO	NOTES
		(CIRCLE)	
BEFORE YOU START:			
1. Have you thought about why you want to own your own business?	Y	N	
2. Are you the kind of person who can get a business started and make it go?	Y	N	
3. Do you want to do this badly enough to keep working long hours without knowledge of how much money you will end up with?	Y	N	
4. Have you worked in a business like you have in mind?	Y	N	
5. Have you worked for someone as a manager?	Y	N	
6. Do you have any business training?	Y	N	
7. Do you know how much money you will need to start the business?	Y	N	
8. Do you know how much money you have to invest and where you will obtain more if needed?	Y	N	
9. Do you know what annual net income to expect from the business?	Y	N	
10. Do other businesses like the one you have in mind do well in your community?	Y	N	
11. Is another business like the one you have in mind needed in your area?	Y	N	
PERSONAL TRAITS			
12. Are you a self-starter?	Y	N	
13. Do you enjoy interacting with other people?	Y	N	
14. Can you lead others?	Y	N	
15. Can you take responsibility?	Y	N	
16. Are you a good organizer?	Y	N	
17. Are you a hard worker?	Y	N	
18. Can you make decisions?	Y	N	
19. Can people trust you?	Y	N	
20. Can you stick with a project even in rough times?	Y	N	
21. Are you healthy enough to regularly work long hours?	Y	N	
WEAKNESSES			
22. Have you had any difficulties in areas that you believe can have an impact on your starting a business?	Y	N	
23. Do you anticipate any difficulties?	Y	N	
24. Do you have a plan to address each area identified above?	Y	N	

Adopted from the Small Business Administration US Government Office of Business Development. Checklist for going into business form #2016. Washington, DC: Author, 1984.

ployee or acquiring a partner or consultant with the skills or personality characteristics you may lack. These efforts allow supplementing natural personal strengths.

Philosophy and Values

Note that values were touched upon in the questionnaire. Each individual should understand and be comfortable with their personal and professional philosophy and values. That is to say, personal and professional philosophy and values should be harmonious. As suggested in Chapter 2, harmony between values and behaviors facilitates psychological comfort.

Goals

A useful conceptualization of goals states that "goals are the destinations and action plans (objectives) are the road maps to get there" (16). Goals are needed for direction and balance between life roles. This, however, is rarely done. Less than 3% of Americans surveyed in 1994 reported having written long-range goals (17).

Goals, to be achieved, have to be defined. Smith (17) provides five criteria for developing goals. Goals should be:

1. Specific
2. Measurable

3. Action-oriented
4. Realistic
5. And time bound

Goals and action plans need to be periodically reviewed and updated. Setting goals in all facets of life will help achieve a balance in the use of energy and time. Six major life goals have been defined as (16, 17):

1. Personal well-being goals: these include physical and mental health which are reasonable prerequisites to achieving other goals.
2. Affiliation goals: families, partners, personal friends.
3. Work group goals: professional associations, community groups, and work related friends
4. Community goals: relationships with fellow community members.
5. Environmental goals: preservation of natural resources, green areas and recreational areas.
6. Spiritual goals: belief in a higher power than mankind.

The preceding discussion has presented a frame of reference for dealing with the next important topic, the business plan. The business plan outline that follows could easily have been presented without a discussion of values and ethics. However, self-understanding will help to focus planning in a direction to which the private practitioner can fully commit his or her time, talent and energy over time.

BUSINESS PLAN: "FAILING TO PLAN IS PLANNING TO FAIL" (18)

To channel dreams into actions, a plan that brings the dream closer to reality is required (13). In business, such a plan is called a business plan. An analogy useful in describing a business plan is planning for a trip. The trip plan should include the destination, method of travel, lodging, cost and source of the funds for the trip. One is likely to be disappointed should they show up at the airport without a reservation or ticket, or at the destination without having made arrangements for accommodations, or without having brought funds to pay expenses. Unfortunately, many individuals spend more time researching a trip than researching a business venture. Information relating to a trip is often found in the itinerary. A business plan should accomplish the same goal as a trip itinerary. The business planning process creates a game plan and a purpose. As discussed in Chapter 6, the plan determines the strategic directions, goals and actions to be taken.

Business plans need to be constructed by the originator of the idea because the planning process can be a form of self-education in all aspects of the business. It assists in realistically and objectively putting the pieces of the business puzzle together. Stern (19) offers 10 reasons to develop a written business plan:

1. It provides an opportunity to take a hard look at the business idea and determine how the idea will progress to reality.
2. It bridges the gap between idea and reality for a business.
3. It helps identify problems and encourages thinking about solutions.
4. It forms a path for management to follow in the early months of operation while serving as a foundation on which to build.
5. It allows performance to be compared to projections and strategies adjusted as the business progresses.
6. It facilitates discussion with associates and family members about what the goals are and how they might be reached.
7. It establishes credibility with investors and contributes to obtaining financial support. This provides lenders with details of the operations and how the loan will impact the firms' goals and improve worth of the company.
8. It helps to avoid errors by identifying problems ahead of time so they may be avoided.
9. It helps to develop a time line for implementation.
10. It acts as a self-assessment tool that evolves as the business progresses.

Once the plan is written, those who have an interest in the business may review it. In addition to the originator of the plan, it is likely to be reviewed by family members, friends, partners, consultants, investors, mentors, bankers and lawyers. Do not become anxious by the thought of having to plan for the future nor by having to defend and explain your plan. Both activities will help refine thinking and enhance the viability of the final product.

Process of Business Planning

Dream

Do not be intimidated by the idea of planning for your future as a physical therapist in private practice. "There's a mystique to the term business plan that makes it sound like you couldn't possibly do one without an MBA or two, but much of what makes up a bona-fide blueprint is probably already in your head" (19). Envision your future practice as if it was already operational and successful. The vision should include the environment, types of patients, staff, referral sources, marketing, image, owners roles, and how the practice will impact your life on a professional and personal level.

Talk and Listen

As part of the planning process, discuss the plans and financial needs with bankers, investors, advisors, partners, other physical therapists, physicians, family and friends. The insights, questions and advice gained from these sources will assist in forming your practice model. The future support of these individuals in the project may also be assessed. For example, if your spouse is planning on making a major purchase in the near future, and you intend to use the funds to finance the practice, this creates a potential problem that needs to be recognized and addressed early in the planning process.

Do Your Homework

Research the current and potential market for the type of physical therapy services you intend to provide. Chapter 3 contains an extensive contemporary overview of marketing principles applicable to health care businesses. A review of Chapter 3, particularly the sections on market orientation, pricing, market segmentation and niche markets, will provide the reader with information on how and what to research for their future physical therapy business.

Write

Reduce the plan to writing. Take the plan from informal notes to an organized document. This can be done by following the 12 steps suggested by Stein (19) which are listed below:

1. Start with whatever information you have at the moment. Even a partial plan in writing gives you a lead in the planning process.
2. Use software, a good book or consultants to help transfer ideas into words. However, the planner must do the work of planning himself or herself.

Software programs such as those by Microsoft for small businesses are available and may assist in compiling the information you gather. The library or local book store will provide resource materials to serve as a guide for your project.

3. Tackle the fun parts first. Write your values and mission statements (see Chapter 2). Pick a location and draw a plan for your office (see Chapter 9).
4. Use plain English in writing. Avoid technical terms that may confuse readers who are not physical therapists. Use references when possible and cite these in the plan.
5. Ask questions that need to be answered before implementing the project. Try to include answers to questions that others will ask when reading the plan. What is needed by others is a way to know if this plan will work. For example, what are the costs to establish and operate this practice? And, where will resources for the project be obtained?
6. Do a marketing plan (Chapter 3) for the initial start-up period of the practice through the first year of operation. Estimate the cost of marketing efforts for the first year.
7. Project cash flow for 3 years on a monthly basis (see Chapter 7). Remember to include a salary for the owner(s) along with staff while considering the lag in time between providing service, billing and collections. Also remember that there will be ongoing personal living expenses to meet in addition to the expenses of the business.
8. Project start-up expenses, including deposits, build out, equipment, supplies, marketing and salaries. Facilities-related information is covered in depth in Chapter 9.
9. Do a break-even analysis (see Chapters 7 and 8) to determine how many patients need to be treated in the practice to cover costs. Determine fees based on your research into reimbursement rates and your projected expenses (see Chapters 7 and 8).
10. Cut to the chase. Make informed estimates of numbers of referrals, patient visits, billing rates and collections.
11. Implement and follow the plan.
12. Continue to refine the plan as new information becomes available.

BUSINESS PLANNING FORMAT

Table 14.2 provides an outline of a process for implementing the 12-step business planning process listed above. This outline reflects the thoughts of several experts (i.e., 3, 4, 15, 18, 20) and the practical experiences of the current authors. The outline and accompanying discussions will guide the reader through the process of developing a concise and substantive business plan.

TABLE 14.2
Business Plan Outline

ELEMENTS	STATUS	NOTES

I. Cover Page
   A. Name of company and status
   B. Address
   C. Phone number
   D. Principal(s)
   E. Logo
   F. Submitted to (only if used for financing purposes)

II. Executive Summary
   A. Describe the business, location, legal status
   B. Mission
   C. Stage of development
   D. Services to be offered
   E. Target market
   F. Marketing strategy
   G. Competitors
   H. Operations and location
   I. Management and organization
   J. Financial information
   K. Long term goals
   L. Funds sought, uses and return on investment

III. Table of Contents

IV. The Business Description
   A. Describe the business (mission)
   B. Industry analysis (describe industry, current trends and opportunities, economic cycles, supply and demand data)
   C. Market analysis and target market (demographics of patients, describe all customers)
   D. Competition analysis (who and where, market distribution, position of competitors, opportunities and barriers to entry)
   E. Marketing plan and strategy (how will services be made known? What is unique to the proposed business?)
   F. Operations and location synopsis (how will the business be run? capacity, productivity, quality control, map, photos, construction plans for location)
   G. Organizational structure (board, advisors, consultants, principles, key employees, lines of authority, management style)
   H. Long term goals and exit plans (vision, what will happen to the business in the future?)

V. Financial Information
   A. Personal capital being applied (personal financial information, how much money is needed?, for what purposes?)
   B. Equipment list (vendors and costs)
   C. Break-even analysis
   D. Balance sheets (personal and business)
   E. Pro-forma cash-flow analysis (estimate of first year month by month and annually for years 1 and 3)
   F. For existing business: current audited financial statements, past 3 years tax returns (and other significant financial data)

VI. Supporting Information
   A. Resume(s)
   B. Letters of intent
   C. Letters of recommendation

continued

TABLE 14.2
Business Plan Outline (continued)

ELEMENTS	STATUS	NOTES
D. Contracts		
E. Job description(s)		
F. Special awards, achievements		
G. Portfolio (newspaper clippings, magazine and journal articles, on principles or type of business)		
H. Equipment photos		
I. Appendices (optional)		

Transmittal Letter

When using the business plan to secure financing, a letter should be enclosed with the business plan explaining why the plan is being sent and what the recipient is expected to do with the plan. The transmittal letter should include the following information:

- Purpose of the business
- Identity of the person requesting funds
- Amount and type of financing requested
- Amount of equity the owners will apply to the business
- The use of the funds
- When the funds will be needed
- Goals and market potential that can be achieved with the new funds
- Collateral available to secure the financing

Elements of a Business Plan

The business plan outlined in Table 14.2 has six major headings: cover letter, executive summary, table of contents, business description, financial information and supporting information. The discussion that follows explains each component of a business plan. Important related points are presented to relate the plan to both a new business and an existing one. To help the reader integrate various business plan concepts, a hypothetical practice example is used. The practice is *XYZ Physical Therapy, Inc.,* a small, local, physical therapy practice owned by a physical therapist. The business plan is being formulated for the purpose of obtaining funding to open a new practice location. The practice will be an outpatient clinic that treats primarily patients with orthopedic and sports related injuries.

Heading I: Cover Letter

The cover page should be neat, short and clear. The cover page includes the items noted under heading I of Table 14.2. There should be an individualized cover sheet for each of the different entities to which the plan is submitted.

Heading II: Executive Summary

After the cover page comes the executive summary. This summary provides an overview of the total business plan. The executive summary:

- Identifies the purpose of the business
- Describes the business and its uniqueness
- States the legal business structure (e.g., corporation, partnership, sole proprietorship)
- States goals
- Establishes time lines
- Identifies the market and competition
- Sets a strategy to approach the market
- Notes key managers and their skill and experience
- Describes financial needs and applications of funds
- Describes the payback time-line supported by earnings projections

Table 14.3 is the executive summary for the example business, *XYZ Physical Therapy, Inc.*

Heading III: Table of Contents

The table of contents is a list of the major areas of the plan and the page numbers where the information begins in the plan. It is organized in standard outline format, including various heading levels.

Heading IV: The Business Description

This very important part of the business plan has the purpose of clearly describing the busi-

TABLE 14.3
Example Executive Summary For *XYZ Therapy, Inc.*

XYZ Physical Therapy, Inc. is a Wisconsin-based corporation providing outpatient physical therapy services. The corporation's mission is to provide the highest possible quality prevention and rehabilitation services using expert, competent, caring, professional staff working as a team with referring physicians. The corporation's core values include integrity, honesty, respect, and courtesy combined with creativity and innovation. Guided by these values, we will strive to assist individuals to achieve their maximal potential physical and emotional well-being. Through efficient, cost-effective services, combined with participative, insightful leadership and strategic planning, we will shape an effective, growing and economically viable health care organization.

The corporation provides outpatient physical therapy services for athletes, workers and others who have been injured. We will specialize in orthopedic care and provide a one-on-one approach to treatment, and build a close relationship with referring physicians. We will also offer specialty services for spinal rehabilitation, knee rehabilitation, hand, upper extremity, and ankle/foot rehabilitation. Occupational therapy will also be offered at the clinic. Athletic training services will be offered at local schools.

Our target market includes persons living, working or attending schools within 5 miles of the clinic who are between 12 to 75 years of age who have musculoskeletal dysfunction and health insurance that will pay for services at our clinic.

Competition located within 5 miles of our proposed location includes four hospitals, seven medical clinics with physical therapy services, three other private physical therapy practices, five chiropractors offering rehabilitation, including physiotherapy services, and four physician-owned physical therapy locations. *XYZ Physical Therapy* will offer personalized attention, specialized care, flexible hours and marketing by the individual therapists to provide unique advantages over the competition.

Our marketing strategy will include establishing relationships with our referral sources through frequent personal contacts. These contacts will be used to emphasize what our services offer the referrer and his or her patients. To maintain these contacts, we will provide referral sources with personalized progress reports related to goals established for each patient. We will also provide athletic training services in the community. Advertising will include articles in local papers and print ads describing our services for common injuries suffered by our target population. We will also have a strong internal marketing approach in obtaining information from our patients, orienting them to the practice, assisting them with their insurance paper work and providing them caring, results-oriented professional services. We will belong to a local network of similar practices that negotiates contracts with local insurance carriers. Management will include one owner-operator physical therapist and one owner-operator occupational therapist. The owners have been in practice for over 5 years and have gained specialty certification in orthopedics and hand therapy, respectively. Together with an advisory board, including referring physicians, consultants and an excellent staff, the practice should have strong, involved leadership.

The business will be located at 655 Beal Street in Anytown, Wisconsin, in a medical professional building housing several medical specialists, including six orthopedists and three general practice physicians. The business plans to open on July 1 and will be open from 8:00AM to 6:00PM Monday through Friday. Staff will include two physical and one occupational therapists, a part-time certified athletic trainer, a secretary and an aide.

Long-term goals include expansion of the practice to include another site within 2 years and additional space within 1 year. Additional partners may be added and future mergers or sale of the practice may be considered within 10 years.

As a start-up operation, we expect to gross $200,000 in revenue the first 12 months with net revenue of $20,000 after expenses, which include an owners' salary and debt payback.

We are seeking a total of $124,000 for the start-up and the first 12 months of operations. The amounts and uses of these funds are: $43,000 in equipment leases, $30,000 in leasehold improvements, $21,000 for operations, and $30,000 invested by the owners to assist with operational expenses until sufficient funds are collected. These funds will be paid back over a 5-year period with interest on a monthly basis starting after 6 months. We feel with adequate funds, the strategic location, the management expertise, the strong local demand for physical therapy services, the aging physically active population, and a well-insured local population, the business will be assured of financial success and future growth.

---

ness in detail. Because of the need for details, this section has eight main components, which include: description (mission), industry analysis, market analysis, competition analysis, marketing plan, operations and location synopsis, structure, goals and exit (termination) plan. Each component is summarized below. Pertinent questions are asked at times to highlight the kind

of information that needs to be provided in each part of the business section of plan.

1. State the philosophy and mission (see Table 14.4) of the practice. Describe what objectives will be accomplished through the business.
2. Define the situation. Is it a start-up practice, an acquisition or an expansion?
3. Identify the owner. If there are multiple owners,

TABLE 14.4
Example Mission Statement for *XYZ Physical Therapy, Inc.*

The mission of *XYZ Physical Therapy, Inc.* is to provide patients the highest possible quality outpatient prevention and rehabilitation services using expert, competent, caring, professional staff working as a team with the referrer. Guided by the core values of integrity, honesty, respect and courtesy, combined with creativity and an innovative and holistic spirit, we will strive to assist individuals to achieve their maximal potential physical and emotional well-being. Through efficiently delivered cost effective services, combined with participative leadership and sound strategic planning, we will shape and effect a growing and economically viable health care organization.

explain how much of the business each will own, what each person will invest, and how and when they will be paid.

4. Describe the legal form of business structure, e.g., corporation, partnership or sole proprietorship.
5. Identify provider payment agreements that exist or will be pursued (e.g., Medicare). Explain if the practice will be making arrangements to contract with hospitals, nursing homes, medical clinics or physician offices. Describe any other types of arrangements that are in existence or anticipated.
6. Explain the benefits of services provided by the practice and why people will buy the services. List services and/or products the practice will offer and an explanation of how these services and/or products are unique (21). Example clinical programs for *XYZ Therapy, Inc.* might include:
    * Cardiac care
    * Fitness programs
    * Hand therapy
    * Industrial rehabilitation/work hardening
    * Pediatrics
    * Pool therapy
    * Spinal rehabilitation
    * Sports Physical Therapy
7. Describe the industry of physical therapy, current trends, and strategic opportunities that are present within the industry. Physical therapy is primarily a service industry and has enjoyed remarkable growth. Is the future growth pattern of physical therapy conducive to supporting new practices? Does regulation and certification impact the industry? Medicare, i.e., ($1500 per year per beneficiary) and other insurance limitations, need to be addressed. Typical referral sources for similar businesses should be identified. Are there industry standards for billings, markups, salaries and profit margins for com-

parison? Identify common barriers for entry into the industry. Address the question, Do you have to be a licensed physical therapist to own a physical therapy practice? If not, what impact does this have on the industry?

8. Market analysis focuses on customers. Who are the customers? Remember the broad concept of customers which may include physicians, patients, healthy individuals, employers, insurance companies, managed care organizations (MCOs), health maintenance organizations, as well as contracting groups. Describe the size of the market population and your expected market share. Demographic data of the target population(s) may be useful. Identify the population base, ages, income levels, large employers, transportation options, housing values and employment rates. Often, demographic information is available through local libraries, internet sources and Chambers of Commerce. For example, a market description might say the practice will target individuals ages 14 to 65 years who have health insurance coverage for physical therapy services and who live within a 5 mile radius of the proposed office site. More specific information on market analysis and targeting segments of the market is contained in Chapter 3.

   Identify physicians by medical specialties that are expected to refer patients to the clinic. In accord with the particular state practice act, consider dentists, chiropractors, podiatrists and others who can prescribe physical therapy as referral sources.

9. List all of the competitors in the local market. These competitors may include national and regional corporate chain practices, hospitals, satellite clinics, chiropractors, massage therapists, occupational therapists and physician owned clinics in which physical therapy is provided. Identify competitor's locations on a map and the distance from the proposed clinic location. Learn from meetings with competitors. Examine their strengths and weaknesses to support your claims of uniqueness and the need for your type of proposed services compared to the competition. See Chapter 3 for more detailed information on conducting an analysis of competitors and how to design a marketing plan and strategy.

10. The operations and location segment of the business plan describes how the business will be run and what is essential to success. This section also includes the description of the proposed clinic's location and physical layout.

   There are several important questions to consider regarding the operation of the business that need to be answered. What leadership style will management use? How will policies and procedures be developed and implemented? How much time will be allocated for managerial responsibilities in addition to patient care responsibilities?

Several questions need to be answered relating to the business' capacity to generate revenue, and include: What type of billing and collections system will be used? Who will handle billing, collections and do follow up work? What will the productivity standards be for patient care employees? Relate this standard to expected numbers of patients to be treated or units of service to be delivered.

11. The next set of questions relate to defining and measuring the quality of the services to be delivered. Several important questions to answer are:
    - What internal and external quality assurance measures will be used?
    - How often will assessments be carried out?
    - What will be done with the information?
    - What kind of follow-up will be done to improve quality?
    - For external assessments, who will be contacted to assess quality?
    - How will they be contacted?

    Chapter 11 offers suggestions that can be used to answer the preceding questions.

    The location synopsis identifies why the location was chosen and provides comparative information regarding competitors locations.

    In this section:
    - Describe the neighborhood, building and the office
    - Provide pictures of the building and office plans
    - Indicate location of major pieces of equipment
    - Compare and contrast the desired facilities to those of local competitors

    Further information on selecting a location, facility planning and space utilization is presented in Chapter 9.

12. The next part of the business description, structure, is very important. It is likely to receive close scrutiny. This scrutiny stems from the general belief that many small business failures are attributable to management weaknesses (4). To detail how the business will operate. Many of the ideas presented in Chapter 3, diversity, Chapter 4, engaging people, and Chapter 6, organizational structure, are used in this section.

    Describe the organization's structure, including how decisions will be made and how company policy will be established and implemented. An organizational chart may be included. Who will be on the board of directors and what will be the role of the board? Will there be a separate advisory board? Describe the management style that will be employed within the

practice. As evidence of a positive track record in managing a business, the organizational structure discussion should include a short personal history of all principles (the owner's). These histories should include:
- Related management experience, including duties and responsibilities with emphasis on those related to the proposed business
- Skills
- Salaries
- Resources the principal will make available to the business

Additional management related resources that will be used can also be noted. Examples of such resources are advisors, consultants (see Chapter 13), community associations, organizations and educational programs.

The final element of section IV deals with the future of the business. Included in the discussion are the long-term aspirations of the owner(s) and what will happen if the owner would go out of business.

Long-term goals may include expansion of space, adding partners, adding other locations, adding specialty programs and changing role of the owner, e.g., retirement or sale of the practice. The vision may express where the owner would like to see the practice in 5 or 10 years. The importance of having a vision of the future was discussed earlier in this chapter, as well as in Chapter 6. A strategy for formulating a vision of the future is presented in the next chapter.

The inclusion of considerations for terminating a business that may not yet exist is not out of context. Thinking about the disposition of a business is similar to what physical therapists do in clinical practice. They think about, and begin planning for, the patient's discharge early in the course of treatment. In business planning, there are several reasons to consider the termination of the business. An owner may retire or die. In a partnership or corporation, a partner or shareholder may wish to leave the business. The business may also be sold. Sale options include outright sale to another practitioner or corporation, selling to employees or partners, merging with another practice while maintaining ownership or liquidating (selling the equipment, fixtures and furniture).

An important consideration in the termination of a business is its value. The value of a practice is often based on referral sources and the ongoing relationship with these sources and contracts with insurance companies, home health agencies or other entities. Consultants can be used to evaluate and set a practices' market value. This is a necessary procedure for determining a price in a buy-sell agreement between partners and for establishing corporate stock value (3, 22–23). Identifying who will fix the market value should the practice ownership change is a foresightful inclusion in a business plan.

Heading V: Financial Information

If a business plan is being used for fund raising, there will be a financial information section that presents personal and business-related income and expenses. The basic purpose of providing such information is to describe how money will be applied and its effect on the business. An explanation of the use of funds includes how much will be spent on various start-up expenses as well as on initial operating costs. If money is borrowed, it is important to explain the effect these borrowed funds will have on making the practice successful.

1. The first information needed is a description of the owner's personal financial situation. A personal financial report includes a personal balance statement. See Chapter 7, Figure 7.1 for the format and contents. This statment shows how much capital owners will invest and how the capital will be used. Capital can come from many sources. The following list identifies typical sources of funds for small businesses (24):
   - Friends and relatives
   - Retirement funds
   - Home equity loan
   - Pre-paid consulting fees (contracts)
   - Delay payment to others 60 to 90 days
   - Lease equipment to others
   - Credit cards
   - Small Business Administration micro loan
   - Small Business Administration guaranteed bank loan
   - Basic bank loan
   - Sell uncollected accounts receivable
   - Venture capitalist
   - Invite shareholders or partners
   - Public stock offering
2. Financial information about the business is also needed. If the practice is already in operation, a current balance sheet for the practice will be needed. Consult Chapter 7, Figure 7.1, to review the contents of a balance sheet.

For a new business, an estimated revenue projection has to be developed. This is called a pro-forma cash-flow analysis. Pro-forma means before formation. The purpose of this analysis is to present the anticipated long-term financial picture of the practice. This involves estimating the anticipated revenues and expenses (see cash flow, Chapter 7, especially Figure 7.3). Accompanying this analysis should be a short narrative description that provides supplementary information about the projected income statement.

Another required analysis is a break-even analysis. This analysis was discussed in Chapter 7 (see Figure 7.15 in particular). Basically, a break-even analysis compares total revenue to total cost. The break-even point refers to the volume point at which total revenue equals total cost. This analysis allows identifying when the business is expected to generate enough revenue to cover expenses. Such an analysis can help identify the sum needed to cover expenses until the break-even point is reached.

Heading VI: Supporting Information

The final section of a business plan is supporting information. This is any information that will make the plan more likely to be supported. Items in this section may include:

- Letters of intent
- Key contracts
- Letters of reference
- Photos
- Drawings of plans
- Complete resumes of management personnel
- Market research data
- Marketing materials
- Newspaper or journal articles relevant to this type of business
- Appendices containing any other materials the planner believes will support the purpose of the plan.

MULTIPLE USES OF A BUSINESS PLAN

The effort of putting together a written plan may save considerable time and money by forcing the planner to examine, in detail, all aspects of the business, anticipate potential problems and formulate solutions. This forethought can be rewarded in the form of financial support from funding agencies.

While securing funding is important to private practice physical therapists, there are other equally important purposes served by a well-developed business plan. One of these purposes is to guide the business in all of its endeavors, from marketing to types of services provided. In this guiding sense, the business plan becomes the blueprint for the business. The plan presents a picture of where the business is going and it provides a basis for tracking progress toward desired goals. Periodic comparisons between the plan and actual occurrences allow identification of variances. This helps determine where changes need to be made to reach the business' goals. A second important purpose a business plan serves is educational. Members of the business and external parties can be introduced to and kept informed of the purpose, goals, mode of operation and status of the business. Providing such information may help keep members of the business focused on goals and it may stimulate support from external parties.

ADDITIONAL PRIVATE PRACTICE PHYSICAL THERAPY CONSIDERATIONS

Planning a private physical therapy practice requires some insight into the options that are available to provide such services. Among the options to consider are providing services on a contractual basis, serving Medicare eligible patients, forming an agency, participating in a joint venture and membership in a network of physical therapists. Each of these options has been discussed in earlier chapters from the perspective of management in large health care organizations. The following discussion focuses on the above options but relates them to small businesses, specifically, to small physical therapy practices.

Contracting to Provide Services

Contracting may involve arranging with hospitals, skilled nursing facilities, outpatient clinics or other types of facilities to provide physical therapy as an independent contractor. To do this successfully, an individual physical therapist or a physical therapy practice owner, must be able to accomplish two things. First, meet the setting's staffing and service needs. And second, do so at a reimbursement level that covers the cost

of personnel, contract administration, and other overhead expenses while also providing a reasonable margin of profit.

Contracting allows a physical therapist to enter private practice with a minimal investment. It is often reasonably easy to arrange a contract with an organization that allows flexibility in scheduling. Such flexibility may allow an employed physical therapist to work as a contractor on a part-time basis. Contracts may be developed for time periods ranging from a few hours a day or for several years. The pay rate for contracted services is usually higher than a typical salary. However, a common risk a contractor takes is that enough work may not always be available. This limits income.

A physical therapy contractor has different legal and tax obligations than does a salaried physical therapist. The distinctions between these classifications have tax and legal implications. The worker classification impacts responsibility for income tax withholding, social security and Medicare taxes, unemployment compensation and workers' compensation premiums. State and federal employment laws, pension benefits and liability are also impacted by classification as contractor or employee. Basically, an employer is responsible for paying the above-mentioned costs for employees. Independent contractors are responsible for paying these costs themselves. In terms of professional liability, a contractor assumes the liability risk and is usually responsible for purchasing liability insurance. In an employment situation, employees are typically provided some professional liability coverage though an employer-paid policy.

There are a variety of tests to determine worker classification. These tests are applied case by case (25). For this reason, it is important to consult an attorney regarding employment status as well as to review any contract to provide services before signing the contract.

Participation in the Medicare Program

For a private physical therapy practice to bill for Medicare services, the physical therapist and the practice must obtain a Medicare billing number and decide how the practice will be classified for Medicare purposes. Each classification has certain advantages and disadvantages. For Medicare reimbursement, the physical therapist in an independent practice (PTIP) classification is the simplest form. However, there is currently a $900 per year maximum limit per Medicare patient for providing services. As a result of the Balanced Budget Act of 1997, on January 1, 1999, the yearly cap on payment will increase to $1500 for physical and other therapies. This cap will be in effect until January 1, 2001, after which a new method of payment is expected which will be based on both diagnostic category and utilization data (26). Updated information on both the $1500 limit and the implementation of the Act should be consulted. Three sources are APTA publications, www.theFOCUSgroup.net and federal government publications.

Form an Agency

Another option available to a PTIP is to form a rehabilitation agency or a certified outpatient rehabilitation facility (CORF). This involves a complex application procedure. These categories of provider are currently reimbursed on a cost-based accrual accounting system rather than on a fee for service or discounted fee basis (see Chapter 8). In 1998, agencies and certified outpatient rehabilitation facilities will be on a transitional payment basis that will likely reduce payments compared to a fee for service method. January 1, 1999 payment will be on a fee schedule basis as mandated by the Balanced Budget Act of 1997 (26). This is expected to further reduce payments for services. Current information on the Act should be consulted because new interpretations and rules are being published at this time.

A rehabilitation agency under Medicare guidelines is a business that provides an integrated multi-disciplinary program designed to upgrade the physical function of handicapped or disabled individuals with a team of specialized rehabilitation professionals. At a minimum, this team includes physical therapy, speech pathology services, and social or vocational services.

A CORF under Medicare guidelines is a nonresidential facility that provides at least medical, physical therapy, and psychological or social services. In addition to the above requirements, PTIP's, rehabilitation agencies and certified outpatient rehabilitation facilities must meet specific requirements relating to clinical records, policies governing services, state and local licensure, plans of care, adequate facilities, equipment, personnel qualifications, budget plan and utilization review.

To gain status as a rehabilitation agency or CORF, an extensive application for accreditation must be completed and a site survey scheduled. Before a site survey, a facility must be operational, financially solvent and have patient records for the site surveyors to review. This certification process may take several months to complete before a practice is accredited and able to bill and collect for services provided to Medicare enrollees.

Home Health Services

Home health physical therapy involves providing services in a person's home. A physical therapist may obtain home health referrals through contracts with local home health agencies or hospitals. Specific accreditation is often required to bill for home health physical therapy services, and the therapist or contracting practice is often paid a fee per visit and, at times, additional payment for mileage. For the most current information on home health services the reader should consult updated information on the Balanced Budget Act of 1997.

Home health practice allows flexibility for the therapist; however, it may require a significant amount of travel, which may result in a small number of patients that can be served per day. Home health practice usually provides a wide variety of patients. However, documentation requirements may differ with each contract source.

Joint Ventures

A joint venture between individuals and organizations involves creating a relationship wherein both groups share risks and benefits. Insurance carriers are seldom interested in negotiating with individual providers for services. Therefore, to survive, private practice physical therapists need to establish linkages with hospitals and other provider groups who contract with managed care organizations (27–29).

The key element in a joint venture for a private practice physical therapist is finding a willing partner who can benefit from the therapist's experience and who will allow the therapist to maintain managerial control over the practice. One form of a joint venture is between groups of physical therapists and physicians. Such a venture provides the physical therapists with a flow of referrals. However, these arrangements may be interpreted as referral for profit or kickback situations. This kind of joint venture needs to be carefully reviewed by an attorney for legality (30) in addition to consideration of the ethical issues associated with the arrangement (10, 22).

Network Participation

Private practice physical therapists, as well as other health care providers, may join forces, i.e., form a network, to negotiate with insurance companies and MCO's to provide services. Groups of therapists can also combine administrative functions to increase efficiency. This consolidation can reduce costs and improve network members' competitiveness on a price basis.

Many local and national physical therapy networks exist. As small, individual, local physical therapy practices find it increasingly more difficult to become a provider in a preferred provider organization, the need to join a network becomes more apparent. The expected benefit of membership in a network of physical therapists is that there will be a regular flow of patients to treat who have insurance that pays for physical therapy services. This becomes possible for two reasons. First, one contract, covering all members of a network, can be developed. By not having to negotiate contracts with individual physical therapy providers as MCO saves time, money and it increases the options available to their members. The members of the MCO have increased choice of physical therapy providers. These are the members of the network. The second benefit physical therapy providers may get from membership in a network is the ability to develop and share outcome data. The network members can pool their data to get large enough numbers of

cases to provide satisfactory evidence of efficacy and cost effectiveness.

Investigating membership in existing local networks could be beneficial for a new or existing practice. For comparative purposes it is important to know:

- The contracts each network holds
- Reimbursement method
- Restrictions on members
- Expenses involved in joining the network

Under network arrangements, reimbursement rates may be based on discounted fee for service, limited fee per visit, case rate or capitated rates (see Chapters 3, 7 and 8). In addition, a fee may have to be paid to the network for membership and ongoing administrative and marketing services. Certain networks may have exclusive arrangements with insurers to send patients to member clinics. Other networks may be nonexclusive and open to other practitioners. Networks may be local, regional or national in the scope of their contracts. Some networks may restrict members from joining competing networks.

CHANGING ENVIRONMENT FOR PRIVATE PRACTICE PHYSICAL THERAPY

One result of the changing health care picture has been that clinicians and non-clinicians, often with conflicting agendas, are becoming more involved in the design of the patient care process, including service determination and outcomes analysis. Employers and insurance companies negotiate for a package of health care services and empower those who authorize services to make decisions regarding services covered and the administration of these services to patients. Health care providers are having less say regarding the types and duration of treatments they provide to patients.

Managerial and clinical work increasingly overlap. Because of this overlap, health care managers and patient care staff need a broader range of knowledge than has been included in traditional educational programs. There is a need for continuous communication between these two groups of workers.

With vast amounts of information available, a need exists for managers and staff to access important information in a timely manner, to have time to analyze the information, and to utilize the information. Change is continuous. As emphasized in Chapter 10, informed choices about future actions require continuous input of up-to-date information.

Shared interests of provider and insurer requires competency in case management, insurance plan interpretation, risk management, outcomes analysis, as well as clinical expertise. Changing ownership and management concepts include diversification and development of interorganizational arrangements and governance structures. In an environment of complex interrelationships between the federal government, insurance companies and health care providers, the traditional view of a small, privately owned physical therapy practice, as presented in this chapter, may not be operational in the future. This thought is developed further in Chapter 15.

SUMMARY

The foundation of any business has been built and presented in the first 13 chapters of this textbook. The basic management principles, i.e., management of finances, understanding values, engaging people, selecting an organizational structure, facility planning, information control and access and consultation, were applied in this chapter to the private practice of physical therapy. The uniqueness of this chapter was its application of the aforementioned principles in a small business setting.

The reader was introduced to entrepreneurship, the benefits and challenges of small business ownership and a process, guided by an outline, to plan a business. Finally, several perceived opportunities available to private practice physical therapists were presented. These opportunities were tempered with a discussion of perceived threats to becoming a successful private practice owner. To gain more experience in thinking about private practice issues, the reader is encouraged to participate in Role-Play 14 in Appendix A. The role-play challenges the reader to integrate many of the business and management concepts presented in the preceding and current chapters.

REFERENCES

1. Wynn KE. Breaking through the barriers. PT Magazine 1997;10(5):44–46,48–50,52–56.
2. Department of Health and Human Services Health Care Financing Administration. Medicare regulations and certification procedures. Division of Health Standards and Quality, 101 Marietta Tower, Atlanta, GA 30323, 1997.
3. Kastantin JT. Physical therapy practice planning. Physical Therapy Today 1994:17–27.
4. Bangs Jr DH. The Business Planning Guide. 7th ed. Chicago, IL: Upstart, 1995:v,x,xi.
5. American Physical Therapy Association. 1993 Active Membership Profile Report. Alexandria VA: Author, 1994:4, 12,17,19,37.
6. American Physical Therapy Association. American Physical Therapy Association omnibus survey 1997. Alexandria VA: Author, 1997.
7. Schneller ES. Accountability for health care: a white paper on leadership and management for the U.S. health care system. Health Care Management Review 1997;22:38–48.
8. Olsen DL. A descriptive survey of management and operations at selected sports medicine centers in the United States. Journal of Orthopedic Sports Physical Therapy 1996:315–322.
9. Anonymous. Hospitals to receive millions for not training physicians. P T Bulletin 1997;12(36):1,10.
10. American Physical Therapy Association. Code of Ethics and Guide to Professional Conduct. APTA core documents. PT Magazine 1997;5:79–87.
11. 42 Code of Federal Regulations Section 1395nn.
12. Black, J. A declaration for independents. Rehab Management 1997;10(4):28–33.
13. Ellis DJ, Pekar Jr PP. Planning for Nonplanners. New York: AMACOM, 1980.
14. McDanial RR, Jr. Strategic leadership: a view from quantum and chaos theories. Health Care Management Review 1997;22:5–9,21–37.
15. Small Business Administration US Government Office of Business Development. Checklist For Going Into Business Form #2016. Washington DC: Author, 1984.
16. Waitley DE. The Psychology of Winning. (audio tape 4) Nightengale-Conant, Chicago, Ill 60648, 1987.
17. Smith HW. The Ten Natural Laws of Successful Time and Life Management. New York: Warner Books, 1994.
18. Pinson L, Jinnett J. Anatomy of a Business Plan Fullerton, CA: Out of Your Mind and Into the Marketplace, 1989.
19. Stern L. Conquer business plan phobia. Home Office Computing 1995(Feb):26–28.
20. Nosse LJ, Friberg DG. Management Principles for Physical Therapists. Baltimore, MD: Williams & Wilkins, 1992:149.
21. Singer DW. Diversifying your practice. Rehab Management 1995(June/July):145–146.
22. Fiebert IM, Zane LJ, Hamby EF. Private Practice Man-

agement in Physical Therapy. New York, NY: Churchill Livingstone, 1990:1.

23. Johnston BE Jr, Lord, PJ. Your Private Practice, Planning and Organization, 1st ed. Lake City, FL: Peter J. Lord and Assoc., 1982.

24. Stern L. Finding cash. Home Office Computing 1995 (Mar):87–90.

25. Von Briesen R, Purtell DJ, Rooper, WJ. Worker Status Classification Handbook. Milwaukee, WI: Von Briesen, Purtell, & Rooper, SC, 1997.

26. Garland N. The Balanced Budget Act: How it affects physical therapy. Alexandria, VA: American Physi-cal Therapy Association, 1997:3–6, Q & A 1–2, 9–10.

27. Sullivan T. Managed care & the survival of private practice. Rehab Management Oct/Nov 1995:22–29.

28. Putvin B. A new beginning for private practice in Michigan. PT Today 1995(Sept/Oct):17–20.

29. Kopet C. Joint venturing with hospitals: Is opportunity knocking? Physical Therapy Today 1994(Sept/Oct): 11–12.

30. Mitchell JM, Scott E. Physician ownership of physical therapy services. Journal of the American Medical Association 1992;268:2055–2059.

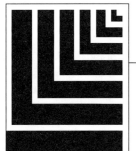

15

FUTURES

PREVIEW

This chapter presents the authors' conceptualizations of what the health care environment will be like in the near future. The reader will be provided with a model for thinking about the future. Our intent is to demystify the process of looking beyond what is and to facilitate thinking about what could or should be. The overall health care environment is the stage upon which current and future physical therapists will play out their careers. While work place issues predominate, physical therapy education is also discussed. The reader is offered many suggestions for succeeding in a complex and ever-changing health care environment.

KEY WORDS

Futures: probable and improbable future trends based on information extrapolated from multiple sources.
Primary Care Physician: the first physician to examine a patient and who decides if further care is needed and if that care will include referral to specialist physicians and other services.
Scenario: synopsis or outline of hypothesized future events or chain of events.
Vision: desired future.

INTRODUCTION

The predictions made in this chapter are based on many information sources that have been modified by the combined considerations of the authors. Our vision of what may be is based on many variables. The major variables that influenced us include the sources of information we consulted, our values and motives and our experiences with making predictions. Our version of the future clearly reflects our common physical therapy background. We are active members of the American Physical Therapy Association (APTA) who advocate for the profession. However, we are cognizant of the fact that managerial skill and interest in managing are not areas limited to physical therapists. Our belief, however, is that physical therapists, because of the breath and depth of their entry level preparation, may offer a wider perspective of patient care than do many other health care professionals.

Our experience in making medium and long-range decisions covers four major areas relevant to physical therapy. We average over 20 years of physical therapy, management and consultative experience and 15 years of teaching experience. Our individual primary interests include education (LN), organizational management (DF), management consulting (PK) and private practice management (DO).

Starting with a model for analyzing current information and melding it with a vision, we gave the future of physical therapy substance. Following the processes associated with the model, we identified specific areas of interest to current and future physical therapists, analyzed relevant information, deliberated about the likelihood of certain outcomes and summarized these possible outcomes. The issues that evolved from our discussions were categorized into seven domains:

- Patients
- Third party payers
- Institutional providers
- Gate keepers/case managers
- Physicians
- Physical therapy practice
- Physical therapy education

Individual lists were formulated to summarize the elements of each of these domains. Pertinent discussions elaborate on the content and meaning of the contents of each list.

FUTURES MODEL

In Chapter 3 we advocated the use of a problem solving approach called a SWOT analysis (strengths, weaknesses, opportunities and threats) (1). Looking at information and trends with an eye on the future can be done using the SWOT concept. Figure 15.1 depicts a generic model for carrying out a futures analysis from the perspective of an organization. An individual considering their personal professional future can also apply this model to formulate their own vision.

The general arrowhead shape of the model reflects movement toward a progressively more defined target. The target in this case is a clearer vision of what is likely to occur based on reasoning organized around multiple SWOT analyses. These analyses can enhance the realization of the vision as they are preludes to creating a desired future (2, 3). As a step toward defining the future, relevant external and internal environmental factors need to be considered. National scenarios and success factors located in the upper half of the model are the external environmental factors. Organizational position and competitive position in the lower half of the model are internal environmental factors.

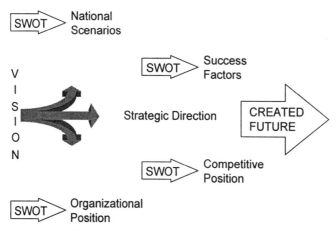

FIGURE 15.1. Futures planning model. [Modified from Bezold C. The future of health care: Implications for the allied health professions. Journal of Allied Health 1989;14(Fall):438. A SWOT analysis involves consideration of strengths, weaknesses, opportunities and threats (1)].

The organizational or personal vision is placed vertically in the model to reflect its influence on all facets of creating a future. This vision is the desired future position of an organization or an individual. The vision is continually called upon during the analysis process to guide decisions. The environments from which the future will evolve are located at the top and bottom of the model. Each element of the model and its use will be described in more detail below. In keeping with the purpose of this text, emphasis will be on an organizations' perspective of defining the future.

External Environment

Starting at the top of Figure 15.1, the first SWOT analysis pertains to the health care industry or the profession nationally. These are factors that are typically outside of the direct control of an individual organization or person. Relevant politically involved associations to which the organization or individual belongs may, however, influence them. The key questions asked about the external environment include:

- What are the known, anticipated, and possible strengths of the industry?
- What are the known, anticipated, and possible weaknesses of the industry?
- What are the known, anticipated, and possible opportunities for the industry?
- What are the known, anticipated, and possible threats to the industry?

After considering an industry-wide picture, the next level of external variables to be analyzed is the characteristics of similar organizations believed to be successful. This SWOT analysis is labeled Success Factors in Figure 15.1. It is an analysis of perceived industry leaders. Those exemplary organizations that have been successful, are likely to continue being successful, and are believed to be able to achieve their proclaimed vision. Information available about each leader can be obtained from trade journals, annual reports, industry reporting services and word of mouth.

Internal Environment

The internal environmental factors are more definitive than external factors because they relate to the organization carrying out the SWOT analysis. Because of internal data management systems, more reliable data is usually available than what is at hand when considering external factors. The SWOT analyses of the organizational position and its competitive position call for consideration of several types of information. Historical information aids trend analysis. Current data from all segments of the organization help in interpreting history as well as identifying present position. The accumulated information allows comparisons between the organizations' position and the industry as a whole (National Scenarios) and between the organizations' competitive position and the industry models (Success Factors). At each step of the process, the vision is used to keep the focus on the desired future.

Created Future

Having assessed the external and internal factors, given consideration to the original vision and thought to the emergent opportunities and threats, a revised or clarified vision of the future can be voiced, disseminated and pursued. A new strategic direction is charted. Periodically, the process is revisited, the vision of the next future is created and strategies are adjusted to bring the updated vision closer to reality.

USING THE MODEL TO ENVISION AND CREATE A VIEW OF THE FUTURE

We used the current health care environment in this country as the National Scenarios portion of the model (Fig. 15.1). Also, we used current issues of particular interest to physical therapists as the Organizational portion of the model. Using the model in this way, we formulated our view of the future. Seven categories of national scenarios emerged from our SWOT analyses. These scenarios are summarized in seven lists. The first national scenario relates to patients because patients are the core members of the health care system. Each succeeding list adds an additional scenario. The sum of these scenarios is a macro view of the future health care environment. Because of interrelationships between the various scenarios, there is some overlap in the content of the seven lists. We purposely placed physical therapy practice and education scenarios at the end so they could be appreciated in the greater context of the health care environment.

National Scenarios For the Near Future in Seven Categories

Patients are the focus of health care. They are the primary customer. Patients are the reason health care organizations and professions exist. Today, the major focus of health care is on managing the care of large groups of patients. Having access to affordable health care is the central issue for Americans. For provider organizations and individual professional providers, having insights about who will be the future patients are critical for planning to meet the patients' needs. List 1 presents patient scenarios. The list is organized around four headings: payment, demographics, other characteristics and when enough is enough.

List 1: Patients

PAYMENT

- Decreasing percentage of the population will be insured resulting in more people uninsured or under-insured
- Increasing need for charity care
- Increasing demands for shrinking government funded health care payment programs
- Increasing cost to patient for health care, i.e., co-payment, deductible and contribution to health insurance premium
- Fewer options in health care providers as the health care delivery system consolidates into regional and national provider groups
- Continuing struggle for more choice within managed care plans

DEMOGRAPHICS

- Growing non-Caucasian populations: Asian, African American, Hispanic
- Increasing number of high risk patients, i.e., cocaine and alcohol syndrome and HIV positive babies, pregnant women with history of substance abuse, HIV positive patients, patients with AIDS
- Increasing percentage of population 65 years and older with greatest increase in 85 and over group
- Increasing numbers of frail elderly (psychosocial, economic and physiological fragility)
- Increasing numbers of patients with chronic illnesses
- Huge end-of-life health care costs

OTHER CHARACTERISTICS

- Increasing patient responsibility for maintaining their own health
- Increasing patient interest in and access to outcome data
- Continuing use of non-traditional health care providers, e.g., acupuncturists, massage therapists, homeopathy, and manual therapies
- Growing availability and willingness to try holistic therapeutic approaches, e.g. mind-body integration approaches
- Increasing interest in prevention and wellness
- Increasing amounts of confusion regarding educational preparation and titles, e.g., PT, MPT, DPT, PTA, PT Aide and PT Technician. Confusion is likey when the therapist extenders administer significant amounts of service compared to the supervising professional

WHEN ENOUGH IS ENOUGH

- Possibility that patients will exert a united front to combat what they believe to be health care decisions being made based on cost rather than on medical necessity
- Possibility that managed care will become unprofitable at some point and for profit organizations may leave health care and invest elsewhere leaving some of their members with fcw affordable health care options

List 2: Third Party Payment

Historically, health care payment plans (secondary customers) have made it possible for patients to have affordable health care. The rising cost of health care has threatened the access of patients and financial well-being of payers. To control costs, providers and payers are shifting their focus from managing the moment of care to managing the disease process and the health of populations. Payers want the best deal for their money. How they try to assure that they are getting what they contracted for is a major part of List 2. A second focus of List 2 is on efforts to control utilization of resources.

MANAGING COSTS

- Continuing focus on cost reduction
- Continuing movement toward managed health care plans
- Continuing control of enrollee access to care (rationing)
- Continuing efforts to decrease utilization of the most expensive types of care (inpatient)
- Continuing movement toward standardized plans

of care and application of best practice models (based on utilization and outcome data)

SCRUTINY

- Increasing sophistication in utilization management programs with a changing focus from controlling the incidence of care to comprehensive disease management
- Increasing accountability of providers for utilization decisions
- Increasing intensity of review of charges for reimbursement
- Increasing amount of monitoring of managed care organization panel providers
- Increasing demand for automated linkages between providers and payers to facilitate billing and data base development and analysis

OTHER FINANCIAL ISSUES

- Phasing out of fee-for-service payment plans
- Continuing decline in reimbursement rates
- Phasing out of indemnity insurance plan options for consumers
- Increasing emphasis on capitation
- Expanding choice of health care plan options for those willing and able to pay a premium rate
- Increasing possibility of outcome driven reimbursement
- Growing numbers of provider and employer based managed health plans

OVERSIGHT

- Increasing importance of managed care accreditation which will help balance efforts to meet patients' health care needs and providers' needs to control expenditures
- Increasing federal governmental regulation of managed care plans
- Increased watchfulness regarding fraud and abuse
- Increased numbers of prosecutions for fraud and abuse

List 3: Institutional Providers

Institutional providers, particularly hospitals, have a need to keep down costs, maintain or increase their patient base and assure sufficient income to meet future needs. To do all of this requires negotiating with third party payers, physician groups and others. These issues and others related to institutional providers are presented in List 3.

MARKET SHARE

- Continuing competition for patients who have higher paying insurance plans or who are able to pay out of pocket for their care

- Accommodations to meet requirements for payment from government payment sources which will likely be based on per diem, per case and capitation reimbursement methods
- Concentration on areas of expertise

OPERATIONS

- Continuing shift of services to ambulatory care settings
- Expanding services in a continuum of care from prevention through hospice
- Slowing of the growth in post-acute care services (e.g., rehabilitation, home care)

STAFFING

- Improved availability of critical staff such as primary care physicians, physical therapists, and case managers
- Changing strategies for meeting work force needs from a primary emphasis on recruitment to more intense and sophisticated selection processes
- Increased emphasis on retention
- Increasing likelihood that traditional associations and loyalties will not supersede the need to operate in the most cost-effective manor

PHYSICIANS

- Increasing importance of primary care physicians and others as gate keepers
- Decreasing demand for physician specialists due to
- dependence on referrals from gate keepers
- Decreasing reimbursement for institutional based physicians especially in managed care organization based centers
- Slowing of physician practice and institutional mergers and acquisitions in favor of other types of business arrangements

FEWER INDIVIDUAL PROVIDERS

- Continuing consolidation of providers in regional market areas
- Increasing importance of national health care corporations in all geographical regions and in all types of health care businesses
- Increasing numbers and types of alternate business structures to coordinate care and negotiate managed care panel access

FINANCIAL ISSUES

- Decreased profit margins
- Decline in net income from traditional operations for organizations and individual providers as reimbursement declines and costs increase
- Increasing efforts to control labor costs, e.g. cross-training of personnel, increasing utilization of non-professional extenders, contracting for services

instead of employing professionals, substituting equipment for employees, e.g., robotic food carts, telemedicine devises and outsourcing
- Labor problems including potential increased unionization of professionals including physicians and physical therapists

NEW PROBLEMS

- Public relations problems due to increased public scrutiny and health care related scandals
- Increasing focus on professional ethics related to resource management decisions regarding scarce resources, e.g., organ transplants, waiting lists and access to specialists
- Increasing need for professional codes of ethics and guides for interpretation to reflect the breadth of issues in which physical therapists and other professionals are involved
- Continued reevaluation of medical specialists' and other health professionals' role in a more global health care system
- Increased scrutiny for fraudulent and abusive business practices

List 4: Gate Keepers and Case Managers

List 4 deals with those who allocate health care resources under most managed care arrangements. The reader is reminded that they will be dealing with physicians and other payer representatives such as case managers who are responsible for assuring overall efficiency of the care patients receive. In addition, there are individuals, often a member of the physical therapy department, who are responsible for assuring the efficient management of each patients' physical therapy services.

ENTRY

- Increasing "power" to primary care physicians, physician assistants and nurse practitioners as they control access to health care services
- Increasing "power" to case managers, typically nurses, to assist in the management and allocation of resources once patients enter into a care system
- Increasing public relations problems when gate keepers' decisions are perceived to be inappropriate or hurtful
- Increasing legal problems for gate keepers
- Increasing requirements for credentialing case managers
- Increasing opportunity for health care professionals, including physical therapists, to become credentialed case managers

List 5: Physicians

The emphasis on managed care has positioned primary care physicians at the entrance to

health care services. This position has increased the demand for physicians with this general medical preparation while at the same time lessening the demand for physician specialists. There is a surplus of some medical specialists in some geographical areas (4). These physicians have great incentive to expand their services beyond those they typically have provided. These issues are summarized below.

SUPPLY AND DEMAND

- Changing perception of a hierarchy among physicians such that there is an increase in the importance of primary care practitioners (gate keepers) relative to medical specialists
- Oversupply of specialists
- Declining reimbursement for specialists
- Increasing percentage of medical students choosing family practice over specialization resulting in a declining percentage of some types of medical specialists
- Increasing numbers of hospitalists, i.e., physicians who stay in the hospital and care for the patients of referring physicians who are off premises

ACCESSING PATIENTS

- Decreasing opportunities for physicians who do not have an association with a hospital-insurance company linked plan to access patients
- Practicing as a member of a group will be the only way to access managed care patients
- Decreasing numbers of independent, solo practice physicians
- Predominance of large-family practice general practice groups
- Groups of physicians controlling health care costs as they control referrals to expensive services such as medical specialists, physical therapy, and diagnostic tests

BUSINESS SKILLS

- Increasing sophistication in service industry business and management practices will be needed to negotiate access to patients and be fairly compensated
- Increasing availability of educational programs to meet the above needs, e.g., continuing education, inservice programs and formal education

NEW PRODUCTS

- Increasing diversity of services offered by physicians, especially specialists, to retain or gain market share
- Increasing attention to holistic care, e.g., nutrition, exercise, meditation, relaxation and non-traditional approaches to health care

- Increasing attention to prevention and wellness
- Improved management of patients with cardiac, neurological, orthopedic and other common diagnoses through new drugs, equipment and techniques

KEEPING COSTS DOWN

- Shifting of responsibilities through the increased use of extenders such as physician's assistants, advanced practice nurses and nurse practitioners to service patients with uncomplicated conditions
- Physician extenders will have increased authority over treatment decisions of patients with uncomplicated conditions

TELEMEDICINE

- Increased use of telemonitoring devices
- Phone and video connections that will allow the transmission of data from a variety of devices from and to multiple locations will become commonplace
- Increased sophistication and variety of physiological montoring devices
- Telemonitoring devices that transmit symptoms directly to emergency transport services for quick response when necessary
- Increased patient self-monitoring with the devices
- 24-hour per day monitoring of patients in their homes
- Monitoring during work

List 6: Physical Therapy Practice

The important scenarios for physical therapy practice (List 6) and physical therapy education (List 7) are presented now that the selected aspects of the health care system have been summarized. This allows discussion of the future issues of physical therapy within the overall context of health care. List 6 presents futures related to physical therapy practice and speaks to issues of interest to salaried and self-employed physical therapists. The impact of a projected oversupply of physical therapists and physical therapist assistants is integrated into the content of the list.

WORK PLACE ENVIRONMENT

- Growing numbers of for-profit regional and national rehabilitation corporations resulting in fewer locally controlled organizations
- Increasing numbers of departments operating as self-managed groups (semi-autonomous and autonomous) as formal first level manager positions are eliminated
- Increasing responsibility delegated (with limits) to the self-managed groups for decisions that previously were made by the department manager

- Continuing decline in the numbers of physical therapists working in inpatient care institutions
- Increasing diversity in service locations
- Increasing numbers of physical therapists working in multiple work settings
- Increasing likelihood of experiencing loyalty conflicts arising from membership in a cohesive interdisciplinary team and loyalty to the concept that physical therapists possess unique skills and knowledge other team members do not have
- Increasing numbers of contract or internal labor pool physical therapists compared to regular full-time employed physical therapists providing services concurrently in all types of physical therapy environments
- Increasing demands on contract physical therapy organizations to demonstrate to purchasers that their personnel meet the same standards as regular full-time employed staff
- Increasing pressure from entry-level educational programs to take students for supervised clinical experiences at various points in their educational preparation
- Increasing necessity to learn and employ preferred practice patterns as defined by the APTA to receive an acceptable job performance rating
- Increasing complexity of ethical issues and new issues not yet covered by the APTA Code of Ethics (9)

COMPETITION

- Increasing competition for jobs and patients from members of various groups, e.g., athletic trainers, occupational therapists, exercise physiologists, massage therapists and chiropractors
- Increasing competition for patients from physicians and physician groups who strive to maintain revenues by offering services traditionally offered by physical therapists and other ancillary providers
- Increasing pressure from chiropractors to have licensure laws altered to recognize them as providers of physical therapy services
- Increasing interprofessional competition and conflict

CONSTRAINTS

- Continuing struggles to meet patients' needs cost effectively, i.e., meets needs in restrained time frames, with fewer resources, less one-to-one time with each patient and by using physical therapist extenders more
- Continuing struggles for technically expert therapists to develop and master non-direct patient care skills e.g., computer use beyond word processing, i.e., accessing internet data bases, spread sheet use; self-managed group skills, team building skills, management skills and appreciation of psychosocial influences (racial, ethnic and economic)

on learning, compliance and choice of management style

- Increasing requirements for all clinicians to act as managers
- Increasing time management pressures, i.e., time needed for self-managed group meetings without changes in productivity
- Increasing accountability for continuing education
- Increasing gap between employer allocations for continuing education and the costs associated with continuing education
- Increasing expectations of employers that if they fund employees to attend courses, e.g. employees will be expected to competently share the new knowledge and skill in an interesting and efficient manor with their colleagues
- Continuing attractiveness of traveling positions to new graduates
- Continuing concern about professional socialization of young traveling physical therapists

CAREER DEVELOPMENT

- Increasing need for life-long career development planning skills to regularly acquire value added skills, i.e., new skills that are useful in many work settings and are in addition to what all other physical therapist applicants would be expected to have: excellent primary physical therapy technical skills and years of clinical experience
- Slowing of the rate of growth of board certified specialists for the same reasons presented in List 5 for medical specialists, i.e., generalist physical therapists, those who can competently treat a wide range of patients, are more valuable to many employers if specialist care adds extra cost
- Increasing emphasis on change management and stress management
- Increasing variety of educational opportunities offered in an organized continuum from beginner through expert on a wide range of topics
- Increasing variety of methods of gaining continuing education, e.g., teleconferences, physical therapy related internet services, organizational internal networks, correspondence courses as well as academic credit, i.e., satellite campuses, evening and weekend advanced courses on campuses or at a health care organizations' site
- Increasing need to personally finance continuing education to maintain or upgrade technical skills as well as to acquire other types of new skills
- Continuing challenge to maintain balance between personal and professional needs

EMPLOYMENT OUTLOOK AND SALARIES

- Increasing likelihood that shortly the physical therapy work force supply will meet the demands of the marketplace at least in the historically most desirable geographical locations and types of work settings
- Increasing competition for jobs in certain practice locations and settings
- Increasing need to develop job search skills, i.e., cover letter and resume writing, informational interviewing, computer job searches, networking skills, interviewing skills and knowledge of prospective employers' track record and prospects for growth
- Slowing of the rate of increases in hourly rates and salaries as the work force supply matches, and then exceeds, job availability
- Equalization of starting pay rates for all rehabilitation therapists, i.e., occupational, speech, physical therapists and possibly athletic trainers
- Increasing use of physical therapist assistants which is likely to limit job opportunities for physical therapists in some situations

PRIVATE PRACTICE

- Decreasing percentage of physical therapists in private practice with those remaining forming networks to negotiate for managed care contracts
- Continuing payment limitations by Medicare to physical therapists in independent practice
- Increasing need for small networks of physical therapists in private practice in outpatient settings to develop outcome data base systems for self-assessment and for managed care negotiation purposes
- Increasing need to treat patients in accord with the APTA preferred practice patterns for reimbursement
- Increasing opportunities for physical therapists in private practice to diversify, i.e., find niches in multiple markets which are not being met by others or which can be met more cost effectively by a small business
- Decreasing utility of efforts to develop a referral base from individual physicians who are not associated with a managed care organization
- Increasing utility of efforts to become a provider for managed care organizations

OTHER SIGNIFICANT ISSUES

- Increasing need for ethical consultation as the dynamics of the work place add new challenges to meeting personal needs as well as those of stakeholders, i.e., clients, peers, the organization and third party payers
- Decreasing percentage of physical therapists maintaining membership in the American Physical Therapy Association as jobs become less plentiful
- Increasing numbers of physical therapist assistants will join the newly configured APTA which will increase their power in the association

List 7: Physical Therapy Education

List 7 is the final list of national scenarios. It presents scenarios for physical therapy students, clinical and academic coordinators of clinical education and academic faculty members. Supply and demand estimations, faculty shortages and the students of the future are important issues considered in the following list.

ACADEMIC PROGRAMS

- Slowing of the growth rate of entry-level physical therapy educational programs followed by a smaller rate decline in the number of new physical therapist assistant programs
- Changing emphasis from selection to recruitment and retention of students as the number of applicants per school declines
- Increasing numbers of second-career students
- Increasing numbers and types of educational products will be offered by academic institutions to gain a market share in continuing education and non-traditional degree program areas, e.g., off-hour educational assistant to therapist conversion programs as well as master's, clinical doctorate and academic doctorate degree programs and advanced courses in all technical areas offered for academic credit on campus, at other locations, domestic and foreign, plus a wide variety of non-credit continuing education courses in person, via internet and on closed circuit television
- Increasing limitations imposed by administrators of established institutions regarding collaboration with new or developing competitor institutions
- Increasing demands on academic programs to increase enrollments without appreciable increases in resources
- Increasing difficulty in securing full and part-time clinical practice sites of any type for students
- Increasing difficulty in integrating classroom knowledge and clinical experiences in a planned progression because of limited clinical sites
- Increasing need to teach the preferred practice patterns developed by the APTA
- Increasing concern about the numbers of graduates who do not successfully pass the licensure examination on their first attempt
- Increasing use of technology in instruction, i.e., computer terminals at each desk, courses on CD ROM discs, use of institutional computer networks for individual and group communications, home pages for each course on internal networks in place of university bulletins, individualized computer generated examinations from pools of items with known degrees of difficulty, video conferences featuring experts at other locations and student video portfolios to demonstrate proficiency in a variety of skills

FACULTY

- Continuing shortage of physical therapists with earned doctorate degrees

- Increasing opportunities for faculty members who are physical therapists with earned doctorates
- Increasing willingness of employers to facilitate faculty members' ability to complete a doctoral degree
- Increasing variety of faculty members teaching in the same level (entry-level) educational program, e.g., non-physical therapist doctorally prepared faculty members, physical therapist faculty members with different mixes of credentials, e.g., bachelors, entry-level masters (MPT), academic masters (MA, MS, etc.), board certified specialists, clinical doctorate (DPT), various academic doctorates (Sc.D. Ed.D, Ph.D) and different blends of full and part-time members
- Declining amounts of funding for physical therapy research
- Increasing numbers of physical therapists with doctorates will leave physical therapy to pursue research in their area of advanced academic preparation
- Increasing demands on faculty members to be engaged in student retention and recruitment activities

QUALITY CONTROL

- Increasing scrutiny by the accrediting body of the educational outcomes attained by educational programs, e.g., investigation of pass-fail rates on the licensure examination, employer satisfaction survey data, patient satisfaction survey data and interviews and surveys of recent graduates.

OTHER ISSUES

- Increasing institutional and state licensing agencies interest in using graduation from a regionally accredited educational institution as the basis for licensure in place of the current costly professional program accreditation process which must be carried out for each individual professional education program
- Continuing state legislative interest in periodically reconsidering the need for state licensure for any category of licensed personnel
- Continuing need for creativity in admissions and academic support processes to increase the racial diversity of the future physical therapy work force

THINKING ABOUT AND PREPARING FOR THE FUTURE

The seven lists of scenarios are intended to stimulate readers to think about their future as a health care provider. Suggestions for clinicians and students were intended to encourage continual efforts to gain skills and experiences to succeed in a dynamic health care environment. Among options to accomplish this for clinicians are continuing education and networking. For current students, options include pursuing academic majors or minors that provide skills and knowledge that are useful in the workplace in addition to physical therapy preparation. The reason for bringing added value to the workplace is that it appeals to employers. The core issue is getting or keeping a job in the future. This important issue merits further consideration.

Supply and Demand

The issue of the supply of physical therapists and physical therapist assistants and the demand for the services of these groups deserves additional discussion. At issue are the prospects for members of both groups to get jobs and earn a reasonable income in the near future. To start this discussion, a short summary of some actions taken by the APTA is helpful.

Background

The APTA has been in the forefront of efforts to increase the number of physical therapy graduates. This role was essential to meet patient needs for access to physical therapy services.

Over the years, a multitude of educational institutions realized that there was a pent up demand for physical therapy educational programs. Having such a program was an almost certain way of increasing university and community college enrollments. Efforts to open new educational programs were supported by federal government projections depicting physical therapy as a field with a very desirable long-range employment outlook. Because of birth rate changes, smaller numbers of students graduated from high school in the 1990s than in the 1980s. Enrollment numbers at many educational institutions declined. For schools dependent on tuition dollars to operate, it became critical to increase enrollments. Armed with a favorable governmental employment outlook, data regarding high physical therapist salaries, and the support of local physical therapist employers who had been chronically understaffed, many schools completed the APTA Commission on Accreditation of Physical Therapy Education (CAPTE) guided process for developing and establishing an educational program.

The APTA voiced the concern that there were inadequate numbers of physical therapists with doctoral degrees to staff existing programs. Where were academically qualified faculty going to come from to staff more educational programs? APTA officials expressed the concern that the federal governments' projections of demand for physical therapists were overly optimistic (5–7). The federal governments' optimistic outlook was inconsistent with the experiences of many APTA members with recruitment and hiring responsibilities.

Part of this concern stemmed from the increasing number of yearly physical therapist and physical therapist assistant graduates. A realistic estimate of the future physical therapy workforce was needed that included consideration of the number of graduates entering the workforce each year. To carry out such a study, the APTA engaged Vector Research, Inc. (Vector) (6,7).

Vector Report

Vector used existing APTA information, interviews with over 40 informed individuals and other resources to carry out their work (6). Using multiple variables in a predictive equation for determining the supply and demand relationship, Vector's equation predicted equilibrium between the number of available physical therapists and physical therapist assistants and the estimated number of jobs by 1998. Thereafter it was predicted that there would be a progressively increasing oversupply of available personnel. According to some, the fault of this equilibium and oversupply lies with the CAPTE for not stopping new schools from developing physical therapist and physical therapist assistant programs. This is, of course, undeserved criticism. The criticism reflects a misunderstanding of the purpose of CAPTE. CAPTE is the accrediting body for physical therapy educational programs in this country. It is recognized by the US Department of Education and Council for Higher Education Accreditation. Its purpose is to accredit physical therapy education programs that meet "established and nationally accepted standards of scope, quality, and relevance" (8). CAPTE provides guidance to interested parties through consultation at each phase of development, from the initial declaration of intent to form a program, through accreditation. The relationship between the APTA and CAPTE is a cooperative one in which CAPTE maintains the decision-making authority regarding educational program accreditation. CAPTE enforces educational standards. Neither CAPTE, nor any other non-governmental body external to an interested educational institution, has authority to discourage the development of new educational programs. It is the administration and board of directors of an educational institution who make the decision regarding which programs to develop or offer.

Threats and Opportunities

For the first time in decades, physical therapists and physical therapist assistants, are becoming concerned about their ability to make a living. The increasing pressures exerted by managed care, limits on physical therapy visits, decreasing reimbursement, increasing non-direct care responsibilities, among other things, all contribute to erode the allure and reward of being a physical therapist or a physical therapist assistant. Some therapists will simply leave the profession. Some therapists will be let go because they are not efficient, unable to work as a member of a team or they are unwilling to make changes necessary in certain situations. The exact impact of the above variables on the work force numbers is not determinable at this time. It is likely, however, that some prospective and current students will discard physical therapy as a career because it may not offer the employment potential or the financial potential it once did. Enrollment numbers will likely decline. The threats to the well-being of physical therapists also provide new opportunities. The strengths of most physical therapists typically include intelligence, creativity and competitiveness. These attributes can be used to develop new markets for physical therapy services, to develop and master new and efficient delivery modes and to engage in life-long improvement in treatment and management skills. Remember, actualizing a desirable future starts with a vision (2).

SUMMARY

A model and process for forming, revising and realizing a vision were discussed. The model and process were applied using information on the American health care system, health care organizations, physical therapy and related topics. The information was organized into seven topical areas: patients, third party payment, institutional providers, gate keepers and case managers, physicians, physical therapy practice and physical therapy education. Based on extrapolations from many sources and the authors' insights, suggestions were offered the reader for enhancing the value they bring to the workplace of the future. While the role play in Appendix A does not have a Chapter 15 portion, planning for the future is integrated throughout the parts. Thus engaging in this role-play exercise will facilitate learning the process of developing an achievable organizational or personal vision.

REFERENCES

1. Peters JA. Strategic Planning Process for Hospitals. Chicago, IL: American Hospital Association, 1985:67, 77, 78, 141.
2. Hoyle JR. Leadership and Futuring: Making Visions Happen. Thousand Oaks, CA: Corwin Press, 1995: 20.
3. Bezold C. The future of health care: Implications for the allied health professions. Journal of Allied Health 1989;14 (Fall):437–457.
4. Anonymous. Hospitals to receive millions for not training physicians. P T Bulletin 1997;12(36):1,10.
5. Silvestri GS. Occupational employment to 2005. Monthly Labor Review 1995;118(11):60–79.
6. Anonymous. APTA workforce study looks at supply and demand of PTs. PT Bulletin 1997;12(20):1, 10.
7. Vector Research, Inc. Physical therapy workforce study executive summary. Ann Arbor, MI: Author, 1997.
8. Commission on Accreditation in Physical Therapy Education. Evaluative criteria for accreditation of educational program of physical therapists. Alexandria, VA: American Physical Therapy Association, October 30, 1996.
9. Tygiel PP. Ethical issues. Letter to the editor. PT Bulletin 1998;13(31):13.

SUGGESTED READINGS

American Physical Therapy Association. American Physical therapy Association environmental statement. Physical Therapy 1992;72:378–394.
American Physical Therapy Association. 1993 Active Membership Profile Report. Alexandria, VA: Author, 1993.
American Physical Therapy Association. A Normative

Model of Physical Therapist Professional Education. Alexandria, VA: Author, 1996.

American Physical Therapy Association. Guide to physical therapy practice. Part one: A description of patient/client management. Part two: Preferred practice patterns. Physical Therapy 1997;77:1165–1650.

Andersen RM, Rice TH, Kominski GF, eds. Changing the U.S. Health Care System. San Francisco CA: Jossey-Bass Publishers, 1996.

Anonymous. Lifelong learning in a changing world. PT Magazine 1994;5:32–47.

Ayers SM. Health Care in the United States: The Facts and the Choices. Chicago, IL: American Library Association, 1996.

Black E. The coming crash in managed care. Biomechanics 1997;IV(5):15–16.

Blayney KD, Beller RE, Bruhn JG, et al. Special issue: Final draft report of the advisory panel for allied health to the Pew health professions commission. Journal of Allied Health 1992;21(Fall):1–66.

Dendtler CE. Physical therapy in the year 2010: Transformation through planned change. PT Magazine 1997;5 (12):32–35, 37.

Finn J, ed. Aging and information technology. Generations 1997;XXI:3–70.

Fosnaught M. PTs as case managers: An evolving role. PT Magazine 1996;4:46–53.

Fowler FJ. The changing role of physicians in rehab alliance and networks. Rehab Management 1996;9:78–79.

Garland N. The Balanced Budget Act: How it affects physical therapy. Alexandria, VA: American Physical Therapy Association 1997.

Glickman LB. Survival strategies for rehab managers looking toward the 21 century. The Resource 1997; 27:6–7.

Goldstein MS. American Physical Therapy Association Omnibus Survey 1997. Alexandria, VA: American Physical Therapy Association, 1997.

Hall DT, Associates. The Career Is Dead-Long Live the Career: A Relational Approach to Careers. San Francisco, CA: Jossey-Bass Publishers, 1996.

Halverson PK, Kaluzny AD, McLaughlin CP, Mays GP. Managed Care and Public Health. Gaithersburg, MD: Aspen, 1998.

Horn J. Draft of long-range plan specifies agenda. PT Bulletin 1991;6(Oct):36–39, 51.

Nosse LJ, Friberg DG. Management Principles for Physical Therapists. Baltimore, MD: Williams and Wilkins, 1992: 231–249.

Temkin AJ, Ulicny GR, Vesmarovich SH. Telerehab: A perspective of the way technology is going to change the future of patient treatment. Rehab Management 1996;9: 28–30.

Triezenberg HL. The identification of ethical issues in physical therapy practice. Physical Therapy 1996;76: 1097–1106.

Walters J. Physical Therapy Management: An Integrated Science. St. Louis, MO: Mosby, 1993:271–274.

Appendix **A**

ROLE PLAYS FOR
CHAPTERS 1 THROUGH 14

Adapted from Kovacek Management, Inc., December, 1997.
Reproduced by permission.

INTRODUCTION TO THE ROLE PLAY

Unique to this book is an ongoing case study, a role play, that covers important concepts from every chapter of the book. Within this ongoing case study, the reader will become familiar with consistent characters who will grow, change and develop as managers, clinicians and individuals.

It is our hope that the role play will prove beneficial to students, clinicians, managers and instructors of courses in physical therapy management and administration. The intent of the role play is to provoke thought and to build a connection between the theory and practice of physical therapy in today's health care environment.

CHAPTER 1: THE HEALTH CARE DELIVERY SYSTEM

Highlights

The characters are introduced. Marty considers the advantages and disadvantages of becoming supervisor. Chris is assigned to Marty who is the clinical instructor. The physical therapy staff say goodbye to Sandy.

The Saga Begins

As the story begins, a large group of healthcare workers are gathered in a festive environment. The location is Memorial Hospital's Physical Therapy Gym. The occasion is a going away party for one of the managers at the hospital. Although the entire staff is assembled to say farewell to Sandy, the departing physical therapy

department manager, there are conflicting feelings among the staff. They liked Sandy well enough, but there is also a feeling that Sandy's leaving may be just what the department needs.

There are about 30 people in attendance. Over the course of this role play, the reader will become familiar with many of them. For now, here is a brief introduction to the key people in the room.

Marty

Marty is a physical therapist with 3-years' experience who is just now moving into a supervisory role. Marty is a strong clinician who is well respected by peers. As Marty begins to assume more responsibility for management of the department, Marty feels poorly prepared for the new responsibilities. Marty has very mixed feelings about Sandy's departure.

Dale

Dale is a physical therapist with 30 years' experience. Dale has been a long-time supervisor and excellent role model to staff. At the onset of the case studies, Dale is the supervisor of the hospital Physical Therapy Department and has been Sandy's right hand (Fig. A.1).

Chris

Chris is a young physical therapy student on affiliation from the local university. Chris will soon graduate. Chris has great potential. Chris has a previous undergraduate degree in business administration and has worked in a physician's office as an office manager. Chris is looking forward to graduation, becoming a physical

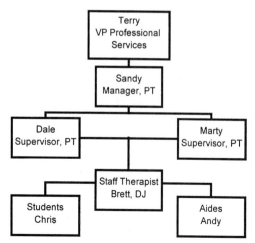

FIGURE A.1. Memorial Hospital Physical Therapy Department organizational structure: Initial.

therapist and moving on to graduate business school. Chris does not know Sandy well but has heard terrible things about Sandy from the staff. Chris is a bit uncomfortable at this party, but agreed to attend at Marty's request. Marty is Chris's clinical instructor.

Sandy

Sandy, the guest of honor at this party, is a long-time physical therapy manager who has not kept up with changes in clinical or management practice. Sandy has been a non attentive, disinterested manager for some time. Sandy knows that the staff is frustrated by what they perceive as a lack of involvement, commitment and interest. The staff has been told that Sandy is leaving voluntarily, but Sandy feels forced out by hospital administration.

Brett

Brett is a physical therapist who has been out of school for 10 years and has never been to a continuing education course.

DJ

DJ is a physical therapist with 20 years' experience who has attained a senior therapist status. DJ is well-respected by peers and is often sought out as a resource to help other staff manage their patients. DJ is struggling with the new paradigms

of physical therapy service delivery. This is especially true for the relationship between quality care, the growing demands for staff productivity, and changes resulting from the Balanced Budget Act of 1997. DJ is very sorry to see Sandy leave. Sandy has always supported DJ in pursuit of clinical advancement. DJ is concerned and suspicious about what will happen next at the hospital. DJ is anxious to know who will replace Sandy and whether they will support DJ's clinical activities. DJ's biggest concern is that the new manager will only care about finances.

Pat

Pat is a physical therapist with 15 years' experience who owns a private practice. Pat has received great financial reward for ownership of the private practice but has begun to notice that the financial environment for the private practitioner is changing rapidly. Pat and Sandy started working together at the hospital many years ago. Pat left the hospital to start a private practice 10 years ago. Pat has worked with Sandy on various projects over the years and was invited to this party by the staff. Sandy is happy that Pat is here. Pat can't help but contemplate the career choice differences that Pat and Sandy made to get to this point.

Andy

Andy is a physical therapy aide who was trained on the job at the hospital. Andy has been a staff member in the department for many, many years. Andy is unsure about what Sandy's leaving will mean to aides at the hospital. Andy is glad to be a union member. To Andy, that means job security.

As the scene unfolds, Marty is involved in an intense conversation with Dale. Marty has expressed concern about the advantages and disadvantages of becoming more involved in the management of the department. Marty is concerned about how to balance the time demands of management activities with the need to continue to develop as a clinician. A major concern for Marty is the potential to focus so much time on the department management that the clinical needs of Marty's patients might become secondary. This is something that Marty had seen happen to Sandy. Dale encourages Marty to consider both the advantages and disadvantages of being a supervisor.

Chapter 1 Role Play Questions

Question 1A. If you were Marty, what would you consider to be the advantages of becoming a supervisor? List at least five.

Question 1B. If you were Marty, what would you consider to be the disadvantages of becoming a supervisor? List at least five.

Dale reviews the list of advantages and disadvantages that Marty has compiled. One of the key points for Dale's success as a supervisor has been to find ways to build upon the advantages and to minimize the disadvantages.

Question 1C. Given the list of advantages created above, what can be done to build upon these advantages to make a supervisory role most successful?

Question 1D. Considering the disadvantages listed above, what can be done to minimize these factors?

In another corner of the room, Chris is thinking about the future, as students often do. Chris's clinical instructor is Marty. The relationship between Chris and Marty is excellent. Marty has been a very good therapist and supervisor. Chris is planning to attend business graduate school after completing physical therapy school. Chris has a strong interest in becoming a manager. As Chris reflects on the role that Marty has as clinical instructor, there are many of Marty's attributes that Chris would like to emulate.

Question 1E. Consider supervisors from the past and present, those that have been successful, and those that have not been as successful. What attributes are needed for someone to be successful as a supervisor in physical therapy? List several.

Question 1F. Again considering past and present supervisors, what attributes must be avoided to be successful as a supervisor in physical therapy?

As the farewell party for Sandy winds down, it is time for the staff to present Sandy with a farewell gift. In addition to the traditional watch engraved with appreciation, the staff has decided to give Sandy an additional gift—the gift of advice. Each person attending this party has been requested to prepare a brief (2 to 3 sentence) statement to be read to Sandy as a means of wishing Sandy well and imparting some advice for future success.

Question 1G. Review what is known about the party goers and indicate what they might wish to say in their statements to Sandy. Marty? Dale? Chris? Brett? DJ? Pat? Andy?

It is now Sandy's turn to address the audience.

Question 1H. What might Sandy wish to say as a means of expressing appreciation and imparting advice to those present?

Question 1I. Considering the changing health care environment of our characters, project scenarios for the future of hospital physical therapy care and private practice physical therapy. Hospital based physical therapy? Private practice physical therapy?

The party ends without incident. The department does not have a plan of succession to replace Sandy. Until a new manager is identified, Dale will be appointed as an acting manager filling Sandy's responsibilities.

CHAPTER 2: VALUES

Highlights

Dale weighs the impact of changing jobs to join a private practice on important personal and family life issues. Dale considers both the stress and financial risks. DJ and Brett discuss the role of continuing education for the professional PT. There is a review of how Sandy loses the job in a restructuring. All the characters struggle with defining high-quality PT.

The Saga Continues

All the excitement has died down after the successful farewell party for Sandy. A week has passed since Sandy's departure. Dale is acting manager for the department (Figure A.2). Thoughts and worries are rushing through

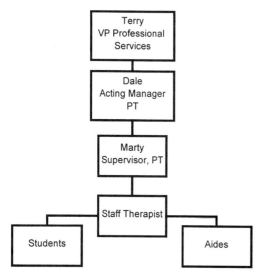

FIGURE A.2. Memorial Hospital Physical Therapy Department organizational structure: Restructured.

Dale's mind during the drive home after a hectic day. A number of events have occurred today that bother Dale.

Pat called Dale today. Pat wants to talk to Dale about joining Pat's private practice as an equity partner. Pat is planning a new site and wants Dale to not only run the site, but to own 50% of it. Financially, it could be a very good move for Dale. However, it would require an investment and there is the risk of losing that investment. Such a loss could seriously affect Dale's family and their plans to retire in 12 years. Dale cannot help but worry about the potential that the new venture might fail. Then Dale would be out of a job and would lose a big part of the money that had been saved for retirement and the children's college education.

Dale also feels a strong sense of loyalty to the staff in the department. They just lost one manager. If Dale left, that would be two management changes in a very short period of time. Would it be fair to them to leave them without leadership? Marty has much talent but little supervisory experience. Would the staff think that Dale was leaving a sinking ship? What about the patients? Who would make sure that they got high-quality care?

Chapter 2 Role Play Questions

Question 2A. What are Dale's responsibilities as Dale contemplates the decision to stay or leave?

Question 2B. Who should Dale include in these deliberations about the future?

Question 2C. Are there some creative solutions to this dilemma that may help Dale feel less anxious about the choices?

Dale thinks back to a meeting attended with Sandy about 3 months before Sandy announced her resignation. This meeting was held in the administration office with Terry, Vice President of Professional Services for the hospital. Terry is a tough, no-nonsense manager who demands results and lets you know it when they don't happen. During this meeting with Sandy and Terry, it became clear that Terry was not happy with Sandy's or the department's performance. Because of some changes in insurance contracts, and changes in Medicare reimbursement, the hospital was not making as much profit from physical therapy as it had in the past. In effect, the physical therapy department was doing the same volume of activity but making less money for the hospital. Terry wanted Sandy and Dale to understand that this was not acceptable. Something was going to have to change.

About a month after that first meeting, Sandy came back from another meeting with Terry very upset. Sandy had chosen to disregard Terry's concerns about the deteriorating profit margin. Terry had asked Sandy to review the plans to address this problem. Sandy had no plans. It was not clear to Dale if Sandy was interested in continuing to try to manage the department or not.

Over time, because of Sandy's consistent failure to act on obvious problems in the department, Dale became concerned that Sandy might be clinically depressed. Dale was unsure of what to do about that.

Question 2D. What should Dale do next?

When Dale went to Terry to discuss Sandy's situation, Terry informed Dale that Sandy's position was going to be eliminated in a restructuring. Sandy would have the option to resign or be laid-off. The rationale given for the change was financial, but Dale believed it was related to Sandy's performance or lack thereof. Terry informed Dale that as the most experienced supervisor in the department, Dale would become the acting manager until a plan could be put in place to restructure the department. Terry thanked Dale for the extra effort but made it clear that this field promotion was not open to discussion or negotiation. Dale would just have to do it.

Dale was concerned about the manner in which Terry made the decision about Sandy. Could Dale be ousted just as easily? Dale was weighing which would be more stressful—staying at the hospital where managers get laid off or taking Pat up on the offer to become a partner in Pat's private practice.

Question 2E. As Dale weighs the options of staying at the hospital or moving into private practice. What moral obligations should be considered here?

Question 2F. What are the ethical principals implicated in each of these options?

Question 2G. What are the primary duties that Dale has? Who are the stakeholders to whom Dale has these duties?

While Dale has a troubled drive home, DJ and Brett are in their usual car pool driving home. Because they live rather close together, they have chosen to share expenses and alternate driving on the days that their schedules coincide. DJ is describing a recent continuing education course that DJ attended. DJ has attended a large number of continuing education courses over a 20-year PT career. Many of the courses that DJ attended were paid for by the hospital as part of the benefit package, but quite a few were not. In those cases, DJ paid for the courses out of pocket. DJ found something worthwhile and useful in every continuing education course attended.

Brett has only attended continuing education when it was offered at inservices or otherwise provided on site by the hospital. Brett has never considered paying for a course. "If it is so important for my job that I know this material, the hospital should pay for it," Brett contends. Brett also feels this way about payment for professional membership dues.

As they navigate through the traffic toward home, DJ and Brett engage in a lively discussion on the value of professional development.

Question 2H. Consider what you know about the two therapists. What are they likely to say regarding who is responsible for continuing education and professional association membership? DJ? Brett?

Question 2I. What impact these issues have on how each defines a good therapist?

Question 2J. What factors should be considered when deciding on a plan of professional development for a staff therapist?

Question 2K. What role should the manager and the employer have in professional development?

After Sandy left, in spite of Sandy's comments indicating that departure was voluntary, several staff began to gossip about Sandy being forced out. When asked, Dale responded appropriately that Sandy had indicated that this was a voluntary departure. At the next staff meeting, staff continued to discuss Sandy's departure. There was significant discussion about how busy the department was and that everything seemed to be going so well. To several staff, it seemed like administration was just trying to get more work out of the staff even if that meant a lower quality of care for the patients. As the staff members continued this discussion, there seemed to be the general feeling that doing more work meant that the work needed to be done less well. This was not acceptable to the staff. DJ made several strong statements about not "giving up quality PT" just to get more done. None of the staff was specific in defining quality care.

Question 2L. How are the staff defining quality?

Question 2M. How should the staff define quality?

Question 2N. How does treating more patients relate to the quality of patient care?

Question 2O. What responsibilities does the staff have in relation to the quality of care and quantity of care?

Question 2P. To whom are these duties owed?

Question 2Q. What role should Dale and Marty play in these discussions?

At the end of the staff meeting, there was no consensus on a course of action. The staff had aired many concerns but nothing had been done to address them. The meeting ended without resolution of staff concerns. In general, there was a continued frustration and dissatisfaction with what was happening in the department.

Question 2R. What might have been done differently to help staff deal with their frustrations?

Question 2S. Dale clearly has responsibilities to many different individuals. Make a list of stakeholders that are important for Dale to interact with throughout the course of the workday.

CHAPTER 3: MARKETING

Highlights

Dale decides to develop several clinical programs that will differentiate the hospital's physical therapy service in the market. Dale reviews the steps of the program development process and prepares a marketing plan. Marty is also faced with some tough decisions about the existing range of hospital-based physical therapy programs as the impact of a merger and a shift in local demographics makes some of the current programs obsolete. Marty must decide which of the current programs will continue and which ones will be terminated. There are many personnel and people issues to consider as part of the termination decisions. After graduation, Chris is hired by Pat to help with a market analysis and marketing plan.

After Dale turns down the offer to open a new site with Pat, Pat approaches the hospital for a potential joint venture. The hospital agrees and assigns Dale to run the new site.

The Saga Continues

Dale has given the private practice opportunity a tremendous amount of thought. In spite of the potential financial return, Dale has decided to stay with the hospital. Dale met with Pat to convey this message. After the meeting with Pat, Dale felt much less anxious. It was as if a weight was lifted. Dale now was able to focus on the work at the hospital—and there was plenty of work to be done. Being able to focus on the tasks at hand feels good to Dale.

The first activity for Dale is to fully analyze the existing types of services that the department offers. Dale finds that many of the services available through the department don't produce the same revenue that they did just a few years ago. Upon review of this situation, Dale decides to develop a plan that will offer a variety of new, better reimbursed programs. Dale will also need to make some decisions about the existing programs that may not be able to pay for themselves. Table A.1 shows the existing physical therapy programs and their reimbursement:

Chapter 3 Role Play Questions

Question 3A. What additional information should Dale consider when making decisions about program closure or rejuvenation?

Question 3B. Who should be included in these discussions?

Marty is working very closely with Dale on this project. It is the feeling of Dale and Marty that the mix of programs that the department offers will have a very big impact on the financial success or failure of the department. To the staff therapists, the idea of closing some of the existing programs in favor of new, untested programs seems to be changing things just to change them. There is significant resistance to discussing termination of some of the larger existing programs—even those that lose money.

Question 3C. What might cause staff resistance to closing programs?

Question 3D. What should Dale and Marty do to reduce this resistance?

As an outcome of potential program closure decisions, Dale and Marty must put together an analysis of the impact that potential program termination will have on staffing levels.

Question 3E. What process should be followed in determining which staff positions would be eliminated if a program is closed? Keep in mind that eliminating positions may result in staff layoffs.

Many new programs are being contemplated.

▦ TABLE A.1
Memorial Hospital Physical Therapy Department Programs And Reimbursement Analysis

PROGRAM	VOLUME	FINANCIAL CONTRIBUTION (LAST FY)	EXPENSE TO REJUVENATE	ACTIONS TO REJUVENATE
Adult Day Rehab	15 patients/day	Loss of $100K	Very high	Increase volume Decrease costs Decrease scope of service offered
Parkinson Education Program	25 patient/month	Profit of $10K	Moderate	Decrease costs Lower staffing level
Back School	15 patients/week	Profit of $25K	Low	Increase volume
Aquatic Program	10 patients/day	Loss of $15K	Very high	Increase volume Decrease costs Decrease overhead
Student Education Program	10 Students/Year	Unknown Suspect loss but difficult to quantify	Unknown	Unknown Increase CI productivity Full analysis of the contribution and costs of the program
Wound Care Program	2 patients/day	Loss of $75K	Very high	Decrease costs Reimbursement very poor Minimize volume

Key: Loss = costs exceed payment for services; Profit = payment exceeds costs for services.

Those that seem to be the most attractive include the following:

- Sports medicine screening and clinics
- Balance and fall prevention programs
- Home care and hospice care

Question 3F. What process should be used to analyze these programs to determine which, if any, should be implemented?

Chris has now completed the academic and clinic education components of the university's physical therapy curriculum. In anticipation of taking the national examination in 2 months, Chris applies for a job in Pat's clinic to assist with market analysis and development of a marketing plan for Pat's private practice.

Question 3G. Where should Chris start in the development of a marketing plan for Pat's clinic? What are the first three actions Chris should take?

Question 3H. What role should Pat play in the development of the marketing plan?

When Dale informed Pat that the proposed partnership for Pat's new clinic site was not possible, Pat was concerned. Pat did not have adequate internal resources to proceed with develop-ment of the new site without a partner. Pat decided to pursue alternate partners in this project.

Several weeks later, Dale is asked to attend a meeting with Terry. Pat is also in attendance. Pat's practice and the hospital have signed an agreement to develop the new site as a joint venture. Pat will oversee the project, but Terry informs Dale that the hospital will provide management and staff for the new site. Terry assigns Dale as the full-time onsite manager for the new site. Marty will assume Dale's responsibilities as acting manager of the hospital's physical therapy department. There will be no increase in salary or other compensation for Dale. Later, Dale learns that Marty will receive a 10% salary increase.

Dale is now faced with the opportunity to pursue the private practice project that was so difficult to turn down. However, Dale will not participate in the risk or financial rewards of private practice. Dale will remain as a salaried hospital employee. This strikes Dale as the worst case scenario of more work for the same pay. Dale is also concerned that this action may be an attempt to force Dale to leave the hospital.

Question 3I. What might Dale do regarding reassignment to the new site?

Question 3J. What should Dale do regarding developing a better working relationship with Terry? With Pat?

Marty's role and departmental leadership has changed again.

Question 3K. Is there a strategy that Marty can use to try to stabilize the department and help it move forward toward success?

Question 3L. Considering the new site, what are the options for coordinating leadership and staff at the new site with those at Pat's private practice and the hospital staff?

Question 3M. How should the decisions regarding staffing and leadership of the new site be made?

As Dale reflects on the events of the day, the feelings of confusion and hopelessness are significant. Dale is feeling like a puppet in a very confusing play. Dale will need to find a way to deal with these feelings. If not, Dale may need to seek employment in an alternate setting.

CHAPTER 4: ORGANIZING AND ENGAGING PEOPLE

Highlights

Dale and Marty discuss the role of PT in the global health care environment. Marty ponders his future as a new manager since Sandy left. Dale is directive in the approach. Marty is a facilitator. Pat is approached by a group of affiliated private practice physical therapists. They want Pat to join their provider network. Memorial Hospital merges with another local hospital. Dale decides that a new job is in order but is unsure of the timing.

The Saga Continues

As we return to our struggling characters, it is 6 months later. Dale is the onsite manager at the new joint venture satellite clinic that is open and running smoothly. Dale feels relieved to be out of the confusion and turmoil of the hospital department. Sometimes, Dale misses the excitement of the hospital and the interaction with its larger staff.

Marty has had several long discussions with Terry. Terry has made it clear that the most important part of Marty's job is to make sure the department stays on budget and performs as expected. Although Marty does not find the relationship with Terry to be comfortable or warm, Marty feels that the relationship works for now.

Marty and Dale continue to work together on a regular basis. Marty represents the hospital department and Dale represents the joint venture satellite. The working and personal relationships have survived the turmoil of the transition very well. Marty and Dale enjoy working together and support each other well. In times of vacation, they cover for each other.

Dale's relationship with Terry continues to be strained. Dale feels Terry was unfair in the decision to move Dale to the satellite. Dale feels Terry should have included Dale in the decision process, not just announced it, particularly because the announcement was made in front of others. Dale now tries to avoid any contact with Terry and often asks Marty to interact with Terry on Dale's behalf. Dale has the convenient excuse of being off site at the new satellite.

Chapter 4 Role Play Questions

Question 4A. What other strategy could Dale use to improve the relationship with Terry?

Marty is growing into the role of manager very well. Marty still has some concern about the balance between management and clinical time, but Marty continues to learn new ways to manage time more efficiently.

Recently Marty has been very reflective. Marty has noticed that there are several different ways in which a manager can lead staff. Marty and Dale have different styles. Marty tends to try to coach staff through problems by counseling them and encouraging them to find the solutions themselves. Dale is much more direct in approach. When staff bring problems, Dale often tells the staff member what to do. So far, both styles have worked well for each of the managers. Marty wonders if one style is better than the other. After discussion with Dale and some additional reading and research, Marty concludes that the best style is the one best fitted to the staff members involved and to the situation at hand.

Question 4B. What are some situational characteristics that might be handled best with a coaching style of management? Of a directive style of management?

Question 4C. What are some characteristics of staff who respond best to a coaching style of management? To a directive style of management?

At the weekly leadership meeting that Dale and Marty have, the two managers find themselves in a discussion on the role of physical therapy in the global healthcare environment. Dale points out that the health care world has changed significantly in the past few years. Changes in reimbursement, changes in clinical care, new management philosophies, and shifts toward more provider accountability and higher productivity have all occurred. Financially, physical therapy is no longer the golden egg it once was. Marty notes that all of these changes make it somewhat harder to manage the department well. Dale agrees.

Question 4D. How have changes in health care and, specifically physical therapy, changed the manner in which a manager must lead staff and direct the department?

Question 4E. What impact have these changes had on physical therapy in larger organizations?

Pat, as a private practitioner, feels somewhat isolated from the organizational turmoil that the hospital is experiencing. Escaping all the bureaucracy is one of the reasons that Pat started the private practice. Pat is beginning to remember how large organizations work now that the joint venture satellite is in place. These are not all pleasant memories. Pat has had to increase contact and interaction with a large number of the hospital staff, including administrators, financial analysts, reimbursement specialists, human resource representatives and legal counsel. One of the things that Pat has noticed is that, unlike the individuals who perform these roles in the private practice, many of the hospital representatives are excellent at global health care issues but unfamiliar with the specifics of running a physical therapy business. Pat finds that all of the hospital staff are very pleasant and competent professionals, but the lack of physical therapy specific knowledge is quite frustrating for Pat.

Question 4F. As Pat interacts with the myriad of hospital staff that do not report to Pat but from whom Pat needs support, what strategies can Pat use to enlist their support and cooperation? Would these strategies be different if Pat was their boss?

In the meantime, Pat receives a phone call from a representative of a consortium of private practice physical therapy clinics. Pat is invited to join their network. The purpose of the network is to allow a single entity, the network, to represent all of the member private practice clinics to insurers and other third party payers. Each member clinic remains independent, but works with the other members of the network toward mutually beneficial goals.

Question 4G. What questions should Pat ask as discussions with the network begin?

At the end of the work day, Pat, Dale and Marty all receive a message about a mandatory meeting the next morning at 8:00 AM. Because these kind of meetings are rare, something important must be happening. Anxiety is high that night as all three managers speculate about the next morning's meeting.

At the mandatory meeting, Terry announces that Memorial Hospital has entered into merger discussions with the competing hospital in town, Community Hospital. More information will be available soon Terry tells all the managers. Until more details are available, Terry asks all the managers to withhold any of this information from staff because "we don't want to unnecessarily excite anyone". Thirty minutes after the mandatory meeting, rumors abound throughout the hospital. Obviously, someone decided to ignore Terry's request to keep the merger information confidential. Staff are excited, anxious and upset.

Question 4H. Each of the managers must now engage in damage control with their respective staffs. How should they proceed? Pat? Marty? Dale?

Question 4I. How might the hospital have shared

information about the merger discussions with managers and staff to decrease staff concern and anxiety?

At the end of a very difficult week, Dale is again driving home, thinking about work life. The job and personal stress that Dale is experiencing is significant. Dale is tired and ready for a change. Dale decides that when the time is right, a job change is needed. Until then, Dale will perform at work as well as possible, but the future is elsewhere for Dale.

CHAPTER 5: DEALING WITH DIFFERENCES

Highlights

Many of the staff state that they want a director like Dale, not a facilitator like Marty. Dale has to resolve a conflict with Marty because of some unfinished tasks that Dale leaves behind. Brett and DJ share a patient and differ in how to treat the patient. Marty has to intervene.

The Saga Continues

This seems to be a time of high energy and emotion for our characters. The environment at the hospital and within the private practice seems to be very unstable. With all the merger activity, an uncertain future, and instability in leadership and structure, everyone seems to be a little frustrated, anxious and testy.

This morning Marty arrives in the department to find a group of staff who demand to meet with Marty immediately. Marty has not even had time to change into a lab coat, the typical dress in the department. Marty asks them to step into the meeting room and they all sit down. There are five staff therapists in the group. Brett is the spokesperson. Brett explains that this is very hard for the staff to do, "but things just can't go on like they are." When Marty asks for more information, Brett explains that Marty is the problem. The staff, Brett says, want more direction and less of Marty's "wishy washy management nonsense." Marty, caught by surprise and taken aback by Brett's statement, asks what that means. Brett goes on to explain that Marty is a good person, the entire staff

knows that. But something changed when Marty became manager. It is not like it used to be. Brett continues, "You never give us good direction or complete information. When we have problems, you end up telling us to figure out the solution. Sandy and Dale always gave us the answers." All the therapists present nod in agreement. "We want you to be more like Sandy and Dale". Marty is at a loss for words.

Chapter 5 Role Play Questions

Question 5A. What should Marty do next?

Question 5B. What will need to happen to resolve this situation? Is it resolvable?

Question 5C. How can Marty use good conflict management skills to facilitate a resolution?

Marty continues to ask questions of the group in an attempt to understand the issues and concerns. Marty is unsure how to proceed at this time, so Marty asks the group for some time to consider what they have shared. A meeting for the next morning is scheduled.

Question 5D. What should Marty do in the next 24 hours to prepare for tomorrow's meeting with the group of therapists?

Later that day, Marty is asked by DJ to help with a problem. While DJ was on vacation last week, Brett covered some of DJ's patients. Many of the treatment plans that DJ had set up for the patients were changed by Brett. DJ feels some of the patients may interpret these changes as Brett overriding DJ's clinical authority. DJ feels that Brett has made DJ look inferior to the patients. When DJ approached Brett on this issue, the response was "I had to do what I thought was best for those patients."

Currently, there are no guidelines for therapist authority while covering someone else's patients. Both DJ and Brett seem upset by this situation. As Marty observes them both, the growing tension between them seems to interfere with their ability to adequately perform their jobs.

Question 5E. What should Marty do to assist Brett and DJ in this situation?

Question 5F. What are the positions that Brett

and DJ are likely to take in this discussion? Brett? DJ?

Question 5G. What are Marty's duties in this situation? To Brett? To DJ? To the patients?

Question 5H. Is there a creative strategy to turn this conflict into a future source of strength for the department and the therapists involved?

Meanwhile, Chris continues to work on the marketing plan for Pat's private practice. As Chris completes the analysis of the geographic market, it becomes very clear that there are very obvious differences in the cultural and socioeconomic compositions of different geographic areas around Pat's practice. There are four major areas and groups that Chris identifies:

1. North section: upper middle class, primarily Caucasian, well-educated, high employment, much private insurance, big houses, low population density, generally healthy population, low crime rate, very poor public transportation.
2. South section: working poor, multi cultural with a large migrant and non-English speaking population, low literacy rate, high unemployment, many uninsured or under insured, small homes and multifamily dwellings, very high population density, significant geriatric population, high proportion of chronic illness, high crime rate, good public transportation.
3. East section: blue collar, multi cultural, high employment rate, primarily dual income families, lower middle class, single family homes, high population density, moderate crime rate, good public transportation.
4. West section: blue collar, multi cultural, high unemployment, area is dominated by industrial complexes, low population density, many lower middle class but significant lower and poverty level families, high crime rate, poor public transportation.

Pat is most interested in development of new satellite sites and new programs. The programs most likely to be developed include sports medicine, injured worker programs and home care.

Question 5I. What additional information will Chris need to consider as the marketing plan is developed?

Question 5J. How would Chris determine which geographic areas will be most likely to match the programs being developed?

Question 5K. Do Chris and Pat have a duty to consider placement of new clinics in all four of the geographic and demographic markets?

Question 5L. Who else should Chris consider to include in the decisions about the marketing plan?

CHAPTER 6: STRUCTURE AND CONTROL

Highlights

Dale decides to start a private practice. Marty is asked to lead the remaining staff at the hospital as a facilitator, not a director. Marty has to review motivation and team building for his new role as a leader, not a manager. Dale has to determine a recruitment and retention plan for the new clinic.

The Saga Continues

With the expansion of clinical services to the new satellite, it will be necessary to hire some new staff to provide the additional services. Marty and Dale agree to work together to develop a recruitment plan. Because of the organizational unrest and perceived low staff morale, Dale suggests that a major component of the recruitment plan be related to retaining the current staff. Marty and Dale work to develop a formal recruitment and retention plan. The focus of the plan is two fold. First, a review of the compensation package offered to staff to make sure that salary and benefits are competitive and not driving potential job candidates or current staff to other employers. Second, to establish an exciting and rewarding professional environment that will allow staff to realize job satisfaction and professional and personal growth.

Chapter 6 Role Play Questions

Question 6A. How should Dale and Marty proceed with determining if the compensation package is adequate?

Question 6B. What factors should be included in discussions related to developing a strong professional environment that will allow staff to grow and succeed?

Dale continues to feel frustration in the role of onsite manager for the hospital/private practice joint venture satellite. Recently, the staff at the satellite have raised questions related to the business structure of the satellite. The staff is aware that the clinic is a joint venture between a not-for-profit hospital, Memorial Hospital, and the for-profit private practice. Many questions have come up related to Pat's role as owner of the private practice. The staff seem to resent the fact that the work they do as hospital employees is directly benefitting the owner of a private practice. The staff approach Dale with these concerns. The first thing that Dale explains to the staff is the structure of the joint venture. See Figure A.3.

Question 6C. Using the organizational chart in Figure A.3, how should Dale explain this structure to the staff?

Question 6D. Referring to the organizational structure in Figure A.3, what alternative structures could exist for the joint venture clinic?

Question 6E. What options might Dale have re-

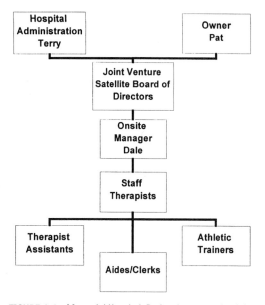

FIGURE A.3. Memorial Hospital: Pat's private practice joint venture organizational structure.

lated to the staff concerns about to Pat profiting from the clinic?

In discussing this situation with Pat, Dale becomes convinced that Pat is not willing to support Dale as manager of the satellite clinic. Given all the past stress and frustrations that Dale has experienced, it seems time for Dale's spouse to be included in discussions related to Dale's continued employment. After some intense soul searching, Dale decides now is the time to leave hospital employment. What Dale is unsure about is what to do next.

Question 6F. List some of the choices available to Dale within the physical therapy profession.

Highest on Dale's list of options are looking for another similar management job or starting a new private practice. Dale does not have a contract with the hospital or with Pat that would preclude competition or starting a new practice. Dale decides that the best choice is to start a new private practice. The practice would be in direct competition with both the hospital and Pat's private practice. This is a big step for Dale.

Question 6G. What are some of the most important issues that Dale must address before being able to make this decision?

Before Dale's resignation from the hospital, Terry had decided to restructure the department. The biggest aspect of this restructuring is to appoint Marty as Physical Therapy Facilitator rather than director or manager. Until this restructuring, Marty had been acting manager of the Physical Therapy Department. Terry attends the next departmental meeting and announces this structural change to the staff.

Question 6H. When asked about the practical implications of having a facilitator rather than director or manager, how is Terry likely to respond?

Terry is also asked why this decision was made.

Question 6I. What could be Terry's rationale for making this decision. What might be Terry's reasons for making this decision at this particular time?

Question 6J. What additional information should Marty request of Terry as Marty assumes this new role?

Question 6K. Given Marty's old and new roles, draw a schematic representation of the department organizational structure before and after the restructuring?

CHAPTER 7: FINANCIAL MANAGEMENT

Highlights

With strong spousal support Dale starts planning for the private practice. Dale analyzes the financial realities of opening a new practice. Dale contacts a bank to acquire working capital. Dale develops a cash flow analysis for the practice based on estimates of practice performance.

The Saga Continues

What an exciting day! Dale has made the decision to start a private practice. The list of priorities is enormous. Dale creates a list of things that need to be done before treating the first patient. As Dale evaluates all the things on the to-do list, they all seem to be very important. In no particular order, Dale's list includes the following:

* Secure an adequate supply of patients
* Acquire insurance contracts so payments can be collected from the top insurers in the area
* Notify potential referrers of the new practice
* Find a location for the practice
* Develop construction and occupancy plans including necessary permits
* Secure startup funding for the new clinic
* Acquire furniture and equipment
* Review and satisfy all legal requirements for establishing a business
* Develop a plan to cover personal living expenses during the practice start up period
* Develop a formal marketing plan
* Develop a formal business plan
* Establish banking privileges, including checking, savings and credit card merchant accounts

Chapter 7 Role Play Questions

Question 7A. What else should Dale consider in preparation for opening the private practice?

Question 7B. Where should Dale start? List the five items that should be Dale's highest temporal priorities.

It is now time to proceed with securing capital (money) for the startup of the clinic. Dale has consulted a local accountant who estimates that the amount needed from outside sources will be $100,000 for the first year of operation.

Question 7C. What options exist for acquiring the startup funds?

Question 7D. What sort of documents will Dale need to secure the necessary loan?

Dale and the accountant estimate the following conditions will exist for at least the first year:

New patients	5 per week increasing at 20% per month for 1 year
Visits per patient	8 per episode of care decreasing by 10% each year
Gross Revenue	$55.00 per visit decreasing by 15% each year
Collections	85% collected with 90 day delay from billing date

Question 7E. Determine the expected cash flow in the practice for the first year of operation by completing the following cash flow table. See Table A.2, Parts A and B (pages 324 and 326).

Dale's accountant also estimates that expenses will be as listed below:

Capital start up	$70,000
Operating Expenses	$15,000 monthly, increasing 15% per month

Question 7F. Estimate the ongoing operational expenses for the first year of operation by completing the expense charts presented in Table A.3, Parts A and B.

Question 7G. Examining the cash flow chart presented in Table A.4, does the monthly flow of cash into the practice (collections) exceed the monthly operating expenses during the first year of operation? What does this say about the break even point for the practice?

Question 7H. Will the accountant's estimate of a $100,000 loan be sufficient for the practice to survive?

TABLE A.2A
Sample Cash Flow Table

	MONTH											
	1	2	3	4	5	6	7	8	9	10	11	12
New Patients												
Visits												
Gross Revenue ($000's)												
Collection ($000's)												
Cumulative Collected ($000's)												

Question 7I. What management actions could Dale take to produce a more favorable financial projection?

What started as an exciting day for Dale has proven to be rather depressing. Dale realizes that the practice will require significantly more working capital than was first anticipated. To acquire this working capital, Dale schedules an appointment with the local bank. Fortunately, the banker is familiar with the excellent potential for success for physical therapy clinics. The bank agrees to work closely with Dale to develop a more formal business plan for the clinic.

CHAPTER 8: FINANCIAL PERFORMANCE

Highlights

Marty has to deal with the financial implications of the merger. Managed care reimbursement is dropping. Dale has to acquire financing for the new practice. Dale has to develop a business plan that includes the critical analyses that are discussed in the text.

Marty finds out that Brett and DJ both have received a substantial number of third party payment rejections. Marty has to work with them to appeal the current rejections and develop a plan to prevent rejections in the future.

The Saga Continues

The merger arrangement between Memorial Hospital and Community Hospital is proceeding along a very aggressive time line. It is now clear to Marty that the merger is very likely to happen. Marty has met with Terry a number of times to review the potential impacts that the merger may have on the physical therapy department. Marty has also met the Director of the Physical Therapy Department at Community Hospital.

It is apparent to Marty that the merged hospitals will only need one department head for the two physical therapy departments. Given the intense work load of the job Marty has at Memorial Hospital, Marty is concerned that the new position over both hospital departments would be too much and too difficult to do suc-

⊞ **TABLE A.3A**
Example Expense Chart

	MONTH											
	1	**2**	**3**	**4**	**5**	**6**	**7**	**8**	**9**	**10**	**11**	**12**
Start Up ($000's)												
Operating Expenses ($000's)												
Total Expenses ($000's)												
Total Cumulative Expenses ($000's)												

cessfully. However, Marty is concerned about financial security. From an ego standpoint, Marty wants to be offered the opportunity to lead both departments.

One of Marty's biggest concerns about the proposed merger is that there would need to be some consolidation of services. This would create a situation in which there was an excess of staff for the volume of services required. A reduction in personnel levels (layoffs) might be necessary.

Chapter 8 Role Play Questions

Question 8A. What options might exist, other than layoffs, to address a situation in which the demand for services is less than the capacity to provide those services?

Question 8B. Before any final staff reduction decision, with whom should Marty consult for advice and guidance?

Until the hospital merger is finalized, Marty is expected to continue to lead the department at Memorial Hospital. It will soon be budget preparation time. To prepare, Marty has been reviewing the financial status of the department. As the environment has been changing, there have been several significant changes within the physical therapy department. Tables A.5 and A.6 show the type of services provided in the physical therapy department in the most

recent fiscal year and the projected change in these volumes.

Question 8C. What staffing changes, if any, are likely to be required to meet these volume projections?

Question 8D. In addition to staffing level changes, what other possible changes should MaFrty anticipate, based on the information in the previous two tables?

Marty is also concerned about changes in the amount of reimbursement for the services that the department provides. Table A.7 shows the predominant reimbursement model for each of the major service areas in physical therapy. There are likely to be further reductions in these reimbursement rates. The finance department at the hospital has made some projections of these changes. Table A.8 shows the projections from the finance department.

Question 8E. What are the likely implications for Marty as the department manager that are suggested by these projected reimbursement changes?

Dale is now preparing to submit the final loan application to the bank for the startup funding of the private practice. The bank officer has asked Dale to include with the application projections of volume and cash flow.

TABLE A.2B
Completed Cash Flow Table

	MONTH											
	1	2	3	4	5	6	7	8	9	10	11	12
New Patients	20	24	29	35	41	50	60	72	86	103	124	148
Visits	160	192	230	276	332	398	478	573	688	826	991	1189
Gross Revenue ($000's)	8.8	10.5	12.6	15.2	18.2	21.9	26.2	31.5	37.8	45.4	54.4	65.3
Collection ($000's)	0	0	0	7.48	8.92	10.7	12.9	15.5	18.6	22.3	26.8	32.1
Cumulative Collected ($000's)	0	0	0	7.48	16.4	27.1	40.0	55.5	74.1	96.4	123.2	155.3

Question 8F. Of all the financial documents available for inclusion with this proposal, which documents are most likely to be helpful to the loan officer in making the decision to grant the loan? Consider all the financial reports and forms that are covered in Chapters 7 and 8.

Back at the hospital, Brett and DJ have both been notified that several third party payers had rejected claims for payment for services provided patients they had treated. This is a relatively new phenomenon for the physical therapy department. There are no guidelines for Brett and DJ to follow. They ask Marty to meet with them to review the actions that should be taken when a claim is rejected. Marty is unsure of the correct procedures.

Question 8G. What should Marty do to prepare for the meeting with Brett and DJ regarding the rejected claims?

Question 8H. Who should Marty and the therapists consult with to determine the appropriate course of action for these rejected claims?

Question 8I. What can be done to minimize the potential for claims rejections in the future?

While reflecting on the way a typical day is spent, Marty is amazed how time intensive some of the financial management activities can become.

Question 8J. What can Marty do to become more time efficient with financial matters?

CHAPTER 9: FACILITIES PLANNING

Highlights

Dale has to determine a location for the clinic. Dale struggles with the decision to build new space versus leasing existing space. Marty has to redesign an existing space for a fall prevention program. It is likely that the renovated space will be used for only a few years or until the final effect of the merger is known. Cost efficiency and design flexibility are critical.

TABLE A.3B
Completed Expense Chart

	MONTH											
	1	2	3	4	5	6	7	8	9	10	11	12
Start Up ($000's)	70	0	0	0	0	0	0	0	0	0	0	0
Operating Expenses ($000's)	15	17.3	19.8	22.8	26.22	30.15	34.7	39.9	45.85	52.7	60.6	69.7
Total Expenses ($000's)	85	17.3	19.8	22.8	26.22	30.15	34.7	39.9	45.85	52.7	60.6	69.7
Total Cumulative Expenses ($000's)	85	102.2	122	144.8	171	201.2	235.9	276	321.7	374.4	435	505

TABLE A.4
Estimated Cash Flow Statement For Dale's Private Practice

	MONTH											
MONTH	1	2	3	4	5	6	7	8	9	10	11	12
Monthly Collection ($000's)	0	0	0	7.48	8.92	10.7	12.9	15.5	18.6	22.3	26.8	32.1
Operating Expenses ($000's)	15	17.3	19.8	22.8	26.2	30.2	34.7	39.9	45.9	52.7	60.6	69.7

TABLE A.5
Memorial Hospital Physical Therapy Department Service Volume By Service Line

SERVICE AREA	AVERAGE MONTHLY VOLUME (TREATMENT UNITS) PREVIOUS FISCAL YEAR	PERCENT OF TOTAL
Acute inpatient care-general	2,281	12.7
Acute inpatient care-hydro	243	1.3
Inpatient rehab unit	2,173	12.1
Outpatient care-main campus	6,321	35.3
Outpatient care-satellite A	4,123	23.0
Outpatient care-satellite B	2,756	15.3
Total	17,897	100

TABLE A.6

Memorial Hospital Physical Therapy Department Service Volume Projections By Service Line

SERVICE AREA	AVERAGE MONTHLY VOLUME (TREATMENT UNITS) PREVIOUS FISCAL YEAR	PROJECTED MONTHLY VOLUME (TREATMENT UNITS) NEXT FISCAL YEAR	CHANGE
Acute inpatient care-general	2,281	2,200	−%
Acute inpatient care-hydro	243	225	−%
Inpatient rehab unit	2,173	2,200	1.2%
Outpatient care-main campus	6,321	6,800	7.5%
Outpatient care-satellite A	4,123	4,800	16.4%
Outpatient care-satellite B	2,756	3,500	26.9%
Total	17,897	19,725	10.2%

TABLE A.7

Memorial Hospital Physical Therapy Department Reimbursement by Service Area

SERVICE AREA	PREDOMINANT REIMBURSEMENT TYPE	AVERAGE REIMBURSEMENT RATE*
Acute inpatient care-general	DRG	0%**
Acute inpatient care-hydro	DRG	0%**
Inpatient rehab unit	Cost Reimbursed	75%
Outpatient care-main campus	Fee Schedule	65%
Outpatient-satellite A	Fee Schedule	68%
Outpatient-satellite B	Fee Schedule	61%

* Percent of charges last fiscal year.
** No individual reimbursement for physical therapy due to DRG bundling. Physical Therapy charges paid as part of a case payment rate.

TABLE A.8

Memorial Hospital Physical Therapy Department Projected Reimbursement Trends

SERVICE AREA	AVERAGE REIMBURSEMENT RATE PREVIOUS FISCAL YEAR*	PROJECTED REIMBURSEMENT RATE NEXT FISCAL YEAR
Acute inpatient care-general	0%	0%
Acute inpatient care-hydro	0%	0%
Inpatient Rehab Unit	75%	70%
Outpatient care-Main campus	65%	63%
Outpatient care-Satellite A	68%	62%
Outpatient care-Satellite B	61%	61%

The Saga Continues

Today is a great day for Dale. The bank has approved a loan for up to $250,000 to cover the first years' expenses related to starting his private practice. The payment schedule has some flexibility in it so that if things go well, Dale can pay off the loan earlier than expected. If the practice is slower to take off than Dale projects, the schedule of repayment can be adjusted so that the payments remain manageable.

As soon as Dale can establish and occupy a treatment facility, patients can be treated. To help with the process, Dale contacts a local commercial real estate agent who handles both new construction and existing commercial buildings. Dale meets with the real estate agent and the first question that comes up is whether Dale prefers to build from the ground up or renovate existing space. The best choice would be to find an existing physical therapy clinic that is no longer in use. That would likely minimize renovation costs. However, the chance of finding an appropriately configured physical therapy space available within the right geographic area is unlikely.

Chapter 9 Role Play Questions

Question 9A. Other than an existing physical therapy clinic, what other types of existing business space would be easily renovated for use by a physical therapy practice? Why?

The decision to build or renovate will have serious financial implications. Dale wants to be sure to consider all the factors in making such an important decision.

Question 9B. What factors should Dale consider in deciding whether to build or renovate?

Question 9C. What are the most important financial differences between building a new site and renovating an existing facility?

Question 9D. What are the advantages of building a new site over renovation?

Question 9E. What are the advantages of renovating an existing site over new construction?

Marty is also involved in a construction project. The hospital has decided to proceed with a new fall prevention program. Marty is now working with the hospital's architect to redesign part of the Radiology Department for use as the programs' treatment site. This will only be a temporary site. It is likely that the fall prevention program will be housed in this site for no more than 2 years. Cost efficiency and design flexibility must be emphasized so that the next renovation of that space will not be overly expensive.

Question 9F. What are the physical requirements of a fall prevention program for outpatients? Feel free to make assumptions about volume, type and age of patients, target population characteristics, etc. Be sure to document these assumptions.

Question 9G. What might be designed differently in the renovated space because it will be temporary rather than permanent?

Question 9H. Because the fall prevention program will be located in the hospital, at least for the short term, what services and processes might be able to be shared with other hospital services that might not be available should the program be housed in a satellite location?

As part of the facility design process, both Marty and Dale will want to consider the equipment and furniture needs. Capital and startup equipment expenses can be substantial.

Question 9I. What can Marty and Dale do to minimize the costs of furniture and equipment at startup while still assuring that there is are adequate furnishings for quality patient care?

CHAPTER 10: INFORMATION MANAGEMENT

Highlights

Marty becomes overwhelmed by the mountain of data that must be reviewed. Marty struggles to set up a system to organize the data into usable information. Dale has computer hardware decisions to make as the new clinic is set up. Dale, Marty and Chris struggle with efficient communications methods and look into potential technological solutions.

The Saga Continues

Marty looks around the office. There are reports, financial statements, productivity data, and other kinds of paperwork everywhere. The departmental secretary brings in a new pile of mail and sets it on Marty's desk. The pile of paper and paperwork grows again. Brett walks into Marty's office and leaves the letters that have been written to insurance companies to appeal payment rejections for Brett and DJ's patients. Marty looks up from behind the piles and says to Brett, "Thanks, I think".

Later that day, Marty receives a phone call from Terry in administration. Terry asks for the medical record on one of Marty's patients to answer a billing question. Marty would be happy to get that file out of the office, but first the file must be found amongst the clutter.

Marty is spending more and more time handling paper and less and less time dealing with information and decision making. Marty needs a system to organize all the data that comes into the office. Marty makes a list of all the different types of paper and data that is already somewhere in the office:

1. Payroll reports
2. Productivity reports
3. Medical records
4. Requests for additional information on current and past patients—Marty's and everyone else's
5. Vacation requests
6. Incident reports
7. Budget reports
8. Revenue and expense reports
9. Department policies
10. Hospital policies
11. Routine memoranda from within the hospital
12. Letters and other communications from peers outside the hospital
13. Meeting minutes and agendas
14. Data from the departmental outcome studies
15. Professional journals and magazines
16. Notices of hospital and community events
17. Thank you notes from patients and care partners
18. Monthly reports on departmental performance
19. Annual reports on departmental performance
20. Information and newsletters from external accrediting agencies and third party payers
21. Instruction manuals for departmental equipment and computers
22. Staff orientation manuals
23. Many, many other individual pieces of paper and snippets of data

Marty wonders if some of this information is more important than the rest or if some of it is unnecessary or irrelevant. Marty decides to review all of the papers and "stuff" in the office and determine which require attention of the department facilitator, which can be handled by someone else, and which can be ignored.

Chapter 10 Role Play Questions

Question 10A. Make a listing of all the above items in Marty's office and indicate which ones Marty must handle, which ones can be delegated and to whom, and which items can be put on a back burner. Items Marty must handle? Items Marty can delegate and to whom? Items for the back burner? Other items?

Marty begins to realize that there is a difference between items to handle and take action on and items to store for future reference.

Question 10B. Which items does Marty need only to have access to for future use?

Question 10C. What other actions can Marty take to organize all the data and paper in the office?

Meanwhile Dale is continuing to plan for the opening of the private practice. The clinic will be approximately 3500 square feet with all the functional areas that are found in a typical outpatient orthopedic physical therapy clinic. Dale is now struggling with computer hardware and software decisions for the information infrastructure of the clinic. Dale has heard many horror stories about clinics that bought state-of-the-art computers only to have everything be outdated and need upgrading within 6 to 12 months. Because of the tight budget, that type of capital expenditures after 6 to 12 months will not be an option for Dale's clinic.

Question 10D. What are the primary information needs that will likely exist in Dale's clinic?

Question 10E. Which of the information systems identified above are most critical for the success of the clinic?

Question 10F. What actions could Dale take to minimize the chances that the computer purchases made today will not be outdated in the near future?

Marty, Dale, Pat, Chris and even Sandy regularly participate in the local PT Managers' Forum. The Forum was established to facilitate communication and professional development of physical therapist managers in the area. At the most recent meeting, the topic was "communicating with and supervising staff who are located at a distant site from that of the manager". Chris pointed out that one potential partial solution for the remote manager is to use technology to enhance communication.

Question 10G. What technological options are currently available to this group of local managers to effectively communicate and supervise staff at remote sites?

Question 10H. What are the relative advantages and disadvantages of each of the potential technologies that could assist managers with supervision of remote site staff? Be sure to consider the cost of acquisition, installation, staff training and equipment maintenance in the discussion.

CHAPTER 11: OUTCOME INFORMATION

Highlights

Dale needs to set up a method to measure therapist effectiveness. Marty is asked to serve on an HMO advisory board to review prospective physical therapy clinicians for inclusion in the HMO panel of providers. Criteria for inclusion must be set up and objectively monitored. Meanwhile, Marty is struggling with DJ and Brett who seem threatened by the functional outcome measurement system that has been put in place. They are marginally compliant with it. Chris has a project as a business graduate student that will involve the examination of patient satisfaction parameters in a physical therapy clinic.

The Saga Continues

Dale has opened the private practice and business is growing as projected. It has been approximately 6 months since the doors opened. Dale is starting to develop working relationships with some of the local third party payers. As Dale approaches many of the managed care organizations in this market, they often question how the practice measures quality. Historically, Dale has always relied on professional judgement to decide if the care being given is of high quality. That just does not seem to be enough anymore.

The managed care companies want objective data that shows that the care given positively impacts the patient's outcome. Additionally, Dale is interested in determining which of the therapists are most effective. This will help identify patterns of practice that are most effective for the patients and that are cost efficient.

Chapter 11 Role Play Questions

Question 11A. As Dale considers establishing quality measurements within the practice, what factors might be included in the collection of outcome data?

Question 11B. What resources might Dale use to develop the outcome/quality management system for the clinic?

Marty is also interested in identifying parameters for measuring quality care for the department at the hospital. Marty has been asked to assist one of the local HMOs to develop criteria to use for screening and selection of physical therapy clinicians who apply for inclusion in the HMOs provider panel. Marty is excited about being in a position to influence the HMO related to physical therapy policy. After discussing the invitation with Terry, Marty agrees to serve on the HMO advisory panel.

Question 11C. What factors should Marty advise the HMO to include in the screening criteria for physical therapists who apply for inclusion in the HMO provider panel?

Question 11D. Are the factors that the HMO should use to monitor ongoing therapist quality different than those that should be used for entrance into the provider panel? If so, how?

Marty has established a comprehensive outcomes management program in the physical therapy department at the hospital. Included in the program are measures of cost, functional outcome, patient satisfaction and referrer satisfaction. Data are collected at the department, by team and individual therapist level, and by patient diagnostic category. Although the program was put in place almost 1 year ago, usable data is just now starting to become available. For the system to benefit the department as much as possible, staff compliance is critical. Only the therapist treating the individual patient is able to provide some of the data that must be collected. During the course of analyzing the outcome data, Marty notices that both DJ and Brett have a relatively small percent of their patient data completed. When Marty questions the two therapists on this issue, they both seem defensive and somewhat threatened by the outcome program. After additional reflection, Marty concludes that both therapists are threatened by the collection of data on their patients. Both seem to feel as if the outcome management program will raise questions about the quality of care they provide and whether or not they are "good" therapists.

Question 11E. What might be the cause of Brett's and DJ's reservations about the outcome management program?

Question 11F. What might Marty do to address the poor data collection compliance of the two therapists?

Question 11G. What should Marty do if the data collection rates for DJ and Brett remain low 6 months later?

Chris is well into graduate school at this time. Working toward an MBA has proven to be very stimulating and exciting. During one of the course assignments on customer satisfaction, Chris, who is now also a licensed physical therapist, has identified a local clinic with very high patient satisfaction rates. As part of the class project, Chris has chosen to study this clinic in closer detail. Chris is excited about identifying the key factors that contribute to such high customer satisfaction.

As Chris observes and reviews the patient care at the clinic, it soon becomes obvious that the patients are receiving less than optimal clinical care. Many of the patients receive only superficial modalities. Rarely is there significant therapeutic exercise included in the plan of care. Most patients receive essentially the same treatment regime, even when their diagnosis and conditions might warrant something different. In Chris's opinion as a therapist, the quality of care is very poor. The patients appear to like the care because they are catered to with coffee, snacks and few de-

mands to work hard in therapy. Chris wonders why the level of patient satisfaction is so high.

Question 11H. What factors might be contributing to a high patient satisfaction rate when the quality of patient care seems to be so poor?

Question 11I. As a graduate student who is studying patient satisfaction at this clinic, what should Chris do about the perceived poor quality care?

CHAPTER 12: RISK MANAGEMENT

Highlights

Sandy files an age discrimination suit against the hospital. A dietary employee comes to see Marty to say that he/she feels Andy is sexually harassing him/her. The entire department reviews the guidelines for appropriate conduct and sexual harassment. A former patient sues the hospital. The patient is suing on the grounds of negligent treatment and injury while undergoing treatment in the physical therapy department. The patient was treated by Chris during Chris' student internship.

The Saga Continues

Today is going to be an interesting day for Marty. First thing this morning, Marty received a call from the hospital's Director of Legal Affairs because Sandy has filed a lawsuit against the hospital. The lawsuit claimed that Sandy was terminated because of age. Sandy was 47 years old at the time of departure from the hospital. Marty is confused because staff were told that Sandy's departure was the result of a voluntary resignation. Marty does remember the meeting in which Terry stated that Sandy was told to quit or be fired.

In reviewing Sandy's lawsuit against the hospital, Sandy's lawyers state that Sandy's rights under the Age Discrimination in Employment Act (ADEA) of 1967 as amended in 1986 were violated. The Director of Legal Affairs informs Marty that to claim this, Sandy's counsel must show four things. That Sandy

1. belonged to a protected class of employee, those over 40 years of age;

2. was qualified for the position of department head of physical therapy;
3. was terminated by the hospital;
4. was replaced by a younger worker.

Marty reviews the situation of Sandy's departure with the hospital attorney. Marty and the lawyer are convinced that all four of these conditions are met. The only one that is questionable is whether Sandy quit or was fired, but Terry's comments to Marty about the ultimatum to Sandy to quit or be fired suggests that Sandy quit under duress. This, the lawyer explained, was the same as termination by the hospital.

Because all four of the conditions were met, the hospital would have to show that Sandy was terminated for reasons other than age. The reason Sandy was terminated was poor performance. Because Marty reported to Sandy during the time in question, Marty was not privileged to what information or counsel Terry had given Sandy regarding job performance.

Chapter 12 Role Play Questions

Question 12A. What documents will be needed by the attorney to show that Sandy's performance on the job was less than satisfactory and justified termination?

Question 12B. Who else will the attorney need to talk to to establish the facts related to Sandy's departure?

Question 12C. What should Marty tell the staff about Sandy's lawsuit?

As Marty is leaving the meeting in Legal Affairs, an employee in the Dietary department hails Marty and asks for a quick meeting. Marty is already seriously behind in the day's schedule, but agrees to a brief meeting. The dietary employee informs Marty that he/she will be filing an employee complaint alleging sexual harassment by Andy, who works as an aide in Physical Therapy. Together, Marty and the employee immediately schedule a meeting with the Director of Human Resources for the hospital.

Marty arrives at the meeting a few minutes early to discuss the situation. Marty is confused and believes that sexual harassment could not be happening because Andy is not someone who su-

pervises the dietary employee. The HR Director explains to Marty that sexual harassment does not only occur when a supervisor or someone in authority requests sexual favors in exchange for preferential treatment in the work place. Sexual harassment also occurs when an employer fails to prevent a hostile work environment. A hostile work environment is one that unreasonably interferes with an individual's work performance by creating an intimidating, hostile or offensive work place. The dietary employee is claiming that Andy has told him/her dirty jokes, shown him/her pictures of scantily clad men/women and repeatedly asked him/her to go out on dates, in spite of his/her repeated requests to stop these behaviors.

Question 12D. What should the HR Director advise Marty regarding this sexual harassment complaint?

Question 12E. Would the situation be different if "Andy" was a nickname for Andrew or for Andrea? Why or why not?

Marty decides to request that the HR Director review the hospital policies related to sexual harassment with the entire staff.

Question 12F. Should the inservice on sexual harassment by the HR Director be mandatory for all staff including Andy? Why or why not?

Still a graduate student, Chris gets a brief visit from a gentleman who identifies himself as a process server. This gentleman gives Chris an envelop that contains documentation of a lawsuit that was filed by a former patient treated by Chris while Chris was a student at the hospital. The lawsuit names Chris, Chris' university, Marty as Chris's clinical instructor and supervisor, and the hospital as defendants in a professional negligence case. The patient claims to have been burned by the electrical stimulation that Chris used in the course of the patient's treatment. Chris remembers the patient, but has no recollection of the patient being injured at any time during the course of treatment. Chris is confused, angry and very upset.

Question 12F. What should be the first things that Chris does in relation to this lawsuit?

Question 12G. What role will Chris' co-defendants play in this suit?

Question 12H. What documents will Chris' legal counsel need to review to adequately prepare for this case?

CHAPTER 13: CONSULTANTS

Highlights

Dale now has a mature private practice. Chris has joined Dale's practice as a partner in the business. They consider hiring a consultant to help them complete a valuation of the practice so they can consider a buy-out offer from a national PT chain. They also consider their values as individuals, partners and clinicians in selling the practice that they have worked so hard to develop. Marty has to work with a large financial consulting group the merged hospitals have engaged to review workgroup efficiency. The relationship between Marty and the consultants is very tense. Marty is resistant to any intervention by the consultants who were hired by someone else. The consultants have little experience with physical therapy practice.

The Saga Continues

Much has changed since we last visited our characters. Dale started the practice and, over the past 3 years, it has become mature and successful. Eighteen months ago Dale invited Chris to join the practice as a partner. Chris gladly accepted the offer and bought into the practice as Dale's equal partner. The two partners have tried to equitably divide the ownership and leadership workload.

Chapter 13 Role Play Questions

Question 13A. Knowing what you know about the clinical and business backgrounds of Chris and Dale, what are some options for division of the workload at their single-site private practice?

Over the past 3 months, Dale and Chris have been repeatedly approached by Big PT, Inc., a national for-profit rehabilitation company. Big PT, Inc. is interested in purchasing their practice. Although Chris and Dale are very satisfied with the practice and the manner in which they have struc-

tured their professional and personal lives, they both feel that it would be prudent to listen to the offer that Big PT, Inc. makes. Before entertaining the sales pitch from Big PT, Inc. Chris feels strongly that they should determine the market value of the practice. Dale agrees but neither of them is sure how to determine the sales value of the practice.

Question 13B. What are some of the factors that should be considered by Chris and Dale as they attempt to determine the sales value of their practice?

Question 13C. How might the overall sales value of the practice vary depending on the after-sale role that the current owners might have?

Question 13D. What should Chris and Dale know about the company that is making an offer to purchase their practice?

Dale and Chris decide to engage a consultant who is experienced in valuing physical therapy private practices for sale. They decide to develop a request for proposal (RFP) to send to consultants who provide these types of services.

Question 13E. What information will Chris and Dale want to include in the RFP to help potential consultants understand the services Dale and Chris desire?

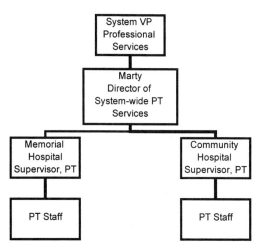

FIGURE A.4. Memorial Hospital–Community Hospital Physical Therapy Services organizational structure.

Question 13F. What resources are available to develop a distribution list of potential consultants for the RFP?

As Dale and Chris begin to develop the RFP, they realize that if they sell the practice, they may be out of work. The possibilities associated with change in both their professional and personal lives both excites and frightens them.

Marty has been named director of the combined physical therapy departments after the merger of Memorial Hospital and Community Hospital. The workload is substantially higher, but some of the efficiency initiatives that Marty put in place before the merger have been very helpful. The revised organizational chart for the merged physical therapy department is shown below in Figure A.4.

In an effort to maximize the efficiency of the merged hospital system, top administration engages a large health care consulting firm to help the staff identify new ways to become more productive. A large team of consultants has been assigned to the entire hospital system. Two consultants have been assigned to work with physical therapy. Marty has met with these consultants and has found them to be deficient in their knowledge of physical therapy practice. They seem to only care about numbers. Because they are not clinicians, Marty fears that they will fail to see the patients as anything more than numbers on a spreadsheet.

Question 13G. Marty is struggling in the relationship with the consultants. What are some things that Marty could do to try to make better use of the resources that the consultants bring?

When the consultants have finished the consulting engagement, they deliver a document that lists all of the recommendations for increasing efficiency in many departments, including physical therapy. Marty reviews this document in great detail and finds many of the suggestions to be inappropriate or to potentially lead to unsafe situations for patients or staff.

Question 13H. What is the role of these recommendations within the physical therapy department? What is Marty's responsibility as a manager in relation to the recommendations of the consultants?

Question 13I. What choices does Marty have in responding to the recommendations of the consultants? What are the potential implications of each of these choices?

CHAPTER 14: ENTREPRENEURIAL PHYSICAL THERAPY

Highlights

Dale and Chris discuss the possible buy-out. They engage other private practitioners in a dialogue on the pros and cons of selling.

The Saga Continues

Dale and Chris have sent out the RFP for the practice valuation consultant. In response, they have received five completed bids for the job. Two of the five bids seem to be exactly what Chris and Dale wanted. They decide to interview each of the candidates in a phone conference call.

Chapter 14 Role Play Questions

Question 14A. Make a list of key questions that Dale and Chris should consider asking each of the consulting candidates. Assume that the proposals received included price, biography information, and references of success in similar types of consulting engagements.

After the phone interview, Chris and Dale find one of the two consulting candidates to be clearly superior to the other.

Question 14B. What actions should Chris and Dale take to finalize the relationship with the chosen consultant and get started with the valuation process?

The valuation is complete. Chris and Dale now have a good estimate of the market value of the practice. A meeting with Big PT, Inc is scheduled and held. The sales pitch of selling to this national chain of PT clinics was very polished and professional. The financial offer is slightly above the market value as determined by the consultant. Chris and Dale will realize significant financial gain by selling the practice.

Question 14C. What non-financial factors should Chris and Dale be considering as they contemplate sale of the practice?

The real issue for Chris and Dale has become whether or not they really want to sell the practice. Financially, there is also concern that the future value of the practice may not be as high as it is now. Chris and Dale are also very anxious about what their lives will be like when if they sell. What will happen to their loyal employees? They wonder if their employees will think that they are bailing out on the practice. They wonder if others will think that they sold out for the "big bucks".

Question 14D. What will be different in the daily lives of Chris and Dale if they sell the practice to Big PT, Inc.?

In an effort to better understand the process of selling the practice and moving on to a new stage in their lives, Chris and Dale decide to contact several other physical therapists who have sold their practice to national chains like Big PT, Inc.

Questions 14E. What questions should Dale and Chris ask of the former private practitioners who have sold their practices?

Question 14F. What are the reasons that Chris and Dale should sell the practice?

Question 14G. What are the reasons that Chris and Dale should not sell the practice?

Question 14H. What other options do Chris and Dale have?

Question 14I. Should Chris and Dale join a network of other private physical therapy practitioners? Why or why not?

Question 14J. What are the implications of each of the options available?

Question 14K. Review your response to the final question in the first role play. Having completed the majority of the text and role plays, how would your answer to the following question be different?

Considering the changing health care environment of our characters, project scenarios for the future of hospital-based physical therapy practice. Do the same for private practice physical therapy. Read Chapter 15 for more on the future.

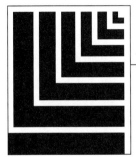

Appendix B

GUIDE FOR PROFESSIONAL CONDUCT

From American Physical Therapy Association.
Physical Therapy 1979;77:1629–1631.
Reproduced by permission.

PURPOSE

This Guide for Professional Conduct (*Guide*) is intended to serve physical therapists who are members of the American Physical Therapy Association (*Association*) in interpreting the *Code of Ethics* (*Code*) and matters of professional conduct. The *Guide* provides guidelines by which physical therapists may determine the propriety of their conduct. The *Code* and the *Guide* apply to all physical therapists who are *Association* members. These guidelines are subject to changes as the dynamics of the profession change and as new patterns of health care diversity are developed and accepted by the professional community and the public. This *Guide* is subject to monitoring and timely revision by the Judicial Committee of the Association.

INTERPRETING ETHICAL PRINCIPLES

The interpretations expressed in this *Guide* are not to be considered all inclusive of situations that could evolve under a specific principle of the *Code* but reflect the opinions, decisions, and advice of the Judicial Committee. While the statements of ethical principles apply universally, specific circumstances determine their appropriate application. Input related to current interpretations, or to situation requiring interpretation, is encouraged from Association members.

Principle 1

Physical therapists respect the rights and dignity of all individuals.

1.1 Attitudes of Physical Therapists

A. Physical therapists shall recognize that each individual is different from all other individuals and shall respect and be responsive to those differences.

B. Physical therapists are to be guided at all times by concern for the physical, psychological and socioeconomic welfare of those individuals entrusted to their care.

C. Physical therapists shall not engage in conduct that constitutes harassment or abuse of, or discrimination against, colleagues, associates or others.

1.2 Confidential Information

A. Information relating to the physical therapist/patient relationship is confidential and may not be communicated to a third party not involved in that patient's care without prior written consent of the patient, subject to applicable law.

B. Information derived from competent-sponsored peer review shall be held confidential by the reviewer unless written permission to release the information is obtained from the physical therapist who was reviewed.

C. Information derived from the working relationships of physical therapists shall be held confidential by all parties.

D. Information may be disclosed to appropriate authorities when it is necessary to protect the welfare of an individual or the community. Such disclosure shall be in accordance with applicable law.

Issued by Judicial Committee, APTA, October 1981. Last Amended September 1997.

1.3 Patient Relations

Physical therapists shall not engage in any sexual relationship or activity, whether consensual or nonconsensual, with any patient while a physical therapist/patient relationship exists.

1.4 Informed Consent

Physical therapists shall obtain informed consent before treatment.

Principle 2

Physical therapists comply with the laws and regulations governing the practice of physical therapy.

2.1 Professional Practice

Physical therapists shall provide consultation, evaluation, treatment, and preventive care, in accordance with the laws and regulations of the jurisdiction(s) in which they practice.

Principle 3

Physical therapists accept responsibility for the exercise of sound judgement.

3.1 Acceptance of Responsibility

A. Upon accepting an individual for provision of physical therapy services, physical therapists shall assume the responsibility for evaluating that individual; planning, implementing, and supervising the therapeutic program; reevaluating and changing that program; and maintaining adequate records of the case, including progress reports.

B. When the individual's needs are beyond the scope of the physical therapist's expertise, or when additional services are indicated, the individual shall be so informed and assisted in identifying a qualified provider.

C. Regardless of practice setting, physical therapists shall maintain the ability to make independent judgements.

D. The physical therapist shall not provide physical therapy service to a patient under the influence of a substance that impairs his or her ability to do so safely.

3.2 Delegation of Responsibility

A. Physical therapists shall not delegate to a less qualified person any activity, which required the unique skill, knowledge, and judgement of the physical therapist.

B. The primary responsibility for physical therapy care rendered by supportive personnel rests with the supervising physical therapist. Adequate supervision requires, at a minimum, that a supervising physical therapist perform the following activities:

1. Designate or establish channels of written and oral communication.
2. Interpret available information concerning the individual under care.
3. Provide initial evaluation
4. Develop plan of care, including short-and long term goals.
5. Select and delegate appropriate tasks of plan of care.
6. Assess competence of supportive personnel to perform assigned tasks.
7. Direct and supervise supportive personnel in delegated tasks.
8. Identify and document precautions, special problems, contradiction, goals, anticipated progress, and plans of reevaluation.
9. Reevaluate, adjust plan of care when necessary, perform final evaluation, and establish follow-up plan.

3.3 Provision of Services

A. Physical therapists shall recognize the individual's freedom of choice selection of physical therapy services.

B. Physical therapists' professional practices and their adherence to ethical principles of the Association shall take preference over business practices. Provisions of services for personal financial gain rather than for the need of the individual receiving their services are unethical.

C. When physical therapists judge that an individual will no longer benefit from their services, they shall so inform the individual receiving their services. Physical therapists shall avoid overutilization of their services.

D. In the event of elective termination of a physical therapist/patient relationship by the physical therapist, the therapist should take steps to transfer the care of the patient, as appropriate, to another provider.

3.4 Referral Relationships

In a referral situation where the referring practitioner prescribed a treatment program, alteration of that program or extension of physical therapy services beyond that program should be undertaken in consultation with the referring practitioner.

3.5 Practice Arrangement

A. Participation in a business, partnership, corporation, or other entity does not exempt the physical therapist, whether employer, partner, or stockholder, either individually or collectively, from the obligation of promoting and maintaining the ethical principles of the Association.

B. Physical therapists shall advise their employer(s) of any employer practice, which causes physical therapists to be in conflict with the ethical principles of the Association. Physical therapist employees shall attempt to rectify aspects of their employment, which are in conflict with the ethical principles of the Association.

Principle 4

Physical therapists maintain and promote high standards for physical therapy practice, education, and research.

4.1 Continued Education

A. Physical therapists shall participate in educational activities, which enhance their basic knowledge and provide new knowledge.

B. Whenever physical therapists provide continuing education, they shall ensure that course content, objectives and responsibilities of the instructional faculty are accurately reflected in the promotion of the course.

4.2 Review and Assessment

A. Physical therapists shall provide for utilization review of their services.

B. Physical therapists shall demonstrate their commitment to quality assurance by peer review and self-assessment.

4.3 Research

A. Physical therapists shall support research activities that contribute knowledge for improved patient care.

B. Physical therapists engaged in research shall ensure:

1. the consent of subjects;
2. confidentiality of the data on individual subjects and the personal identified of the subjects;
3. well-being of all subjects in compliance with facility regulations and laws of the jurisdiction in which the research is conducted;
4. the absence of fraud and plagiarism;
5. full disclosure of support received;
6. appropriate acknowledgement of individuals making a contribution to the research;
7. that animal subjects used in research are treated humanely and in compliance with facility regulations and laws of the jurisdiction in which the research experimentation is conducted.

C. Physical therapists shall report to appropriate authorities any acts in the conduct or presentation of research that appear unethical or illegal.

4.3 Education

A. Physical therapists shall support quality education in academic and clinical settings.

B. Physical therapists functioning in the education role are responsible to the students, the academic institutions and the clinical settings for promoting ethical conduct in educational activities. Whenever possible, the educator shall ensure:

1. the right of students in the academic and clinical setting;
2. appropriate confidentiality of personal information;
3. professional conduct toward the student during the academic and clinical educational process;
4. assignment to clinical settings prepared to give the student a learning experience.

C. Clinical educators are responsible for reporting to the academic program student conduct which appears to be unethical or illegal.

Principle 5

Physical therapists seek remuneration for their services that is deserved and reasonable.

5.1 Fiscally Sound Remuneration

A. Physical therapists shall never place their own financial interest above the welfare of individuals under their care.

B. Fees for physical therapy services should be responsible for the service performed, considering the setting in which it is provided, practice costs in the geographic area, judgement of other organizations, and other relevant factors.

C. Physical therapists should attempt to ensure that providers, agencies, or other employers adopt physical therapy fee schedules that are reasonable and that encourage access to necessary services.

5.2 Business Practices/Fee Arrangements

A. Physical therapists shall not:

1. directly or indirectly request, receive or participate in the dividing, transferring, assigning, and rebating of an unearned fee;
2. profit by means of a credit or other valuable consideration, such as unearned commission, discount, or gratuity in connection with furnishing of physical therapy services.

B. Unless laws impose restriction to the contrary, physical therapists who provide physical therapy services in a business entity may pool fees and moneys received. Physical therapists may divide or apportion these fees and moneys in accordance with the business agreement.

C. Physical therapists may enter into agreements with organizations to provide physical therapy services if such agreements do not violate the ethical principles of the Association.

5.3 Endorsement of Equipment or Services

A. Physical therapists shall not use influence upon individuals under their care of their families for utilization of equipment or services based upon the direct or indirect financial interest of the physical therapists in such equipment or services. Realizing that these individuals will normally rely on the physical therapists' advice, their best interest must always be maintained as well as their right of free choice relating to the use of any equipment or service. While it cannot be considered unethical for physical therapists to own or have a financial interest in equipment companies or services, they must act in accordance with law and make full disclosure of their interest whenever such companies or services become the source of equipment or services for individuals under their care.

B. Physical therapists may be remunerated for endorsement or advertisement of equipment or services to the lay public, physical therapists, or other health professionals provided they disclose any financial interest in the production, sale, or distribution of said equipment or services.

C. In endorsing or adverting equipment or services, physical therapists shall use sound professional judgement and shall not give the appearance of Association endorsement.

5.4 Gifts and Other Considerations

A. Physical therapists shall not accept nor offer gifts or other considerations with obligatory conditions attached.

B. Physical therapists shall not accept nor offer gifts or other considerations that affect or give an objective appearance of affecting their professional judgement.

Principle 6

Physical therapists provide accurate information to the consumer about the profession and about those services they provide.

6.1 Information about the Profession

Physical therapists shall endeavor to educate the public to an awareness of the physical therapy profession through such means as publication of articles and participation in seminars, lectures, and civic programs.

6.2 Information about Services

A. Information given to the public shall emphasize that individual problems cannot be treated without individualized evaluation and plans/programs of care.

B. Physical therapists may advertise their services to the public.

C. Physical therapists shall not use, or participate in the use of, any form, of communication containing a false, plagiarized, fraudulent, misleading, deceptive, unfair, or sensational statement or claim.

D. A paid advertisement shall be identified as such unless it is apparent from the context that it is a paid advertisement.

Principle 7

Physical therapists accept the responsibility to protect the public and the profession from unethical, incompetent, or illegal acts.

7.1 Consumer Protection

A. Physical therapist shall report any conduct, which appears to be unethical, incompetent, or illegal.

B. Physical therapists may not participate in any arrangements in which patients are exploited due to the referring sources enhancing their personal incomes as a result of referring for, prescribing, or recommending physical therapy.

C. Physical therapists shall be obligated to safeguard the public from underutilization or overutilization of physical therapy services.

7.2 Disclosure

The physical therapists shall disclose to the patient if the referring practitioner derives compensation from the provision of physical therapy. The physical therapist shall ensure that the individual has freedom of choice in selecting a provider of physical therapy.

Principle 8

Physical therapists participate in efforts to address the health needs of the public.

8.1 Pro Bono Service

Physical therapists should render pro bono publico (reduced or no fee) services to patients lacking the ability to pay for services, as each physical therapist's practice permits.

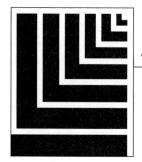

Appendix C

CODE OF ETHICS

From American Physical Therapy Association.
Physical Therapy 1979;77:1628.
Reproduced by permission.

PREAMBLE

This *Code of Ethics* sets forth ethical principles for the physical therapy profession. Members of this profession are responsible for maintaining and promoting ethical practice. This *Code of Ethics,* adopted by the American Physical Therapy Association, shall be binding on physical therapists who are members of the Association.

Principle 1

Physical therapists respect the rights and dignity of all individuals.

Principle 2

Physical therapists comply with the laws and regulations governing the practice of physical therapy.

Principle 3

Physical therapists accept responsibility for the exercise of sound judgement.

Principle 4

Physical therapists maintain and promote high standards for physical therapy practice, education, and research.

Principle 5

Physical therapists seek remuneration for their services that is deserved and reasonable.

Principle 6

Physical therapists provide accurate information to the consumer about the profession and about those services they provide.

Principle 7

Physical therapists accept the responsibility to protect the public and the profession from unethical, incompetent, or illegal acts.

Principle 8

Physical therapists participate in efforts to address the health needs of the public.

⬛ Glossary

Abuse: neglect or harm of a minor or vulnerable adult.

Accounting: the process of collecting, summarizing, analyzing, reporting and interpreting, in monetary terms, information about the enterprise.

Accounts Receivable: monies owed to a business.

Adverse Patient Outcomes (APOs): undesirable results of care such as death, infection, overmedication or fracture.

Allocation Basis: the common measure used to divide allocated cost among unit level budgets. For example, the cost of an employee picnic is divided among departments based on the number of employees assigned to that department. If physical therapy has 50% of the employees, it will be allocated 50% of the cost of the picnic.

Ambulatory care: services that require less than a 24-hour period for delivery and recovery after which the patient is ready for discharge home.

Application: a computer program designed to help people perform a certain type of work. An application thus differs from an operating system (which runs a computer), a utility (which performs maintenance or general-purpose chores), and a programming language (with which computer programs are created). Depending on the work for which it was designed, an application can manipulate text, numbers, graphics or a combination of these elements. Some application packages offer considerable computing power by focusing on a single task, such as word processing; others, called integrated software, offer somewhat less power but include several applications, such as a word processor, a spreadsheet and a database program.

Appropriateness: degree to which care provided is relevant to a patient's clinical care needs, given the current state of knowledge.

Assault: any threat made by another that a person fears or expects to cause them immediate harm.

Automated Medical Record: system of data collection, storage, protection, verification of accuracy, and retrieval of medical information concerning a single individual or group of individuals in an electronic format.

Basis: book value of any asset.

Battery: unjustified, offensive, unwanted intentional contact.

Beneficiary: individual who is enrolled and is eligible to receive health care insurance coverage under the Medicare and/or Medicaid programs.

Best Practices: approaches to care delivery identified when the practices of clinical care providers are reviewed and analyzed to identify those that produce the best clinical and financial outcomes. Best practices are used to guide the practices of clinicians.

Blueprint: architect's planning document that graphically represents the layout of a facility.

Board of Directors: also referred to as a Board of Trustees, is the governing body of an organization.

Breach: violation of a law or legal obligation.

Browser: software programs used on an Internet or intranet network to retrieve information in the form of text, graphics and other data formats.

Building Codes: rules and regulations that govern the methods, materials and designs used in construction.

Building Permits: legal record that construction has been approved according to the local building codes. Permits may require the contractor to have inspections at various stages of the work.

Business Plan: formatted explanation of the steps that will be taken to meet the objective of starting and running a business.

Case Mix: the percentage of total patient services by diagnostic category.

Cause and Effect Diagram: a problem-solving statistical tool that indicates effects and causes and how they interrelate. Also known as a fish bone diagram.

Certified Public Accountant (CPA): an individual who has passed state licensure exams and meets continuing education requirements in the area of finance and accounting.

Chief Executive: the highest ranking member in the management structure. Usually the owner or accountable to the owner or board of directors of a business.

Civil Law: involves legal actions brought about by private citizens (plaintiffs) against a person (defendant) or group (defendants) deemed liable (see below). To correct civil wrongs, the remedy in civil cases is monetary.

Civil Rights Act (1964): Title VII established the Equal Employment Opportunity Commission (EEOC) to define and enforce acceptable employment policies and practices as they affect minorities and women.

Claim: demand based on a right to payment or right to an equitable remedy for breach of performance.

Closed Panel Managed Health Care Plan: a health insurance plan that restricts enrollee choice of health care providers to those who have participation agreements with the plan. The group of participating providers is sometimes referred to as a panel.

Closing: when a contract is transacted and each person fulfills his or her role under the terms and conditions of the agreement. In a sale, it is the moment when the title is deeded to the buyer and the seller gets the proceeds of the sale.

Closing Costs: broker fees and the cost of preparation of all the documents between the buyer and seller to effect a transfer between the two parties.

Code of Ethics: guidelines formulated by members of a group with common interests that expresses the groups' ideals and moral code or obligations to the public to self-regulate while advancing the interests of the group.

Code Violation: breach of a current city building code that must be corrected prior to successful completion of a building inspection.

CARF, The Rehabilitation Commission (CARF): Nonprofit organization for the promotion of quality services for people in need of rehabilitation. Formerly known as the Commission on Accreditation of Rehabilitation Facilities (CARF). CARF accreditation is voluntary.

Common Cause Variation: normal variation in the number of undesirable outcomes, errors and deviations from standards.

Communications Systems: systems related to the efficient flow of communication though a facility, including, telephone, intercom, background music, mail delivery, signal lights, and data transmission.

Consultant: a person who gives professional or technical advice.

Consulting Engagement: the arrangement between the parties seeking consulting services and the parties providing consulting services for a particular project or scope of work to be completed.

Contingency Plan: alternative plan prepared and used in case initial assumptions are not accurate.

Continuous Quality Improvement: a system in which individuals in an organization look for ways to do things better, usually based on understanding of processes, process improvement, and control of variation.

Contractor: parties from outside of the organization used to augment existing resources to perform specific tasks on a short- or long-term basis. An independent contractor's involvement is generally temporary until the company can hire employees. The temporary need for contract services disappears or the companys' employees are trained to perform the contracted work.

Control Chart: a graphic method for evaluating whether a process is or is not in a state of statistical control.

Co-Payments: an amount or percentage of the service cost a patient and/or family must pay after the deductible has been satisfied.

Cost: money spent.

Cost Allocation: the process of dividing, distributing or assigning indirect or general costs to revenue center level budgets.

Coverage Guidelines: written descriptions of the types of service and terms under which health care services qualify for payment under a health insurance plan.

Creditor: an individual or company to whom something is owed.

Cross-Functional: organizational work, processes, groups that involve representatives from diverse departments, disciplines and/or job categories.

Cultural Diversity: the representation, in one social system, of people with distinctly different group affiliations of cultural significance.

Culture: people who come together to achieve a common purpose.

Culture Group: an affiliation of people who collectively share certain norms, values, or traditions that differ from those of other groups.

Culture Identity Groups: groups of individuals that are different from the majority group in which the differentiating factors are based on shared norms, values, and common socio-cultural heritage (i.e., subjective culture).

Customers: individuals or groups who directly or indirectly may need or want to use a product or service.

Data: information in its most basic form.

Data Aggregation: the process of collecting and analyzing data as a collective or data grouping.

Data Base: any collection of data organized for storage in an electronic format and designed for easy access by authorized users. The data may be in the form of text, numbers, or encoded graphics.

Deductible: an amount that the patient or family has agreed to pay out of pocket for covered health care services before the insurer must pay any part of the bill.

Deductible Payments: cover that portion of the health care costs that must be paid by the subscriber before their health plan assumes any financial responsibility for covered care health services.

Disease Management: a term used to describe utilization management efforts that are targeted at controlling the cost of care for patients who have a chronic disease or disability.

Dividend Payments: made when a company distributes net revenue to its owners based on the number of shares of stock owned on or before a specified date.

Easement: an interest in land that gives another public or private entity the right to either use another person's land for a limited and specific purpose, or to prevent another person from using his land in a specified way. The most common easements are rights of way that give a person the right to pass over or under another's land, such as driveways, roads, sidewalks, and footpaths.

Efficacy: the degree to which the care of a patient has been shown to accomplish the desired or projected outcome.

Electronic Data Transfer: movement of information from one location to another, either within a computer (as from a disk drive to random access memory) or between a computer and an external device (as between two computers or a file server and a computer on a network).

Endowment: wealth that is given to provide a permanent income to an individual or organization.

Enrollee: an individual who is enrolled in a health care plan and is entitled to receive health care payment coverage under an individual or group insurance plan for a specific period of time.

Entity: for the purpose of financial reporting, a business is considered to be an entity capable of economic action.

Entrepreneur: someone who is willing to take risks or try new things in pursuit of business gains.

Escrow: something held by a third party for a specific purpose. See Escrow Deposit.

Escrow Deposit: The amount of deposit held by another party. In buying or leasing property, the owner or their agent usually holds a deposit (escrow deposit) from the buyer or tenant.

Ethical: a descriptor of behaviors that is in keeping with accepted standards of conduct.

Ethical Principles: guidelines or rules based on moral philosophies used to compare alternative options.

Ethics: branch of philosophy focusing on morality (see morality below). Ethics relate to what ought to be done in the ideal sense.

Expenses: costs incurred by a business during a specific period of time.

Facility Plan: a comprehensive plan of the construction project.

Fiduciary Duty: requirement to act primarily for another's benefit in a professional relationship. This requirement is based on trust, confidence or responsibility wherein fairness is required in dealing with the other party.

Financial report: a statement of financial performance and position.

Financial (Budget) Variance: the difference between planned and actual performance.

Fire Wall: systems, including hardware and software, designed to prevent unauthorized access to information systems within an organization.

Floor Plan: detailed, graphical representation of the layout of a facility that is used to construct the facility.

Flow Chart: a problem-solving statistical tool that shows the way things go through the organization (the current process), the way they should go (the improved process) or the difference between the two. Also known as a work flow diagram.

Forecasting: the process of using scientific systems and data to predict changes in a market.

Full-Time Equivalent (FTE): represents 52 weeks of full time employment at 40 hours per week. It is equal to 2080 hours of paid time per year. The 2080 hours represents time when the employee is available to work (productive time) as well as time when the employee is paid but not available (non-productive time).

Futures: probable and improbable future trends based on information extrapolated from multiple sources.

Gantt Chart: a horizontal bar chart that graphically displays the time relationship of steps in a project. Also known as a time line chart.

Geriatrician: a physician who specializes in the provision of health care to the elderly.

Goal: statement of what is to be accomplished. The target toward which effort is directed.

Gross revenue: the sum of all the income earned by a business during a specific time period.

Hardware: physical components of a computer system, including any peripheral equipment such as printers, modems, and mice.

Health Care Provider: an individual or organization that provides products and/or services used to maintain or improve health.

Health Information System: electronic medical record.

Health Maintenance Organization (HMO): a health insurance plan that assumes responsibility for all of the subscribers health care cost for a fixed, all inclusive price. The HMO is responsible for the quality and cost of care provided to enrollee. To control both of these elements, the HMO restricts enrollee choice of health care providers to those who have participation agreements with the plan. The group of participating providers is sometimes referred to as a panel.

Health Plan Employer Data and Information Set (HEDIS): the HEDIS tool is a set of standardized performance measures designed to ensure that purchasers and consumers have the information they need to reliably compare the performance of managed health care plans.

Hospital Information System: the system of data collection, storage, protection, verification of accuracy, and retrieval of medical and financial and other types of performance information concerning a hospital system, its employees, medical staff and patients in an electronic format.

Human Resources: members of an organization as a potential input to produce an output. It recognizes people as an asset to the organization. Human resources may also be the name of the organizational segment that manages employee related functions such as recruitment and benefits.

HVAC: heating, ventilation, and air conditioning systems.

Incident Report: also called an occurrence report, is a factual written summary of an unusual event.

Incorporation: the process by which a business venture receives recognition as a legal entity.

Industry Analysts: individuals whose career is related to the evaluation of the performance trends of a specific industry. They may also perform evaluations of a company's performance in relation to industry standards.

Information: data that has been manipulated into a useful form, i.e., the knowledge that resides in the human brain, in all written and electronic records.

Information Flow: passage of information and communication through an organization. The system of data collection, storage, protection, verification of accuracy, and retrieval of medical information concerning the health status, history, potential risks and behaviors of a defined population in an electronic format.

Information Superhighway: terms popularly used to refer to the availability and use of advanced information services by means of a variety of high-capacity data transport facilities, especially computers and computer networks. Often confused with Internet or World Wide Web.

Input: represents the resources used to produce an outcome.

Integrated Delivery Network (IDN): an affiliated group of health care providers who together are able to meet the comprehensive health care needs of patients within a specific geographical region.

Internet: an open interconnection of networks that enables connected computers to communicate directly. There is a global, public Internet and many smaller-scale, controlled-access internets, known as enterprise internets or intranets.

Investment: the money paid for the purchase of financial instruments such as stock for personal gain.

Joint Commission on Accreditation of Healthcare Organizations (JCAHO): non-profit accrediting body covering seven types of health care, i.e., ambulatory care, home care and hospice care, long-term care, psychiatric facilities, hospital care and managed care. JCAHO accreditation is voluntary. Also known as The Joint Commission.

Leader: a term used in reference to any individual who has the ability to lead others regardless of organizational position and/or authority.

Liability: the state of being bound by law or justice to do, pay or make good.

Liable: obliged, compelled or bound in law or equity to make good.

Local Area Network (LAN): a group of computers and other devices dispersed over a relatively limited geographic area and connected by a communications link that enables any device to interact with any other on the network. LANs may include microcomputers and shared resources such as laser printers and large hard disks. Most LANs can support a wide variety of computers and other devices. Each device must use the proper physical and data-link protocols for the particular LAN, and all devices that want to communicate with each other on the LAN must use the same communications protocol. Although single LANs are geographically limited (to a department or an office building, for example), separate LANs can be connected to form larger networks (See WAN).

Loss: denotes a negative financial margin.

Majority Group: numerically largest group represented in the social system, typically the group in power.

Malpractice: professional negligence or misconduct, i.e., unreasonable lack of skill or knowledge, fidelity, or fiduciary responsibility which results in injury, loss or damage to a recipient of services.

Management: the formally recognized leadership of an organization.

Management Information System: the system of data collection, storage, protection, verification of accuracy, and retrieval of financial performance information concerning an organization, its employees and customers in an electronic format.

Management Style: the behaviors a manager exhibits as a leader within the organization (e.g., dictatorial, collaborative, controlling, influenced by others, etc.).

Manager: any individual who has been assigned organizational authority to direct other members of the organization.

Managing Diversity: planning and implementing organizational systems and practices to manage people so that the potential advantages of diversity are maximized while the potential disadvantages are minimized.

Margin: in relation to financial performance, this term is used to describe the difference between total revenue and total expenses. The terms net income, net revenue, profit and loss are also used to describe this difference.

Market Mix: the combination of those factors that determine a market strategy-product or service, price, place and promotion.

Market Orientation: a philosophy seen in companies that hold that the main task of the organization is to determine the needs and wants of target markets and to satisfy them through design, communication, pricing and delivery of appropriate and competitively viable products and services.

Market Segmentation: the process of dividing a market into submarkets according to target market characteristics.

Market Share: the percentage of the entire market that is served by a single organization.

Market Value: presumed value for which a specific property will sell in any given market condition.

Marketing: the process of planning and executing the conception, pricing, promotion, and distribution of ideas, goods, and services to create exchanges that satisfy individual and organizational objectives.

Marketing Campaign: the process by which a marketing strategy is carried out.

Master Plan: overall comprehensive plan for the development or redevelopment of a community. Master plans indicate the zoning that is allowed for each area of a community.

Minority Group: group with fewer members than the majority group, lower status or less power in the social system compared to the majority group.

Mission Statement: written document identifying why an organization exists. This statement tells the reader what the business does (products, services), who the customers or patients are, the geographical location(s) where the business operates, it's specialty, and it expresses the collective aspirations (goals) of the organization. This statement also may contain values related to interpersonal relations.

Moral Issues: conflicts stemming from human interactions which involve matters of fairness, harm, just claims and rights.

Morality: in its most general form morality involves assumptions about what is good and right and duties or obligations present in a situation. Moral obligations are behavior related. These behavioral obligations are universal and apply without exception to everyone alike.

Motivation: a psychological construct term that refers to biological, interpersonal and societal goals people strive to fulfill. Values (see below) support motivations.

Motivational Types of Values: empirically derived groups of values that serve different motivations. A value typology that groups values according to their common motivational goal.

National Committee for Quality Assurance (NCQA): an accrediting body for managed care organizations. NCQA accreditation is voluntary.

Negligence: failure to exercise ordinary care, i.e., failure to do or refrain from doing what a competent, careful person would do or not do.

Net revenue: equal to gross revenue less total expense for a specific time period.

Network: group of health care providers joining together under a common structure to better accomplish common goals such as negotiating contracts with managed care organizations.

Niche Marketing: the targeting of a specific group (subset) of consumers with a product or service.

Occurrence Screening: identifying variances from what is expected through the inspection of multiple reports and interviews.

Operating Margin: the ratio of net income to total revenue. See Chapter 7 for the formula to calculate margin.

Operating System: software responsible for controlling the allocation and usage of hardware resources such as memory; central processing unit (CPU) time, disk space, and peripheral devices. The operating system is the foundation on which applications, such as word-processing and spreadsheet programs, are built. Popular operating systems include MS-DOS, Windows-NT, the Macintosh OS, OS/2, and UNIX.

Opportunity Cost: the potential that is lost because of the path you take.

Ordinances: laws within a community that govern many aspects of construction.

Organizational Culture: the set of behavioral norms that guide the action of an organization's employees.

Organizational Restructuring: occurs when the management of an organization changes the relationships between employees in one or more segments of the organization or the relationships between segments of the organization.

Organizational Structure: how the segments and employees of an organization relate to each other in the performance of their work.

Outlier: event that falls outside of the normal range of variance for similar events.

Output: what is produced when resources are used.

Pareto Chart: bar graph that helps focus the user's attention on the few most important factors rather than on many less important factors.

Participating Provider: a provider of health care products and/or services who has applied, met criteria for participation and has a signed agreement with a government or private health care insurance plan for the provision of specific health care services to its enrollees (beneficiaries).

Participation Agreement: a contract between an insurance plan and a provider that allows a health care provider to participate in the care of the plans enrollees.

Payer Mix: percentage breakdown of total patient service revenue by payer type.

Performance Benchmarks: local, regional, national or international industry standards against which the performance of a similar entity can be compared. A therapy practice can determine if it offers competitive outcomes if it compares its performance to the outcomes achieved by other providers for similar services.

Performance Standard: the expectation of how a job or task should be done according to objective requirements and specifications.

Program Evaluation and Review Technique (PERT) Chart: graphic representation of a project, its tasks and deadlines. Performance standards can also be used to plot and communicate the progress of a project. Also known as a time plot.

Personal Information Manager: software programs used to store information typically used by a single individual about that individual's schedule, personal contacts and projects, similar to a personal organizer.

Phenotype Identity Groups: groups of individuals that are different from the majority group in which the differentiating factors are physically and visually observable. For example, gender specific groups, racial-ethnic groups, and persons with differing abilities.

Philanthropist: an individual who has a natural love of people that is expressed through practical efforts to improve the well-being of others.

Physiatrist: a physician who specializes in physical medicine and rehabilitation.

Physical Therapist in Independent Practice (PTIP): according to the Health Care Financing Administration (HCFA) is a physical therapist that (a) renders services on his or her own. One who is free of the administrative and professional control of an employer; (b) treats his/her own patients; (c) collects a fee or other compensation for services rendered; (d) maintains at their own expense an office or office space and the necessary equipment to provide an adequate program of physical therapy.

Plan Member (Enrollee): an individual who is enrolled in a health care plan and is entitled to receive health care coverage under an individual or group insurance plan for a specific period of time.

Planning: forming a scheme or method of doing or an arrangement of means or steps for the attainment of a goal.

Potentially Compensable Events (PCOs): situations that may lead to legal actions.

Prejudice: an attitudinal bias and tendency to prejudge something or someone on the basis of some differentiating characteristics. Although prejudice may be manifested as either a positive or negative predisposition, it is most often defined as a negative predisposition.

Primary Care Physician: the first physician to examine a patient and who decides if further care is needed and if that care will include referral to specialist physicians and other services.

Private Practice: providing services in an environment where the practice owner(s) has/have taken the financial risk to develop the practice for which they have managerial responsibilities.

Private Practitioner: a health care professional who has ownership in a private practice.

Product Line: a group of similar products that are often functionally presented together or thought of as a collective.

Productivity: the relationship between the value of resources used (INPUT) to the value of what is produced (OUTPUT).

Profit: positive net revenue.

Provider Participation Agreements: contracts between health care providers and government or private health care insurance plans for the provision of specific health care services to its enrollees (beneficiaries).

Public Accountant: an accountant who is not certified but frequently has received formal education in accounting and related subjects.

Punch List: a document that lists all the changes and incomplete items in a construction project.

Reference Laboratory: provides highly specialized analytic services and accepts referral work from other laboratory providers.

Risk: possibility of suffering harm or loss.

Risk Management: in a health care entity this involves coordinated efforts to identify, assess and minimize, where possible, the risk of suffering harm or loss to patients, visitors, staff, and the organization.

Safety Systems: systems within a building that address occupant and general community safety, including fire, disaster, weather, and security.

Scatter Diagram: diagram that shows the relationship between two variables with data plotted in two dimensions.

Scenario: synopsis or outline of hypothesized future events or chain of events.

Scope: the breadth of the organization or part of an organization. Scope may range from a small element of the organization up to and including the entire organization.

Security: processes involved in protecting an information systems from unauthorized access, damage or misuse.

Self-Employed: working for oneself rather than being employed to work for someone else. A business owner is self-employed.

Self-View: a constructed word meaning all aspects of one's psychological self. Groups also have self-views. Self-view is a global cognitive concept that is sustained by engaging in behaviors that are congruent with self-view.

Senior Management: often called executive management, refers to those individuals near the top of the management structure. Senior managers often report directly to the chief executive or another member of senior management.

Service Line: groups of similar services or treatments that are often functionally presented together or thought of as a collective.

Sexual Harassment: a form of sex discrimination in the workplace involving unwelcome sexual advances or demands or other verbal or physical conduct of a sexual nature.

Software: computer programs; instructions that cause the hardware to do work Software as a whole can be divided into a number of categories based on the types of work done by programs. The two primary software categories are operating systems (system software), which control the workings of the computer, and application software, which addresses the multitude of tasks for which people use computers.

Sound Abatement: processes and structures to reduce excess noise and noise pollution inside a facility.

Special Cause Variation: unexpected variation in the number of undesirable outcomes, errors, and deviations from standards due to an event that can be identified and, hopefully, rectified.

Spreadsheet: type of computer software program in which numerical or text data or formulas are displayed in rows and columns.

Stakeholder: any individual or group with something to gain or lose as a result of a decision.

Stockholder: an individual or organization that owns stock in a company or corporation.

Strategic Plan: the result of an organizational planning process which is intended to fulfill the organization's values, mission and move the organization toward the realization of it's vision (see below).

Stratification: breakdown of information into meaningful categories or classifications to better develop an interpretation and action plan.

Structural Systems: structural components of a facility, including wall, ceilings, floors, floor coverings. windows, window coverings and doors.

Subscriber: the individual who holds or joins a group that holds, subscribes to, an insurance policy for health care coverage. A subscriber may enroll others under the policy or into the group that holds the policy. An employee who signs up for insurance as an employment benefit is the subscriber. All of the employer's employees and those they enroll will be part of the employer's group.

Suit: court proceeding by a person or group against a person or group in which a legal remedy is pursued. A suit is often called an action.

System Administrator: the person responsible for administering use of a multiuser computer system, communications system, or both. A system administrator performs such duties as assigning user accounts and passwords, establishing security access levels, and allocating storage space, as well as being responsible for other tasks such as watching for unauthorized access and preventing virus programs from entering the system.

Target Market: a selected group who share specific characteristics that may affect their interest in a specific product or service.

Tele Medicine: use of electronic, computerized remote communications and teleconferencing tools to practice medicine from a geographically distant location.

Temporary Employee: an individual hired for a limited period of time after which employment automatically terminates.

Third Party Payer: refers to employers, health insurance plans or any other entity that pays health care providers for services provided to another party, the patient. The consumer (the first party) unable to pay for services of the provider (the second party) relies on the health care plan (the third party) for payment (3).

Title Insurance: insurance designed to protect the buyer against problems following the acquisition of a property.

Value Priority: relative importance given by an individual or group to the motivational goal served by a particular value.

Values: words expressing enduring goals that carry sufficient psychological reward to serve as guiding principles in the life of a person, group or culture. Values stimulate emotions, serve as cognitive standards for judging and justifying actions and lead to actions that fulfill desired personal, social, and societal motivational goals.

Values Statement: a document adapted by the highest managerial level of an organization focusing on moral issues. A values statement, also known as a philosophical statement, proclaims the organization's beliefs about morality, i.e., what behaviors are right and what behaviors are wrong.

Vendor: an individual or company that offers a product or service for sale to others.

Venture Capitalist: an investor who provides business financing in return for an ownership interest in the company.

Vision: an organization's view of what it can and should strive to become in the future.

Vision Statement: a simple, brief, written inspirational document intended to advance a futuristic view of an organization to its members and other stakeholders.

Wealth: refers to all things having monetary value.

Wide Area Network (WAN): a group of computers or computer networks and other devices dispersed over a large geographic area and connected by a communications link that enables devices to interact with each other. Similar to a local area network except covering a much larger geographic area.

Word Processing Program: an application program for manipulating text-based documents. All word processors offer at least limited facilities for document formatting, such as font changes, page layout, paragraph indentation, etc. Some word processors can also check spelling, find synonyms, check grammar, incorporate graphics created with another program, correctly align tables, charts, and mathematical formulas, create and print form letters and perform calculations. Example word processing programs are Microsoft Word© and WordPerfect©.

Work Design: the process of determining the specific job duties of the employees of an organization.

Work Flow Chart: graphic representation of the progression of the work in a project.

World Wide Web: a system of resources available to computer users who are connected to an Internet. It is accessed primarily through the public Internet and enables users to view and interact with a variety of information, including magazine archives, public and university library resources, professional organization home pages, current world and business news, and programs.

Zoning: process by which a municipality regulates the use of property including the development of land within its jurisdiction.

Zoning Ordinance: a law that establishes the parameters of use of any property.

Index

Page numbers in *italics* denote figures; those followed by a "t" denote tables.